Lecture Notes in Computer Science 1915

Edited by G. Goos, J. Hartmanis and J. van Leeuwen

T0073450

Springer

Berlin
Heidelberg
New York
Barcelona
Hong Kong
London
Milan
Paris
Singapore
Tokyo

Sandhya Dwarkadas (Ed.)

Languages, Compilers, and Run-Time Systems for Scalable Computers

5th International Workshop, LCR 2000
Rochester, NY, USA, May 25-27, 2000
Selected Papers

Springer

Series Editors

Gerhard Goos, Karlsruhe University, Germany
Juris Hartmanis, Cornell University, NY, USA
Jan van Leeuwen, Utrecht University, The Netherlands

Volume Editor

Sandhya Dwarkadas
University of Rochester
Department of Computer Science
Rochester, NY 14627-0226, USA
E-mail: sandhya@cs.rochester.edu

Cataloging-in-Publication Data applied for

Die Deutsche Bibliothek - CIP-Einheitsaufnahme

Languages, compilers, and run time systems for scalable computers :
5th international workshop ; selected papers / LCR 2000, Rochester,
NY, USA, May 25 - 27, 2000. Sandhya Dwarkadas (ed.). - Berlin ;
Heidelberg ; New York ; Barcelona ; Hong Kong ; London ; Milan ;
Paris ; Singapore ; Tokyo : Springer, 2000
   (Lecture notes in computer science ; Vol. 1915)
   ISBN 3-540-41185-2

CR Subject Classification (1998): F.2.2, D.1.3, D.4.4-5, C.2.2, D.3, F.1, C.2.4

ISSN 0302-9743
ISBN 3-540-41185-2 Springer-Verlag Berlin Heidelberg New York

Springer-Verlag Berlin Heidelberg New York
a member of BertelsmannSpringer Science+Business Media GmbH
© Springer-Verlag Berlin Heidelberg 2000
Printed in Germany

Typesetting: Camera-ready by author, data conversion by Christian Grosche, Hamburg
Printed on acid-free paper   SPIN: 10722769   06/3142   5 4 3 2 1 0

Preface

It is an honor and a pleasure to present this collection of papers from LCR 2000, the fifth workshop on Languages, Compilers, and Run-Time Systems for Scalable Computers, held in Rochester, N.Y., U.S.A., on May 25–27, 2000. The LCR workshop is a bi-annual gathering of computer scientists who develop software systems for parallel and distributed computers, held in the off-year for the ACM Symposium on the Principles and Practice of Parallel Programming (PPoPP).

This fifth meeting was held in cooperation with ACM SIGPLAN on the University of Rochester campus. A total of 38 six-page abstracts were submitted, of which 22 were chosen for presentation and publication. Each paper received a minimum of 3 reviews, with 122 reviews in total. There were 44 registered attendees.

Local arrangements were coordinated by Kristen Wondrack, along with Sara Sadick and Mary Albee, from the University of Rochester conference and events office, and JoMarie Carpenter from the University of Rochester department of computer science. Grigorios Magklis was the webmaster for the workshop. I would like to thank all of them for an excellent job, and in particular, Kristen Wondrack, for helping ensure an enjoyable workshop that also proceeded smoothly. I hope the participants were able to take advantage of some of the attractions in Upstate New York as well.

The program committee provided prompt reviews and participation. In addition, the following people participated in the reviewing process — George Almasi, Angelos Bilas, Calin Cascaval, DeQing Chen, Shun Yan Cheung, Sarah E. Chodrow, Marcelo Cintra, Ceriel J.H. Jacobs, Jaejin Lee, Yuan Lin, Jason Maassen, Grigorios Magklis, Srinivasan Parthasarathy, Umit Rencuzogullari, Robert A. Shillner, Yefim Shuf, Paul Stodghill, Ronald Veldema, Peng Wu, Jianxin Xiong, and Ivan Zoraja. My thanks to all of them, and in particular, Dave O'Hallaron (the previous LCR chair), Jaspal Subhlok, Michael L. Scott, Alan L. Cox, Thomas Gross, and Willy Zwaenepoel, for their invaluable input and advice.

The workshop was organized into eight contributed paper sessions, the keynote address, and a panel session. John Mellor-Crummey, Lawrence Rauchwerger, Angelos Bilas, Michael L. Scott, Peter Keleher, Gagan Agrawal, David Lowenthal, and myself chaired the sessions. The keynote, titled "Software Shared Memory: Successes, Failures, Future Directions", was put together by Alan Cox and Willy Zwaenepoel. The panel on "New and Renewed Applications and Challenges for Scalable Computing" was moderated by Jaspal Subhlok, and included Alan Cox, David O'Hallaron, Keshav Pingali, and Michael Scott as panelists.

Finally, many thanks to the authors, presenters, and participants for providing a great start to the new millennium by making the workshop interesting, interactive, and of excellent quality.

August 2000   Sandhya Dwarkadas

Organization

LCR 2000 was organized and sponsored by the Department of Computer Science, University of Rochester, in cooperation with ACM/SIGPLAN.

Program/General Chair

Sandhya Dwarkadas, University of Rochester

Program Committee

Henri Bal, Vrije University
Alan L. Cox, Rice University
Sandhya Dwarkadas, University of Rochester
Thomas Gross, Carnegie-Mellon University, ETH Zurich
Mary Hall, ISI, University of Southern California
David O'Hallaron, Carnegie-Mellon University
Vijay Karamcheti, New York University
Carl Kesselman, ISI, University of Southern California
David Padua, University of Illinois at Urbana-Champaign
Keshav Pingali, Cornell University
Lori Pollock, University of Delaware
Michael L. Scott, University of Rochester
Jaswinder Pal Singh, Princeton University
Jaspal Subhlok, University of Houston
Vaidy Sunderam, Emory University
Willy Zwaenepoel, Rice University

Table of Contents

Session 6 - Heterogeneous/Meta-Computing

Session 7 - Issues of Load

Session 8 - Compiler-Supported Parallelism

A Collective I/O Scheme Based on Compiler Analysis

Mahmut Taylan Kandemir

Computer Science and Engineering Department
The Pennsylvania State University
University Park, PA 16802-6106, USA
E-mail: kandemir@cse.psu.edu
WWW: http://www.cse.psu.edu/~kandemir

Abstract. Current approaches to parallel I/O demand extensive user effort to obtain acceptable performance. This is in part due to difficulties in understanding the characteristics of a wide variety of I/O devices and in part due to inherent complexity of I/O software. While parallel I/O systems provide users with environments where persistent datasets can be shared between parallel processors, the ultimate performance of I/O-intensive codes depends largely on the relation between data access patterns and storage patterns of data in files and on disks. In cases where access patterns and storage patterns match, we can exploit parallel I/O hardware by allowing each processor to perform independent parallel I/O. To handle the cases in which data access patterns and storage patterns do not match, several I/O optimization techniques have been developed in recent years. Collective I/O is such an optimization technique that enables each processor to do I/O on behalf of other processors if doing so improves the overall performance. While it is generally accepted that collective I/O and its variants can bring impressive improvements as far as the I/O performance is concerned, it is difficult for the programmer to use collective I/O in an optimal manner.

In this paper, we propose and evaluate a compiler-directed collective I/O approach which detects the opportunities for collective I/O and inserts the necessary I/O calls in the code automatically. An important characteristic of the approach is that instead of applying collective I/O indiscriminately, it uses collective I/O selectively, only in cases where independent parallel I/O would not be possible. We have implemented the necessary algorithms in a source-to-source translator and within a stand-alone tool. Our experimental results demonstrate that our compiler-directed collective I/O scheme performs very well on different setups built using nine applications from several scientific benchmarks.

1 Introduction

Todays' parallel architectures comprise fast microprocessors, powerful network interfaces, and storage hierarchies that typically have multi-level caches, local and remote main memories, and secondary and tertiary storage devices. In going from upper levels of a storage hierarchy to lower levels, average access times

S. Dwarkadas (Ed.): LCR 2000, LNCS 1915, pp. 1–15, 2000.
© Springer-Verlag Berlin Heidelberg 2000

increase dramatically. For instance, typical DRAM access times are in tens of nanoseconds whereas typical disk access times can climb up to tens of milliseconds. Because of their cost effectiveness, magnetic disks have dominated the secondary storage market for the last several decades. Unfortunately, their access times have not kept pace with performance of the processors used in parallel architectures. Consequently, a large performance gap between secondary storage access times and processing unit speeds has emerged.

To address this imbalance, hardware designers focus on improving parallel I/O capabilities using multiple disks, I/O processors, and large bandwidth I/O busses [DC94]. It is generally agreed upon that an optimized I/O software can also play a major role in bridging this performance gap. For example, parallel file systems use several optimization techniques such as data striping, caching, and prefetching to reduce/hide I/O latencies [Rullman,CFP93,NK96]. In order to eliminate the difficulty in using a parallel file system directly, several research groups proposed high-level parallel I/O libraries and runtime systems that allow programmers to express access patterns of their codes using program-level data structures such as rectilinear array regions [CBH94,SCJ95,MPI-IO95]. While all these software supports provide an invaluable help to boost the I/O performance in parallel architectures, it remains still programmer's responsibility to select appropriate I/O calls to use, to insert these calls in appropriate locations within the code, and to manage the data flow between parallel processors and parallel disks. Some previous work focused on compiler optimizations for out-of-core applications [BCK95,PKK95,BCR95].

One of the most important optimizations in MPI-IO [MPI-IO95], an emerging parallel I/O standard, is *collective I/O,* an optimization that allows each processor to do I/O on behalf of other processors if doing so improves the overall performance [CBH94]. This optimization has many variants [Nitzberg95,Kotz94,SCJ95]; the one used in this study is *two-phase I/O* as implemented in MPI-2 standard [MPI-2]. In this implementation, I/O is performed in *two phases*: an I/O phase and a communication phase. In the I/O phase, processors perform I/O in a way that is most beneficial from the storage layout point of view. In the second phase, they engage in a many-to-many type of communication to ensure that each piece of data arrives in its destination. Previous experiences with collective I/O and its variants show impressive improvements in I/O latencies, and that the extra time spent in performing inter-processor communication is, in most cases, negligible. While collective I/O and its variants might be very effective if used properly, almost all previous studies considered a *user-oriented* approach in applying collective I/O. For example, Thakur et al. suggest programmers to use collective I/O interfaces of MPI-IO instead of easy-to-use Unix-like interfaces [TGL98]. Apart from determining the most suitable collective I/O routine and its corresponding parameters, this also requires, on the user part, analyzing access patterns of her code, detecting parallel I/O opportunities, and finally deciding a parallel I/O strategy.

In this paper, we propose and evaluate a *compiler-directed* collective I/O strategy whereby an optimizing compiler and MPI-IO cooperate to improve I/O performance of scientific codes. The compiler's responsibility in this work is to analyze the data access patterns of individual applications and determine suitable file storage patterns and I/O strategies. Our approach is *selective* in the sense that it activates collective I/O selectively, only when necessary. In other cases, it ensures that processors perform *independent parallel I/O,* which has almost the same I/O performance as collective I/O but without extra communication overhead. In this approach, MPI-IO provides collective I/O and independent parallel I/O interfaces that are utilized by the compiler. Preliminary results on an SGI/Cray Origin 2000 NUMA multiprocessor show that we can achieve most benefits of a user-oriented approach where a qualified user would direct the I/O activity using MPI-IO in an optimal manner.

The remainder of this paper is organized as follows. In the next section, we review collective I/O and discuss under what circumstances it is most useful. In Section 3, we explain our compiler analyses to detect access patterns and suitable storage patterns for multidimensional datasets considering multiple, related applications together. In Section 4, we describe our experimental framework, benchmarks, and different code versions, and present our experimental results. In Section 5, we present our conclusions.

2   Collective I/O

In many I/O-intensive applications that access large, multidimensional, disk-resident datasets, the performance of I/O accesses depends largely on the layout of data in files (*storage pattern*) and distribution of data across processors (*access pattern*). In cases where these patterns are the same, potentially, each processor can perform *independent parallel I/O.* However, the term 'independent parallel I/O' might be misleading, as, depending on the I/O network bandwidth, the number of parallel disks available, and the data striping strategies employed by the parallel file system, two processors may experience a conflict in accessing different data pieces residing on the same disk [DC94]. What we mean by 'independent parallel I/O' instead is that the processors can read/write their portions of the dataset (dictated by the access pattern) using only a few I/O requests *in the code,* each for a large number consecutive data items in a file. How these independent source-level I/O calls to files are broken up into several system-level calls to parallel disks. This last aspect, however, is architecture and operating system dependent and is not investigated in this paper. Note that, in independent parallel I/O, there is *no* interprocessor communication (or synchronization) during I/O. In this paper, an access pattern which is the same as the corresponding storage pattern is called a *conforming* access pattern.

In cases where storage and access patterns do not match, allowing each processor to perform independent I/O will cause processors to issue many I/O requests, each for a small amount of consecutive data. Collective I/O can improve the performance in these cases by first reading the dataset in question in a conforming (storage layout friendly) manner and then redistributing the data among the processors to obtain the target access pattern. Of course, in this case, the total data access cost should be computed as the sum of I/O cost and communication cost. The idea is that the communication cost is typically small as compared to I/O cost, meaning that the cost of accessing a dataset becomes almost independent from its storage pattern. The decision to use or not to use collective I/O depends on how a given dataset will be used (or shared) by different applications (or program modules). For example, if a dataset is accessed by every application exactly the same fashion (i.e., using the same access pattern), it might be beneficial to store the data in that fashion in file. This, of course, assumes that we have the flexibility of determining the storage pattern. If this is the case, we do not need collective I/O and each processor can do independent parallel I/O. If this is not possible, that is, different applications have different access patterns for the same dataset, we have to select a suitable storage pattern so that the majority of applications will still be able to use independent parallel I/O. For each of the remaining applications, however, we need to use collective I/O as the storage pattern and the access pattern will be different.

Consider Fig. 1 that shows both independent parallel I/O and collective I/O for a four processor case using a single disk-resident two-dimensional dataset. In Fig. 1(a), the storage pattern is row-major (each circle represents an array element and the arrows denote the linearized file layout of elements) and the access pattern is row-wise (i.e., each of the four processors accesses two full-rows of the dataset). Since the access pattern and the storage pattern match, each processor can perform independent parallel I/O without any need of communication or synchronization. Fig. 1(b), on the other hand, shows the case where collective I/O is required. The reason is that in this figure the storage pattern is row-major and the access pattern does not match it (i.e., each processor requires a four-by-four sub-array, elements of which are not fully consecutive in file). As explained earlier, the I/O is performed in two phases. In the first phase, each processor accesses the data in a layout conforming way (i.e., row-wise, as if this was the original access pattern), and in the second step, an all-to-all communication is performed between the processors and each data item is delivered to its final destination.

3   Compiler Analysis

Our approach to collective I/O utilizes a directed graph called *weighted communication graph* (WCG). Each node of a weighted communication graph is a *code block*, which can be defined as a program fragment during which we can keep the datasets in memory; however, between executions of code blocks, the datasets should be stored on disks. Depending on the applications, the datasets in question, and the available memory, a code block can be as small as a loop nest or can be as large as a full-scale application. An example for the latter is shown in Fig. 2 that depicts a typical scenario from a scientific working environment. There is a directed edge, $e_{1,2}$, between two nodes, cd_1 and cd_2, of the WCG if and only if there exists at least a dataset that is produced (i.e., created and stored on disk) in cd_1 and used (i.e., read from disk) in cd_2. The *weight*

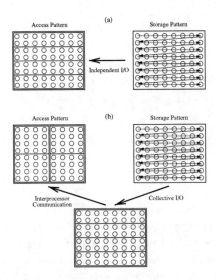

Fig. 1. (a) Independent parallel I/O and (b) Collective (two-phase) I/O.

associated with $e_{1,2}$ (written as $w_{1,2}$) corresponds to total number of dynamic control-flow transitions between code blocks cd_1 and cd_2 (e.g., how many times cd_2 is run after cd_1 in a typical setup). Depending on the granularity of code blocks, these weights can be calculated using profiling with typical input sets, can be approximated using weight estimation techniques, or can be entered by a user who observed the scientific working environment for a sufficiently long period of time.

For each dataset of interest, we also mark all the nodes that produce it (called *producers*) and use it (called *consumers*). Note that a given dataset can be produced and consumed *multiple times* and by *multiple nodes* in the WCG. For each producer, we determine all the consumers that use the values coming from that particular producer. *Since, in general, we may have more than one consumer for a given dataset and producer, and each consumer may access the dataset using a different access pattern, selecting an appropriate storage pattern for this dataset in the producer code block is of extreme importance.* For example, suppose that, in Fig. 2, node 0 produces a dataset which is later consumed by nodes 3, 4, and 5. Depending on the access patterns exhibited by these three nodes, we may or may not need to use collective I/O. In the fortunate case where all these three nodes have the same access pattern for the dataset, we can store the dataset in node 0 using this particular pattern (when we create it), resulting in independent parallel I/O in nodes 3, 4, and 5. However, if, say node 5, has a different access pattern than the other two, and we happen to select a storage pattern that is the same as the access pattern of nodes 3 and 4, then we need to perform collective I/O in node 5 in accessing the dataset in question. Nodes 3 and 4 can, on the other hand, still perform independent parallel I/O.

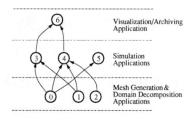

Fig. 2. Scientific working environment.

3.1   Access Pattern Detection

Access patterns exhibited by each code block can be determined by considering individual loop nests that make up the code block. The crucial step in this process is taking into account the parallelization information [Anderson97]. Individual nests can either be parallelized explicitly by programmers using compiler directives [ACI93,CCC97], or can be parallelized automatically (without user intervention) as a result of intra-procedural and inter-procedural compiler analyses [Anderson97,GB92,HMA95]. In either case, after the parallelization step, our approach determines the data regions (for a given dataset) accessed by each processor involved. Three typical access patterns for a given reference to a disk-resident array U are depicted in Fig. 3 for abstract form of a loop nest taken from a Specfp benchmark, Swim.256. Although, in principle, we can have a wide variety of I/O access patterns (e.g., banded, diagonal, block-cyclic, etc.), for simplicity, we confine ourselves to *blocked* access patterns in which each dimension (of the disk-resident dataset in question) is either shared between processors (denoted $block(p)$) or not shared (denoted $*$), where p is the number of processors sharing the dimension. With this notation, the two access patterns shown in Figures 1(a) and (b) can be expressed as $(block(4), *)$ and $(block(2), block(2))$, respectively. In addition to the access pattern information, the compiler also records information about inter-processor communication patterns [Anderson97].

For each array reference in each loop nest, our compiler determines an access pattern as explained above. Afterwards, it utilizes a *conflict resolution scheme* to resolve intra-nest and inter-nest access pattern conflicts. To achieve a reasonable conflict resolution, we associate a *count* with each reference indicating (or approximating) the number of times that this reference is touched in a typical execution. In addition to that, for each access pattern that exists in the code block, we associate a *counter* that is initialized to zero and incremented by a count amount each time we encounter a reference with that access pattern. In this way, for a given array, we determine the most preferable (or most prevalent) access pattern (also called *representative access pattern*) and mark the code block with that information. Although, at first glance, it seems that, in a typical large-scale application, there will be a lot of conflicting patterns that would make compiler's job of favoring one of them over the others difficult, in reality, most scientific codes have a few preferable access patterns.

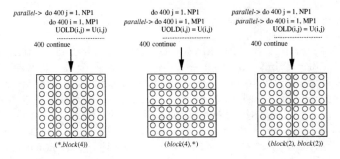

Fig. 3. Three parallelization strategies and corresponding I/O access patterns.

3.2 Storage Pattern Detection

Having determined an access pattern for each disk-resident dataset in each consumer code block, the next step is to select a suitable storage pattern for each dataset in its producer code block. We have built a prototype tool to achieve this.[1] For a given dataset, the tool takes the representative access patterns detected in the previous step by the compiler for each code block and runs a storage layout detection algorithm. Since this algorithm can be run for each disk-resident dataset separately, without loss of generality, in the following discussion, we focus only on a single dataset. The first step in our approach is to determine *producer-consumer subgraphs* (PCSs) of WCG for the dataset in question. A PCS for a dataset consists of a producer node and a number of consumer nodes that use the data produced by this producer. For instance, suppose that a dataset is produced by node 0 in Fig. 2 and consumed by nodes 3, 4, and 5. In that case, the PCS, as shown in Fig. 4(a), contains the nodes 0, 3, 4, and 5 and the edges from 0 to 3, 4, and 5. In the second step, we associate a count with each possible access pattern and initialize it to zero. Then, we traverse all the consumer nodes in turn and for each consumer node add its weight to the count of its access pattern. At the end of this step, for each access pattern, we obtain a count value.

In the third step, we set the storage pattern in the producer node to the access pattern with the highest count. Continuing with our current example, suppose that we have the following weights for the PCS as shown in Fig. 4(a): $w_{0,3} = 5$, $w_{0,4} = 5$, and $w_{0,5} = 15$. Assume further that the access patterns (found using the technique presented in the previous subsection) for the nodes 3, 4, and 5 are $(*, block(4))$, $(*, block(4))$, and $(block(4), *)$, respectively. Therefore, the final count values for the patterns $(*, block(4))$, and $(block(4), *)$ are 10,

---

[1] Note that building a separate tool is necessary only if the granularity of code blocks is a full-application. If, on the other hand, the granularity is a single nested-loop or a procedure, the functionality of this tool can be embedded within the compiler framework itself. Our current implementation supports three code block granularities, namely, full-application granularity, single procedure granularity, and loop nest granularity.

and 15, respectively. Considering these values, we select $(block(4), *)$ as the final storage pattern in node 0.

Note that, for a given dataset, we need to run the storage pattern detection algorithm multiple times, *one for each producer node* for this dataset. Note also that a given node can be both producer and consumer for for a dataset. For instance, assume that, in Fig. 2, node 0 produces a dataset which is later used by nodes 3 and 4, and the same dataset is overwritten (i.e., updated on the secondary storage) by node 4 and this updated dataset is later consumed by node 6. In this case, for this dataset, we have two PCSs as shown in Fig. 4(b).

3.3   I/O Insertion

The next step is to determine suitable I/O strategies for each consumer node. Let us focus on a specific dataset. If the access pattern (for this dataset) of a consumer node is the same as the storage pattern in the producer node, we perform independent parallel I/O in this consumer node. Otherwise, that is, if the access and storage patterns are different, we perform collective I/O. For our running example in Fig. 4(a), the final I/O strategies are shown in Fig. 4(c). We perform this step for each dataset and each PCS. Once the suitable I/O strategies have been determined, the compiler automatically inserts corresponding MPI-IO calls in each code block. Due to lack of space, this last step is not discussed in this paper.

3.4   Discussion

Although, our approach is so far mainly discussed for a setting where individual code blocks correspond to individual applications, it is relatively easy to adapt it to different settings as well. For example, if we consider each code block as a procedure in a given application, then a WCG can be processed using algorithms similar to those utilized in processing *weighted call graphs* [GBS97], where each node (code block) represents a procedure and an edge between two nodes correspond to dynamic control-flow transitions (e.g., procedure calls and returns) between the procedures represented by these two nodes. In an out-of-core environment where processor memories are at premium, on the other hand, each node may represent an individual loop nest and edges might represent dynamic control-flow between nests; in this case, the WCG is similar to a control-flow graph. In all cases, though, the weights between edges can be obtained either by using profiling with representative inputs (dynamic approach) [GBS97] or by static weight estimation techniques. For the latter, the control-flow prediction heuristics proposed by Ball and Larus [BL93] might be useful.

Another important issue that needs to be addressed is what to do (inside a code block) when we come across a reference whose access pattern is not the same as the representative (prevalent) access pattern for this code block. Recall that we assumed that, within a code block, we should be able to keep the datasets in memory. When the access pattern of an individual reference is different from the representative access pattern determined for a code block, we can re-shuffle the

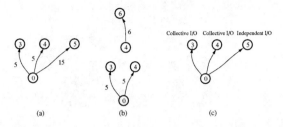

Fig. 4. (a) A producer-consumer subgraph (PCS). (b) Two PCGs for a dataset. (c) Final I/O strategies for the PCG in (a).

Table 1. Platform used in the experiments.

Number of Processors	32
Processor Type	MIPS R10000
Clock Rate	195 MHz
Out-of-Order Issue	4 instructions
Functional Units	5
L1 Cache	32 KB split, 2-way associative
L2 Cache	4 MB unified, 2-way associative
L1 Latency	2-3 cycles
L2 Latency	$\sim$10 cycles
Memory Capacity	256 MB per two processors
Network	100 Mbs Ethernet and 800 Mbs HiPPI
Disk Space	9 GB per node
Operating System	IRIX 6.5
Parallel File System	XFS
I/O Subsystem	2 RAID units with SCSI-2 interfaces

data in memory. This may not be a correctness issue for SMP or NUMA shared machines as each processor has full-access to the global memory space, rather, it may increase the number of nonlocal references, thus, may cause performance degradation. In distributed-memory message-passing architectures, on the other hand, this data re-shuffling in memory is necessary to ensure the correct data accesses in subsequent computations.

4 Experiments

We used the MPI-2 library and an SGI/Cray Origin 2000 to evaluate our scheme proposed in this paper. The important characteristics of our experimental platform are shown in Table 1.

Table 2. Benchmark codes used in the experiments.

Benchmark	Source	Lines	Brief Description	CB
tomcatv	Specfp	190	Mesh Generation	cb_0
vpenta	Specfp	166	Nasa Ames Fortran Kernel	cb_1
btrix	Specfp	188	Nasa Ames Fortran Kernel	cb_2
mxm	Specfp	35	Quantum Physics	cb_3
tis	Perfect Club	485	Electron Integral Transform	cb_4
eflux	Perfect Club	122	Molecular Dynamics of Water	cb_5
transpose	Nwchem (PNL)	321	Computational Chemistry	cb_6
cholesky	Miscellaneous	34	Cholesky Factorization	cb_7
ADI	Miscellaneous	56	Alternate Direction Integral	cb_8

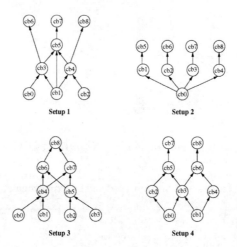

Fig. 5. Setups (communication graphs) used in the experiments.

4.1   Setups and Configurations

In this study, we used 4 different *setups (communication graphs)*, each built up using 9 different benchmark codes in different ways. Important characteristics of the benchmark codes used are given in Table 2. The last column (CB) gives a code block name for each benchmark that will be used in the remainder of this paper. We manually forced these codes to be I/O-intensive by increasing the input sizes and by making all input and output datasets disk-resident. The setups built from these benchmarks are given in Fig. 5. For each setup given in Fig. 5, we conducted experiments using three *configurations (weighted communication graphs)*. As shown in Table 3, for a given setup, the configurations differ from each other only in the weights of the edges in the graph. However, these weights are chosen such that the storage patterns detected by the algorithm for different configurations (of the same setup) are different. The details are omitted due to lack of space.

The access pattern detection was implemented as a stand-alone pass in a source-to-source translator that uses the Omega Library [KMP95] whenever necessary. After access pattern detection, the resulting representative patterns are written into a permanent data structure along with necessary information about code blocks. After that, the storage pattern detection algorithm is run. This algorithm uses the permanent data structure created in the previous step and also takes the WCG as input. The resulting storage patterns are written on another permanent data structure. The final step is the insertion of the necessary I/O calls in the code. This is also implemented as a separate pass in the source-to-source translator.

Table 3. Configurations used in each setup.

Setup 1:

	$w_{0,3}$	$w_{1,3}$	$w_{1,4}$	$w_{1,5}$	$w_{2,4}$	$w_{3,5}$	$w_{4,5}$	$w_{3,6}$	$w_{5,7}$	$w_{4,8}$
Configuration 1.1	5	5	10	5	12	15	5	6	10	10
Configuration 1.2	10	1	10	5	5	15	5	12	10	4
Configuration 1.3	10	10	10	10	10	15	15	5	5	5

Setup 2:

	$w_{0,1}$	$w_{0,2}$	$w_{0,3}$	$w_{0,4}$	$w_{1,5}$	$w_{2,6}$	$w_{3,7}$	$w_{4,8}$
Configuration 2.1	4	4	4	4	10	4	4	4
Configuration 2.2	1	1	10	10	10	1	1	4
Configuration 2.3	10	10	10	10	15	15	15	15

Setup 3:

	$w_{0,4}$	$w_{1,4}$	$w_{2,5}$	$w_{3,5}$	$w_{4,6}$	$w_{4,7}$	$w_{5,6}$	$w_{5,7}$	$w_{6,8}$	$w_{7,8}$
Configuration 3.1	10	1	1	1	4	4	4	4	5	5
Configuration 3.2	5	5	5	5	1	1	1	1	10	10
Configuration 3.3	10	10	10	10	15	15	15	15	8	8

Setup 4:

	$w_{0,2}$	$w_{0,3}$	$w_{1,3}$	$w_{1,4}$	$w_{2,5}$	$w_{3,5}$	$w_{3,6}$	$w_{4,6}$	$w_{5,7}$	$w_{6,8}$
Configuration 4.1	2	2	2	2	4	4	4	4	8	8
Configuration 4.2	8	8	8	8	4	4	4	4	2	2
Configuration 4.3	10	10	10	10	12	12	12	12	10	10

4.2   Versions

We used three different code versions as explained below.

Version 1. In this version, each processor performs independent (non-collective) I/O regardless whether the access pattern and the storage pattern are the same or not. This strategy may in general result in an excessive number of I/O calls issued by each processor. We call this version the *naive I/O strategy.*

Version 2. This version performs indiscriminate collective I/O. While we expect this version to bring significant improvements over the naive I/O strategy, in cases where the access pattern and the storage pattern match, the collective I/O is not necessary as the processors can perform independent parallel I/O.

Version 3. This is the strategy explained in this paper. The collective I/O is performed selectively, only if the access pattern and the storage pattern do not match. In all other cases, we perform independent parallel I/O.

4.3   Results

Performance Improvement. Fig. 6 presents the percentage improvements provided by version 3 (our approach) over version 1 for both I/O times and total execution times for all the configurations experimented with. Note that **C I.J** denotes the Jth configuration of setup **I** (see Table 3). For each dataset (array) used in these experiments, the size of each array dimension is set to 4K double-precision elements except for dimensions whose sizes were fixed at small values (i.e., not modifiable). We observe that the average improvements for I/O times and total times are 61.30% and 26.82%, respectively, showing that our approach performs much better than the naive I/O strategy that lets each processor to do independent I/O. The largest improvements are obtained with setup 4 as there is more I/O activity in this setup and this setup has the highest 'consumers per producer' rate. Also, for a given setup, the last (third) configuration shows the largest improvements (as it has the largest edge weights). Our additional experiments revealed that our approach is more effective with large processor sizes. For example, using 16 processors and 25 processor, we are able to obtain 66.91% and 70.82%, respectively, improvements in I/O times.

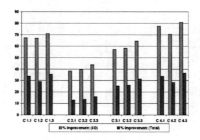

Fig. 6. % improvements of version 3 over version 1 using 9 processors.

Effectiveness of Storage Pattern Detection. We now compare the performance of our approach with that of version 2. Recall that the version 2 differs from our technique in that it applies collective I/O indiscriminately. We used the same input size as before (4K double-precision elements per array dimension) and nine processors. Fig. 7 shows the I/O time (%) improvements (over version 1) caused by version 2 with three different storage schemes. In the first scheme, all the arrays are stored as column-major in file. In the second scheme, they are stored as row-major, and in the third, in blocked fashion. For comparison purposes, we also repeat the performance improvements of version 3. We note that version 3 performs better than version 2 with any storage scheme. We also observe that column-storage and row-storage versions of version 2 behave similarly and one cannot choose one over the other in general for a given setup. The additional improvements brought about by version 3 over version 2 are 17.74%, 17.76%, and 21.07% for column-major, row-major, and blocked-layout cases, respectively.

Effectiveness of Access Pattern Detection. So far, for all versions we experimented, we used an access pattern detection scheme (a pass in the source-to-source translator) to determine the optimal I/O access pattern. This is important as a suboptimal access pattern can result in a lot of inter-processor communication (in message-passing machines) or nonlocal accesses (in NUMA architectures). In a new set of experiments, we ran five different 'version 3 algorithms', each is similar to the version we used so far except that the access

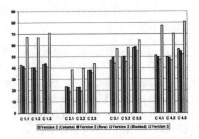

Fig. 7. Comparison of percentage improvements of versions 2 and 3 over version 1 using 9 processors.

pattern detection scheme is different in each. The results are given in Fig. 8 in terms of improvements in the overall execution time over the version 1. The first three algorithms always use fixed column-wise, row-wise, and blocked access patterns, respectively. The fourth algorithm (called `First-Nest`) determines the access pattern for a dataset in an application by considering the access pattern exhibited by the first nest that accesses this dataset in the application. The fifth one (called `Most-Costly`), on the other hand, sets the access pattern of the application to that of the most important nest (i.e., the nest that would consume the most cycles—among all the nests—during execution) in the application. We used profiling to detect the most important nest. We also give the improvements of the version 3 algorithm that we used earlier. It should be mentioned that all these five new version 3 algorithms utilize the *same storage pattern detection scheme* as the original algorithm. The only difference is in the representative access patterns for each code block. We note that our access pattern detection algorithm performs better than the other approaches. The results indicate that only `Most-Costly` can come close to access pattern detection. Our approach brings a 2.84% additional improvement over `Most-Costly`, and 6.40% and 6.19% additional improvement over fixed row-wise and column-wise access patterns.

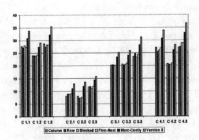

Fig. 8. % improvements for different version 3 algorithms.

5   Conclusions

In this paper, we present a compiler-directed collective I/O technique to improve I/O latencies of large-scale scientific codes. Our observation is that, in many scientific codes, the way that the datasets are accessed is, in general, different from the way they are stored in files. This disparity between storage and access patterns can cause huge runtime latencies, if, in accessing a dataset, each processor performs independent I/O. While collective I/O might be very effective in reducing these I/O latencies at the expense of some extra communication, there are cases where an indiscriminate use of collective I/O may not be the best choice. In those cases, a solution is to store the datasets in files in the fashion that they will be accessed in the future. We show that the required information to detect access patterns can be provided by a compiler analysis, and a graphical representation, called weighted communication graph (WCG), can be utilized by an optimizer tool to determine the most suitable storage strategies. Then, the compiler can build and insert necessary I/O calls (MPI-IO calls) in each code automatically. Our preliminary performance results are very promising and encourage us to focus more on compiler-directed I/O optimization techniques.

References

ACI93. A. Ancourt, F. Coelho, F. Irigoin, and R. Keryell. A linear algebra framework for static HPF code distribution. *Scientific Prog.,* 6(1):3–28, Spring 1997.

Anderson97. J. Anderson. *Automatic Computation and Data Decomposition for Multiprocessors.* Ph.D. dissertation, Computer Systems Lab., Stanford Univ., March 1997.

BL93. T. Ball and J. Larus. Branch prediction for free. In *Proc. the SIGPLAN'93 Conf. on Prog. Lang. Design and Implementation,* pp. 300–313, June 1993.

BCK95. R. Bordawekar, A. Choudhary, K. Kennedy, C. Koelbel, and M. Palecnzy. A model and compilation strategy for out-of-core data parallel programs. In *Proc. ACM-SIGPLAN Symposium on Principles and Practice of Parallel Programming,* Santa Barbara, CA, 1995.

BCR95. R. Bordawekar, A. Choudhary, and J. Ramanujam. Automatic optimization of communication in out-of-core stencil codes, In Proc. *10th ACM International Conference on Supercomputing,* pages 366–373, Philadelphia, PA, May 1996.

CCC97. R. Chandra, D. Chen, R. Cox, D. Maydan, N. Nedeljkovic, and J. Anderson. Data-distribution support on distributed-shared memory multi-processors. In *Proc. Prog. Lang. Design and Implementation,* Las Vegas, NV, 1997.

CBH94. A. Choudhary, R. Bordawekar, M. Harry, R. Krishnaiyer, R. Ponnusamy, T. Singh, and R. Thakur. Passion: Parallel and scalable software for input-output. *NPAC Technical Report SCCS-636,* Sept 1994.

CFP93. P. F. Corbett, D. G. Feitelson, J-P. Prost, and S. J. Baylor. Parallel access to files in the Vesta file system. In *Proc. Supercomputing'93,* pp. 472–481, Nov 1993.

MPI-IO95. P. Corbett et al. Overview of the MPI-IO parallel I/O interface, In *Proc. Third Workshop on I/O in Par. and Dist. Sys.,* IPPS'95, Santa Barbara, CA, April 1995.

DC94. J. del Rosario and A. Choudhary. High performance I/O for parallel computers: problems and prospects. *IEEE Computer,* March 1994.

GBS97. N. Gloy, T. Blackwell, M. D. Smith, and B. Calder. Procedure placement using temporal ordering information. In *Proc. Micro-30,* Research Triangle Park, North Carolina, December 1–3, 1997.

GB92. M. Gupta and P. Banerjee. Demonstration of automatic data partitioning techniques for parallelizing compilers on multicomputers. *IEEE Transactions on Parallel and Distributed Systems,* 3(2):179–193, March 1992.

HMA95. M. W. Hall, B. Murphy, S. Amarasinghe, S. Liao, and M. Lam. Interprocedural analysis for parallelization. In *Proc. 8th International Workshop on Lang. and Comp. for Parallel Computers,* pages 61–80, Columbus, Ohio, August 1995.

KMP95. W. Kelly, V. Maslov, W. Pugh, E. Rosser, T. Shpeisman, and David Wonnacott. The Omega Library interface guide. Technical Report CS-TR-3445, CS Dept., University of Maryland, College Park, March 1995.

Kotz94. D. Kotz. Disk-directed I/O for MIMD multiprocessors. In *Proc. the 1994 Symposium on Operating Systems Design and Implementation,* pages 61–74, November 1994. Updated as Dartmouth TR PCS-TR94-226 on November 8, 1994.

MPI-2. Message Passing Interface Forum. MPI-2: Extensions to the Message-Passing Interface. July 1997. On the WWW at
http://www.mpi-forum.org/docs/docs/html.

NK96. N. Nieuwejaar and D. Kotz. The Galley parallel file system. In *Proc. the 10th ACM International Conference on Supercomputing,* pages 374–381, Philadelphia, PA, May 1996. ACM Press.

Nitzberg95. B. J. Nitzberg. *Collective Parallel I/O.* PhD thesis, Department of Computer and Information Science, University of Oregon, December 1995.

PKK95. M. Paleczny, K. Kennedy, and C. Koelbel. Compiler support for out-of-core arrays on data parallel machines. In *Proc. the 5th Symposium on the Frontiers of Massively Parallel Computation,* McLean, VA, February 1995, pp. 110-118.

Rullman. B. Rullman. Paragon parallel file system. *External Product Specification,* Intel Supercomputer Systems Division.

SCJ95. K. E. Seamons, Y. Chen, P. Jones, J. Jozwiak, and M. Winslett. Server-directed collective I/O in Panda. In *Proceedings of Supercomputing'95,* December 1995.

TGL98. R. Thakur, W. Gropp, and E. Lusk. A case for using MPI's derived data types to improve I/O performance. In *Proc. of SC'98: High Performance Networking and Computing,* November 1998.

Achieving Robust, Scalable Cluster I/O in Java

Matt Welsh and David Culler

University of California at Berkeley, Berkeley CA 94618, USA
{mdw,culler}@cs.berkeley.edu
http://www.cs.berkeley.edu/~mdw

Abstract We present *Tigris*, a high-performance computation and I/O substrate for clusters of workstations that is implemented entirely in Java. Tigris automatically balances resource load across the cluster as a whole, shielding applications from asymmetries in CPU, I/O, and network performance. This is accomplished through the use of a *dataflow programming model* coupled with a work-balancing *distributed queue*. To meet the performance challenges of implementing such a system in Java, Tigris relies on *Jaguar*, a system that enables direct, protected access to hardware resources, including fast network interfaces and disk I/O. Jaguar yields an order-of-magnitude performance boost over the Java Native Interface for Java bindings to system resources. We demonstrate the applicability of Tigris through a one-pass, parallel, disk-to-disk sort exhibiting high performance.

1   Introduction

Realizing the performance potential of workstation clusters as a platform for incrementally scalable computing presents many challenges. While the performance aspects of communication [9,27], I/O [16], and process scheduling [4] have been addressed in specific settings, maintaining good performance across a range of different applications has proven difficult [3]. Applications tend to be fragile with respect to performance imbalance across the cluster; a single overloaded node can easily become a bottleneck for the entire application [2].

At the same time, Java has emerged as attractive platform allowing heterogeneous resources to be harnessed for large-scale computation. Java's object orientation, type and reference safety, exception handling model, code mobility, and distributed computing primitives all contribute to its popularity as a base upon which novel, component-based applications can be readily deployed. Increasingly, Java is becoming pervasive as a core technology supporting applications such as high-performance numerical computing [17], database connectivity [6], and scalable Internet services [14,19]. Unfortunately, most efforts in this direction focus on interfaces to legacy servers by encapsulating them in Java contexts, rather than the ability to construct large, I/O-intensive services directly in Java.

We present *Tigris*, a high-performance computation and I/O substrate for clusters of workstations, implemented entirely in Java. Tigris automatically balances resource load across the cluster as a whole, shielding applications from

S. Dwarkadas (Ed.): LCR 2000, LNCS 1915, pp. 16–31, 2000.

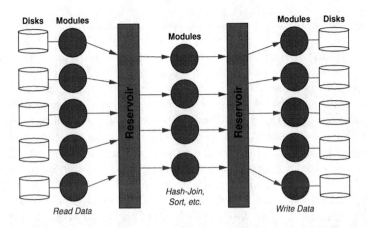

Figure 1. A sample Tigris application. *Tigris applications consist of a series of module stages connected by reservoirs. Reservoirs are realized as a distributed queue which allows data to flow from producers to consumers at autonomously adaptive rates.*

asymmetries in CPU, I/O, and network performance. This is accomplished through the use of a *dataflow programming model* coupled with a work-balancing *distributed queue*. By exploiting the use of Java as the native execution and control environment in Tigris, we believe that cluster application development is greatly simplified and that applications can take advantage of code mobility, strong typing, and other features provided by Java. The key ideas in Tigris build upon those River [5], a system which was implemented in C++ on the Berkeley Network of Workstations [25]. We describe the major differences between Tigris and River in Section 6.

Tigris achieves high-performance communication and disk I/O through the use of *Jaguar* [28], an extension of the Java programming environment which enables direct, protected access to hardware resources, such as fast network interfaces. Jaguar yields an order-of-magnitude performance boost over the Java Native Interface and eliminates the use of native methods, which raise protection concerns.

We evaluate the communication and load-balancing performance of Tigris on an 8-node workstation cluster and demonstrate its applicability through *Tigris-Sort*, a one-pass, parallel, disk-to-disk sort.

2   The Tigris System

The goal of Tigris is to automatically overcome cluster resource imbalance and mask this behavior from the application. This is motivated by the observation that cluster applications tend to be highly sensitive to performance heterogeneity; for example, if one node in the cluster is more heavily loaded than others, without some form of work redistribution the application may run at the rate of the slowest node. The larger and more heterogeneous a cluster is, the more evident this problem will be. Often, performance imbalance is difficult to prevent; for example, the location of bad blocks on a disk can seriously affect its bandwidth. This imbalance is especially serious for clusters which utilize nodes of varying CPU, network, and disk capabilities. Apart from hardware issues, software can cause performance asymmetry within a cluster as well; for example, "hot spots" may arise due to the distribution of data and computation in the application.

Tigris employs a dataflow programming model wherein applications are expressed as a series of *modules* each supporting a very simple input/output interface. Modules are organized into *stages*, each of which is a set of identical modules replicated across the nodes of a cluster. Increasing the number of modules in a stage can increase the effective bandwidth of that stage. Module stages communicate through the use of *reservoirs*, which are virtual communication channels through which data packets can be pushed or or pulled. A simple data-transformation application might consist of three distinct stages: one which reads data from disk and streams it out to a reservoir; one which reads packets from a reservoir and performs some transformation on that data; and one which writes data from a reservoir back onto disk. Figure 1 depicts this scenario.

Tigris addresses resource imbalance in a cluster by implementing reservoirs as a *distributed queue* (DQ), which balances work across the modules of a stage. The DQ allows data to flow at autonomously adaptive rates from producers to consumers, thereby causing data to "flow to where the resources are." In Tigris, the DQ is implemented by balancing outgoing data from a module across multiple communication channels.

2.1   Using Type-Safe Languages for Scalable Applications

Designers of robust, scalable systems can take advantage of the features provided by a type-safe language such as Java. Language protection and automatic memory management eliminate many common sources of bugs, and object orientation allows code to be built in a modular, reusable form. Within a cluster, Java's Remote Method Invocation (RMI) provides an elegant programming model for harnessing distributed resources. A JVM can export remote interfaces to local objects which are accessed through method invocation on a client-side stub. Java's portability simplifies the process of tying multiple heterogeneous architectures into a single application. The use of bytecode mobility allows an application to push new code modules into a JVM on demand. This is particularly valuable for building flexible cluster applications, as the binding between application modules and cluster nodes can be highly dynamic. For example, the number of nodes devoted to running a particular task can be resized based on application demand.

There are a number of challenges inherent in the use of Java for scalable server applications. A great deal of previous work has addressed problems with Java processor performance, including the efficiency of compiled code, thread

```
public class PrintModule implements ModuleIF {
  public void init(ModuleConfig cfg) { /* Empty */ }
  public void destroy() { /* Empty */ }
  public String getName() { return "PrintModule"; }

  public void doOperation(Water inWater, Stream outStream)
    throws ModuleException {
    for (int i = 0; i < inWater.getSize(); i++) {
      System.out.println("Read: " + inWater.readByte(i));
    }
    outStream.Put(inWater);
  }
}
```

Figure 2. An example of a Tigris module. *This module displays the contents of each packet it receives, and passes the packet along to the outgoing stream.*

synchronization, and garbage collection algorithms [20,22]. Java compilers, including both static and "just-in-time" (JIT) compilers, are now capable of generating code which rivals lower-level languages, such as C++, in performance [17]. However, obtaining high-performance I/O and efficient exploitation of low-level system resources remain as important performance problems. In this paper we describe *Jaguar*, our approach to obtaining high I/O performance in Java. Other issues include memory footprint, the binding between Java and operating system threads, and resource accounting. We believe that despite these issues, Java provides a compelling environment for the construction of cluster-based applications.

In Tigris, each cluster node runs a Java Virtual Machine which is bootstrapped with a receptive execution environment called the *MultiSpace* [14]. MultiSpace allows new Java classes to be "pushed into" the JVM remotely through Java Remote Method Invocation. A Security Manager is loaded into the MultiSpace to limit the behavior of untrusted Java classes uploaded into the JVM; for example, an untrusted component should not be allowed to access the filesystem directly. This allows a flexible security infrastructure to be constructed wherein Java classes running on cluster nodes can be given more or fewer capabilities to access system resources.

2.2   Design Overview

Tigris is implemented entirely in Java. Tigris modules are Java classes that implement the `ModuleIF` interface, which provides a small set of methods that each module must implement. The code for an example module is shown in Figure 2. `init` and `destroy` are used for module initialization and cleanup, and `getName` allows a module to provide a unique name for itself. The `doOperation` method is the core of the module's functionality: it is called whenever there is incoming data for the module to process, and is responsible for generating any outgoing data and pushing it down the dataflow path that the module is on.

Communication is managed by the `Stream` class, which provides two methods, `Get` and `Put`, allowing data items to be read from and written to a single, point-to-point communications channel. The `Water` class represents the unit of data which can be read from or written to a `Stream`; this is also the unit of work that is processed by the module `doOperation` method. A `Water` can be thought of as containing one or more data buffers that can be accessed directly (similarly to a Java array) or from which other Java objects can be allocated. This allows the contents of a `Water` to represent a structure with typed fields that have meaning to the Java application, rather than as an untyped collection of bytes or integers.

By subclassing `Stream` and `Water`, different communication mechanisms can be implemented in Tigris. Our prototype implementation includes three stream implementations:

- `ViaStream` provides reliable communications over Berkeley VIA [8], a fast communications layer implemented on the Myrinet system area network. This is accomplished through Jaguar (see below).
- `MemoryStream` implements communications between modules on the same JVM, passing the data through a FIFO queue in memory.
- `FileStream` associates the `Get` and `Put` stream operations with data read from and written to a file, respectively. This is a convenient way to abstract disk I/O. Each `Get` or `Put` operation accesses file data in FIFO order; random access is provided by a separate seek method.

`Waters` are initially created by a `Spring`, an interface which contains a single method: `createWater(int size)`. Every `Stream` has associated with it a `Spring` implementation that is capable of creating `Waters` which can be sent over that `Stream`. This allows a stream to manage allocation of `Waters` which will be eventually transmitted over it; for example, a stream may wish to initialize data fields in the `Water` to implement a particular communications protocol (e.g., sequence numbers). The implementation of `Water` can ensure that a module is unable to modify these "hidden" fields once the `Water` is created, by limiting the range of data items that can be accessed by the application.

2.3   Reservoir Implementation

Reservoirs are used as a virtual communication channel between stages of a Tigris application. Logically, modules pull data from their upstream reservoir, process it, and push data to their downstream reservoir. Reservoirs are implemented as a Distributed Queue (DQ), which dynamically balances communication between individual modules in a stage. Each Tigris module has multiple incoming and outgoing streams; the DQ is realized through the stream selection policy used by each module. Each module has an associated thread that is responsible for repeatedly issuing `Get` on one of the module's incoming streams, and invoking

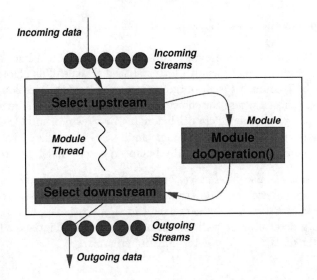

Figure 3. Tigris Reservoir implementation. *Tigris modules have an associated thread which repeatedly selects an incoming stream, reads data from it, invokes the module's* doOperation *method, and sends outgoing data to one of the outgoing streams. The reservoir is implemented through the stream selection policy used by this thread. Module authors are required only to implement the* doOperation *method.*

doOperation with two arguments: the input Water, and a handle to the outgoing stream to which any new data should be sent. This logic is invisible to the application, which is only responsible for implementing the doOperation method for each module.

By passing a handle to the current outgoing stream to doOperation, the module is capable of emitting zero or more Waters on each iteration. Also, this permits the module to obtain a handle to the stream's Spring to create new Waters to be transmitted. Note that the module may decide to re-transmit the same Water which it took as input; because a stream may not be capable of directly transmitting an arbitrary Water (for example, a ViaStream cannot transmit a FileWater), the stream is responsible for transforming the Water if necessary, e.g., by making a copy.

There are three implementations of the DQ scheduler in our prototype:

- *Round-Robin*: Selects the incoming and outgoing stream for each iteration in a round-robin fashion.
- *Random*: Selects the incoming stream for each iteration using round-robin, and the outgoing stream at random. The algorithm maintains a credit count for each outgoing stream. The credit count is decremented for each Water sent on a stream, and is incremented when the Water has been processed by the destination (e.g., through an acknowledgment). On each iteration,

a random stream S with a nonzero credit count is chosen from the set of
downstream reservoirs.

- *Lottery*: Selects the incoming stream for each iteration using round-robin,
  and the outgoing stream using a lottery-based scheme. The algorithm maintains a credit count for each outgoing stream. On each iteration, a random
  stream S is chosen where the choice of S is weighted by the value $w = (c_S/C)$
  where c_S is the number of credits belonging to stream S and $C = \sum c_S$. The
  intuition is that streams with more credits are more likely to be chosen,
  allowing bandwidth to be naturally balanced across multiple streams.

A reservoir may also be *Deterministic*, in which packets are sent between
modules of a stage based on a deterministic routing. Deterministic reservoirs do
not perform load balancing, but are useful for applications which require data
to flow along a deterministic path between modules. The TigrisSort benchmark
described later makes use of a deterministic reservoir.

2.4   Initialization and Control

A Tigris application is controlled by an external client which contacts the MultiS-
pace control interface of each cluster node through Java RMI, and communicates
with the `TigrisMgr` service running on that node. `TigrisMgr` provides methods
to create a module, to create a stream, to add a stream as an incoming or
outgoing stream of a given module, and to start and stop a given module. In
this way the Tigris application and module connectivity graph is "grown" at
runtime on top of the receptive MultiSpace environment rather than hardcoded.
Each cluster node need only be running the MultiSpace environment with the
`TigrisMgr` service preloaded.

Execution begins when the control client issues the `moduleStart` command
to each module, and ends when one of two conditions occur:

- The control client issues `moduleStop` to every module; or,
- Every module reaches the "End of Stream" condition.

"End of Stream" (EOS) is indicated by a module receiving a null `Water` as
input. This can be triggered by a producer pushing a null `Water` down a stream
towards a consumer, or by some other event (such as the DQ implementation
itself declaring an EOS condition). A module may indicate to its control thread
that EOS has been reached by throwing an `EndOfStreamException` from its
`doOperation` method; this obviates the need for an additional status value to
be passed between a module and its controlling thread.

3   Jaguar: High-Performance Communication and I/O in Java

Efficient communication and I/O in Tigris is provided by *Jaguar* [28], an extension of the Java environment that enables direct access to system resources such

as fast network interfaces and disk I/O. Traditionally, Java applications make use of low-level system functionality through the use of *native methods*, which are written in a language such as C. To bind native method code to the Java application, a *native method interface* is used, which has been standardized across most JVMs as Sun Microsystems' Java Native Interface [21]. However, the use of native methods raises two important concerns. The first is performance: the cost of traversing the native method interface can be quite high, especially when a large amount of data must be copied across the Java-native code boundary. The second is safety: invoking arbitrary native code from a Java application effectively negates the protection guarantees of the Java Virtual Machine. These two problems conflate, as programmers tend to write more application code in the native language to amortize the cost of crossing the native interface.

Jaguar overcomes these problems by providing applications with efficient and safe access to low-level system resources. This is accomplished through a bytecode specialization technique in which certain Java bytecode sequences are translated to low-level code which is capable of performing functions not allowed by the JVM, such as direct memory access. Because this low-level code is inlined into the Java application at compile time, the overhead of the native interface is avoided. Also, the compiler can perform aggressive optimizations on the combined application and inlined Jaguar code. Low-level code is expressed as a type-exact, portable superset of Java bytecode, *Jaguar bytecode*, which includes additional instructions required for direct memory access. Application programmers are not permitted to make use of these instructions; they are only used within Java-to-Jaguar bytecode translation rules.

Tigris makes use of Jaguar in two ways: to implement efficient network and disk I/O, and to avoid Java object serialization. Network I/O is provided by the `ViaStream` class, which is implemented using the Jaguar interface to the Berkeley VIA communications architecture. Jaguar's VIA interface provides direct, zero-copy access to the Myrinet system area network, and obtains a round-trip time of 73 microseconds for small messages, and a peak bandwidth of over 488 mbits/second. This is identical to the performance of Berkeley VIA as accessed from C code. Jaguar translates access to certain Java classes (representing VIA registers, packet descriptors, and network buffers) into low-level code which directly manipulates these system resources.

Likewise, disk I/O in Tigris is provided by the `FileStream` class; this is implemented by memory-mapping the contents of a disk file (using the *mmap* system call) into the application address space. Jaguar specializes accesses to the `Water` objects representing file data to direct access to this memory-mapped region.

Jaguar is also used to map Java objects onto the raw byte streams transferred over network and disk streams. Rather than employ Java object serialization, which involves data copying and is very costly, Tigris uses Jaguar's *Pre-Serialized Objects* feature, which translates Java object field access into direct access to a low-level network, disk, or memory buffer. No copies are required to map a Pre-

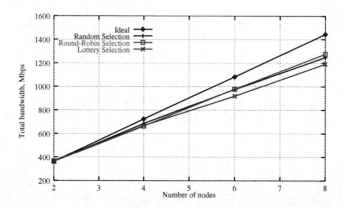

Figure 4. Reservoir performance under scaling. *This figure shows the aggregate bandwidth through the reservoir as the number of nodes reading and writing data through the reservoir is scaled. From 1 to 4 nodes write data into a reservoir implemented on top of the VIA network interface, and 1 to 4 nodes read data from the reservoir. The three DQ implementations (round-robin, randomized, and lottery) are shown, along with the ideal bandwidth under perfect scaling.*

Serialized Object onto an I/O buffer. In this way, Tigris streams are used to efficiently transfer Java objects rather than raw bytes.

4   Reservoir Performance

Figure 4 shows the performance of the Tigris reservoir implementations (round-robin, randomized, and lottery) as the number of nodes passing data through the reservoir is scaled up. All experiments were performed on a cluster of 500 MHz Pentium III systems with 512 MB of memory running Linux 2.2.13, connected using Myrinet with the Berkeley VIA communications layer. The Blackdown port of Sun JDK 1.1.7v3 is used along with a Jaguar-enabled JIT compiler. The `ViaStream` stream type is used, which implements a simple credit-based flow-control scheme over VIA. End-to-end peak bandwidth through a `ViaStream` is 368 Mbits/sec, or 75% of the peak bandwidth of raw VIA, which implements no flow-control or reliability.

In each case an equal number of nodes are sending and receiving data through the reservoir. The results show only a slight bandwidth loss (12% less than ideal) in the 8-node case, demonstrating that the presence of a reservoir does not seriously affect performance when the system is perfectly balanced. The bandwidth loss is partially due to the DQ implementation itself; in each case, the receiving node selects the incoming stream from which to receive data in a round-robin manner. Although the receive operation is non-blocking it does require the receiver to test for incoming data on each incoming stream until

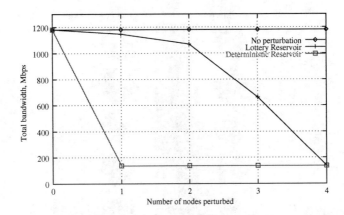

Figure 5. Reservoir performance under perturbation. *This figure shows the performance of the lottery reservoir as consumer nodes are artificially perturbed. 4 nodes are pushing data into a reservoir and 4 nodes are pulling data from the reservoir. When 3 out of 4 consumers are perturbed, 56% of the total bandwidth can be achieved. With the deterministic reservoir, performance drops as soon as a single receiver is perturbed.*

a packet arrives. We also believe that a portion of this bandwidth loss is due the VIA implementation being used; as the number of active communication channels increases, the network interface must poll additional queues to test for incoming or outgoing packets.

The second benchmark demonstrates the performance of the lottery reservoir in a scenario that models a performance imbalance in the cluster. This is accomplished by artificially loading nodes by adding a fixed delay to each iteration of the module's doOperation method. In this benchmark, 4 nodes are pushing data into the reservoir, and 4 nodes are pulling data from the reservoir; the receiving nodes are perturbed as described above. Figure 5 shows the aggregate bandwidth through the reservoir as the number of perturbed nodes is increased.

The total bandwidth in the unperturbed case is 1181.58 Mbits/second (4 nodes sending 8Kb packets at the maximum rate to 4 receivers through the reservoir), or 295.39 Mbits/sec per node. Perturbation of a node limits its receive bandwidth to 34.27 Mbits/sec. The lottery reservoir balances bandwidth automatically to nodes which are receiving at a higher rate, so that when 3 out of 4 nodes are perturbed, 56% of the total bandwidth can be achieved. Over 90% of the total bandwidth is obtained with half of the nodes perturbed. With the use of a non-load-balancing deterministic reservoir, the total bandwidth is limited by the slowest node, as shown in the figure.

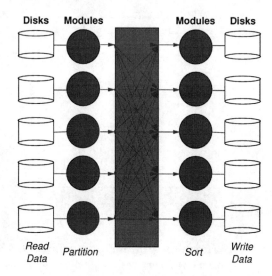

Figure 6. TigrisSort structure. *The application consists of two types of modules: partitioners and sorters. Partitioning nodes read data from their local disk and partition it into buckets based on the record key. Full buckets are transmitted to the appropriate sorting node, which sort the local data set and write it to the local disk. Communication is accomplished using a deterministic reservoir which routes packets to the appropriate sorting node based on the bucket's key value.*

5   TigrisSort: A Sample Application

In order to evaluate Tigris more generally, we have implemented *TigrisSort*, a parallel, disk-to-disk sorting benchmark. As with Datamation [12] and NOWSort [3], sorting is a good way to measure the memory, I/O, and communication performance of the complete system. While the existence of previous sorting results on other systems yields a yardstick by which the Tigris system can be compared, we were also interested in understanding the functional properties of the Tigris and Jaguar mechanisms in the context of a "real application."

5.1   TigrisSort Structure

The structure of TigrisSort is shown in Figure 6. TigrisSort implements a one-pass, disk-to-disk parallel sort of 100-byte records, each of which contains a 10-byte key. Data is initially striped across the input disks with 5 megabytes of random data per node.[1] The application consists of two sets of nodes: *partitioners* and *sorters*. Partitioning nodes are responsible for reading data from

---

[1] This amount is arbitrary; the software has no limitation in the amount of data that can be partitioned or sorted per node. 5 megabytes is a convenient value that limits the amount of memory that must be devoted to pinned VIA network buffers, which simplifies the benchmark structure somewhat.

# nodes	Amount sorted	Avg time/node	Total sort bw
2	5 MBytes	762 msec	52.49 Mbps
4	10 MBytes	734.5 msec	108.91 Mbps
6	15 MBytes	733 msec	163.71 Mbps
8	20 MBytes	725 msec	220.68 Mbps

Figure 7. TigrisSort performance results.

their local disk and partitioning it based on the record key; the partition "buckets" from each node are transmitted to the sorting nodes which sort the entire data set and write it to the local disk. This results in the sorted dataset being range-partitioned across the nodes, with each partition in sorted order. Communication is accomplished using a deterministic reservoir between the partitioning and sorting stages; this reservoir routes Waters representing full buckets to the appropriate sorting node based on the bucket's key value. This application cannot make use of a load-balancing reservoir, as data must be deterministically partitioned across the sorting modules.

File I/O is implemented by a class which maps a file into the address space of the JVM and exposes it directly to the Java application, through Jaguar, using methods such as readByte and writeByte. Operations on this class correspond to disk reads and writes through the memory-mapped file. This is the same mechanism used by the FileStream class. A special method is provided, flush(), which causes the contents of the memory-mapped file to be flushed to disk.

This approach has several limitations. One is that the operating system being used (Linux 2.2.13) does not allow the buffer cache to be circumvented using memory-mapped files, meaning that file data may be double-buffered. Another is that a particular write ordering cannot be enforced. Currently, Linux does not provide a "raw disk" mechanism which provides these features. Rather than concerning ourselves with these details, we assume that performance differences arising because of them will be negligible. This seems to be reasonable: first, disk I/O is just one component of the TigrisSort application, which does not appear to be disk-bandwidth limited. Secondly, double-buffering of sort data in memory is not problematic with the small (5 megabyte) per-node data partitions being dealt with. Third, write ordering is not important for implementing parallel sort; it is sufficient to ensure that all disk writes have completed.

The actual partitioning and sorting of records are implemented using native methods which manipulate I/O buffers directly, using pointers. This was necessary to avoid performance limitations of our Java compiler, which does not perform aggressive optimizations such as array bounds-check elimination. No data copying between Java and C is necessary as both Java (through Jaguar) and native code can directly manipulate the contents of the I/O buffers.

5.2 TigrisSort Performance

Figure 7 shows the performance of TigrisSort as the benchmark is scaled up from 2 to 8 nodes. In each case, half of the nodes are configured as partitioners, and half as sorters; 5 megabytes of data are partitioned or sorted per node. The total time to complete the sort averaged 738 milliseconds; as more nodes are added to the application, more data can be sorted in constant time. Given this result we feel that with careful tuning, TigrisSort can compete with the current world-record holder of the Datamation sort record, Millennium Sort [7], which was implemented on the same hardware platform using Windows NT and C++. However, the dominant cost of Datamation sort on modern systems is application startup; the results above do not include the cost of starting the Tigris system itself. Because Tigris is implemented in Java, which involves higher application startup cost (for class loading and JIT compilation), there is some question as to what should be included in the startup measurements. For instance, for traditional Datamation sort implementations, the cost of compiling the application and cold-booting the operating system are not measured.

6   Related Work

Tigris relates most closely to work in the areas of cluster programming frameworks and parallel databases.

Tigris' design is based on River [5], a robust cluster-based I/O system implemented in C++ on the Berkeley Network of Workstations [25]. While facially quite similar, Tigris differs from the original River system in a number of important respects, mainly stemming from the use of Java and Jaguar. In River, communication channels transmit raw byte streams (using Active Messages [9]), and the application must extract typed values from them through the use of a "data dictionary" class which maps field names onto byte offsets in the stream. In Tigris, modules map Java objects directly onto I/O buffers represented by the Water class through the use of Jaguar's *Pre-Serialized Object* mechanism. Type checking is therefore enforced by the compiler and modules operate directly on "true" Java objects, rather than using a library for indirection.

River made use of a single DQ algorithm (randomized), while Tigris introduces the round-robin and lottery DQ variants. Tigris additionally provides stream interfaces to shared memory segments and memory-mapped disk files, both enabled using Jaguar.

Other projects have considered support for parallel and distributed computing in a type-safe language. JavaParty [18] is an extension to Java providing transparent remote object access and object mobility. cJVM [1] is a cluster-based JVM which implements DSM-like remote object access and thread migration. DOSA [15] is a DSM system which provides fine-grain sharing at the granularity of objects which could be applied to languages such as Java. Titanium [30] is a dialect of Java for large-scale scientific computing; it is focused on static compilation and automated techniques for optimization of parallel programs expressed in the Titanium language. Other models for Java-based parallel computing, such as work stealing in JAWS [29] and agents in Ninflet [23], have also been considered. Tigris is the first dataflow and I/O-centric programming model to our knowledge to have been explored in the Java environment.

Parallel databases have made use of some of the dataflow concepts found in Tigris. Systems such as Bubba [10], Gamma [11], and Volcano [13] made use of static data partitioning techniques, rather than runtime adaption, to balance load across multiple physical resources. Static partitioning techniques form the foundation for all commercial shared-nothing parallel RDBMS products to our knowledge. Relational database queries have long been viewed as a dataflow graph; Eddies [6] build on the concepts in Tigris and River by dynamically reordering operators in a parallel database query plan to adapt to runtime performance fluctuations.

7   Conclusion

Cluster programming is by its nature a difficult task; obtaining good performance in the face of performance perturbations is even harder. Compounding this problem is the increasing use of clusters for irregular applications such as hosting Internet services and databases, which must tolerate fluctuations in resource availability and performance. Java has proven to be a viable platform for constructing such applications; what remains now is to bridge the gap between application demands and the mechanisms provided the underlying platform.

Tigris takes the idea of cluster programming in Java a step further by introducing dynamic resource adaptation to the programming model, as well as the use of high-performance networking and disk I/O through Jaguar. Several novel applications are being developed using Tigris as a base; the Telegraph [26] and Ninja [24] projects at UC Berkeley are both incorporating Tigris into their design for cluster-based scalable services.

We believe that through our experience with TigrisSort, as well as the low-level benchmarks of the Tigris DQ performance, that Tigris is an effective platform upon which to construct adaptive cluster applications. Moreover, the use of Jaguar allows us to build interesting data-intensive applications entirely in Java, which opens up new possibilities for developing flexible cluster programming environments.

References

1. Y. Aridor, M. Factor, A. Teperman, T. Eilam, and A. Schuster. A high performance cluster jvm presenting a pure single system image. In *Proceedings of the ACM 2000 JavaGrande Conference*, San Francisco, CA, June 2000.
2. R. H. Arpaci, A. Dusseau, A. M. Vahdat, L. T. Liu, T. E. Anderson, and D. A. Patterson. The interaction of parallel and sequential workloads on a network of workstations. In *Proceedings of SIGMETRICS/PERFORMANCE*, May 1995.

3. A. Arpaci-Dusseau, R. Arpaci-Dusseau, D. E. Culler, J. M. Hellerstein, and D. A. Patterson. Searching for the sorting record: Experiences in tuning NOW-Sort. In *Proceedings of the 1998 Symposium on Parallel and Distributed Tools (SPDT '98)*, 1998.

4. A. C. Arpaci-Dusseau, D. E. Culler, and A. Mainwaring. Scheduling with implicit information in distributed systems. In *1998 SIGMETRICS Conference on the Measurement and Modeling of Computer Systems*, pages 233–243, June 1998.

5. R. Arpaci-Dusseau, E. Anderson, N. Treuhaft, D. Culler, J. Hellerstein, D. Patterson, and K. Yelick. Cluster I/O with River: Making the fast case common. In *IOPADS '99*, 1999.
   http://www.cs.berkeley.edu/~remzi/Postscript/river.ps.

6. R. Avnur and J. M. Hellerstein. Eddies: Continuously Adaptive Query Processing. In *Proceedings of the 2000 ACM SIGMOD International Conference on Management of Data*, Dallas, TX, May 2000.

7. P. Buonadonna, J. Coates, S. Low, and D. E. Culler. Millennium Sort: A Cluster-Based Application for Windows NT Using DCOM, River Primitives and the Virtual Interface Architecture. In *Proceedings of the 3rd USENIX Windows NT Symposium*, July 1999.

8. P. Buonadonna, A. Geweke, and D. Culler. An implementation and analysis of the Virtual Interface Architecture. In *Proceedings of SC'98*, November 1998.

9. B. Chun, A. Mainwaring, and D. Culler. Virtual network transport protocols for Myrinet. *IEEE Micro*, 18(1), January/February 1998.

10. G. Copeland, W. Alexander, E. Boughter, and T. Keller. Data Placement in Bubba. *SIGMOD Record*, 17(3):99–108, September 1988.

11. D. J. DeWitt, S. Ghanderaizadeh, and D. Schneider. A Performance Analysis of the Gamma Database Machine. *SIGMOD Record*, 17(3):350–360, September 1988.

12. Anon *et. al.* A measure of transaction processing power. In *Datamation, 31(7): 112-118*, February 1985.

13. G. Graefe. Encapsulation of Parallelism in the Volcano Query Processing System. *SIGMOD Record*, 19(2):102–111, June 1990.

14. S. Gribble, M. Welsh, D. Culler, and E. Brewer. Multispace: An evolutionary platform for infrastructural services. In *Proceedings of the 16th USENIX Annual Technical Conference*, Monterey, California, 1999.

15. Y. Charlie Hu, Weimin Yu, Dan Wallach, Alan Cox, and Willy Zwaenepoel. Runtime support for distributed sharing in typed languages. In *Proceedings of the Fifth ACM Workshop on Languages, Compilers, and Run-time Systems for Scalable Computers*, Rochester, NY, May 2000.

16. J. Huber, C. L. Elford, D. A. Reed, A. A. Chien, and D. S. Blumenthal. PPFS: A high performance portable parallel file system. In *Proceedings of the 9th ACM International Conference on Supercomputing*, pages 385–394, July 1995.

17. J. Moreira, S. Midkiff, and M. Gupta. From flop to megaflops: Java for technical computing. In *Proceedings of the 11th Workshop on Languages and Compilers for Parallel Computing (LCPC'98)*, 1998. http://www.research.ibm.com/ninja/.

18. M. Philippsen and M. Zenger. JavaParty - transparent remote objects in Java. In *Concurrency: Practice and Experience, 9(11):1225-1242*, November 1997.

19. Sun Microsystems Inc. Enterprise Java Beans Technology.
    http://java.sun.com/products/ejb/.

20. Sun Microsystems Inc. Java HotSpot Performance Engine.
    http://java.sun.com/products/hotspot/index.html.

21. Sun Microsystems Inc. Java Native Interface Specification.
    http://java.sun.com/products/jdk/1.2/docs/guide/jni/index.html.

22. Sun Microsystems Labs. The Exact Virtual Machine (EVM).
    http://www.sunlabs.com/research/java-topics/.
23. H. Takagi, S. Matsuoka, H. Nakada, S. Sekiguchi, M. Satoh, and U. Nagashima.   Ninflet: A migratable parallel objects framework using Java.   In *ACM 1998 Workshop on Java for High-Performance Network Computing*, 1998.
    http://www.cs.ucsb.edu/conferences/java98/papers/ninflet.eps.
24. UC Berkeley Ninja Project. http://ninja.cs.berkeley.edu.
25. UC Berkeley NOW Project. The UC Berkeley Network of Workstations Project.
    http://now.cs.berkeley.edu.
26. UC Berkeley Telegraph Project. http://db.cs.berkeley.edu/telegraph/.
27. T. von Eicken, A. Basu, V. Buch, and W. Vogels. U-Net: A user-level network interface for parallel and distributed computing. In *Proceedings of the 15th Annual Symposium on Operating System Principles*, December 1995.
28. M. Welsh and D. Culler. Jaguar: Enabling efficient communication and I/O from Java. *Concurrency: Practice and Experience*, 2000. Special Issue on Java for High-Performance Network Computing, To appear,
    http://www.cs.berkeley.edu/~mdw/proj/jaguar.
29. A. Woo, Z. Mao, and H. So. The Berkeley JAWS Project.
    http://www.cs.berkeley.edu/~awoo/cs262/jaws.html.
30. Yelick, Semenzato, Pike, Miyamoto, Liblit, Krishnamurthy, Hilfinger, Graham, Gay, Colella, and Aiken. Titanium: A high-performance Java dialect. In *ACM 1998 Workshop on Java for High-Performance Network Computing*, February 1998.

High Level Programming Methodologies for Data Intensive Computations*

Gagan Agrawal[1], Renato Ferreira[2], Ruoming Jin[1], and Joel Saltz[2]

[1] Department of Computer and Information Sciences
University of Delaware, Newark DE 19716
[2] Department of Computer Science
University of Maryland, College Park, MD 20742

1   Introduction

Solving problems that have large computational and storage requirements is becoming increasingly critical for advances in many domains of science and engineering. By allowing algorithms for such problems to be programmed in widely used or rapidly emerging high-level paradigms, like object-oriented and declarative programming models, rapid prototyping and easy development of computational techniques can be facilitated.

Our research focuses on an important class of scientific and engineering problems, *data intensive computations*. The datasets associated with these applications are usually multi-dimensional. The data dimensions can be spatial coordinates, time, or varying experimental conditions such as temperature, velocity or magnetic field. The increasing importance of such applications has been widely recognized. Runtime systems like the Active Data Repository [5,6] and the Passion runtime library [18,19] allow high performance on data intensive applications, but do not address the need for programming with high-level abstractions.

We target two high-level programming models for this important class of computations:

1. Object-Oriented (Java Based): Object-oriented features like encapsulation and polymorphism can ease software development and allow better long-term management of large computational projects. We target a dialect of Java for expressing data intensive computations. This dialect of Java includes extensions for allowing multidimensional collection of objects, parallel loops over such collections and reduction interface. An initial prototype compiler for this dialect of Java has been built using the Titanium infrastructure. We have been able to successfully compile templates from medical image processing and scientific simulation domains through our compiler. Our compiler uses static interprocedural slicing technique for extracting required functions for an existing runtime system, called the Active Data Repository (ADR). ADR is responsible for optimizing utilization of system resources.

* This work was supported by NSF grant ACR-9982087 awarded jointly to University of Maryland and University of Delaware. Authors Agrawal and Jin were also supported by NSF CAREER award ACI-9733520.

S. Dwarkadas (Ed.): LCR 2000, LNCS 1915, pp. 32–43, 2000.

2 Declarative (XQL Based): The very high-level nature of declarative languages can allow rapid prototyping of new computational techniques. XML (Extensible Markup Language) is getting accepted as the format for logical lay-out of data which may be made available over the web or is exchanged between organizations. XML Schemas provide facilities for describing the structure and constraining the contents of XML documents. Many declarative languages are being proposed for querying and processing XML documents and schemas, the one likely to get widely accepted is the XML Query Language (XQL). We propose extensions to XML Schemas to allow expressing multidimensional collections of elements and to XQL for allowing expression of computations. In this paper we describe how XQL with such extensions can be translated to our dialect of Java. Our current compiler and ADR runtime support can then be used for optimizing execution of computations expressed using XQL.

The rest of this paper is organized as follows. In Section 2, we describe the target application class. Object-oriented and declarative language support for data intensive computing is presented in Section 3. A brief overview of the design of current compiler, including performance, is presented in Figure 4. We conclude in Section 5.

2 Data Intensive Applications

Data intensive computations arise in many domains of scientific and engineering research. Typical examples of very large scientific datasets include long running simulations of time-dependent phenomena that periodically generate snapshots of their state hydrodynamics and chemical transport simulation for estimating pollution impact on water bodies, magnetohydrodynamics simulation of planetary magnetospheres, simulation of a flame sweeping through a volume, airplane wake simulations; archives of raw and processed remote sensing data, MODIS [13]), and archives of medical images (e.g. high resolution light microscopy, CT imaging, MRI, sonography) [8,9,17,15].

Data intensive applications in these and related scientific areas share many common charactestics. The datasets are usually multi-dimensional. The data dimensions can be spatial coordinates, time, or varying experimental conditions such as temperature, velocity or magnetic field. Access to data items is described by a *range query*, namely a multi-dimensional bounding box in the underlying multi-dimensional space of the dataset. Only the data items whose associated coordinates fall within the multi-dimensional box are retrieved. The basic computation consists of (1) mapping the coordinates of the retrieved input items to the corresponding output items, and (2) aggregating, in some way, all the retrieved input items mapped to the same output data items. The computation of a particular output element is a reduction operation, i.e. the correctness of the output usually does not depend on the order input data items are aggregated.

Another common characteristic of these applications is their extremely high storage and computational requirements. For example, ten years of global coverage satellite data at a resolution of four kilometers for our satellite data processing application Titan consists of over 1.4TB of data [6]. For our Virtual Microscope application, one focal plane of a single slide requires over 7GB (uncompressed) at high power, and a hospital such as Johns Hopkins produces hundreds of thousands of slides per year [9]. Similarly, the computation for one ten day composite Titan query for the entire world takes about 100 seconds per processor on the Maryland sixteen node IBM SP2.

3   Language Support

We now describe our current solution towards providing high-level language support for data intensive computations, including Java extensions, extensions to XML, DTD and query language for XML data.

3.1   Java Extensions for Data Intensive Computing

We borrow two concepts from object-oriented parallel systems like Titanium [22], HPC++ [3] and Concurrent Aggregates [7].

- *Domains* and *Rectdomains* are collections of objects of the same type. *Rectdomains* have a stricter definition, in the sense that each object belonging to such a collection has a *coordinate* associated with it that belongs to a pre-specified rectilinear section of the domain.
- The *foreach* loop, which iterates over objects in a domain or rectdomain, and has the property that the order of iterations does not influence the result of the associated computations. We further extend the semantics of foreach to include the possibility of updates to *reduction variables*, as we explain later.

We introduce a Java interface called *Reducinterface*. Any object of any class implementing this interface acts as a *reduction variable* [11]. The semantics of a reduction variable are analogous to those used in version 2.0 of High Performance Fortran (HPF-2) [11] and in HPC++ [3]. A reduction variable has the property that it can only be updated inside a *foreach* loop by a series of operations that are associative and commutative. Furthermore, the intermediate value of the reduction variable may not be used within the loop, except for self-updates.

Figure 1 outlines an example code with our chosen extensions. This code shows the essential computation in a virtual microscope application [9]. A large digital image is stored in disks. This image can be thought of as a two dimensional array or collection of objects. Each element in this collection denotes a pixel in the image. The interactive user supplies two important pieces of information. The first is a bounding box within this two dimensional box, this implies the area within the original image that the user is interested in scanning. The first 4 arguments provided to the main are integers and together, they specify the *points* lowend and hiend, the two extreme corners of the rectangular bounding box. The second information provided by the user is the subsampling factor, an integer denoted by subsamp, which tells the granularity at which the user is interested

```
Interface Reducinterface {
// Any object of any class implementing
// this interface is a reduction variable
}
public class VMPixel {
 char[] colors;
 void Initialize() {
  colors[0] = 0 ;
  colors[1] = 0 ;
  colors[2] = 0 ;
 }
 void Accum(VMPixel Apixel, int avgf) {
  colors[0] += Apixel.colors[0]/avgf ;
  colors[1] += Apixel.colors[1]/avgf ;
  colors[2] += Apixel.colors[2]/avgf ;
 }
}
public class VMPixelOut extends VMPixel
        implements Reducinterface;
public class VMScope {
 static int Xdimen = ... ;
 static int Ydimen = ... ;
 static Point[2] lowpoint = [0,0];
 static Point[2] hipoint = [Xdimen-1,Ydimen-1];
 static RectDomain[2] VMSlide = [lowpoint : hipoint];
 static VMPixel[2d] VScope = new VMPixel[VMSlide];
 public static void main(String[] args) {
  Point[2] lowend = [args[0],args[1]];
  Point[2] hiend = [args[2],args[3 ]];
  int subsamp = args[4];
  RectDomain[2] Outputdomain = [[0,0]:(hiend -
         lowend)/subsamp];
  VMPixelOut[2d] Output = new VMPixel[Outputdomain] ;
  RectDomain[2] querybox ;
  Point[2] p;
  foreach(p in Outputdomain) {
   Output[p].Initialize();
  }
  querybox = [lowend : hiend] ;
  foreach(p in querybox) {
   Point[2] q = (p - lowend)/subsamp ;
   Output[q].Accum(VScope[p],subsamp*subsamp) ;
  }
 }
}
```

Fig. 1. Example Code

in viewing the image. A `querybox` is created using specified points `lowend` and `hiend`. Each pixel in the original image which falls within the `querybox` is read and then used to increment the value of the corresponding output pixel.

3.2   XML/XQL Based Interface

We now describe how the persistent data accessed by our class of applications can be represented, at a logical level, by using and extending the emerging *Extensible Markup Language* (XML) [4] and the associated XML schemas that provide *Document Type Definition* (DTD) [1,2]. We also show how the processing performed on these datasets can be expressed by using and extending *XML Query Language* (XQL).

Background: XML, Schemas, and XQL. XML provided a simple and general facility which is useful for data interchange between organizations or over the web. XML models data as a tree of *elements*. Each element contains *character data* and can have *attributes* composed of *name-value* pairs. An XML document represents elements, attributes, character data, and the relationship between them by simply using angle brackets.

Note that XML does not specify the actual lay-out of large file on the disks. Rather, if a system supports certain data-set in an XML representation, it must allow any application expecting XML data to properly access this data-set.

Applications that operate on XML data often need guarantees on the structure and content of data. XML Schema proposals [1,2] describe facilities for describing the structure and constraining the contents of XML documents.

Though XML documents can be processed by common procedural languages, it is convenient to use declarative syntax for selecting and processing elements from XML documents. XML Query Language (XQL) [16] is a rapidly emerging declarative language for this purpose.

XML and XQL Based Interface for Data Intensive Computing. We propose to use XML, XML Schemas with some extensions, and XQL with some proposed extensions for logically representing, accessing and processing data for our target class of applications. We have two major reasons behind choosing XQL based syntax as the declarative model for expressing data intensive computations:

- Allow, at a logical level, representation of persistent data from fields like medical informatics, satellite data processing, and scientific simulations as XML documents. This will enable this data to be accessed by rapidly emerging distributed applications that specifically access XML format.
- Allow expression of processing of data in a form consistent with the widely accepted standard for processing data available over the web or interchanged between organizations. The processing of data thus specified can actually be performed on a local uniprocessor or multiprocessor, or can be performed on a remote site where the data repository may reside.

A typical VMPixel Element

<**VMPixel**>
  <XCoord> ...   </XCoord>
  <YCoord> ...   </YCoord>
  <Color1> ...   </Color1>
  <Color2> ...   </Color2>
  <Color3> ...   </Color3>
</**VMPixel**>

Schema Declaration

<**archetype name** = ”VMPixel”>
  <element name=”XCoord” type =’integer’
  range=”0””999” rangetype=”unique_all_incl” >
  <element name=”YCoord” type =’integer’
  range=”0””999” rangetype=”unique_all_incl” >
  <element name=”Color1” type = ’char’ >
  <element name=”Color2” type = ’char’ >
  <element name=”Color3” type = ’char’ >
</**archetype**>

XQL Query

VMPixel[XCoord ge arg1 and
  XCoord le arg3 and
  YCoord ge arg2 and
  YCoord le arg4 and
  (XCoord - arg1) mod subsamp eq 0 and
  (YCoord - arg2)mod subsamp eq 0].
  setvalue[XCoord = (.XCoord - arg1)/subsamp ;
  YCoord = (.YCoord - arg3)/subsamp ;]

Fig. 2. XML Data, Schema and XQL Query

We now propose several extensions to XML Schemas and XQL for expressing our target class of applications. We use the virtual microscope application
initially presented in Figure 1 to demonstrate our proposed extensions. XML
data format, XML schema and XQL query for this applications is presented in
Figure 2.

The logical lay-out of a VMPixel element is presented at the top of left hand
side. The type of this element is <VMPixel>. It has 5 fields of character data
associated with it, which are the X and Y coordinates (of type integer) and the
values of 3 colors (of type character).

XML Schema declaration for such data-set is shown at the bottom of the left
hand side of Figure 2. This schema specifies that the 5 fields, XCoord, YCoord,
Color1, Color2, and Color3 are all required. It also specifies types of these 5

fields. The current XML Schema proposals [1,2] do not provide any mechanism for specifying multi-dimensional collection of objects. We propose additional syntax for this purpose. In the Schema declaration, we can add a *range*, which specifies the range of values an integer field can take. Further, we specify that in the data-set, this range is `unique_all_incl`, which means that only all values for `XCoord` and `YCoord` must be present within the data-set, and no two elements have the same value of both `XCoord` and `YCoord`.

The processing over such data set is specified using extensions to XQL, which are shown in right hand side of Figure 2. The term `VMPixel` means that elements of type VMPixel are chosen. The square brackets denotes the filter for elements of this type. Using the `XCoord` and `YCoord` fields, the $subsamp^{th}$ elements along each dimension from the query range are selected. Current version of XQL allows filtering of elements in this fashion, but does not allow assignment of new values to the fields. We propose a new directive, `setvalue`, for this purpose. This directive is used to assign new values to `XCoord` and `YCoord`. Unlike the code presented in Figure 1, the values of `Color1`, `Color2`, and `Color3` are not calculated by averaging the neighboring elements, but by simply picking $subsamp^{th}$ element along each dimension.

The processing involved in this this example is extremely simple. An obvious question is, "How can the expressiveness of XQL be improved for more complex applications ?". We propose to use Java with embedded XQL for this purpose. An example of the use of Java with embedded XQL is available at `http://xml.darmstadt.gmd.de/xql/xql-examples.html`. The basic ideas are as follows. XML data can be imported in Java programs using the *Document Object Model (DOM)*. DOM is an application programming interface (API) for XML documents. It defines the logical structure of documents and the way a document is accessed and manipulated. DOM data-structures can be accessed from Java programs. XQL operations can be applied to the DOM data-structures imported inside Java programs and can be used to: 1) Request a result object or set of objects, which may then be iterated over or processed by Java program segments, or 2) Create a new XML/DOC data structure containing the results. Note that the operations in XQL are analogous to data parallel expressions, because the filtering and computations are applied to all elements in the data-set. So, we expect that Java with embedded XQL and without any data parallel extensions can be used to express data intensive computations and the compiler can conveniently extract useful parallelism from such programs.

4   Compiler Design

We now give a very brief overview of the current prototype compiler, including the performance from some templates written using Java extensions.

Our compiler effort targets an existing runtime infrastructure developed at University of Maryland, called the *Active Data Repository (ADR)* [5], that integrates storage, retrieval and processing of multi-dimensional datasets on a parallel machine. Processing of a data intensive data parallel loop is carried

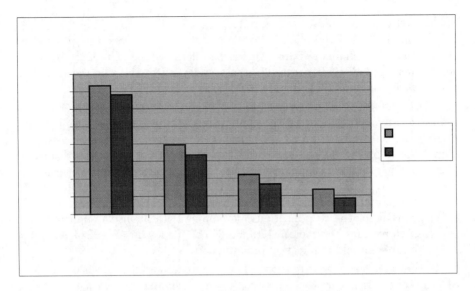

Fig. 3. Comparison of Compiler and Hand Generated Versions for VMScope

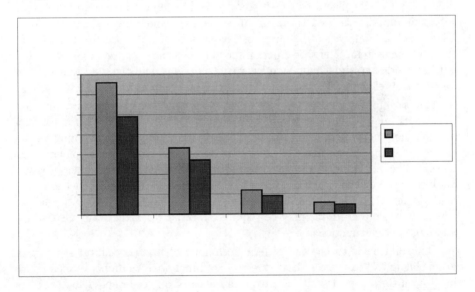

Fig. 4. Comparison of Compiler and Hand Generated Versions for Bess

out by ADR in two phases: *loop planning* and *loop execution*. The objective of loop planning is to determine a schedule to efficiently process a loop based on the amount of available resources in the parallel machine. The loop execution service manages all the resources in the system and carries out the loop plan generated by the loop planning service.

ADR allows customization for application specific processing, while leveraging the commonalities between the applications to provide support for common operations. Customization in ADR is achieved through C++ class inheritance. Current examples of data intensive applications implemented with ADR include Titan [6], for satellite data processing, the Virtual Microscope [9], for visualization and analysis of microscopy data, and coupling of multiple simulations for water contamination studies [12]. Though high performance has been achieved by using ADR for these applications, developing data intensive applications in this fashion requires very detailed knowledge of the low-level API of ADR and is not suitable for end application programmers.

In contrast, our Java extensions allow programming at a much higher level of abstraction. Our current compiler uses the technique of *loop fission* [21] to break the loop into a series of loops such that a unique subscript function is used to access all collections which are modified in the loop and another unique subscript function is used to access all collections which are read in the loop. Given such a loop, we need to extract several sets of functions to be passed to the runtime system. The three most important ones are, the *range function*, the left hand side and right hand side *subscript functions*, and the functions used to *aggregate* an element of each collection of object which is written in this loop.

Similar information is often extracted by various data-parallel Fortran compilers. One main difference in our work is that we are working with an object-oriented language (Java), which is significantly more challenging to analyze because of two main reasons: 1) Unlike Fortran, Java has a number of language features like object references, polymorphism, and aliases, which make program analysis more difficult, and 2) The object-oriented programming methodology leads to small procedures and frequent procedure calls. As a result, analysis across multiple procedures may be required in order to extract range, subscript and aggregation functions.

Our solution is to use the general technique of interprocedural static program slicing [20] to extract these three sets of functions. A number of techniques have been developed for slicing in the presence of object-oriented features like object references and polymorphism. Harrold *et al.* and Tonnela *et al.* have particularly focused on slicing in the presence of polymorphism, object references, aliases, and across procedure boundaries [10,20,14]. Thus, the use of slicing for extracting range, aggregatation and subscript functions enables our compiler to work accurately in the presence of object-oriented features and frequent procedure boundaries.

We briefly present some of the experimental results demonstrating the performance of our current compiler. Results from two templates are presented here: 1) VMScope models a virtual microscope, which provides a realistic digital emulation of a microscope, by allowing the users to specify a rectangular window and a subsampling factor, and 2) Bess models computations associated with water contamination studies over bays and estuaries. The computation performed determines the transport of contaminants, and accesses large fluid velocity datasets generated by a previous simulation. For both these applications, the performance of compiler generated ADR customization was compared against the performance of hand-coded versions.

Our experiments were performed using the ADR runtime system ported on a cluster of dual processor 400 MHz Intel Pentium nodes connected by gigabit ethernet. Each node has 256MB main memory and 18 GB of internal disk. Experiments were performed using 1, 2, 4 and 8 nodes of the cluster.

The results comparing the performance of compiler generated and hand customized VMScope are shown in Figure 3. A microscope image of $19,760 \times 15,360$ pixels was used. A query window of $10,000 \times 10,000$ was used for our experiments, with a subsampling factor of 8. The results comparing performance of compiler generated and hand coded version for Bess are shown in Figure 4. The dataset comprises of a grid with 2113 columns, each with 46,080 time-steps. Each time-step on each column has 4 4-byte floating point numbers, denoting simulated hydrodynamics parameters previously computed. The number of time-steps used for our experiments was 30,000.

As an average over these two templates and 1, 2, 4, and 8 processor configurations, the compiler generated versions are 21% slower than hand coded ones. Considering the high programming effort involved in managing and optimizing disk accesses and computation on a parallel machine, we believe that a 21% slow-down from automatically generated code is extremely good for the first prototype of the compiler. Further, our analysis of the differences between compiler generated and hand coded versions has pointed us to a number of directions for future research.

We are currently developing a translator for generating our dialect of Java from XML Schemas and XQL queries. The operations in XQL are analogous to data parallel expressions, because the filtering and computations are applied to all elements in the data-set. Translation from XQL queries to data parallel Java can be performed in three steps: (a) Use XML Schemas to create data members for Java classes, (b) Convert filtering operations of XQL to loop bounds and conditionals, and (c) Convert setvalue operations to Java assignment statements.

5   Summary

In this paper, we have addressed the problem of expressing data intensive computations in a high-level languages and then compiling such codes to efficiently manage data storage, retrieval and processing on a parallel machine. We have developed data-parallel extensions to Java for expressing this important class of applications. We have also proposed how XML, XML Schemas, and XQL can be extended to express such computations. Using these extensions, the programmers can specify the computations assuming that there is a single processor and infinite flat memory.

References

1. D. Beech, S. Lawrence, M. Maloney, N. Mendelsohn, and H. Thompson. XML Schema part 1: Structures, W3C working draft. Available at http://www.w3.org/TR/1999/xmlschema-1, May 1999.
2. P. Biron and A. Malhotra. XML Schema part 2: Datatypes, W3C working draft. Available at http://www.w3.org/TR/1999/xmlschema-2, May 1999.
3. Francois Bodin, Peter Beckman, Dennis Gannon, Srinivas Narayana, and Shelby X. Yang. Distributed pC++: Basic ideas for an object parallel language. *Scientific Programming*, 2(3), Fall 1993.
4. T. Bray, J. Paoli, and C. Sperberg-McQueen. Extensible Markup Language (XML) 1.0. Available at http://www.w3.org/TR/REC-xml, February 1998.
5. Chialin Chang, Renato Ferreira, Alan Sussman, and Joel Saltz. Infrastructure for building parallel database systems for multi-dimensional data. In *Proceedings of the Second Merged IPPS/SPDP (13th International Parallel Processing Symposium & 10th Symposium on Parallel and Distributed Processing)*. IEEE Computer Society Press, April 1999.
6. Chialin Chang, Bongki Moon, Anurag Acharya, Carter Shock, Alan Sussman, and Joel Saltz. Titan: A high performance remote-sensing database. In *Proceedings of the 1997 International Conference on Data Engineering*, pages 375–384. IEEE Computer Society Press, April 1997.
7. A.A. Chien and W.J. Dally. Concurrent aggregates (CA). In *Proceedings of the Second ACM SIGPLAN Symposium on Principles & Practice of Parallel Programming (PPOPP)*, pages 187–196. ACM Press, March 1990.
8. Srinivas Chippada, Clint N. Dawson, Monica L. Martínez, and Mary F. Wheeler. A Godunov-type finite volume method for the system of shallow water equations. *Computer Methods in Applied Mechanics and Engineering (to appear)*, 1997. Also a TICAM Report 96-57, University of Texas, Austin, TX 78712.
9. R. Ferreira, B. Moon, J. Humphries, A. Sussman, J. Saltz, R. Miller, and A. Demarzo. The Virtual Microscope. In *Proceedings of the 1997 AMIA Annual Fall Symposium*, pages 449–453. American Medical Informatics Association, Hanley and Belfus, Inc., October 1997. Also available as University of Maryland Technical Report CS-TR-3777 and UMIACS-TR-97-35.
10. M. J. Harrold and Ning Ci. Reuse-driven interprocedural slicing. In *Proceedings of the International Conference on Software Engineering*, 1998.
11. High Performance Fortran Forum. Hpf language specification, version 2.0. Available from, January 1997,
http://www.crpc.rice.edu/HPFF/versions/hpf2/files/hpf-v20.ps.gz.
12. Tahsin M. Kurc, Alan Sussman, and Joel Saltz. Coupling multiple simulations via a high performance customizable database system. In *Proceedings of the Ninth SIAM Conference on Parallel Processing for Scientific Computing*. SIAM, March 1999.
13. The Moderate Resolution Imaging Spectrometer.
http://ltpwww.gsfc.nasa.gov/MODIS/MODIS.html.
14. R. Fiutem P. Tonnela, G. Antonio and E. Merlo. Flow-insensitive c++ pointers and polymorphism analysis and its application to slicing. In *Proceedings of the International Conference on Software Enginering*, 1997.

15. G. Patnaik, K. Kailasnath, and E.S. Oran. Effect of gravity on flame instabilities in premixed gases. *AIAA Journal*, 29(12):2141–8, Dec 1991.
16. J. Robie, J. Lapp, and D. Schach. XML Query Language (XQL). Available at http://www.w3.org/Style/XSL/Group/1998/09/XQL-proposal.html, September 1998.
17. T. Tanaka. Configurations of the solar wind flow and magnetic field around the planets with no magnetic field: calculation by a new MHD. *Jounal of Geophysical Research*, 98(A10):17251–62, Oct 1993.
18. R. Thakur, A. Choudhary, R. Bordawekar, S. More, and S. Kutipudi. Passion: Optimized I/O for parallel applications. *IEEE Computer*, 29(6):70–78, June 1996.
19. Rajeev Thakur and Alok Choudhary. An extended two-phase method for accessing sections of out-of-core arrays. *Scientific Programming*, 5(4):301–317, Winter 1996.
20. F. Tip. A survey of program slicing techniques. *Journal of Programming Languages*, 3(3):121–189, September 1995.
21. Michael Wolfe. *High Performance Compilers for Parallel Computing*. Addison-Wesley, 1995.
22. K. Yelick, L. Semenzato, G. Pike, C. Miyamoto, B. Libit, A. Krishnamurthy, P. Hilfinger, S. Graham, D. Gay, P. Colella, and A. Aiken. Titanium: A high-performance Java dialect. *Concurrency Practice and Experience*, 9(11), November 1998.

Static Analysis for Guarded Code*

Ping Hu

INRIA Rocquencourt, 78153 Le Chesnay, France
Ping.Hu@inria.fr

Abstract. *Guarded(predicated) execution*, as a new hardware feature, has been introduced into today's high performance processors. *Guarded execution* can significantly improve the performance of programs with conditional branches, and meanwhile also poses new challenges for conventional program analysis techniques. In this paper, we propose a static semantics inference mechanism to capture the semantics information of guards in the context of guarded code. Based on the semantics information, we extend the conventional definitions regarding program analysis in guarded code, and develop the related guard-aware analysis techniques. These analyses include control flow analysis, data dependence analysis and data flow analysis as well.

1   Introduction

High performance compilation techniques rely heavily on effective program analysis. Sufficient and precise information on a program is critical to program optimization as well as to program parallelization.

Guarded(predicated) execution [10,9], as a new hardware feature, has been introduced into more and more high performance processors. This hardware feature provides an additional boolean register for each operation to guard whether the operation will be executed or not. If the value of the register is *true*, then the operation will be executed normally, otherwise the operation will be collapsed after initiating the execution of the operation. Such a register in an operation is termed the *guard* of the operation and the operation is said to be a *guarded(predicated) operation*. To support *guarded execution*, a compiler algorithm, called *if-conversion* [2,9,3,6], converts programs with conditional branches into guarded code. As a result, *if-conversion* removes conditional branches from programs. Figure 1 shows an example of guarded code, which has been if-converted from the control flow graph given on the left of the figure.

Guarded execution can significantly improve the performance of a program with conditional branches due to two main facts. First, *if-conversion* enlarges the size of basic blocks and thereby provides a large number of opportunities to extract the available parallelism from the enlarging scheduling scope. Second, the elimination of branches can avoid high branch misprediction penalties so as to

---

* This research was partially supported by the ESPRIT IV reactive LTR project OCEANS, under contract No. 22729.

S. Dwarkadas (Ed.): LCR 2000, LNCS 1915, pp. 44–56, 2000.

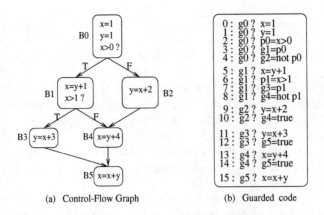

(a) Control-Flow Graph   (b) Guarded code

Fig. 1. An example of guarded code

improve branch dynamic behavior. However, the introduction of *guarded execution* also proposes new challenges for conventional program analysis techniques when applied to guarded code.

For instance, for two successive guarded operations below,

$$g1? \ x = y + 1$$
$$g2? \ x = x * 2$$

does there exist any data-dependence between them? Will the value of variable x defined in the first operation be redefined by the second operation? If we ignore the effect of guards on the operations, the answer should be 'yes' to both questions. However, if the two guards $g1$ and $g2$ are disjoint(i.e. they never evaluate to *true* at same time), there is indeed no data-dependence between them. Only when $g2$ is always *true* as long as $g1$ is *true*, will the variable x in the first operation be redefined(killed) by the second operation and is not reachable(alive) after the second one. Hence, the logical relations among guards have to be taken into consideration in the analysis techniques.

The authors in [4] have suggested P-facts to extract and represent the disjointedness relations between guards. These P-facts are used to analyze live-variable ranges for register allocation. But the extraction mechanism for disjointedness relations of guards is very sensitive to the instruction set architecture since it depends upon the instruction scheme of the HPL PlayDoh architecture [8]. Another data-structure for tracking guard relations, proposed in [7], is the *predicate partition graph*. This graph-based data-structure is used to provide query information for data-flow analysis and register allocation in [5]. Similar to [4], the construction of the partition graph is based upon the HPL PlayDoh instruction set. A rather different approach developed in [12] is to apply *reverse if-conversion* to convert guarded code back to an explicit conditional branch structure where traditional analysis techniques can be applicable. In contrast, we expect to develop analysis techniques that would be directly applicable to guarded code.

In this paper, we propose a static semantics inference mechanism in the context of guarded code, which can capture the semantics information of guards directly from guarded code, and allows us to analyze the logical relations among guards.

Based on the semantics information, we extend the conventional definitions regarding program analysis in the context of guarded code, and develop the related guard-aware analysis techniques. These guard-aware analyses include not only data-flow analysis but also control-flow and data-dependence analysis. The guard-aware control-flow analysis enables us to achieve the traditional results of control-flow analysis, such as dominance, post-dominance and control-equivalence, etc. The control-equivalence analysis has been used to reduce the number of guards required in guarded code. The guard-aware data-dependence analysis can avoid a lot of dependences so as to provide more opportunities for exploiting and extracting parallelism in guarded code.

The remainder of the paper is organized as follows. Section 2 presents the semantics inference mechanism. Section 3 presents the guard-aware control-flow analysis. The guard-aware data-dependence and data-flow analysis will be presented in Sect. 4 and Sect. 5, respectively. The last section gives the concluding remarks and outlines our future work.

2   Semantics Analysis for Guards

The semantics of a guard is a logical proposition which consists of predicate variables(i.e. branch conditions, e.g. p_1 and p_2 in the example of Fig. 1) and three basic logical operators($\wedge, \vee$ and $\neg$). That implies an operation will be executed only when its guard's semantics is *true*, i.e. the proposition evaluates to *true*.

A judgment $C \vdash S$ is introduced to denote that, from C, a given segment of guarded code, one can deduce S, a set of semantics of all guards in the guarded code. We have defined three inference rules for the reduction of guard semantics as follows.

Table 1. Guard semantics analysis

$$\vdash \{g_0 = true\} \qquad \text{(taut)}$$

$$\frac{C \vdash S \cup \{g_1 = l_1\}}{C; (g_1? \ g_2 = l_2) \vdash S \cup \{g_1 = l_1\} \cup \{g_2 = dnf(l_1 \wedge l_2)\}} \quad \text{(fork)}$$

$$\frac{C \vdash S \cup \{g_1 = l_1\} \cup \{g_2 = l_2\}}{C; (g_1? \ g_2 = l_3) \vdash S \cup \{g_1 = l_1\} \cup \{g_2 = dnf((l_1 \wedge l_3) \vee l_2)\}} \quad \text{(join)}$$

Rule *taut* identifies that g_0 is a true-guard whose value is always true. Rule *fork* describes, if the semantics of guard g_1 is known as l_1 in S, after the execution of the guarded operation $(g_1? \ g_2 = l_2)$, the semantics of guard g_2 is the proposition $dnf^1(l_1 \wedge l_2)$, i.e. the conjunction of the g_1's semantics l_1 and the condition l_2 under which the operations guarded by g_2 will be executed. The difference of the third rule *join* from the second rule *fork* is that guard g_2 has already had a semantics definition l_2 in S. Hence, the new semantics of g_2 after the guard operation $(g_1? \ g_2 = l_3)$ should be $dnf((l_1 \wedge l_3) \vee l_2)$, i.e. the disjunction of the current g_2's semantics $(l_1 \wedge l_3)$ and the previous g_2's semantics l_2.

These three inference rules are applied to deduce the guard semantics for the above example in Fig. 1. The detail for the inference procedure is demonstrated in the following table.

Table 2. The deduction for the semantics of the guards

C	S	Rule
	$g_0 = true$	taut
$g_0? \ x = 1$ $g_0? \ y = 1$ $g_0? \ p_0 = x > 0$		
$g_0? \ g_1 = p_0$	$g_1 = dnf(true \wedge p_0) = p_0$	fork
$g_0? \ g_2 = \neg p_0$	$g_2 = dnf(true \wedge \neg p_0) = \neg p_0$	fork
$g_1? \ x = y + 1$ $g_1? \ p_1 = x > 1$		
$g_1? \ g_3 = p_1$	$g_3 = dnf(p_0 \wedge p_1) = p_0 \wedge p_1$	fork
$g_1? \ g_4 = \neg p_1$	$g_4 = dnf(p_0 \wedge \neg p_1) = p_0 \wedge \neg p_1$	fork
$g_2? \ y = x + 2$		
$g_2? \ g_4 = true$	$g_4 = dnf((\neg p_0 \wedge true) \vee$ $(p_0 \wedge \neg p_1)) = \neg p_0 \vee \neg p_1$	join
$g_3? \ y = x + 3$		
$g_3? \ g_5 = true$	$g_5 = dnf((p_0 \wedge p_1) \wedge true)$ $= p_0 \wedge p_1$	fork
$g_4? \ x = y + 4$		
$g_4? \ g_5 = true$	$g_5 = dnf(((\neg p_0 \vee \neg p_1) \wedge true)$ $\vee (p_0 \wedge p_1)) = true$	join
$g_5? \ x = x + y$		

The guarded operations in the first column have been analyzed one by one via the use of the inference rules. The names of the rules applied to the operations are shown in the third column. The details of how to apply the rules to the operations are given in the second column. For instance, the only applicable rule is *taut* at the beginning of all the operations, as shown in the first line. For the operation $(g_0? \ g_1 = p_0)$, we can apply rule *fork* to obtain g_1's semantics

---

[1] Function dnf returns a logical proposition in disjunction normal form.

$dnf(true \wedge p_0)$, i.e. p_0. For the operation $(g_2? \; g_4 = true)$, g_4 has a semantic definition $(p_0 \wedge \neg p_1)$ in S at this moment, we thus apply rule $join$ and obtain its new semantics $dnf((\neg p_0 \wedge true) \vee (p_0 \wedge \neg p_1))$, i.e. $(\neg p_0 \vee \neg p_1)$.

The final semantics set for all the guards is achieved as follows,

$$\{g_0 = true, \; g_1 = p_0, \; g_2 = \neg p_0, \; g_3 = p_0 \wedge p_1, g_4 = \neg p_0 \vee \neg p_1, \; g_5 = true\}$$

A function Sem is employed to return the semantics of a guard. For example, $Sem(g_0) = true$, $Sem(g_1) = p_0$ and $Sem(g_2) = \neg p_0$, etc.

An immediate application of the semantics set is dead-code elimination in the context of guarded code. We can eliminate those operations whose guards are $false$ in the semantics set, because it is clear that this kind of operations will never be executed in any cases.

The semantics sets of guards also provides a good foundation for the analysis of guarded code. They enable us to analyze the logical relations between guards, and to develop the guard-aware analysis techniques. These analyses include control-flow, data-dependence and data-flow analysis, which are presented respectively in the following sections.

3   Guard-Aware Control Flow Analysis

Although a lot of information about control flow paths has been lost in if-converted code, we can still achieve some conventional results of control flow analysis, such as dominance, post-dominance and control-equivalence, etc, with the support of the semantics sets of guards obtained in the previous section.

3.1   Dominance Analysis

Dominance is a fundamental concept in control flow analysis. A node m of a flow graph $dominates$ node n if every path from the initial node of the flow graph to n goes through m, see [1]. This definition implies that if node n is visited from the initial node along an arbitrary path, then m must have been visited along the path as well. We extend the definition to guarded operations,

Definition of $Dominator$

A guarded operation $op1$ $dominates$ guarded operation $op2$ if each time $op2$ is executed, then $op1$ has definitely been executed.

$$Dom(op1, op2) =_{df}$$
$$(op1 \preccurlyeq op2) \wedge Taut(Guard(op2) \rightarrow Guard(op1))$$

The definition of $Dominator$ is represented by a boolean function $Dom(op1, op2)$, which returns $true$ if $op1$ $dominates$ $op2$, otherwise returns $false$. The symbol $\preccurlyeq$ denotes the execution initiation order of operations, for instance, $op1 \preccurlyeq op2$ represents that an execution initiation for $op1$ is not later than that for $op2$. The boolean function $Taut$ verifies whether a logical proposition is a tautology(i.e. the proposition always evaluates to true),

$$Taut(p) =_{df} \begin{cases} true & \text{proposition } p \text{ is a tautology} \\ false & \text{otherwise} \end{cases}$$

It is a decidable problem to check whether a given logical proposition is a tautology or not. Its computational complexity is $O(2^n)$ in the worst case, where n is the number of predicate variables in the proposition.

The function $Guard$ returns the semantics of the guard of an operation from the semantic sets of guards, which are obtained after the semantics analysis of guards presented in Sect. 2. The symbol $\rightarrow$ is used to denote the logical implication operator.

For the above given example, we can verify that the first operation $op0$ *dominates* all the operations. For instance, $op0$ *dominates* $op5(g_1? \ x = y+1)$ because

$$Taut(Guard(op5) \rightarrow Guard(op0))$$
$$\Rightarrow Taut(Sem(g_1) \rightarrow Sem(g_0))$$
$$\Rightarrow Taut(p_0 \rightarrow true) \Rightarrow true$$

It can be further verified that $op5$ *dominates* all the operations guarded by g_3 because

$$Taut(Sem(g_3) \rightarrow Sem(g_1))$$
$$\Rightarrow Taut((p_0 \wedge p_1) \rightarrow p_0) \Rightarrow true$$

But $op5$ does not dominate the operations guarded by g_4 because

$$Taut(Sem(g_4) \rightarrow Sem(g_1))$$
$$\Rightarrow Taut((\neg p_0 \vee \neg p_1) \rightarrow p_0) \Rightarrow false$$

The dual *dominator* notion is *post-dominator*. A node n of a flow graph *post-dominates* node m if every path from m to any exit of the flow graph goes through n, see [1]. The definition of *post-dominator* is extended to guarded code in the same manner as *dominator*.

Definition of *Post-dominator*

A guarded operation $op2$ *post-dominates* guarded operation $op1$ if each time $op1$ is executed, then $op2$ will definitely be executed.

$$Pdom(op2, op1) =_{df}$$
$$(op1 \preccurlyeq op2) \wedge Taut(Guard(op1) \rightarrow Guard(op2))$$

Let us have a look again at the example. It can be seen the last operation $op15$ *post-dominates* all the operations. In addition, the operations guarded by g_4 *post-dominate* those guarded by g_2 because

$$Taut(Sem(g_2) \rightarrow Sem(g_4))$$
$$\Rightarrow Taut(\neg p_0 \rightarrow (\neg p_0 \vee \neg p_1)) \Rightarrow true$$

As a corollary, it is trivial to verify that any guarded operation *dominates* and *post-dominates* itself.

3.2 Control-Equivalence

In general, we are interested in two kinds of control-flow relationships in the analysis of control-flow, control-dependence and control-equivalence. Most control-dependences have been converted into data-dependences in if-converted code. The analysis of data-dependence will be presented in the next section. Here, we focus on the analysis of control-equivalence.

Definition of *Control-equivalence*

An operation $op1$ is *control-equivalent* to operation $op2$ iff

1. $op1$ *dominates*(or *postdominates*) $op2$
2. $op2$ *postdominates*(or *dominates*) $op1$

Analysis of *Control-equivalence*

A boolean function $ConEq$ is used to verify whether two guarded operations are *control-equivalent*.

$$ConEq(op1, op2) =_{df} (Dom(op1, op2) \wedge Pdom(op2, op1)) \\ \vee (Dom(op2, op1) \wedge Pdom(op1, op2))$$

According to the above definitions of Dom and $Pdom$, the function $ConEq$ can be simplified as

$$ConEq(op1, op2) =_{df} Taut(Guard(op1) \leftrightarrow Guard(op2))$$

Moreover, a guard g_1 is *control-equivalent* to guard g_2 iff $Sem(g_1) \leftrightarrow Sem(g_2)$ is a tautology, i.e.

$$ConEq(g_1, g_2) =_{df} Taut(Sem(g_1) \leftrightarrow Sem(g_2))$$

In the above example, g_0 is *control-equivalent* to g_5 as $(true \leftrightarrow true)$ is a tautology. The operations guarded by g_0 are thus *control-equivalent* to those guarded by g_5.

All guards that are mutually *control-equivalent* form a *control-equivalence* class. Because the guards in a *control-equivalence* class are *control-equivalent*, they can share the same name so as to reduce the number of required guards. Therefore, the guarded code in the example can be improved by renaming g_5 to the control-equivalent guard g_0, and eliminating all the operations for the assignment of g_5. The improved guarded code as well as the original code are shown in Fig. 2.

Remark: The functions Dom, $Pdom$ and $ConEq$ are applicable only to the operations in the same loop iteration. More precisely, given two operations $op1$ and $op2$ from a loop body, if $Dom(op1, op2)$ evaluates to $true$, that just means $op1$ dominates $op2$ in the same iteration, and does not mean $op1$ from an iteration dominates $op2$ from another different iteration. This is not surprising because the traditional dominance relationship based on a control flow graph is also limited in the same iteration. It is possible that there is no dominance between two nodes from different iterations, even though conventional dominance analysis determines that one node dominates the other.

```
 0 : g0 ? x=1              0 : g0 ? x=1
 1 : g0 ? y=1              1 : g0 ? y=1
 2 : g0 ? p0=x>0           2 : g0 ? p0=x>0
 3 : g0 ? g1=p0            3 : g0 ? g1=p0
 4 : g0 ? g2=not p0        4 : g0 ? g2=not p0

 5 : g1 ? x=y+1            5 : g1 ? x=y+1
 6 : g1 ? p1=x>1          6 : g1 ? p1=x>1
 7 : g1 ? g3=p1            7 : g1 ? g3=p1
 8 : g1 ? g4=not p1        8 : g1 ? g4=not p1

 9 : g2 ? y=x+2            9 : g2 ? y=x+2
10 : g2 ? g4=true        10 : g2 ? g4=true

11 : g3 ? y=x+3          11 : g3 ? y=x+3
12 : g3 ? g5=true        12 : g3 ? g5=true

13 : g4 ? x=y+4          13 : g4 ? x=y+4
14 : g4 ? g5=true        14 : g4 ? g5=true

15 : g5 ? x=x+y          15 : g0 ? x=x+y

    (a)  original              (b)  improved
```

Fig. 2. The improved guarded code

4   Guard-Aware Data Dependence Analysis

A data-dependence holds between two operations when one of them computes values needed by the other. Data-dependences directly determine the available parallelism in a program since they decide the execution order of operations. To guarantee the semantic correctness of a program, scheduling the operations for extracting parallelism must honor data-dependences.

Traditionally, data-dependences are divided into three classes,

1. *Flow-dependence*
   An operation *flow-depends* on another operation if a variable used in the former is defined by the latter.

2. *Anti-dependence*
   An operation *anti-depends* on another operation if a variable defined in the former is used by the latter.

3. *Output-dependence*
   An operation *output-depends* on another operation if the former defines the same variables as the latter.

In fact, as Wolfe mentions in [13], there does not exist a data-dependence between two operations respectively from *then* and *else* edges of a conditional branch since they will never be executed at the same time. We further extend this fact as:

> *there exists no data-dependence between two operations that are never executed along the same execution path.*

If two guarded operations are not executed along the same execution path, then the two guards of both operations don't evaluate to *true* at same time. Such operations are said to be disjoint. We use a boolean function $Disjoint$ to determine whether two guarded operations are disjoint, i.e.

$$Disjoint(op1, op2) =_{df} Taut(\neg(Guard(op1) \wedge Guard(op2)))$$

We formally extend the above data-dependence definitions in the guard-aware data-dependence analysis.

1. **Flow-dependence:** $Dflow(op1, op2) =_{df}$
   $(op2 \prec op1) \wedge (Use(op1) \cap Def(op2) \neq \phi) \wedge \neg Disjoint(op1, op2)$

2. **Anti-dependence:** $Danti(op1, op2) =_{df}$
   $(op2 \prec op1) \wedge (Def(op1) \cap Use(op2) \neq \phi) \wedge \neg Disjoint(op1, op2)$

3. **Output-dependence:** $Doutput(op1, op2) =_{df}$
   $(op2 \prec op1) \wedge (Def(op1) \cap Def(op2) \neq \phi) \wedge \neg Disjoint(op1, op2)$

where $(op2 \prec op1)$ represents that an execution initiation for $op2$ is earlier than that for $op1$, as mentioned above. The function Use returns the set of all variables used(read) in an operation and the function Def returns the set of all variables defined(written) in an operation.

Return to the example. The operation $op9(g_2? \ y = x + 2)$ would have depended on $op5(g_1? \ x = y + 1)$ if we had not taken take into account the effects of the guards. However,

$$Disjoint(op5, op9)$$
$$\Rightarrow Taut(\neg(Guard(op5) \wedge Guard(op9)))$$
$$\Rightarrow Taut(\neg(Sem(g_1) \wedge Sem(g_2)))$$
$$\Rightarrow Taut(\neg(p_0 \wedge \neg p_0)) \Rightarrow true$$

$op5$ and $op9$ are disjoint, and thus $op9$ is not data-dependent on $op5$. Moreover, we can deduce that g_2 and g_3 are also disjoint, and thus the operations guarded by g_3 do not depend on those guarded by g_2. For the same reason, there is no data-dependence between the operations guarded by g_3 and those guarded by g_4.

From this example, we can see the guard-aware analysis for data-dependences has effectively got rid of a large number of data-dependences between the disjoint operations. That will provide more opportunities for exploiting and extracting parallelism in guarded code.

Remark: It is not possible to statically determine two operations from different loop iterations are disjoint, even though they are known to be disjoint in the same iteration. Hence, when the function $Disjoint$ is applied to the operations from different iterations, its value has to be conservatively supposed to be *false* in order to guarantee the correction of the static guard-aware data-dependence analysis.

5   Guard-Aware Data-Flow Analysis

5.1   Reaching Definition

The notion of *reaching definition* concerns whether a definition in an operation can reach some point of a program. Conventionally, a value of a variable defined in an operation $op1$ can reach another operation $op2$ if this variable is not redefined along an execution path from $op1$ to $op2$, refer an example in [11].

We represent the *reaching definition* in the presence of guarded code by a boolean function *Reach*.

$$Reach(op1, op2) =_{df}$$
$$(op1 \prec op2) \wedge (Def(op1) \neq \phi) \wedge \neg Kill(op1, op2)$$

where the additional condition $(Def(op1) \neq \phi)$ is used to guarantee that there is a variable definition in the operation. The boolean function $Kill$ represents whether or not a variable definition in $op1$ would be killed by some operation between $op1$ and $op2$. A variable definition in $op1$ is killed before reaching $op2$

when the guard of op1 evaluates to true, there is some operation between op1 and op2 that would redefine this variable, and its guard always evaluates to true.

Suppose $\bigvee \phi = false$,

$$Kill(op1, op2) =_{df} Taut(Guard(op1) \rightarrow$$
$$\bigvee \{ Guard(op) \mid (op1 \prec op \prec op2) \wedge (Def(op) \cap Def(op1) \neq \phi) \})$$

A similar *reaching definition* proposed in [4] is that the variable definitions in a guarded operation can reach some point in a guarded code when the guard of the operation evaluates to *true*, and meanwhile all the guards of the operations that would redefine the variable evaluate to *false*. For the example,

```
0 : g0? x = 1
......
5 : g1? x = y + 1
......
9 : g2? y = x + 2
```

the value of variable x defined in $op0$ can reach $op9$ only when g_0 evaluates to *true*, and g_1 evaluates to *false*. Here, the question is how to determine statically that the value of $(g_0 \wedge \neg g_1)$, i.e. $(true \wedge \neg p_0)$, is *true* or *false*. In fact, this is an undecidable problem at compile time even if we had the semantics set for the guards.

Compared with our *reaching definition*, the value of x in $op0$ can reach $op9$ if g_1 does not always evaluate to *true* while g_0 evaluates to *true*. This implies that there exists a path(when g_1 is *false*) so that this value of x can flow through $op5$ and reach $op9$. This obviously agrees with the original *reaching definition*.

Conversely, if g_1 always evaluates to *true* while g_0 evaluates to *true*, this implies that $op5$ post-dominates $op0$. In this case, the value of x in $op0$ will definitely be killed by $op5$ in any case, and therefore can not reach $op9$. Moreover, it is a decidable problem to check whether a logical proposition is a tautology or not, as mentioned above.

Here, we have

$$Kill(op0, op9)$$
$$\Rightarrow Taut(Sem(g_0) \rightarrow Sem(g_1))$$
$$\Rightarrow Taut(true \rightarrow p_0) \Rightarrow false$$

the value of x in $op0$ thus can reach $op9$. In contrast, this value can not reach the last operation $op15$ since

$$Kill(op0, op15)$$
$$\Rightarrow Taut(Sem(g_0) \rightarrow \bigvee\{Sem(g_1), Sem(g_4)\})$$
$$\Rightarrow Taut(true \rightarrow \bigvee\{p_0, (\neg p_0 \vee \neg p_1)\}) \Rightarrow true$$

In the next subsection, we utilize the two functions *Reach* and *Kill* to define the guard-aware data-flow equations.

5.2   Guard-Aware Data Flow Equations

Before giving the guard-aware data-flow equations, we recall the conventional equation for data-flow analysis. The information(for instance, variable definitions) reaching the end of a basic block is that information which is either generated within the block or enters the beginning but is not killed by the block. The formal expression of this statement is the following well-known data-flow equation [1],

$$Out(B) =_{df} Gen(B) \cup (In(B) - Kill(B)) \quad where$$

– $Out(B)$: the set of all operations whose variable definitions can reach the end of B;

– $Gen(B)$: the set of the operations in B whose variable definitions can reach the end of B;

– $In(B)$: the set of all operations whose variable definitions enter at the beginning of B;

– $Kill^2(B)$: the set of the operations in $In(B)$ whose variable definitions are killed by B.

---

[2] For the sake of avoiding too many notations, the function names can be overloaded here.

In the context of guarded code, a basic block should be a maximal set of consecutive guarded operations with one entry point and one exit point, which is a so-called guarded block. Given such a guarded block GB, we can obtain the variable definitions reaching the end of the guarded block via the analysis of the *reaching definition* presented in the previous subsection. Suppose *end* is a virtual empty operation to represent the end point of GB, *end* is thus the successor of the last operation in GB. Table 3 gives the guard-aware data-flow equations.

Table 3. Guard-aware data-flow equations

$$Out(GB) =_{df} Gen(GB) \cup (In(GB) - Kill(GB)) \qquad \text{where}$$

$$Gen(GB) =_{df} \{\ op_i \mid (op_i \in GB) \wedge Reach(op_i, end)\ \}$$

$$In(GB) =_{df} \bigcup_{P \in pred(GB)} Out(P)$$

$$Kill(GB) =_{df} \{\ op_i \mid (op_i \in In(GB)) \wedge Kill(op_i, end)\ \}$$

The guarded code in the example of Fig. 1 forms a guarded block GB. Its $Gen(GB)$ is

$$\{1,\ 2,\ 3,\ 4,\ 6,\ 7,\ 8,\ 9,\ 10,\ 11\}$$

since the definitions of variable x in operations 0,5,13 are killed before reaching the end of the block. The final $Out(GB)$ is same as the $Gen(GB)$ because its $In(GB)$ is empty.

An important application of data-flow equations is to analyze live-variable ranges for register allocation. We believe the above guard-aware data-flow analysis would form an essential base for developing guard-aware register allocation techniques.

6   Conclusion

In this paper, we have presented a static semantics inference mechanism to capture the semantics information on guards, which provides a unified framework to develop the guard-aware analysis techniques, such as control flow analysis, data dependence analysis and data flow analysis. These guard-aware analyses provide the essential information to support optimizing and parallelizing compilation techniques on processors with guarded execution.

Guarded execution actually provides more opportunities and greater flexibility for program optimization. In future work, we intend to develop the optimization techniques especially for guarded code.

Acknowledgements

The author would like to thank Christine Eisenbeis and François Thomasset for their insightful comments and suggestions which improved the quality of this paper. The author would also like to thank Gang Chen and Michael Liebelt for their support in the work. Special thanks to Richard James for the correction of English faults.

References

1. A.V. Aho, R. Sethi, and J.D. Ullman. *Compilers: Principles, Techniques, and Tools.* Addison Wesley, 1986.
2. J.R. Allen, K. Kennedy, C. Portefied, and J. Warren. Conversion of control dependence to data dependence. In *Proceedings of the 10th ACM Symposium on Principles of Programming Languages*, pages 177–189, January 1983.
3. J.C. Dehnert and R.A. Towle. Compiling for the Cydra 5. *Journal of Supercomputing*, 7(1/2):181–227, May 1993.
4. A.E. Eichenberger and E.S. Davidson. Register allocation for predicated code. In *Proceedings of the 28th Annual International Symposium on Microarchitecture*, pages 180–191, November 1995.
5. D.M. Gillies, D.R. Ju, R. Johnson, and M. Schlansker. Global predicate analysis and its application to register allocation. In *Proceedings of the 29th Annual International Symposium on Microarchitecture*, pages 114–125, December 1996.
6. J. Hoogerbrugge and L. Augusteijn. Instruction Scheduling for TriMedia. *Journal of Instruction-Level Parallelism*, 1, February 1999.
7. R. Johnson and M. Schlansker. Analysis techniques for predicated code. In *Proceedings of the 29th Annual International Symposium on Microarchitecture*, pages 100–113, December 1996.
8. V. Kathail, M.S. Schlansker, and B.R. Rau. HPL PlayDoh architecture specification: Version 1.0. Technical Report HPL-93-80, Hewlett Packard Laboratories, February 1994.
9. J.C.H. Park and M. Schlansker. On predicated execution. Technical Report HPL-91-58, Hewlett Packard Software and Systems Laboratory, May 1991.
10. B.R. Rau, W.L. Yen, and R.A. Towle. The cydra 5 departmental supercomputer. *IEEE Computer*, pages 12–35, January 1989.
11. F. Thomasset. Analyse de flots de données : introduction. *Notes de cours : DEA d'Informatique*, March 1999. http://www-rocq.inria.fr/~thomasse/DEA/.
12. N.J. Warter, S.A. Mahlke, W.W. Hwu, and B.R. Rau. Reverse if-conversion. In *Proceedings SIGPLAN 1993 Conference on Programming Language Design and Implementation*, pages 290–299, June 1993.
13. M. Wolfe. *High performance compilers for parallel computing.* Addison Wesley, 1996.

A Framework for Efficient Register Allocation through Selective Register Demotion

Deepankar Bairagi, Santosh Pande, and Dharma P. Agrawal

Department of Electrical and Computer Engineering and Computer Science
University of Cincinnati, Cincinnati, OH 45221
{dbairagi,santosh,dpa}@ececs.uc.edu

Abstract. Decisions made during register allocation greatly influence the overall quality of compiled code. Standard graph-coloring allocators often make spilling decisions which are not guided by program structure or path-sensitive control flow information. This can result in generation and placement of load and store instructions which is inefficient from a global perspective. Quite often, allocation decisions get heavily influenced by the choice of candidates for register residency. We propose a framework which selectively demotes variables in a contained manner to maintain balanced register pressure. The decisions for selective demotion are made through a flow-analytic approach and the loads and stores are inserted in strategic points such that degrading effect of spill code on overall code quality is sufficiently reduced. Our approach tries to keep variables as candidates for register allocation only along the paths where it is profitable to do so. We attempt to identify good local candidates for demotion, however, decisions are taken only after their global demotion costs are captured. We have implemented the framework inside the SGI MIPSPRO compiler and have obtained very encouraging results in improving the allocation of a Briggs-style allocator.

1 Introduction

Register allocation is a very important phase of an optimizing compiler. Good register allocation is likely to provide the single most conducive factor in improving code quality in terms of speed as well as size. Strategies, such as graph coloring [2,3,5,6,7], neatly capture the concept of simultaneous liveness or lack thereof. They provide a reasonably good allocation at a moderate cost when the demand for registers is not very high. However, such strategies fall short of providing an adequately efficient global allocation of registers when demand for registers is high and spills are forced. Spill code is generally expensive and can lead to excessive latency problems interfering with other prefetching mechanisms. The negative effect of memory access instructions on system performance is even more pronounced for pipelined and superscalar machines. The mere number of loads and stores is not necessarily an indication of the quality of the generated code. The placement of the loads and stores is often as important a factor in dictating performance. Effects of spill code can severely degrade instruction pipeline

S. Dwarkadas (Ed.): LCR 2000, LNCS 1915, pp. 57–69, 2000.
© Springer-Verlag Berlin Heidelberg 2000

due to memory access latency slowing down the whole pipeline. An instruction scheduler for a pipelined machine is often forced to insert "nop"s in the pipeline to allow availability of program variables after memory access instructions. A multiple instruction issue machine often fails to issue instructions due to the fact that operands are not available in registers yet.

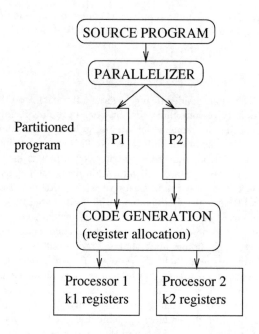

Fig. 1. Code generation for scalable computers

1.1   Register Allocation and Other Transformations

A parallelizing compiler for scalable distributed memory machines often partitions programs and assigns them to different processors. Such a model is shown in Figure 1. In a heterogeneous system, the processors may have different capabilities, including the size of the register set. While the code generator generates code for different processors, the driving force behind partitioning is usually parallelizability rather than the lower level architectural details. In an attempt to reduce communication, variables are often duplicated across partitions in the restructured program. This does not help the case of reducing register demands and the allocator is still expected to do a good job of register assignment.

The effectiveness of a register allocator is not just reflected in the generation and placement of loads and stores. Many other compiler optimizations, such as partial redundancy elimination (PRE) or common subexpression elimination (CSE), depend on the register allocator to find registers for temporaries that are generated during the optimization phase. The efficacy of such expensive optimizations are lost if the temporaries are spilled to memory. Loop restructuring optimizations which expose parallelism may also lead to increase in demand for registers.

1.2   Register Pressure and Register Candidates

Besides coloring or spilling decisions, register allocation is intricately linked with decisions made during *register promotion* [8]. Register promotion identifies which program variables are safe to be kept in registers and the program segments over which a particular variable can be safely kept in registers. Profitability of register promotion, particularly in the context of register pressure, is usually not addressed because promotion is carried out as a machine independent optimization. It is the profitability issue where our work is directed at. Even though register promotion assists register allocation by placing program variables in pseudo registers, the job of the register allocator is far from trivial. Forced spills not only undo the job performed through register promotion earlier, but can also lead to bad spilling decisions and introduce non-optimally placed spill code. Thus, register promotion, in a way, works against good allocation by promoting far too many variables and by increasing register pressure beyond a reasonable limit. Our approach, therefore, is centered around the idea of *containing register pressure* such that a reasonable amount of register pressure is maintained through the whole program.

In this paper we present a framework for global register allocation based on *selective demotion*. We propose a flow-analytic approach wherein global allocation of registers is guided by judicious placement of loads and stores along the different paths of control-flow in the program to improve overall code quality. We do not seek to build a new allocator; however, we attempt to positively influence an underlying graph-coloring allocator by augmenting it with a phase of selective demotion. In situations where register allocation forces spill of variables, we achieve more efficient allocation by *selective demotion* of program variables along regions of high register pressure. A Variable is kept promoted only along those paths of control-flow where it is profitable to keep the variable in registers. Live ranges of variables or temporaries promoted to pseudo-registers constitute the candidates for register allocation. The global information about profitability or spill cost is fed into the register allocator by influencing the formation of live ranges, and thus guiding the allocator to generate globally efficient spill code. We also minimize the effect of spill code by placing it outside regions of heavy execution frequency whenever possible. The novelty of our approach is highlighted by the following points:

- The idea of demotion before allocation, which is essentially spilling or splitting the live ranges of certain variables before a traditional graph-coloring allocator.
- Identification of the variables to be demoted.
- Identification of the program segments over which demotion is carried out.

1.3   Outline

We limit our analysis to register allocation within procedure boundaries. In the next section, we briefly discuss the anatomy of a representative register allocator and introduce some terminology widely used in the literature. We also motivate our approach by using an example. In the third section, we discuss our approach in detail. In the fourth section, we discuss implementation issues and results. In the fifth and the last section, we draw conclusions and discuss future work.

2   Background

Most of the work on register allocation as graph coloring are variants of or extensions to Chaitin's or Chow's work [5,6]. Chaitin's graph coloring approach [5] is based on the concept of an *interference graph*. The nodes of an interference graph represent the *live ranges* of the variables in a program. Two nodes of an interference graph are connected by an edge if the corresponding live ranges are simultaneously live. Given k physical registers, register allocation is reduced to k-coloring the interference graph. Nodes with *degree* < k are guaranteed to find a color. Such a node is termed an *unconstrained* node. All the unconstrained nodes and their edges are removed from the graph and pushed down a stack for making coloring decisions later. If the resulting graph is empty, then the original interference graph can be trivially colored. Once the coloring blocks, the allocator attempts to reduce the the degree of the interference graph by *spilling* a live range. A spilled live range is assigned to memory and the corresponding node is removed from the interference graph. If the spill frees up some other constrained nodes, the algorithm proceeds as above by putting those nodes in the stack. Otherwise, it continues to spill till the interference graph is empty. Nodes in the stack are then assigned colors so that no two neighbors have the same color.

Briggs [3] suggests an *optimistic spilling heuristic* which postpones the actual insertion of spill code for a node marked for spilling. Such a node is removed from the interference graph, however, it is pushed in the same stack as the unconstrained nodes. Later, when nodes are removed from the stack, it is likely that there could still be a color left to color the constrained node. Briggs's heuristic exposes one weakness of Chaitin style approaches - interference graph may give an excessively conservative view of the "simultaneously live" information. Briggs's allocator always performs at least as good as Chaitin's and sometimes better.

The number of colors needed to color an interference graph without spilling is called the *register pressure* of the program. *spill_cost/degree* is a criterion which often guides the choice of a spilling candidate. Another commonly used spilling heuristic is that - if the use of a live range is easy to recompute, it should be recomputed rather than reloaded.

In majority of the graph coloring allocators, the spilling strategy is "all-or-nothing". Once a node is spilled, it is spilled everywhere. A few approaches [2,6]

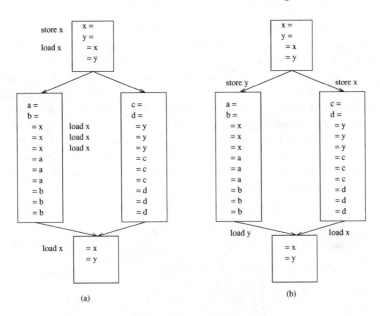

Fig. 2. Control-flow-sensitive allocation

attempt to spill only along the interfering regions. While that is an improvement, all of them suffer from a basic limitation - *the choice of which variables should be kept in registers and which variables should be spilled is going to be different along different paths of control-flow in the program.* Most of the approaches are not sufficiently sensitive to program structure. Hierarchical approaches [4,11] try to overcome this drawback by performing register allocation over portions of code separately and then by merging these allocation decisions over the entire program or routine. An obvious benefit of doing so is that a variable can possibly be spilled only locally. The hierarchical approaches do address the issue of spilling less frequently used variables around regions by giving priority to local variables. However, spilling decisions are performed early in the allocation phase and variables which may appear to be good candidates for spilling in the bottom-most hierarchy may introduce spill code which is inefficient from the viewpoint of the complete program. Lueh et al. [9] propose a sophisticated approach called *fusion-based register allocation* which tries to capture the benefits both Briggs-and Chow-style coloring. It fuses interference graphs of contiguous regions and attempts to preserve cost-effectiveness of spilling or splitting across fused regions. Unlike the fusion-based model, our framework reduces register pressure before the interference graph is built.

2.1 Motivating Example

We illustrate the limitations of standard algorithms with an example. In figure 2, we show a small segment of code and an ideal allocation of registers. Assuming that there are three registers available, either x or y needs to be spilled, and should be spilled only along the high register pressure region. Variables a, b, c, d have sufficient uses so that they are not considered for spilling. In this example we choose to spill x (y is as good a candidate) and the spill code is inserted around basic block 2. In figure 2 (a), we show how a Briggs-style allocator would spill the variable x. x is spilled over its entire live range. Our objective is to reach an allocation as shown in figure 2 (b). x and y are demoted along the boundaries of the regions where they are profitable to be considered for register allocation. As obvious, we reduce the number of spill code from 6 to 4. However, the run-time gains of such an allocation is also significant since only 2 spill instructions are executed in 2 (b).

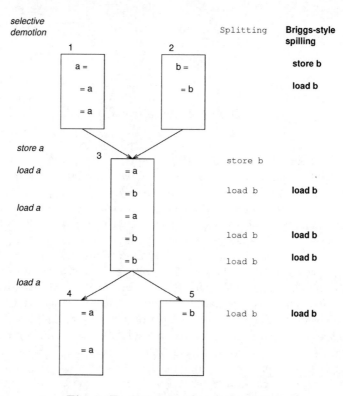

Fig. 3. Traditional spilling or splitting

In yet another example shown in figure 3, we illustrate the limitations of traditional algorithms. We assume that basic block 3 has high register pressure and one of the two variables a or b needs to be spilled. In a splitting-allocator a has 6 uses as opposed to b which has 5 uses. Therefore a has higher priority than b and is allocated a register. The splitting algorithm then recognizes that b can still be allocated a register in basic block 2. Thus, the live range of b is split, allocated a register in basic block 2, and spilled in basic block 3. In a Briggs-style spilling allocator, b has lower spill cost than that of a, and therefore, is spilled entirely over basic blocks 2-3-5. However, more efficient code is generated if a, which has fewer uses in the high register pressure region (basic block 3), is spilled. Selective register demotion attempts to achieve this by demoting a in basic block 3 before the register allocator attempts coloring.

3   Our Approach

In this section we discuss our framework of selective demotion. The crux of our approach is on selectively demoting variables around regions of high register pressure:

- heavy use favors promotion
- sparse use favors demotion

The promotion phase has already promoted variables optimistically. The demotion phase is carried out as a pre-pass of actual global register allocation (GRA). Some of the known register allocators attempt to optimize the placement of spill code or try to move them out of regions of high execution frequency as a post-pass of GRA. However, spilling decisions are already made and it may not be possible to move spill code thus introduced. The major benefit obtained by our approach is that unlike trying to repair the damage of non-optimal spill code, we try to avoid making such decisions by judiciously demoting variables. In the underlying framework, similar to hierarchical approaches, we start at the basic block granularity to identify the candidates for demotion and try to merge or propagate the areas of demotion into larger regions. However, unlike the Tera [4] or RAP [11] allocator, we delay the actual demotion decision till global profitability has been captured. Following this, the register allocator takes over and works on the modified live ranges.

3.1   High Register Pressure Region

The first step of our framework consists of identification of the areas of high register pressure. For every basic block, we construct the sets reg_candidate for every register candidate, namely, the variables or temporaries already in pseudo registers and expected to be in a register in that basic block. The reg_candidate information is essentially *live range* information calculated at per basic block granularity. It is the set of live ranges passing through that basic block. The reg_candidate information is gathered by using traditional data-flow analysis to compute *liveness* and *reaching-definition* attributes [1]. The analysis is similar to the one performed in the Chow allocator [6].

A variable v is *live* at a basic block B if it is referred at B or at some succeeding block without preceded by a redefinition. Global *liveness* information is computed by backward iteration over the control flow graph.

A definition d of a variable v is *reaching* a basic block B if a definition or use of the variable reaches B. Global *reaching-definition* information is computed by forward iteration over the control flow graph.

The intersection of the two attributes, that is, if a variable is both live and reaching a basic block, gives whether the variable is a candidate at the basic block. These variables were already placed on pseudo registers earlier and will be considered for register allocation in that block by the succeeding allocation phase. Thus, for every basic block B, we have a set reg_candidate[B] saying which variables are candidates in that block. And for every variable v v we also construct a set reg_candidate_in saying in which blocks it is a candidate.

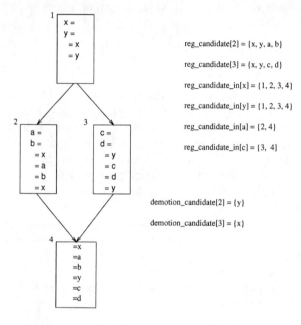

reg_candidate[2] = {x, y, a, b}

reg_candidate[3] = {x, y, c, d}

reg_candidate_in[x] = {1, 2, 3, 4}

reg_candidate_in[y] = {1, 2, 3, 4}

reg_candidate_in[a] = {2, 4}

reg_candidate_in[c] = {3, 4}

demotion_candidate[2] = {y}

demotion_candidate[3] = {x}

Fig. 4. Example of reg_candidate attribute

Figure 4 illustrates the reg_candidate and reg_candidate_in information in a simple example. The cardinality of the reg_candidate set gives the *register_pressure* of the basic block. Assuming there are k physical registers available for allocation, a basic block with *register_pressure* $> k$, is marked as a high register pressure region.

3.2   Demotion Candidates

For every region of high register pressure, we identify the variables which are promoted through the region and have the least number of uses or definitions. These variables constitute the initial set of demotion candidates for that particular basic block. We try to identify at least *register_pressure* - k initial candidates.

In figure 4, we show the initial demotion candidates for basic blocks 2 and 3 where register pressure is 4 (assuming there are 3 available registers). We also compute the tentative estimate of demotion cost if a particular variable were to be demoted across the region. Many of the register allocators use a spill cost estimate given by $(\#loads + \#stores).10^{depth}$, assuming so many additional loads and stores will be inserted as a result of spilling and depth indicates the depth of loop nesting. Our estimation of demotion cost is similar except that it is weighted by the static frequency estimate of that basic block. The weighing factor is a number between 0 and 1 indicating the likelihood of the basic block being executed. The particular basic block forms the initial *tentative* demotion region for a demotion candidate. In the following discussion, a demotion region is a *tentative* demotion region unless otherwise specified. We assume that besides a load preceding every use of a variable, demotion of a variable in a particular block would result in a store in the entry of the basic block and a load in the exit of the basic block.

3.3   Merger of Demotion Regions

Following the initialization of the demotion candidates, we attempt to enlarge the demotion regions for the candidates, if it leads to better overall demotion cost. In particular, we attempt to merge two contiguous or disjoint demotion regions for a particular variable if it happens to be a demotion candidate for both the regions. A merger would lead to the elimination of a load and a store at the edge connecting the merging regions. In order to maintain safety, every exit point of a demotion region has a load for the particular variable under consideration. These mergers of demotion regions are final, however, the decision whether the particular variable will be demoted at all is taken later. We illustrate with a simple example in figure 5 how merger of demotion regions may lead to better allocation.

The shaded nodes in the control flow graph are high register pressure regions. x is a demotion candidate in both the nodes 2 and 4. The dotted region shows the merged demotion region 2-4-6. The numbers in the second and third column indicate the number of loads and stores that would be executed if the control follows any one of the paths as represented by the first column. Obviously, in this particular example, merger of the demotion regions is always as good as demoting them only in the blocks 2 and 4. If there were more uses of x in nodes 1 and 8, demotion in 2 and 6 or 2-4-6 far outweigh any benefit of spilling x all over place. However, merger of demotion regions is not always profitable. If there were multiple uses of x in node 4, demotion along 2 and 6 would be more profitable than demoting along 2-4-6. If there was just one use of x in node 4, it is still worthwhile demoting along 2-4-6. For, it may be possible to enlarge the demotion region further and move the spill code at the entry and exit out of a loop if such a situation exists.

For a given demotion candidate, merging of demotion regions is attempted along any path joining two demotion regions. If the static estimate of demotion cost for the merged region is cheaper than the sum of the two individual demotion

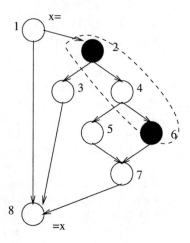

	2 & 6	2-4-6
1-8	0	0
1-2-3-8	2	2
1-2-4-5-7-8	2	2
1-2-4-6-7-8	4	2

Fig. 5. Merger of demotion regions

regions, the merger is carried out. Otherwise, merger of the two regions for that variable is aborted. As obvious from the discussion, if there are several uses or definitions of a variable along a path, the estimate for demotion will go up and it will eventually prevent the variable from being demoted. This is desirable since demotion is deemed beneficial only for global variables with sparse or no uses along a particular path or region.

3.4   Demotion Decisions

Having determined the various demotion regions, we sort the spill cost estimates associated with each demotion region. We also keep a count of the number of high register pressure regions a demotion region spans. A good candidate for demotion is one which has the least demotion cost estimate and spans most number of high register pressure regions. Guided by this heuristic, we demote the best possible candidate. Then we check if register pressure has gone down sufficiently or candidate demotion regions are still available. This process is continued till we run out of demotion region candidates or register pressure has gone down sufficiently across the program. This is the phase when loads and stores are inserted.

The steps discussed above may appear to be costly or time-consuming. However, such a situation is likely only if in a fairly complex control-flow graph, the

Table 1. Results: Mediabench

program	demotion	static		dynamic			
		loads	stores	loads	stores	instr. count	cycles
adpcm	ON	170	52	552257	146251	10123343	5171507
	OFF	174	59	554310	149869	10135661	5194090
epic	ON	2514	1309	7509874	1141173	65800703	34451393
	OFF	2547	1433	7916368	1151733	66810779	36163595
ghostscript	ON	38860	16995	199040025	10654972	946420682	681700703
	OFF	45987	22998	201713409	10722031	947287048	703361906
mpeg2	ON	4443	1262	25420246	4933359	95450129	63150280
	OFF	4521	1298	25566009	5567736	97055575	65299771

high register pressure region with a candidate x are scattered far apart with very sparse or no use at all. Nearby high register pressure regions are the ones which are most likely to be merged successfully. And merger with the further ones are likely to be given up if sufficient uses are encountered on the way.

The procedure we describe above will work with any kind of demotion candidates so far as merging them along a sparse-use path is concerned. The idea guiding our demotion algorithm is to gather the global view of the spill cost associated with locally good candidates.

4   Implementation and Results

Our framework is implemented within the backend of the MIPSPRO compiler from Silicon Graphics (SGI). The code generator of the MIPSPRO compiler comprises a framework for global scheduling called Integrated Global Local Scheduling (IGLS) [10]. GRA is preceded by a round of global and local scheduling which also provides an estimate for local register demands to GRA. Our framework is implemented following this round of scheduling as a frontend to GRA. GRA is followed by another round of global and local scheduling.

Table 1 shows the improvement in various parameters in test runs of a few programs from the Mediabench suite of benchmarks (from UCLA). The benchmarks consist of commonly used programs from multimedia applications. The comparison is against a Briggs-style allocator. We have carried out the experiments in an SGI O2 with a MIPS R12000 processor which is 4-way superscalar. We have implemented our own version of a Briggs-style allocator. Various allocators also work on different levels of intermediate representation and depend upon the optimizations performed before and after allocation. We have tried our best to provide a fair comparison with our Briggs-style allocator.

The number of loads and stores reported in the table, both static and dynamic, are absolute number of loads and stores and not just the ones due to spilling. As the numbers indicate, the code quality is never worse than the underlying allocator. A general observation is that there is room for improvement when the register pressure is fairly high. Ghostscript is considerably larger than the other benchmarks, and as the number of static loads and stores indicate, the improvement is considerable. Loads and stores constitute a good amount of the actual instructions executed and any improvement in their generation and placement also improves the dynamic instruction count and cycles. In mpeg2, improvement in dynamic stores is much better than that of static stores. This indicates that these instructions were probably moved out of loops, or the improved segments of code were frequently executed. The cases when improvement in dynamic loads and stores is worse than that of static loads and stores is probably because the weighing of demotion cost with static estimates did not work out at run-time. It is possible that a branch assumed to be less likely was taken at run-time. This can possibly be improved upon by using profile-driven estimates.

5 Conclusion

We have presented a framework which assists register allocation by keeping down register pressure. Selective demotion chooses variables which are less likely to be used along a certain path and inserts loads and stores at strategic points to reduce the demand for registers. The choice is carried out by identifying locally good candidates for demotion and by capturing their global cost of demotion. Thus, we achieve the goal of spilling variables only along the areas of high register pressure and lead to more efficient generation and placement of spill code. We are working on modeling and studying the effect of program partitioning on register allocation in general and our framework in particular. We also intend to analyze the effect of selective demotion on different suites of benchmarks.

Acknowledgement

We would like to thank SGI for allowing us to use the MIPSPRO backend compiler.

References

1. Alfred V. Aho, Ravi Sethi, and Jeffrey D. Ullman. *Compilers Priciples, Techniques, and Tools*. Addison-Wesley Publishing Company, 1986.
2. P. Bergner, P. Dahl, D. Engebretsen, and M. O'Keefe. Spill Code Minimization via Interference Region Spilling. In *Proceedings of the 1997 ACM SIGPLAN Conference on Programming Languages Design and Implementation*, pages 287–295, June 1997.
3. P. Briggs, K. Cooper, and L. Torczon. Improvements to Graph Coloring Register Allocation. *ACM Transactions on Programming Languages and Systems*, 16(3):428–455, May 1994.
4. D. Callahan and B. Koblenz. Register Allocation via Hierarchical Graph Coloring. In *Proceedings of the 1991 ACM SIGPLAN Conference on Programming Languages Design and Implementation*, pages 192–203, June 1991.

5. G. Chaitin, M. Auslander, A. Chandra, J. Cocke, M. Hopkins, and P. Markstein. Register Allocation via Coloring. *Computer Languages*, 6:47–57, January 1981.

6. F. Chow and J. Hennessy. The Priority-based Coloring Approach to Register Allocation. *ACM Transactions on Programming Languages and Systems*, 12(4):501–536, October 1990.

7. P. Kolte and M. J. Harrold. Load/store Range Analysis for Global Register Allocation. In *Proceedings of the 1993 ACM SIGPLAN Conference on Programming Languages Design and Implementation*, pages 268–277, June 1993.

8. R. Lo, F. Chow, R. Kennedy, S. Liu, and P. Tu. Register Promotion by Sparse Partial Redundancy Elimination of Loads and Stores. In *Proceedings of the 1998 ACM SIGPLAN Conference on Programming Languages Design and Implementation*, pages 26–37, May 1998.

9. Guei-Yuan Lueh. Fusion-based register allocation. PhD Thesis CMU-CS-97-135, Carnegie Mellon University, 1997.

10. S. Mantripragada, S. Jain, and J. Dehnert. A New Framework for Integrated Global Local Scheduling. In *Proceedings of the 1998 International Conference on Parallel Architectures and Compilation Techniques*, pages 167–175, October 1998.

11. C. Norris and L. L. Pollock. RAP: A PDG-based Register Allocator. *Software - Practice and Experience*, 28(4):401–424, April 1998.

A Comparison of Locality Transformations for Irregular Codes*

Hwansoo Han and Chau-Wen Tseng

Department of Computer Science, University of Maryland, College Park, MD 20742

Abstract. Researchers have proposed several data and computation transformations to improve locality in irregular scientific codes. We experimentally compare their performance and present GPART, a new technique based on hierarchical clustering. Quality partitions are constructed quickly by clustering multiple neighboring nodes with priority on nodes with high degree, and repeating a few passes. Overhead is kept low by clustering multiple nodes in each pass and considering only edges between partitions. Experimental results show GPART matches the performance of more sophisticated partitioning algorithms to with 6%–8%, with a small fraction of the overhead. It is thus useful for optimizing programs whose running times are not known.

1 Introduction

As microprocessors become increasingly fast, memory system performance begins to dictate overall performance. The ability of applications to exploit locality by keeping references in cache becomes a major factor affecting performance. Computational scientists, however, are writing programs with increasingly irregular memory access patterns as they attempt to create more complex simulations. These *irregular* computations arise in several application domains. In computational fluid dynamics (CFD), meshes for modeling large problems are sparse to reduce memory and computations requirements. In n-body solvers such as those arising in astrophysics and molecular dynamics, data structures are by nature irregular because they model the positions of particles and their interactions.

Unfortunately, irregular computations have poor temporal and spatial locality because they do not repeatedly access data in memory with small constant strides. Researchers recently showed locality can be improved for irregular codes using compiler and run-time data layout and computation reordering transformations [1,8,27,28]. In this paper, we form a framework for applying locality optimizations to irregular codes and experimentally evaluate the impact of a number of optimization techniques. The contributions of this paper are:

---

* This research was supported in part by NSF CAREER Development Award #ASC9625531 in New Technologies, NSF CISE Institutional Infrastructure Award #CDA9401151, and NSF cooperative agreement ACI-9619020 with NPACI and NCSA.

- Experimentally evaluate the effectiveness of several locality optimizations for a range of input data and programs. We are the first to use RCB for improving cache performance, and the first to combine RCM and METIS with computation reordering.
- Develop GPART, a new locality transformation based on hierarchical clustering which nearly matches the performance of more sophisticated partitioning algorithms, but with a small fraction of the overhead.

We begin with a refresher on existing optimization techniques, then present our new algorithm and evaluate its performance.

2   Locality Optimizations

A number of locality optimizations have been developed for irregular computations. We can decide which are needed based on application structure.

Application Structure. Irregular scientific computations are typically composed of loops performing reductions such as SUM and MAX which can be safely reordered [6,8]. For locality optimizations, it turns out the number of distinct irregular accesses made by each loop iteration can be used to choose the proper optimization algorithm.

In some codes, each iteration makes only one irregular access to each array. The NAS integer sort (IS) and sparse matrix vector multiplication found in conjugate gradient (CG) fall into this category. More often, scientific codes access two or more distinct irregular references on each loop iteration. Such codes arise in PDE solvers traversing irregular meshes or N-body simulations, when calculations are made for pair of points. In such cases loop iterations may be considered edges connecting the data accessed on that iteration.

Figure 1 shows an example of data/computation reordering for these computations. Circles represent computations (loop iterations), squares represent data, and arrows represent data accesses. Notice how computations can be viewed as edges connecting data nodes, resulting in a graph. Partitioning the graph and putting nodes in a partition close in memory can then improve spatial locality. Sorting the loop iterations can improve temporal locality further.

Lexicographical Sorting. One optimization is to reorder loop iterations. If each iteration performs only one irregular access, sorting the loop iterations by data accessed results in optimal locality. Bucket sorting with cache-sized buckets can also be used, producing similar improvements with low overhead [28]. For computations with two or more irregular accesses, lexicographically sorting the loop iterations will improve temporal locality. Sorting is so effective that data meshes provided by applications writers are frequently presorted, eliminating the need to apply sorting at run time. When we perform experiments, we use presorted input meshes, and always apply lexicographical sorting after data reordering.

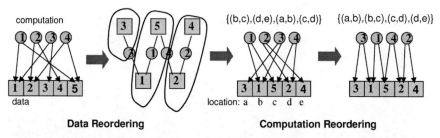

Data Reordering   **Computation Reordering**

Fig. 1. Overview of Data and Computation Transformations

Consecutive Packing (CPACK). In addition to computation reordering, the compiler can also reorganize data layout. Ding and Kennedy proposed *consecutive packing* (CPACK), where data is moved into adjacent locations in the order they are first accessed (first-touch) by the computation [8]. CPACK can be applied with very low overhead, since it just requires one pass through the loop marking the order in which data is accessed. However, CPACK does not explicitly take into account the underlying graph or geometric structure of the data.

Reverse Cuthill-McKee (RCM). Reverse Cuthill-McKee (RCM) methods have been successfully used in sparse matrix reorganization [5,17,24]. RCM simply uses reverse breadth-first search (BFS) to reorder data in irregular computations, by viewing iterations as graph edges. Performance is improved with low overhead [1,6].

Recursive Coordinate Bisection (RCB). Space-filling curves (*e.g.*, Hilbert, Morton) are continuous, non-smooth curves that pass through every point in a finite k-dimensional space [15,27,32]. Because interactions tend to be local, arranging data using space-filling curves reduces the distance (in memory) between two geometrically close points in space, yielding better locality [27]. When geometric coordinate information is available, sorting data and computation using space-filling curves is the locality optimization of choice, since it achieves good locality with very low overhead simply using a multidimensional bucket sort. However, geometric coordinate information is not necessarily available, and will probably require user intervention to identify. In addition, space-filling curves may not work well for unevenly distributed nodes, due to the fixed size grid.

As an alternative, we propose using recursive coordinate bisection (RCB). RCB recursively splits each dimension into two partitions by finding the median of data coordinates in that dimension. The process is recursively repeated, alternating dimension [2,3]. After partitioning, data items are stored consecutively within each partition. Subpartitions are also arranged consecutively, creating a recursive hierarchical layout similar to Z-ORDERING, a space-filling curve for dense array layouts. RCB has higher overhead, but is likely to work well for unevenly distributed data.

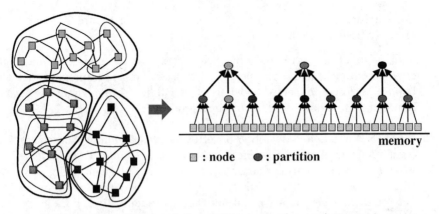

Fig. 2. Low-Overhead Graph Clustering (GPART) Example

*Multi-level Graph Partitioning (*METIS*).* A major limitation of RCB and space-filling curves is that geometric coordinate information is needed for each node. This information may not be available for some applications. Even if it is available, user annotations may be needed since the compiler may not be able to automatically derive coordinate information for each data item.

In comparison, graph partitioning algorithms can be applied automatically based on the loop data access pattern. Partitioning algorithms were first developed for load balancing in parallel codes [32]. Spectral partitioning methods can be effective but are computationally intensive [31]. More recently, people have employed multi-level graph partitioning algorithms encapsulated in library packages such as METIS [19,20] to achieve good partitions with low overhead. These algorithms compute a succession of coarsened graphs (with fewer nodes) which approximate the original graph, compute a partition on the coarsened graph, and then expand back to the original graph.

3   Low-Overhead Graph Partitioning (GPART)

Previous graph partitioning algorithms were designed for load-balancing in parallel computations, VLSI circuits, and other high cost applications. As a result, greater processing time is acceptable. Experiments indicate the overhead of preprocessing for RCB and METIS are 5–40 times higher than CPACK, the lowest overhead algorithm. Since our goal is to improve cache performance at run-time for irregular applications, we desire partitioning algorithms with lower overhead. We have developed a hierarchical graph clustering algorithm (GPART) that has low overhead and produces quality ordering for cache locality.

3.1   Algorithm

The GPART algorithm performs a number of passes. On each pass, it clusters several adjacent nodes into a single partition. Each partition is then treated as a single node in the next pass, creating a hierarchical structure. An example of data partitioned by the GPART algorithm is shown in Figure 2. The GPART algorithm consists of the following steps:

1. SORT: Nodes are sorted once by their vertex degrees (number of incipient edges) from most number of neighbors to least. Sorting improves the likelihood that closely connected nodes are clustered first through multiple passes, improving the quality of the partitions produced.

2. MERGE: Visiting nodes in order of vertex degree, randomly choose partition containing neighboring node on adjacency list. If combined size is less than *pLimit* (current partition size limit), merge partitions containing the node and its chosen neighbor. Mark the neighbor as merged. Random selection may result in lower quality partitions than more sophisticated methods, but reduces overhead.

3. FILTER: While visiting nodes to cluster, mark neighbors as merged if they have already been merged into the partition of the current node. After visiting all nodes, marked neighbors are eliminated from the adjacency list. Fewer nodes need to be searched on each pass, speeding up future passes.

4. LOOP: Repeat STEP 2 and STEP 3, increasing the current limit on partition size (*pLimit*) by factor *growFac*, up to the maximum desired partition size (*maxLimit*). Initial *pLimit* is set to the cache line size, and *maxLimit* is set to L1 cache size divided by data accessed on each loop iteration. If *pLimit* is small, overhead increases as the algorithm iterates many times. If *pLimit* is large, the quality of partition degrades. *growFac* is experimentally set to eight.

5. LAYOUT: Finally, arrange nodes according to the resulting hierarchical layout. Nodes in a partition are recursively laid out nearby in memory, maintaining the partition hierarchy.

The full GPART algorithm is shown in Figure 3. The partitions produced by GPART are used to improve locality by generating data layouts that put neighboring nodes in nearby memory locations. The hierarchical structure in GPART is similar to that of RCB. Each partition in a level keeps all its subpartitions in lower levels close together in memory, which further improves locality. Since applications visit nodes according to the storage order due to lexicographical sorting, maintaining the hierarchical structure of the clustered graph increases the chances of visiting neighbor nodes that have already been recently accessed. These nodes are more likely to remain in cache, improving performance.

GPART is similar to the coarsening phase in METIS, but fewer clustering passes are required because more nodes are collapsed at once. Because we form clusters in a bottom-up fashion, we capture most of the locality immediately and can stop after a small number of passes. The quality of the partition produced is slightly less than that produced by METIS, but the overhead is significantly less.

```
sort nodes by descending degree
pLimit = cacheLineSize
while (pLimit <= maxLimit) {
  for each node N (in sorted order) {
    P = partition containing N
    if (size(P) < pLimit) {
      for each neighbor M of N in adj. list {
        // pick partner in random order
        Q = partition containing M
        if (P == Q)
          mark M as merged neighbor
        else if (size(P) + size(Q) <= pLimit) {
          merge Q into P
          mark M as merged neighbor
          if (size(P) == pLimit)
            break (exit for loop)
        }
      }
    }
  }
  eliminate merged neighbors in adjacency list
  pLimit = pLimit * growFac  // new partition size
}
recursively lay out nodes according to hierarchy
```

Fig. 3. Hierarchical Graph Clustering Algorithm

We chose our parameters for GPART experimentally by performing a large number of experiments. We found that stopping after partitions reach the size of L1 cache and using a coarsening factor of eight reduced the number of passes without significantly degrading the quality of the partitions [11].

4   Experimental Evaluation

4.1   Evaluation Environment

We have begun implementation of our prototype compiler using the Stanford SUIF compiler. The prototype can identify and parallelize irregular reductions, generating parallel *pthreads* programs. The compiler can also determine where inspectors need to be inserted, based on when memory access patterns are changed. However, we have not implemented the actual inspector generation phase using techniques developed by Chaos [13,14]. As a result, we currently insert inspectors by hand for both the sequential and parallel versions of each program.

We used two machine configurations, DEC multiprocessor with 275MHz Alpha 21064 processors and an SGI Origin2000 with 195MHz MIPS R10000 processors. The Alpha has a 16K direct-mapped L1 cache and a 4M direct-mapped L2 cache. The R10000 has a 32K two-way set associative L1 cache and a 4M L2 cache. We also simulate cache performance using a cache simulator based on the Shade utility from Sun Microsystems.

Table 1. Input Data Sets for Irregular Kernels

Name	# Nodes	# Edges	Description
FOIL	144649	1074393	3D mesh of a parafoil
AUTO	448695	3314611	3D mesh of GM's Saturn
MOL1	131072	1179648	semi-uniform 3D molecule distribution (sm)
MOL2	442368	3981312	semi-uniform 3D molecule distribution (lg)

4.2   Applications and Input Characteristics

We examine three irregular applications, IRREG, NBF, and MOLDYN. All applications contain an initialization section followed by the main computation enclosed in a sequential time-step loop. The main computation is thus repeated each iteration of the time-step loop. Statistics and timings are collected after the initialization section in order to investigate main computation execution.

IRREG is a representative of iterative partial differential equation (PDE) solvers found in computational fluid dynamics (CFD) applications. NBF is a kernel abstracted from the GROMOS molecular dynamics code [13]. MOLDYN is abstracted from the non-bonded force calculation in CHARMM, a key molecular dynamics application used at NIH to model macromolecular systems.

To test the effects of data reordering, we experiment with a variety of input data meshes described in Table 1. FOIL and AUTO are 3D meshes of a parafoil and GM Saturn automobile, respectively. MOL1 and MOL2 are small and large 3D meshes derived from semi-uniformly placed molecules of MOLDYN using a 1.5 angstrom cutoff radius. FOIL and AUTO are used for IRREG, and MOL1 and MOL2 are used for NBF and MOLDYN.

4.3   Experimental Results

In our experiments, we evaluated several locality reordering algorithms with three kernels. The different optimizations are as follows: ORIG is the original program, which corresponds to the result of computation reordering, since input meshes are presorted. RCB, METIS, and GPART apply recursive coordinate bisection, multi-level graph partitioning algorithm, and hierarchical graph clustering algorithm, respectively. After partitioning graphs, nodes in a partition are arranged nearby memory locations. RCM applies Reverse Cuthill-McKee, and CPACK arranges nodes by consecutive packing. As we mentioned earlier, computation reordering is always applied after each data reordering algorithm.

RCB and METIS are both configured to create partitions so that the data accessed is roughly the L1 cache size. For instance, if the 16K L1 cache holds 4K elements, and each loop iteration accesses 2 node arrays, the partition size is 2K. In GPART we start from a partition containing 4 nodes. Since each node in our applications contains an 8-byte double-precision floating point number, 4 nodes will fit into a 32-byte cache line. 8 partitions are merged into a new partition at each pass and the final partition size is determined in the same manner as RCB and METIS.

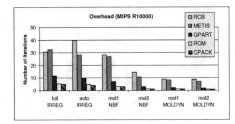
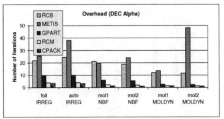

Fig. 4. Overhead of Data Reordering (relative to time-per-iteration of ORIG)

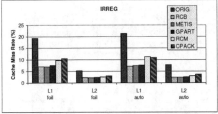
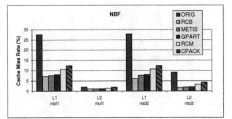

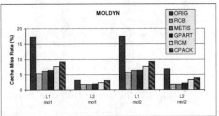

Fig. 5. L1 and L2 Cache Miss Rates (percentage of all memory references)

Overhead of Optimizations. Figure 4 displays the costs of data reordering techniques measured relative to the time per iteration of ORIG. The overhead includes the cost to update edge structures and transform other related data structures to avoid the extra indirect accesses caused by the data reordering. The overhead also includes the cost of computation reordering.

The least expensive data layout optimization is CPACK. RCM has almost same overhead as CPACK. In comparison, partitioning algorithms have rather high overhead. RCB and METIS are quite expensive when used for cache optimizations, on the order of 5–45 times higher than CPACK. The overhead of GPART is much less than METIS and RCB, but 3–5 times higher than CPACK.

Impact on Miss Rates. We also simulated cache miss rates, using the cache configuration of the DEC Alpha 21064: 16K direct-mapped L1 cache with 32 byte cache lines and 4M direct-mapped L2 cache with 64 byte cache lines. Figure 5 shows L1 and L2 cache miss rates side by side for the same input. L1 cache miss rates of original, unoptimized programs are about 15%–28%. All partitioning techniques, RCB, METIS, and GPART reduce miss rates to 6%–8%, outperforming RCM and CPACK by 1%–6%. RCB and METIS achieve the best over all perfor-

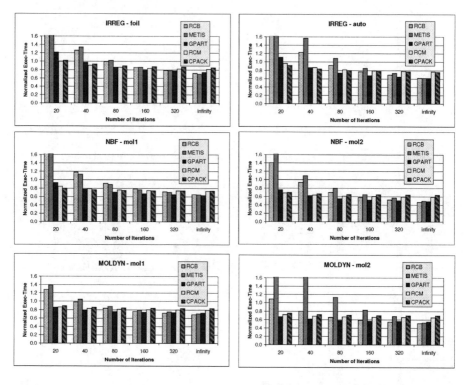

Fig. 6. Normalized Execution Times on DEC Alpha 21064 (including overhead)

mance. but GPART obtains nearly the same performance. L2 cache miss rates are calculated as the percentages of all memory references, not the percentages of L2 cache references. L2 miss rates are higher for larger data sets, around 7%–8%. They are reduced by optimizations to around 2%–3%. L2 miss rates are reduced by applying partitioning techniques, outperforming RCM and CPACK. RCB and METIS show the best performance, but GPART also achieves nearly the same performance.

Impact on Performance. Next we look at sequential execution times on the DEC Alpha and MIPS R10000. Figures 6 and 7 present normalized execution times calculated relative to the execution time of ORIG. Results are presented for programs executing different numbers of iterations. Since results include the overhead of locality optimizations performed at the beginning of each program, performance improves as the number of iterations increases.

The set of results when the number of iterations is *infinity* represent the quality of each optimization when overhead is ignored. The results show partitioning algorithms perform better than RCM and CPACK in quality of data reordering. RCB, METIS, and GPART achieve 30%–50% improvements on the DEC Alpha and 20%–80% on the MIPS R10000. In comparison, RCM improves less than the partitioning algorithms, but a bit better than CPACK. CPACK shows the least

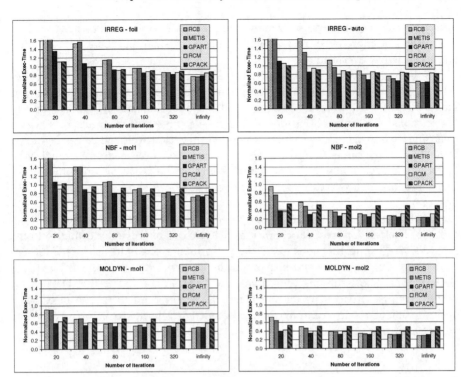

Fig. 7. Normalized Execution Times on MIPS R10000 (including overhead)

Table 2. Average improvement over ORIG and GPART

	Compared to ORIG				Compared to GPART			
	SGI Origin2000		DEC Alpha 21064		SGI Origin2000		DEC Alpha 21064	
	Avg	Range	Avg	Range	Avg	Range	Avg	Range
RCB	14%	-161% ~ 78%	10%	-84% ~ 54%	-35%	-152% ~ 7%	-22%	-86% ~ 8%
METIS	18%	-137% ~ 78%	-7%	-194% ~ 51%	-28%	-99% ~ 6%	-46%	-338% ~ 6%
GPART	39%	-36% ~ 77%	28%	-21% ~ 52%	-	-	-	-
RCM	35%	-11% ~ 70%	24%	-0% ~ 41%	-11%	-34% ~ 18%	-8%	-25% ~ 18%
CPACK	26%	-11% ~ 51%	22%	-2% ~ 36%	-34%	-117% ~ 18%	-11%	-32% ~ 11%

improvement among all algorithms. We also measured parallel performance, and found locality optimizations improve performance even more than for sequential codes. On a on a 4-processor DEC Alpha multiprocessor, partitioning algorithms achieve 110%–130% improvements in speedups, while CPACK achieves only 60% improvements.

Optimization Technique Selection. When applying locality optimizations in practice, we must consider overheads for each optimization. Even though RCB and METIS generate higher quality orderings, they require hundreds of iterations to be competitive with RCM or CPACK. Meanwhile, GPART begins to outperform RCM and CPACK around 40 iterations due to its low overhead. RCB and METIS will be most beneficial for long running scientific applications where their high overheads can be can be amortized over many loop iterations. GPART, RCM, and CPACK will be more effective for applications with small numbers of iterations due to their low overhead.

Table 2 summarizes performance for each optimization relative to both the original performance and GPART. Results are computed as the average over the six versions of each program (running 20, 40, 80, 160, 320, and an infinite number of iterations). The range of improvements are also presented, ranging from negative values (short-running programs where optimization overhead cause degradations) to positive values (long-running programs where overheads are amortized). We see that GPART has the best overall results over a range of program executions, because it provides good performance for both short and long-running programs.

GPART has good performance compared to other optimizations, on average 11%–35% better. Under ideal conditions, GPART can improve performance from 25%–338%. Even in the worst case, the performance of GPART is close to other algorithms. For very long-running programs RCB and METIS do 6%–8% better, while for very short-running programs CPACK and RCM do 11%–18% better.

On average GPART's performance is 11% better than RCM, the next best optimization. For long-running applications GPART is up to 25% faster than RCM. Based on these results, we feel GPART is the preferred optimization in the most cases, particularly when the number of iterations executed is not known.

5   Related Work

Irregular scientific codes were first encountered in the context of message-passing systems. It was discovered these codes typically performed reduction operations which can be automatically parallelized and reordered in a compiler [25]. Researchers have investigated compiler analyses [22,23] and ways to provide efficient run-time and compiler support [4,29]. Libraries which can efficiently communicate data between processors using an inspector/executor approach were key to achieving good performance [7,16,21]. Compiler techniques for automatically generating and inserting these inspectors were developed [16,13,14].

Most research on improving data locality has focused on dense arrays with regular access patterns, applying either loop [26,33] or data layout [18,30] transformations. Locality optimizations have also been developed n the context of sparse linear algebra. The Reverse Cuthill-McGee (RCM) method [5] improves locality in sparse matrices by reordering columns using reverse breadth-first search (BFS). More sophisticated versions of the algorithm have since been developed [5,24,17].

A few researchers have investigated irregular scientific application. Das *et al.* investigated data/computation reordering for unstructured Euler solvers [6]. They combined data reordering using RCM and lexicographical sort for computation reordering with communication optimizations to improve performance of parallel codes on an Intel iPSC/860. Al-Furaih and Ranka studied partitioning data using METIS and BFS to reorder data in irregular codes [1].

They conclude METIS yields better locality, but did not include computation reordering or account for processing overhead.

Ding and Kennedy explored applying dynamic copying (packing) of data elements based on loop traversal order, and show major improvements in performance [8]. They were able to automate most of their transformations in a compiler, using user provided information. In comparison, we show partitioning algorithms can yield better locality, albeit with higher processing overhead. Ding and Kennedy also developed algorithms for reorganizing single arrays into multi-dimensional arrays depending on their access patterns, improving the performance of many irregular applications [9]. Their technique might be useful for Fortran codes where data are often single dimension arrays, not structures as in C codes.

Mellor-Crummey *et al.* used a geometric partitioning algorithm based on space-filling curves to map multidimensional data to memory [27]. They also blocked computation using methods similar to tiling. In comparison, our graph-based partitioning techniques are more suited for compilers, since geometric coordinate information and block parameters for space-filling curves do not need to provided manually. When coordinate information is available, using RCB is better because space-filling curves cannot guarantee evenly balanced partition when data is unevenly distributed, which may cause significant performance degradation in parallel execution.

Mitchell *et al.* improved locality using bucket sorting to reorder loop iterations in irregular computations [28]. They improved the performance of two NAS applications (CG, and IS) and a medical heart simulation. Bucket sorting works only for computations containing a single irregular access per loop iteration. In comparison, we investigate more complex cases where two or more irregular access patterns exist. For simple codes lexicographic sort yields improvements similar to bucket sorting.

6 Conclusion

Our research demonstrates the benefits of improving data locality in irregular scientific applications by applying compiler and run-time transformations to partition data and computation. We develop GPART, a new partitioning algorithm based on hierarchical graph partitioning, which produces partitions which almost match the performance of the best partitioning strategies, but with much lower overhead. On experiments with a number of applications and input data sets, GPART improved performance by an average of 28% and 39% on the DEC Alpha 21064 and MIPS R10000, respectively.

Experiments also find partitioning algorithms (RCB, METIS, GPART) generate better quality ordering for cache locality than simple traversing algorithms (RCM, CPACK). Partitioning algorithms improve performance by an average of 38% on DEC Alpha 21064 and 49% on MIPS R10000, while traversing algorithms improve only 26% and 35%, respectively. These results show that as processors continue to increase in speed relative to memory, using graph partitioning to improve data layout will increase in importance since processing costs go down while benefits increase. For very large graphs, we should also obtain benefits by reducing TLB misses and paging in the virtual memory system. Locality optimizations for irregular computations can be effectively for parallel computations [10,34]. Low-overhead transformations such as GPART will be especially useful for *adaptive* irregular applications, where optimizations may need to be reapplied after access patterns changes [12].

References

1. I. Al-Furaih and S. Ranka. Memory hierarchy management for iterative graph structures. In *Proceedings of the 12th International Parallel Processing Symposium*, Orlando, FL, April 1998.
2. M. Berger and S. Bokhari. A partitioning strategy for pdes across multiprocessors. In *Proceedings of the 1985 International Conference on Parallel Processing*, August 1985.
3. M. Berger and S. Bokhari. A partitioning strategy for non-uniform problems on multiprocessors. *IEEE Transactions on Computers*, 37(12):570–580, 1987.
4. S. Chandra and J.R. Larus. Optimizing communication in HPF programs for fine-grain distributed shared memory. In *Proceedings of the Sixth ACM SIGPLAN Symposium on Principles and Practice of Parallel Programming*, Las Vegas, NV, June 1997.
5. E. Cuthill and J. McKee. Reducing the bandwidth of sparse symmetric matrices. In *Proceedings of the 24th National Conference of the ACM, ACM Publication P-69*, Association for Computing Machinery, NY, 1969.
6. R. Das, D. Mavriplis, J. Saltz, S. Gupta, and R. Ponnusamy. The design and implementation of a parallel unstructured Euler solver using software primitives. In *Proceedings of the 30th Aerospace Sciences Meeting and Exhibit*, Reno, NV, January 1992.
7. R. Das, M. Uysal, J. Saltz, and Y.-S. Hwang. Communication optimizations for irregular scientific computations on distributed memory architectures. *Journal of Parallel and Distributed Computing*, 22(3):462–479, September 1994.
8. C. Ding and K. Kennedy. Improving cache performance of dynamic applications with computation and data layout transformations. In *Proceedings of the SIGPLAN '99 Conference on Programming Language Design and Implementation*, Atlanta, GA, May 1999.
9. C. Ding and K. Kennedy. Inter-array data regrouping. In *Proceedings of the Twelfth Workshop on Languages and Compilers for Parallel Computing*, San Diego, August 1999.
10. H. Han and C.-W. Tseng. Improving compiler and run-time support for adaptive irregular codes. In *Proceedings of the International Conference on Parallel Architectures and Compilation Techniques*, Paris, France, October 1998.
11. H. Han and C.-W. Tseng. Improving locality for adaptive irregular scientific codes. Technical Report CS-TR-4039, Dept. of Computer Science, University of Maryland at College Park, September 1999.
12. H. Han and C.-W. Tseng. Improving locality for adaptive irregular codes. In *Proceedings of the Thirteenth Workshop on Languages and Compilers for Parallel Computing*, White Plains, NY, August 2000.

13. R. v. Hanxleden. Handling irregular problems with Fortran D — A preliminary report. In *Proceedings of the Fourth Workshop on Compilers for Parallel Computers*, Delft, The Netherlands, December 1993.
14. R. v. Hanxleden and K. Kennedy. Give-N-Take — A balanced code placement framework. In *Proceedings of the SIGPLAN '94 Conference on Programming Language Design and Implementation*, Orlando, FL, June 1994.
15. Y. Hu, S. L. Johnsson, and S.-H. Teng. High Performance Fortran for highly irregular problems. In *Proceedings of the Sixth ACM SIGPLAN Symposium on Principles and Practice of Parallel Programming*, Las Vegas, NV, June 1997.
16. Y.-S. Hwang, B. Moon, S. Sharma, R. Ponnusamy, R. Das, and J. Saltz. Runtime and language support for compiling adaptive irregular programs on distributed memory machines. *Software—Practice and Experience*, 25(6):597–621, June 1995.
17. E. Im and K. Yelick. Model-based memory hierarchy optimizations for sparse matrices. In *Proceedings of the 1998 Workshop on Profile and Feedback-Directed Compilation*, Paris, France, October 1998.
18. M. Kandemir, A. Choudhary, J. Ramanujam, and P. Banerjee. Improving locality using loop and data transformations in an integrated framework. In *Proceedings of the 31th IEEE/ACM International Symposium on Microarchitecture*, Dallas, TX, November 1998.
19. G. Karypis and V. Kumar. A fast and high quality multilevel scheme for partitioning irregular graphs. In *Proceedings of the 24th International Conference on Parallel Processing*, Oconomowoc, WI, August 1995.
20. G. Karypis and V. Kumar. Multi-level k-way hypergraph partitioning. In *Proceedings of SC'98*, Orlando, FL, November 1998.
21. A. Lain and P. Banerjee. Exploiting spatial regularity in irregular iterative applications. In *Proceedings of the 9th International Parallel Processing Symposium*, Santa Barbara, CA, April 1995.
22. Y. Lin and D. Padua. On the automatic parallelization of sparse and irregular Fortran programs. In *Proceedings of the 4th Workshop on Languages, Compilers, and Run-time Systems for Scalable Computers*, Pittsburgh, PA, May 1998.
23. Y. Lin and D. Padua. Compiler analysis of irregular memory accesses. In *Proceedings of the SIGPLAN '00 Conference on Programming Language Design and Implementation*, Vancouver, Canada, June 2000.
24. W. Liu and A. Sherman. Comparative analysis of the cuthill-mckee and the reverse cuthill-mckee ordering algorithms for sparse matrices. *SIAM Journal on Numerical Analysis*, 13(2):198–213, April 1976.
25. B. Lu and J. Mellor-Crummey. Compiler optimization of implicit reductions for distributed memory multiprocessors. In *Proceedings of the 12th International Parallel Processing Symposium*, Orlando, FL, April 1998.
26. K. S. McKinley, S. Carr, and C.-W. Tseng. Improving data locality with loop transformations. *ACM Transactions on Programming Languages and Systems*, 18(4):424–453, July 1996.
27. J. Mellor-Crummey, D. Whalley, and K. Kennedy. Improving memory hierarchy performance for irregular applications. In *Proceedings of the 1999 ACM International Conference on Supercomputing*, Rhodes, Greece, June 1999.
28. N. Mitchell, L. Carter, and J. Ferrante. Localizing non-affine array references. In *Proceedings of the International Conference on Parallel Architectures and Compilation Techniques*, Newport Beach , LA, October 1999.
29. M. Rinard and P. Diniz. Commutativity analysis: A new analysis technique for parallelizing compilers. *ACM Transactions on Programming Languages and Systems*, 19(6):942–992, November 1997.

30. G. Rivera and C.-W. Tseng. Data transformations for eliminating conflict misses. In *Proceedings of the SIGPLAN '98 Conference on Programming Language Design and Implementation*, Montreal, Canada, June 1998.

31. H. Simon. Partitioning of unstructured mesh problems for parallel processing. In *Proceedings of the Conference on Parallel Methods on Large Scale Structural Analysis and Physics Applications*. Permagon Press, 1991.

32. J. P. Singh, C. Holt, T. Totsuka, A. Gupta, and J. Hennessy. Load balancing and data locality in adaptive hierarchical n-body methods: Barnes-hut, fast multipole, and radiosity. *Journal of Parallel and Distributed Computing*, June 1995.

33. M. E. Wolf and M. Lam. A data locality optimizing algorithm. In *Proceedings of the SIGPLAN '91 Conference on Programming Language Design and Implementation*, Toronto, Canada, June 1991.

34. H. Yu and L. Rauchwerger. Adaptive reduction parallelization techniques. In *Proceedings of the 2000 ACM International Conference on Supercomputing*, Santa Fe, NM, May 2000.

UPMLIB: A Runtime System for Tuning the Memory Performance of OpenMP Programs on Scalable Shared-Memory Multiprocessors*

Dimitrios S. Nikolopoulos[1], Theodore S. Papatheodorou[1],
Constantine D. Polychronopoulos[2], Jesús Labarta[3], and Eduard Ayguadé[3]

[1] Department of Computer Engineering and Informatics
University of Patras, Greece
{dsn,tsp}@hpclab.ceid.upatras.gr
[2] Department of Electrical and Computer Engineering
University of Illinois at Urbana-Champaign
cdp@csrd.uiuc.edu
[3] Department of Computer Architecture
Technical University of Catalonia, Spain
{jesus,eduard}@ac.upc.es

Abstract. We present the design and implementation of UPMLIB, a runtime system that provides transparent facilities for dynamically tuning the memory performance of OpenMP programs on scalable shared-memory multiprocessors with hardware cache-coherence. UPMLIB integrates information from the compiler and the operating system, to implement algorithms that perform accurate and timely page migrations. The algorithms and the associated mechanisms correlate memory reference information with the semantics of parallel programs and scheduling events that break the association between threads and data for which threads have memory affinity at runtime. Our experimental evidence shows that UPMLIB makes OpenMP programs immune to the page placement strategy of the operating system, thus obviating the need for introducing data placement directives in OpenMP. Furthermore, UPMlib provides solid improvements of throughput in multiprogrammed execution environments.
Keywords: OpenMP, scalable shared-memory multiprocessors, memory management, runtime systems, operating systems.

1 Introduction

Scalable shared-memory multiprocessor architectures converge remarkably to a common model, in which nodes with commodity microprocessors and memory are connected via a fast network and equipped with additional hardware support to provide

* This work was supported by the E.C. through the TMR Contract No. ERBFMGECT-950062 and in part through the IV Framework (ESPRIT Programme, Project No. 21907, NANOS), the Greek Secretariat of Research and Technology (Contract No. E.D.-99-566) and the Spanish Ministry of Education through projects No. TIC98-511 and TIC97-1445CE. The experiments were conducted with resources provided by the European Center for Parallelism of Barcelona (CEPBA).

S. Dwarkadas (Ed.): LCR 2000, LNCS 1915, pp. 85–99, 2000.
© Springer-Verlag Berlin Heidelberg 2000

the communication abstraction of a shared address space to the programmer [2]. High-level programming models for scalable parallel computers converge also to a small set of standards that represent essentially two programming methodologies with different communication abstractions, namely message-passing and shared-memory. MPI [3] and OpenMP [13] are the most popular representatives of these programming methodologies.

There is a considerable debate going on recently with respect to the programming model of choice for scalable shared-memory multiprocessors. Interestingly, contemporary systems such as the SGI Origin2000 [8] support programming models based on both message-passing and shared-memory, via customized runtime systems provided by the vendors. Performance experiences on these systems indicate that implementations of parallel programs with MPI perform often better than implementations of the same programs with OpenMP. This is true especially for large industrial codes [14].

The most prominent problem that OpenMP are faced with on scalable shared-memory multiprocessors is the non-uniformity of memory access latencies (NUMA). Although the shared-memory communication abstraction hides data distribution details from the programmer, the programs are very sensitive to the page placement strategy of the operating system. A poor page placement scheme may exacerbate the number of remote memory accesses, which cost two to ten times as much as local memory accesses on state-of-the-art systems. It is therefore critical to ensure that threads and data are aligned in the nodes of the system, so that each thread is collocated with the data that the thread accesses more frequently.

Unfortunately, in order to achieve the aforementioned goal with a plain shared-memory programming model, the programmer must be aware of the page placement strategy of the operating system and either modify the program to adapt its memory reference pattern to the enforced system policy, or bypass the operating system and hand-code a customized page placement scheme [6]. Both approaches compromise the simplicity of shared-memory programming models and jeopardize their portability across different platforms. Nevertheless, vendors of shared-memory multiprocessors are already facing the dilemma of whether data distribution directives should be introduced in OpenMP or not [9].

The question that motivates the work presented in this paper is whether OpenMP can be enhanced with runtime capabilities for the transparent improvement of data locality at the page level, without exporting data distribution details to the programmer. We present the design and implementation of UPMLIB (User-Level Page Migration library), a runtime system with mechanisms and algorithms that transparently optimize at runtime the page placement of OpenMP programs, using feedback from the compiler, the operating system and dynamic monitoring of the memory reference pattern of the programs. UPMLIB leverages dynamic page migration [16] at user-level [10] to correct suboptimal page placement decisions made by the operating system.

The notable difference between UPMLIB and previously proposed kernel-level page migration engines, is that the employed dynamic page migration algorithms correlate the memory reference information obtained from hardware counters with the semantics of the parallel computation and scheduling information provided by the operating system. This is accomplished by integrating the compiler, the runtime system and the operating system in the page migration engine. The compiler drives the page migration mechanism, by identifying memory regions which are likely to contain pages candidate for migration and instrumenting the programs to invoke the page migration engine of UPMLIB. The operating system provides scheduling notifications to the runtime system in order to trigger aggressive page migration schemes upon thread migrations. Thread migrations incur bursts of remote memory accesses due to cache reloads and the misalignment between migrated threads and the set of pages for which these threads exhibit memory affinity. The overall approach improves the accuracy and timeliness of page migrations, amortizes well the cost of page migrations over time, and makes the page migration engine responsive to unpredictable runtime events that may harm data locality. Furthermore, implementing the page migration engine entirely at user-level provides us with a great deal of flexibility in testing and customizing memory management schemes without requiring kernel source code and without compromising the well-tuned resource management policies of the operating system.

We have implemented UPMLIB on the SGI Origin2000, using the IRIX 6.5.5 memory management control interface. As a case study, we have used UPMLIB with unmodified OpenMP implementations of the NAS benchmarks [7]. Our results show that UPMLIB embeds the desirable immunity of OpenMP codes to the page placement strategies of the operating system. In addition, UPMLIB provides solid and in some cases significant performance improvements compared to the native IRIX page placement and migration schemes for standalone parallel programs and multiprogrammed workloads, scheduled with space- or time-sharing by the IRIX kernel.

The rest of this paper is organized as follows. Section 2 outlines the design of UPMLIB. Section 3 provides implementation details. Section 4 presents results with OpenMP codes that utilize UPMLIB to improve their data locality in dedicated and multiprogrammed execution environments. Section 5 concludes the paper.

2   UPMLIB **Design and Algorithms**

The key design issue of UPMLIB is the integration of the compiler, the runtime system and the operating system in a unified framework that enhances the effectiveness of dynamic page migration. The page migration engine of UPMLIB correlates the dynamic reference pattern of a parallel program with the semantics of the program and the scheduling status of its threads at runtime. UPMLIB implements feedback-guided optimization of page placement in a local scope, in order to arm OpenMP programs with invulnerability to the global memory management strategy of the operating system and interventions of the kernel scheduler, when parallel programs are executed in multiprogrammed environments. Figure 1 shows the main modules and interfaces of UPMLIB. These are explained in detail in the following paragraphs.

2.1   Compiler Support

The OpenMP compiler identifies areas of the virtual address space which are likely to contain pages candidate for migration and instruments the programs to call the page

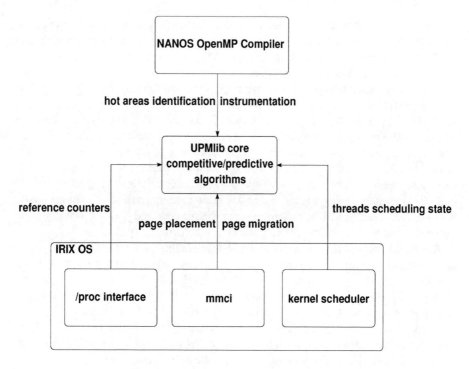

Fig. 1. UPMLIB modules and interfaces.

migration services of UPMLIB at specific points during their execution. In our first prototype, the compiler locates shared arrays which are both read and written in possibly
disjoint sets of OpenMP parallel/work sharing constructs, thus incurring interprocessor
communication of shared data. The compiler identifies these arrays as *hot* memory areas
and inserts calls to UPMLIB for activating dynamic monitoring of page reference activity and page migration on these areas. The implementation is flexible enough to exploit
advanced compiler knowledge, in case the compiler can provide accurate boundaries
for parts of the hot areas which are likely to concentrate the most significant fraction of
remote memory accesses, and the exact points of the program at which page migration
could improve locality by emulating data distribution and redistribution schemes.

The compiler exploits the semantics of the parallel program in order to migrate
pages accurately and ahead in time. The associated mechanisms distinguish between
iterative and non-iterative parallel programs. The former represent the vast majority of
parallel codes. For iterative programs, the compiler applies page migration at a coarse-
grain scale, namely at the ends of the outer iterations of the parallel program. At these
points of execution the runtime system can obtain an accurate view of the complete
page reference pattern of the parallel computation by reading the hardware counters.
Therefore, the runtime system is in a position to take successful decisions for migrating
pages and achieve an *optimal* page placement, where *optimal* is defined with respect
to the observed repetitive memory reference pattern of the program. The optimal page

placement is achieved when each page is placed in a node so that the maximum latency due to remote memory accesses by any node in the system to this page is minimized.

For strictly iterative parallel computations and in the absence of page-level false-sharing or thread migrations, the runtime system attains the best page placement with respect to the observed reference pattern after executing a single iteration of the parallel computation. Besides to the advantage of timeliness, this strategy amortizes well the cost of page migrations over time. Cost amortization is of particular importance, since page migrations are overly expensive operations on state-of-the-art systems. Since page migration is performed based on the reference trace of the complete parallel computation, the page migration engine is not biased by temporary effects such as cold-start or phase changes[1] in the reference pattern [10].

UPMLIB handles non-iterative codes, as well as iterative codes with non-repetitive access patterns, using a sampling-based mechanism for migrating pages. The runtime system wakes up periodically a thread, which scans a fraction of the pages in the hot memory areas and migrates some of these pages if needed. The sampling frequency and the amount of pages scanned upon each invocation of UPMLIB can be adjusted by the user to fit the characteristics of the application. Programs with frequent changes in the communication pattern between processors benefit from short sampling intervals, while programs with infrequent changes in the communication pattern can utilize longer sampling intervals. The amount of pages scanned upon each invocation is selected to limit the cost of checking and migrating pages to at most a small fraction of the sampling interval. The algorithm for scanning pages can vary from sequential to stride to randomized scanning, in order to enable the runtime system to adapt the page migration engine to the distribution of hot pages in the virtual address space.

Practically, the duration of the sampling interval must be at least a few hundred milliseconds. This holds due to the high cost of page migrations. The sampling interval must be selected to give the runtime system enough time to migrate a reasonable amount of pages ahead in time, so that a good fraction of the cost of remote memory accesses to these pages is moved off the critical path of the program. The sampling mechanism is beneficial for programs in which phases in the memory reference pattern last for at least a few seconds. Programs that exhibit fine-grain phase changes do not provide usually enough time to the runtime system for migrating pages.

The compiler is in a position to apply more aggressive data locality optimizations using page migration as its vehicle. As an example, the compiler can apply phase-driven optimization of page placement. The compiler can analyze the communication patterns of each phase, detect phase changes due to changes in the communication pattern across phases, and invoke the page migration mechanism between phases [5]. The effectiveness of such optimizations depends on the granularity of the phases in terms of execution time. The compiler analysis should be quite conservative when optimizing page placement across phase changes, because page migrations have to be performed on the critical path of the parallel program, thus making the amortization of the cost of the runtime system a critical performance parameter. Optimization of page placement across phase changes is a subject of investigation in our current version of UPMLIB.

---

[1] In OpenMP, we define a phase as a sequence of parallel or worksharing constructs that have the same communication pattern among processors.

2.2   Page Migration Algorithms

UPMLIB uses by default a competitive algorithm for migrating pages. The criterion of competitiveness in the algorithm is the estimated latency seen by each node in the system due to remote memory accesses. This criterion incorporates the number of references, the estimated cost of each remote reference according to the distance in hops between the referencing node and the referenced page, and contention at the nodes to which references are issued. The competitive thresholds used in the algorithm are tunable and may change at runtime, according to the observed effectiveness of page migrations on reducing the rate of remote memory accesses. In addition, the page migration algorithms include a self-deactivation mechanism, which disables the page migration mechanisms when it detects that the memory reference pattern is stabilized so that no further page migrations are needed by the runtime system. More details can be found in [10].

UPMLIB circumvents page-level false-sharing with a ping-pong prevention mechanism. The idea is to avoid migrating a page if it is likely to bounce between the same nodes more than once. The ping-pong prevention mechanism ensures that unless the threads of a parallel program migrate between nodes, each page will be placed at the appropriate node within the first two iterations of the program, assuming a strictly iterative program with a repetitive reference pattern. For the more general case in which pages can ping-pong between more than two nodes due to wide false-sharing, UPMLIB uses a bouncing threshold to limit the maximum number of times a page can move before the runtime system pins the page to a node. The bouncing threshold of UPMLIB is also a tunable parameter of the runtime system, to handle cases in which ping-pong of a page can actually be beneficial, for improving data locality across distinct phases.

2.3   Operating System Support

On scalable shared-memory multiprocessors, the page placement strategy establishes an implicit association between threads and data in a parallel program. In principle, a thread is associated with its *memory affinity set*, that is, the set of pages that the thread accesses more frequently than any other thread of the same program. On a multiprogrammed system in which multiple parallel and sequential programs execute simultaneously, the operating system arbitrarily preempts and migrates threads between nodes, thus breaking the association between these threads and their memory affinity sets. Thread migrations incur the cost of reloading the working sets of migrated threads from remote memory modules, as well as satisfying most cache misses incurred from migrated threads remotely. A page migration mechanism can alleviate this problem by forwarding the pages that belong to the memory affinity set of a migrated thread to the new node that hosts the thread. Unfortunately, a competitive page migration algorithm may fail to perform timely page migrations in this case. The reason is that the page reference counters may have accumulated obsolete reference history that prevents a page from migrating, unless the new home node of the migrated thread issues a sufficiently large amount of remote references to meet the competitive criterion.

UPMLIB uses a lightweight communication interface with the operating system to obtain scheduling information, which is used as a trigger for activating aggressive page

Table 1. UPMLIB interface.

Call	Functionality
`upmlib_init()`, `upmlib_end()`	UPMLIB initialization and termination.
`upmlib_memrefcnt(va, size)`	Initializes reference counting and activates dynamic page migration for the range [va,va+size-1].
`upmlib_migrate_pages(pol)`	Runs the specified page migration policy for all hot memory areas.
`upmlib_check_pset()`	Polls the effective processor set on which the program executes from shared memory and records thread migrations.
`upmlib_switch()`	Switches the page migration policy from competitive to predictive and vice-versa using OS information.
`upmlib_record_counters()`	Records per-page/per-node reference counters for statistics collection.

forwarding algorithms upon migrations of threads from the operating system. The runtime system polls a vector in shared-memory which stores the instantaneous mapping of threads to processors and switches on the fly the default competitive algorithm, if it detects that some threads have migrated. In that case, UPMLIB activates a predictive algorithm which forwards pages in the memory affinity sets of migrated threads. The idea is to have the pages of a memory affinity set of a thread follow the thread in case this thread migrates. In the actual implementation, the runtime system detects *permanent* thread migrations, that is, thread migrations that move a thread to a node for an amount of time sufficiently long to justify the activation of the page forwarding mechanism. The associated algorithms and implementation issues are available in [11].

Table 2. UPMLIB environment variables.

Variable	Functionality
`UMIGR_POLICY`	Page migration criterion
`UMIGR_THRESHOLD`	Competitive criterion threshold
`UMIGR_PING_PONG_LIMIT`	Bouncing threshold for ping-pong
`UMIGR_SAMPLING_PERIOD`	Period for the sampling-based mechanism
`UMIGR_PAGES_PER_SAMPLE`	Number of pages sampled per invocation of the sampling-based mechanism
`UMIGR_THREAD`	Thread that executes UPMLIB code

Table 1 summarizes the UPMLIB user-level interface. This interface is meant to be used by the compiler, in the process of instrumenting OpenMP programs to use the page migration engine. Table 2 shows the runtime environment variables used to set the tunable parameters of UPMLIB. Figure 2 gives an example of the use of UPMLIB in the NAS BT benchmark. In this example, the compiler identifies three arrays of the application (u, rhs, forcing) as hot memory areas and activates the monitoring of page reference rates on these areas using the `upmlib_memrefcnt()` call to the runtime

```
call upmlib_init()
call upmlib_memrefcnt(u, size_of_u)
call upmlib_memrefcnt(rhs,size_of_rhs)
call upmlib_memrefcnt(forcing,size_of_forcing)
 ...
do step=1,niter
 call compute_rhs
 call x_solve
 call y_solve
 call z_solve
 call addi
 stat=upmlib_check_pset()
 if (stat .gt. 0) then
   call upmlib_switch(PREDICTIVE)
 else
   call upmlib_switch(COMPETITIVE)
 endif
 call upmlib_migrate_pages()
enddo
```

Fig. 2. Usage of UPMLIB in the NAS BT benchmark.

system. The function upmlib_check_pset() polls the scheduling information provided by the operating system and returns a positive value in case the operating system has performed at least one thread migration and the migrated thread has stayed on the same node for a sufficiently long amount of time. If no such thread migration has occurred, the default competitive page migration algorithm is invoked at the end of every iteration of the outer do loop, by calling the function upmlib_migrate_pages(). The page migration engine scans the hot memory areas, identifies pages candidate for migration and migrates pages according to the competitive criterion. In the event of a thread migration, the compiler switches the page migration algorithm to use the aggressive predictive criterion for page forwarding, by calling upmlib_switch(). The same function is called to switch back to the competitive algorithm in the absence of thread migrations by the operating system.

3   Implementation

UPMLIB is implemented on the SGI Origin2000, using the user-level memory management services of the Cellular IRIX operating system. The runtime system is integrated with the NANOS OpenMP compiler [1], which implements the instrumentation pass for using UPMLIB.

3.1   Interfaces

The page migration facilities of UPMLIB use the memory management control interface (mmci) of IRIX (see Figure 1). The IRIX mmci provides significant flexibility in managing physical memory at user-level, by virtualizing the topology of the system. The user can create high-level abstractions of the physical memory space, called *Memory Locality Domains* (MLDs). MLDs can be statically or dynamically mapped to physical nodes of the system. After establishing a mapping between MLDs and nodes, the user can associate ranges of the virtual address space with MLDs in order to implement application-specific page placement schemes. The runtime system requests the coherent migration of a range of the virtual address space of the program with the `migr_range_migrate(addr,size,node)` system call. The requested memory migration is subject to the global resource management policies of IRIX. This practically means that IRIX may reject a request for migrating pages if it detects that there is not enough available memory in the target node. In general, IRIX follows a best-effort scheme for migrating pages. If the target node has insufficient free physical memory, IRIX tries to migrate the pages to a node as physically close as possible to the target node [15].

UPMLIB uses the `/proc` interface for accessing hardware reference counters. The Origin2000 memory modules are equipped with 11-bit hardware counters. There is one counter per node for each page in memory, for system configurations of up to 64 nodes. The hardware counters are memory-mapped to 32-bit software-extended counters by the operating system. When a hardware counter overflows, the system adds the contents of the counter as well as the contents of all the counters of the same page to the corresponding software-extended counters and resets the hardware counters. This implementation introduces a hysteresis of the values of the software-extended counters, compared to the actual number of references to the corresponding pages. The runtime system polls both the hardware and the software-extended counters, to cope with this asynchrony that might affect page migration decisions.

The asynchrony between hardware and software-extended counters is circumvented in the following way. Let $n_{h,t}$, $n_{s,t}$ be the contents of a hardware and the corresponding software-extended counter at time t. If $n_{s,t} < n_{h,t}$, the system uses $n_{h,t}$ in the page migration criteria, since the value of the hardware counter is up-to-date with the actual number of references in this case. Suppose that $n_{s,t} \geq n_{h,t}$. Also, let $n_{s,t-1}, n_{h,t-1}$ be the values of the counters the last time the runtime system retrieved a snapshot of them. If $n_{s,t-1} = n_{s,t}$, the runtime system uses the formula $n_{s,t-1} + n_{h,t} - n_{h,t-1}$, to compute the actual number of references to the page. Note that in the same scenario, it is impossible to have $n_{h,t} < n_{h,t-1}$. This would mean that the hardware counter has overflowed at least once, and therefore $n_{s,t} > n_{s,t-1}$, which is impossible according to the original hypothesis. If the two consecutive snapshots of the counters indicate that $n_{s,t} > n_{s,t-1}$, the runtime system uses the formula $n_{s,t} + n_{h,t}$ to compute the actual number of references, since $n_{h,t}$ is the amount of references after the counter overflow in this case.

The size of the hardware page in the Origin2000 memory modules is 4 Kbytes. The page size used by the operating system to manage virtual memory is 16 Kbytes. Each virtual memory page is stored in four consecutive physical memory pages. UPMLIB combines the values of the counters of the physical memory pages that cache a virtual memory page, to compute reference rates. Furthermore, UPMLIB tries to batch multiple page migrations for consecutive pages in the virtual address space into a single invocation of the IRIX memory migration facility to reduce the runtime overhead.

The communication between UPMLIB and the IRIX kernel is realized via polling shared variables in the private data areas (prda) of IRIX threads, using the sched-ctl() interface. The operating system updates a flag in the prda of each thread, which stores the physical CPU on which the thread was scheduled during the last time quantum. UPMLIB uses this information in conjunction with hints provided by the IRIX kernel for defining the number of threads that execute OpenMP parallel/work sharing constructs. The latter can be obtained using the mp_suggested_numthreads() call to the IRIX parallelization runtime library. In this way, UPMLIB detects thread preemptions and migrations at the boundaries of parallel constructs to trigger the page forwarding algorithms.

3.2   Mechanisms for Executing Page Migrations

UPMLIB uses two mechanisms for executing page migration algorithms. By default, the runtime system overlaps the execution of page migrations with the execution of the threads of a parallel program. We measured with microbenchmarks the average cost of a user-level page migration on the SGI Origin2000 to be equal to approximately 1–1.3 milliseconds, including the cost for reading reference counters and executing the page migration algorithm. This makes evident that UPMLIB can not execute a large number of page migrations on the critical path of the program. Therefore, the runtime system uses a separate thread, called the *memory manager*, for executing page migrations. This thread is created in sleep mode when UPMLIB is initialized and wakes up upon every invocation of UPMLIB by the OpenMP program. The memory manager executes in parallel with the application threads. This strategy works well for standalone parallel programs running on moderate to large processor scales, at which the program can gracefully sacrifice one processor for executing operating system code [6].

In loaded multiprogrammed systems in which the total number of active threads may be higher than the number of processors , the memory managers created by UPM-LIB may undesirably interfere with the threads of parallel programs. To cope with this problem, UPMLIB supports also the execution of page migration algorithms from the master thread of the OpenMP program. According to the OpenMP specification, the master thread participates in the execution of parallel constructs. It is therefore important to minimize the interference between the master thread and UPMLIB code. To achieve this, the runtime system uses stripmining of the buffers that store the reference counters, in order to reduce the size of the working set size of UPMLIB and avoid erasing completely the cache footprint of the master thread. The same technique is used when the compiler uses UPMLIB for phase-driven optimization of page placement , since in this case page migrations must be performed before phase changes to ensure proper data distribution [12].

4   Experimental Results

In this section we provide a small set of experimental results, as case studies that demonstrate the potentials of UPMLIB.

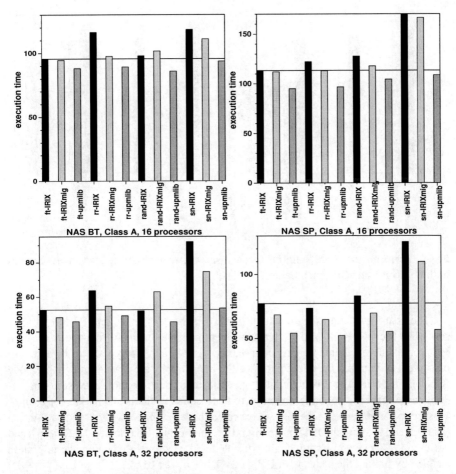

Fig. 3. Performance of the NAS BT and SP benchmarks, with different page placement and migration strategies on 16 and 32 processors of the Origin2000.

Figure 3 illustrates the performance of two application benchmarks from the NAS suite, BT and SP, both parallelized with OpenMP [7]. BT is a simulated CFD application which solves Navier-Stokes equations using the Beam-Warming method. SP solves the same equations using approximate API factorization. The applications are strictly iterative, in the sense that they perform the same parallel computation for a number of time steps. Both programs are optimized by their providers, to exploit the first-touch page placement strategy, which is used by default in the Origin2000. This is done by executing a cold-start iteration of the parallel computation before the beginning of the time-stepping loop, in order to warm up the caches and place pages appropriately. The experiments were conducted on a 64-processor SGI Origin2000 with MIPS R10000 processors. Each processor had a clock frequency of 250 MHz, 32 Kbytes of primary and 4 Mbytes of secondary cache. The system had 8 Gbytes of main memory, uniformly distributed among the nodes.

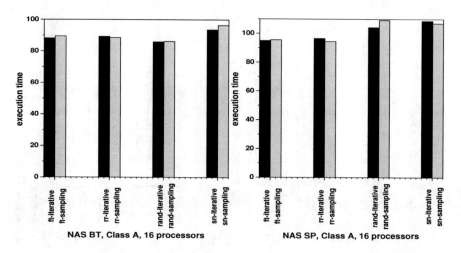

Fig. 4. Performance of the sampling mechanism with different page placement schemes in the NAS BT and SP benchmarks.

The charts plot the execution time of the benchmarks on 16 and 32 idle processors with four different initial page placement schemes, namely first-touch (labeled `ft`), round-robin (labeled `rr`), random (labeled `rand`) and the hypothetical worst-case placement in which all resident pages of the benchmarks are placed on a single node (labeled `sn`), thus exacerbating contention and latency due to remote accesses. The random and worst-case page placement were hand-coded in the benchmarks. For each of the three page placement schemes, we executed the benchmarks without page migration (labeled `IRIX`), with the IRIX page migration engine enabled (labeled `IRIXmig`), and with the IRIX page migration engine disabled and user-level dynamic page migration enabled by linking the codes with UPMLIB (labeled `upmlib`).

The primary outcome of the results is that the benchmarks exhibit sensitivity to the page placement strategy of the operating system and in the cases in which the page placement scheme is harmful, the IRIX page migration engine is unable to close the performance gap. For example, worst-case page placement incurs slowdowns of 1.24 to 2.10 even if dynamic page migration is enabled in the IRIX kernel. With round-robin page placement, the slowdown compared to first-touch ranges between 1.08 and 1.38, while with random page placement the slowdown ranges between 1.02 and 1.14.

The iterative page migration engine of UPMLIB brings the slowdown factor in the case of worst-case page placement down to at most 1.06. With round-robin and random page placement schemes, slowdown is less than 1.01 when the user-level page migration engine is employed. The results show that user-level page migration makes the OpenMP implementations of the benchmarks immune to the page placement strategy of the operating system and the associated problems with data locality. Furthermore, UPMLIB provides sizeable performance improvements (28% in the case of BT) over the best-performing page placement and migration scheme of IRIX.

Figure 4 illustrates the performance of the sampling mechanism of UPMLIB, against the performance of the iterative mechanism. The duration of the sampling in-

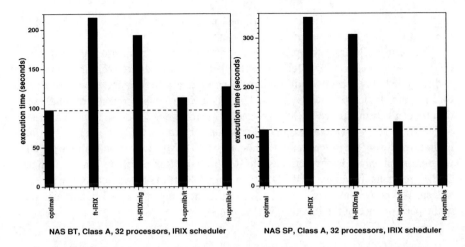

Fig. 5. Average execution time of the NAS BT and SP benchmarks, in multiprogrammed workloads executed with the native IRIX scheduler.

terval used in these experiments was 1 second and the mechanism scanned 100 pages in the hot memory areas per invocation by the runtime system. The hot memory areas were scanned by the page migration engine in a round-robin fashion. The performance of the sampling-based mechanism inferior to the performance of the iterative mechanism by at most 17%. Considering the fact that the iterative mechanism is well tuned for applications like the ones evaluated in these experiments, we can conclude that the sampling-based mechanism constitutes an effective alternative in cases in which the iterative mechanism is not applicable.

Figure 5 illustrates the results from executions of multiprogrammed workloads with the NAS BT and SP benchmarks. Each workload includes four identical copies of the same benchmark, plus a sequential background load consisting of an I/O-intensive C program. The workloads were executed on 64 processors. All instances of the parallel benchmarks requested 32 processors for execution, however the benchmarks enabled the dynamic adjustment of the number of threads that execute parallel code, via the OMP_SET_DYNAMIC call [13]. In these experiments, IRIX initially started all 128 threads of the parallel benchmarks, relying on time-sharing for the distribution of processor time among the programs. In the course of execution, IRIX detected that the parallel benchmarks underutilized some processors and reduced accordingly the number of threads, reverting to space-sharing for executing the workload. However, some processors were still time-shared due to the interference of the background load.

The results show the average execution time of the parallel benchmarks in the workloads with plain first-touch page placement (ft-IRIX), first-touch and the IRIX page migration engine enabled (ft-IRIXmig) and first-touch with the page forwarding heuristic, enabled with the iterative and the sampling-based mechanisms used in the page migration engine (labeled ft-upmlib/it and ft-upmlib/s respectively). The theoretical optimal execution time of the benchmarks is also illustrated in the charts. The optimal time is computed as the standalone execution time of each benchmark on 32 processors with the best page placement strategy (ft-upmlib, see Figure 3), divided by the degree of multiprogramming in the workload.

The results illustrate the performance implications of multiprogramming on the memory performance of parallel programs when their threads are arbitrarily preempted and migrated between nodes by the operating system. The average execution time of the programs is slowed down by 2.1 to 3.3 compared to the theoretically optimal execution time, when the native IRIX page management schemes are used. Instrumentation of UPMLIB has shown that the IRIX kernel performed on average about 2500 thread migrations during the execution of each workload. UPMLIB with the iterative page forwarding mechanism is very effective in dealing with this problem. The performance of the programs linked with UPMLIB is within 5% off the theoretical optimal performance. The performance of the sampling-based mechanism is inferior, although close to the performance of the iterative mechanism.

5   Conclusion

This paper outlined the design and implementation of UPMLIB, a runtime system for tuning the page placement of OpenMP programs on scalable shared-memory multiprocessors, in which shared-memory programming models are sensitive to the alignment of threads and data in the system. UPMLIB takes a new approach by integrating the compiler and the operating system with the page migration engine, to improve the accuracy, timeliness, and effectiveness of dynamic page migration. The experiments have shown that a smart page migration engine can obviate the need for introducing data distribution directives in OpenMP, thus preserving the simplicity of the shared-memory programming model. Moreover, dynamic page migration has demonstrated its potential as a means to provide robust performance of parallel programs in multiprogrammed environments, in which the programs can not make any safe assumptions on resource availability.

Our current efforts are oriented towards three directions: utilizing the functionality of UPMLIB in codes with fine-grain phase changes in the memory access pattern; customizing UPMLIB to the characteristics of specific kernel-level scheduling strategies; and integrating a unified utility for page and thread migration in UPMLIB, with the purpose of biasing thread scheduling decisions by page reference information to achieve better memory locality.

References

1. E. Ayguade et.al. *NanosCompiler: A Research Platform for OpenMP Extensions*. Proc. of the First European Workshop on OpenMP, pp. 27–31. Lund, Sweden, October 1999.
2. D. Culler, J. P. Singh and A. Gupta. *Parallel Computer Architecture: A Hardware/Software Approach*. Morgan Kaufmann Publishers, 1998.
3. W. Gropp et.al. *MPI: The Complete Reference, Vol. 2*. MIT Press, 1998.
4. High Performance Fortran Forum. *High Performance Fortran Language Specification. Version 2.0*. Technical Report CRPC-TR92225. Center for Research on Parallel Computation, Rice University. January 1997.

5. G. Howard and D. Lowenthal. *An Integrated Compiler/Run-Time System for Global Data Distribution in Distributed Shared Memory Systems.* Proc. of the 2nd Workshop on Software Distributed Shared Memory, in conjunction with ACM ICS'2000. Santa Fe, New Mexico, May 2000.
6. D. Jiang and J. P. Singh. *Scaling Application Performance on a Cache-Coherent Multiprocessor.* Proc. of the 26th International Symposium on Computer Architecture, pp. 305–316. Atlanta, Georgia, May 1999.
7. H. Jin, M. Frumkin and J. Yan. *The OpenMP Implementation of NAS Parallel Benchmarks.* Technical Report NAS-99-011, NASA Ames Research Center. October 1999.
8. J. Laudon and D. Lenoski. *The SGI Origin2000: A ccNUMA Highly Scalable Server.* Proc. of the 24th Int. Symposium on Computer Architecture, pp. 241–251. Denver, Colorado, June 1997.
9. J. Levesque. *The Future of OpenMP on IBM SMP Systems.* Invited talk. First European Workshop on OpenMP. Lund, Sweden,October 1999.
10. D. Nikolopoulos et.al. *A Case for User-Level Dynamic Page Migration.* Proc. of the 14th ACM International Conference on Supercomputing, pp. 119–130. Santa Fe, New Mexico, May 2000.
11. D. Nikolopoulos et.al. *User-Level Dynamic Page Migration for Multiprogrammed Shared-Memory Multiprocessors.* To appear in the 29th International Conference on Parallel Processing. Toronto, Canada, August 2000.
12. D. Nikolopoulos et.al. *Leveraging Transparent Data Distribution in OpenMP via user-level Dynamic Page Migration.* To appear in the 3rd International Symposium on High Performance Computing, Workshop on OpenMP Experiences and Implementations. Tokyo, Japan, October 2000.
13. OpenMP Architecture Review Board. *OpenMP FORTRAN Application Programming Interface.* Version 1.1, November 1999.
14. M. Resch and B. Sander. *A Comparison of OpenMP and MPI for the Parallel CFD Case.* Proc. of the First European Workshop on OpenMP. Lund, Sweden, October 1999.
15. Silicon Graphics Inc. *Origin2000 Performance Tuning and Optimization Guide.* IRIX 6.5 Technical Publications, http://techpubs.sgi.com. Accessed January 2000.
16. B. Verghese, S. Devine, A. Gupta and M. Rosenblum. *Operating System Support for Improving Data Locality on CC-NUMA Compute Servers.* Proc. of the 7th International Conference on Architectural Support for Programming Languages and Operating Systems, pp. 279–289. Cambridge, Massachusetts, October 1996.

Performance Evaluation of OpenMP
Applications with Nested Parallelism

Yoshizumi Tanaka[1], Kenjiro Taura[1], Mitsuhisa Sato[2], and Akinori Yonezawa[1]

[1] Department of Information Science, Faculty of Science, University of Tokyo
{y-tanaka,tau,yonezawa}@is.s.u-tokyo.ac.jp
[2] Real World Computing Partnership
msato@trc.rwcp.or.jp

Abstract. Many existing OpenMP systems do not sufficiently implement nested parallelism. This is supposedly because nested parallelism is believed to require a significant implementation effort, incur a large overhead, or lack applications. This paper demonstrates Omni/ST, a simple and efficient implementation of OpenMP nested parallelism using StackThreads/MP, which is a fine-grain thread library. Thanks to StackThreads/MP, OpenMP `parallel` constructs are simply mapped onto thread creation primitives of StackThreads/MP, yet they are efficiently managed with a fixed number of threads in the underlying thread package (e.g., Pthreads). Experimental results on Sun Ultra Enterprise 10000 with up to 60 processors show that overhead imposed by nested parallelism is very small (1-3% in five out of six applications, and 8% for the other), and there is a significant scalability benefit for applications with nested parallelism.

1 Introduction

OpenMP is increasingly becoming popular for high performance computing on shared memory machines. Its current specification, however, is restrictive in many ways [16]. Specifically, the current OpenMP specifies that nested parallelism is optional, which means that implementation can ignore parallel directives encountered during the execution of another parallel directive. Many existing OpenMP systems in fact support no nested parallelism or a very limited form of it based on load-based inlining [1,11,4].

The basic justification will presumably be as follows:

Benefit: Assuming that sufficient parallelism is obtained at the outermost loop, extracting nested parallelism does no good for overall performance.

Cost: Efficient implementation of nested parallelism is difficult or complex, because it needs a thread management that can comfortably handle a very large number of threads. Standard thread libraries such as Pthreads [9] or Win32 threads [12] do not meet this criteria; they incur a large overhead for thread creation and do not tolerate a large number of threads.

While these arguments are reasonable, we nevertheless believe efficient implementation of nested parallelism is both beneficial (many applications can benefit from it) and not costly (its implementation is not that difficult).

S. Dwarkadas (Ed.): LCR 2000, LNCS 1915, pp. 100–112, 2000.

As for the benefit, an obvious benefit is that nested parallelism supports programs that do not have sufficient parallelism at the outermost level (e.g., parallel recursion). Perhaps more important is the fact that it enhances performance transparency of parallel libraries, and in general promotes reuse of black box code, users of which do not know whether it is parallel or not. Without nested parallelism, parallel libraries called during the execution of another parallel directive simply give up the opportunities of parallel execution. Therefore the library provider must expose parallelism of the library to the user, and the user must make the right choice on how to extract parallelism—call the library in parallel and run each call sequentially, or call the library sequentially and run each call in parallel. With nested parallelism, the library user does not have to know whether the library is parallel or not.

As for the implementation cost, a large body of existing literature in parallel programming language community indicates that nested parallelism, and dynamic parallelism management in general, can be implemented efficiently [10,2,19,8,5,13,6]. In particular, our previous work on fine-grain thread library StackThreads/MP [18,17,20] shows that this can be done using regular sequential compilers, imposing almost no overhead for serial execution.

This paper describes implementation of nested parallelism using fine-grain thread library StackThreads/MP. Specifically, we introduce StackThreads/MP into Omni [14,15], an OpenMP implementation which originally supports only a limited form of nested parallelism as described later. We call the Omni equipped with StackThreads/MP Omni/ST. In the experiments shown later, the original Omni and Omni/ST exhibit a similar sequential performance and speedup for applications with flat parallelism. For applications with nested parallelism, the scalability of Omni/ST was significantly better than Omni, as expected.

The rest of this paper is organized as follows. Section 2 discusses possible implementation schemes of nested parallelism and section 3 describes our implementation. Section 4 shows experimental results. Section 5 mentions related work and section 6 states summary and future work.

2   Implementation Schemes for Nested Parallelism

We discuss three representative implementation strategies of nested parallelism, from the simplest to the most involved, and clarify a necessary condition to fully support nested parallelism.

For the sake of clarity we will define some terminologies used throughout the paper. A *lightweight process* (LWP) refers to a thread created by a thread creation primitive of a thread package commonly supported on many operating systems, such as Pthreads, Solaris threads, or Win32 threads. A lightweight process keeps its own stack space so its creation is fairly costly, both in terms of space and time. A *thread*, on the other hand refers to a *logical* thread of control seen by the programmer. For example, in OpenMP, the programmer expects to observe that OMP_NUM_THREADS logical threads of controls are created at parallel sections.

Under this terminology, implementing nested parallelism means the programmer observes OMP_NUM_THREADS *logical* threads are created at *every* parallel section. Here are several implementation possibilities.

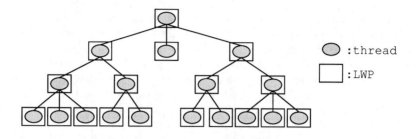

Fig. 1. Dynamic LWP Creation

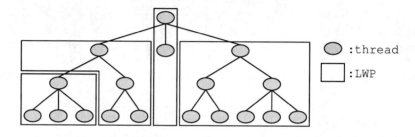

Fig. 2. Fixed LWP Pool

Dynamic LWP Creation: The simplest approach is to map each thread to an LWP like figure1. That is, each `parallel` construct creates `OMP_NUM_THREADS` LWPs using whatever thread package is available on the platform. However, in most thread packages, an LWP creation is expensive both in terms of space and time, and the scheduler does not schedule a large number of threads in a space efficient manner. Simply implemented, this approach easily runs out of memory when `parallel` constructs are deeply nested (e.g., parallel recursion). This approach will not be pursued further in this paper.

Fixed LWP Pool: A simple way to overcome the problem in the above approach is to bound the number of LWPs. This strategy is adopted by the original Omni implementation [15]. More specifically, an OpenMP program creates a fixed number of LWPs (typically as many as the number of processors) at the beginning, and keeps a pool of idle LWPs. When a program encounters a `parallel` construct, it is parallelized when there are idle LWPs at that moment. This effectively implements a limited form of nested parallelism, because if the number of logical threads created at an outermost level `parallel` construct is less than the number of LWPs, some LWPs will be left unutilized and available for nested `parallel` constructs. Figure 2 shows such an example. First, three LWPs are assigned at top level and one LWP is idle yet. Then this idle LWP is assigned at inner level. In this way nested parallelism is at least supported.

Lazy Task Creation Based Methods: Lazy Task Creation (LTC)[10], which is adopted by Omni/ST, is a technique that defers paying the cost of thread

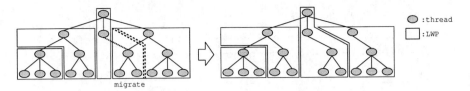

Fig. 3. Lazy Task Creation

creation until an idle LWP appears. As long as all LWPs are active, a thread creation amounts to just a regular procedure call + a trivial amount of bookkeeping instructions. The cost is paid only when a thread created by an LWP actually migrates to another. It also schedules threads in LIFO order to achieve space efficiency. In figure 3, thread assignment is just like figure 2 at first. The difference is that unexecuted threads can migrate to idle LWP later.

Fixed LWP pool approach appears to be attractive because it is not difficult to implement and nested parallelism is supported to some degree. So what is the problem? The problem is that the decision as to whether a `parallel` construct gets parallelized is made too early. Suppose there are no idle LWPs at the beginning of a `parallel` construct P, and later some become idle. These idle LWPs cannot be used by P because the decision not to parallelize P has already been made.

In general we must implement a *greedy* scheduler, which guarantees that whenever there are more logical threads than the number of specified LWPs, all LWPs are (or soon become) active, and otherwise all tasks are being scheduled by LWPs. Implementing this greedy scheduler without creating too much stacks requires a compact (stackless) representation of a thread and thread migration between LWPs. This is basically what LTC is all about.

LTC has so far been implemented for specific programming languages, with custom stack frame formats, procedure call conventions, and so on. This is reasonable because LTC generally needs to operate on procedure call frames. Therefore, packages readily available for implementation of other languages did not exist. StackThreads/MP was developed to improve this situation. It is a *library* that supports LTC with an API that exactly looks like regular thread libraries, such as thread creation and synchronizations.

3   Implementation of Omni/ST

3.1   StackThreads/MP

This section briefly describes StackThreads/MP library. It is a thread package that has basically the same API with other regular thread packages. The difference is that a thread creation cost is very low, and it tolerates a very large

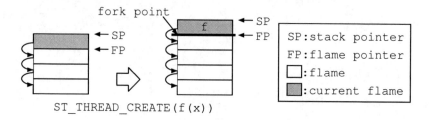

ST_THREAD_CREATE(f(x))

Fig. 4. Creation of fine-grain threads

number of threads, such as 10,000 or even more. Therefore it enables a programming style in which many threads are created as necessary and ceased as finished, no matter how many actual processors exist. See [18] for details.

The basic execution model of StackThreads/MP is as follows, and this basic scheme was invented by Mohr et al. [10]. When a program starts, it creates a fixed number of LWPs, one of which executes the 'main' procedure and others stay idle. When a program creates a thread by the thread creation primitive of StackThreads/MP, called ST_THREAD_CREATE, the executing LWP simply begins its execution sequentially. Parallelism is then extracted by task stealing, when there is an idle LWP. In general, idle LWPs repeatedly try to steal a thread from other LWPs and each busy LWP gives a thread when it has two or more threads.

In order to support a large number of threads, a thread creation overhead must be very small, both in terms of space and time. Yet, we must retain greedy property, which says LWPs should not stay idle for a long time if there are more logical threads than the number of LWPs. Below we describe how Stack-Threads/MP achieves this goal.

Creation of Fine-Grain Threads: As mentioned above, a thread is created by a primitive ST_THREAD_CREATE($f(x)$), which is actually a C macro. This creates a logical thread of control that executes the body of this procedure call (f).

While semantics is the same as the similar primitive found in regular thread packages, such as pthread_create, implementation is quite different; when an LWP encounters ST_THREAD_CREATE($f(x)$), it initially executes procedure call $f(x)$, as if it is a sequential call. (See figure 4) Each LWP counts the number of threads that it is currently in charge of, so a thread creation cost at this point is merely a procedure call + a counter increment.

If other LWPs are all busy, the original LWP keeps executing it until it finishes or blocks. If it finishes without blocking, its parent resumes just as is the case in a sequential procedure call. In this case, we effectively eliminate most of thread creation overhead. Moreover, this LIFO scheduling is typically much more space efficient than FIFO scheduling commonly used in regular thread packages.

Thread Migration: Each LWP keeps track of the number of threads it is managing. When the counter becomes zero, it means that LWP is idle. Idle LWPs randomly select an LWP and ask it to give one of its threads, if it has more

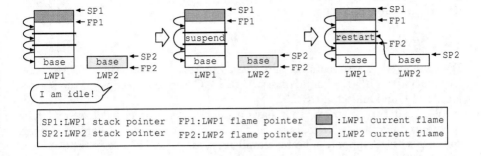

Fig. 5. Thread migration

than one. Each busy LWP that has more than one thread periodically checks if an idle processor is requesting a thread, and if one is, it gives one of its managing threads to the requesting LWP.

In this way, we implement a greedy scheduler; when some LWPs are idle while there are actually more logical threads than the number of LWPs, those idle LWPs sooner or later successfully obtain a thread to work on.

We refer the reader to [18] for the exact mechanism of thread migration, but in essence, we pass the address of the stack frame and the values of registers necessary to continue the execution of the migrating thread like figure 5.

3.2   Omni/ST: Nested Parallelism Using StackThreads/MP

With StackThreads/MP's support of extremely light-weight threads, it becomes quite straightforward to implement nested parallelism. We merely create the specified number of (OMP_NUM_THREADS) threads at *every* parallel constructs.

For applications with only a flat parallelism, OMP_NUM_THREADS threads are created at the first encounter to a parallel construct. Since all but one LWPs are idle at that moment, they will be migrated to other LWPs via the task stealing mechanism mentioned above. Therefore, Omni/ST has a relatively large startup overhead for parallel construct. Once each thread gets its LWP assigned, no more task stealing will occur and they keep running.

For applications with nested parallelism, or in more general, applications with much more logical parallelism than the number of LWPs, threads created at parallel construct may or may not migrate, depending on the runtime condition. When sufficient parallelism exists in outer levels and therefore all LWPs are already busy, subsequent parallel constructs create logical threads, but these threads do not migrate. So the only cost incurred for those inner, excess parallel constructs are that of ST_THREAD_CREATE, which is only a dozen of instructions per thread. Yet, if other LWPs become idle later, task stealing takes place, so we never lose parallelism.

4   Experiments

4.1   Settings

We conducted experiments on Sun Ultra Enterprise 10000 (Ultra SPARC 250 MHz, 64CPUs, 10GB Main Memory, 1MB L2 Cache) and compared the performance of Omni and Omni/ST.

We used two programs that have enough outermost parallelism and four programs that do not. Programs in the former group should exhibit a good speedup without support of nested parallelism, so our goal is to keep the overhead of Omni/ST as small as possible. The later group requires nested parallelism support to achieve good speedup.

The following two programs have enough outermost parallelism.

Matrix Product: This program simply calculates a matrix product. This program has triply-nested `for` loops, and the task size of each iteration is nearly equal so that we parallelize this program inserting a `parallel for` directive only at the outermost loop.

In the experiments, matrix elements are integers and each matrix size is 1000×1000.

Molecular Dynamics: This program simulates simple molecular dynamics [3]. It records the positions and velocity of whole molecules at a phase and calculates new positions and velocity at the next phase by molecular dynamics. And it simulates the transition of the total kinetic and potential energy. We parallelize this program by inserting `parallel for` directive only at outermost level.

In the experiments, the number of molecules is 8192 and we simulate for ten steps.

The following four programs are taken from KAI benchmark [16], which was originally from Cilk [2] benchmark suite. They do not have enough parallelism in the outermost level, but do have nested parallelism, so should benefit from nested parallelism support. Since they were originally written using KAI's workqueuing pragmas, we simply replaced them with standard OpenMP pragmas.

Queens: The n-queens problem is to find the way of putting n queens on an $n \times n$ chess board not to attack each other. The basic strategy is following: (1) put a queen at the left column, and (2) put the next queen at the next column if possible (see figure 6). (2) is recursively applied until the search reaches the right column. In this process, we use a backtracking search algorithm to avoid useless searches. We parallelize this program by inserting a `parallel for` directive at (2) phase.

In the experiments, the board size is 13 and we measure the time taken to find all answers.

Multisort: Multisort is basically a variation of mergesort. The algorithm is that (1) an array of elements is divided to four subarrays and each subarray is sorted, (2) two groups of two subarrays are merged respectively and the merged subarrays are merged again. (2) phase is recursively applied until array size becomes smaller than a lower limit. And then quick sort is used

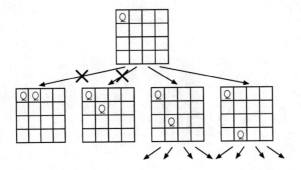

Fig. 6. Queens

to sort the small array. We parallelize this program by inserting a `parallel sections` directive at (1) to sort four subarrays in parallel. And the first step of (2) are also executed in parallel.

In the experiments, the array element is integer and the array size is 512MB.

Strassen: This program calculates a matrix product by strassen's algorithm. While the simple algorithm described above consumes $O(n^3)$ time to multiply $n \times n$ matrices, Strassen's algorithm achieves a runtime complexity of $O(n^{2.807})$. The key point is to translate multiplication to addition. When matrices are multiplied like following, the number of times of multiplication is eight.

$$\begin{pmatrix} A_{11} & A_{12} \\ A_{21} & A_{22} \end{pmatrix} \times \begin{pmatrix} B_{11} & B_{12} \\ B_{21} & B_{22} \end{pmatrix} = \begin{pmatrix} C_{11} & C_{12} \\ C_{21} & C_{22} \end{pmatrix}$$

$$C_{11} = A_{11}B_{11} + A_{12}B_{21}$$
$$C_{12} = A_{11}B_{12} + A_{12}B_{22}$$
$$C_{21} = A_{21}B_{11} + A_{22}B_{21}$$
$$C_{22} = A_{21}B_{12} + A_{22}B_{22}$$

However Strassen's algorithm requires only seven submatrix multiplications instead of eight.

$$P_1 = (A_{11} + A_{22})(B_{11} + B_{22})$$
$$P_2 = (A_{21} + A_{22})B_{11} \qquad C_{11} = P_1 + P_4 - P_5 + P_7$$
$$P_3 = A_{11}(B_{12} - B_{22}) \qquad C_{12} = P_3 + P_5$$
$$P_4 = A_{22}(B_{21} - B_{11}) \qquad C_{21} = P_2 + P_4$$
$$P_5 = (A_{11} + A_{12})B_{22} \qquad C_{22} = P_1 + P_3 - P_2 + P_6$$
$$P_6 = (A_{21} - A_{11})(B_{11} + B_{12})$$
$$P_7 = (A_{12} - A_{22})(B_{21} + B_{22})$$

This program is parallelized by inserting `parallel sections` directive and submatrices are multiplied in parallel. And applying this algorithm recursively, submatrices are decomposed to fine-grain tasks.

In the experiments, the matrix size is 1024×1024 of double floating point numbers.

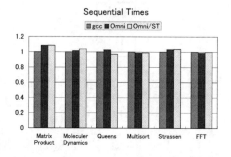

Fig. 7. Sequential Execution Times

Fast Fourier Transformation: This program practices Fast Fourier Transformation (FFT) by using Cooley-Tukey algorithm. In this program, the first phase is to scramble data for an in-place operation. An array is first divided into two subarrays and each subarray is divided in parallel until the array size is smaller than a certain size. Then the data is scrambled and the first phase ends. The second phase is to multiply these data. This phase is similar to the first phase. An array is splited small in parallel and then calculated. In the experiments, the size of element is 256MB.

4.2   Sequential Overhead

As a baseline to compare scalability, we compare single processor performance of Omni, Omni/ST, and gcc. Figure 7 shows execution time of each, normalizing the execution time of gcc to one (the smaller the faster). Both Omni and Omni/ST use gcc as the backend, so there should not be significant difference in serial performance.

The overhead of Omni/ST against gcc is 8% in Matrix Product and 1-3% in other applications. And the difference of Omni and Omni/ST is 5% in Queens and 1-2% in the others. This result indicates both Omni and Omni/ST deliver almost the same serial performance as the backend C compiler.

4.3   Scalability

Figure 8 shows speedup of the applications. The horizontal axis of each graph corresponds to the number of processors and the vertical axis shows the speedup. According to a graph of Matrix Product and Molecular Dynamics, Omni's performance is scalable and Omni's and Omni/ST's performance are almost equal. Both systems achieve about 50-fold speedup on 60 processors. However when the number of processors is 60, Omni/ST's performance is a little worse than Omni's in Molecular Dynamics. Supposedly the reason is that the overhead of reduction is a little larger than Omni.

From the results of Queens, Multisort, Strassen, and FFT, Omni/ST's performance is considerably better than Omni's. The characteristics of these applications are that the outermost level parallelism is small, nest level is deep, and

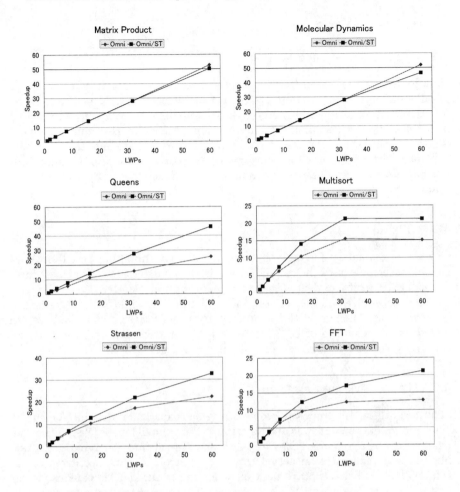

Fig. 8. Speedup of six applications by parallelization. Each graph compares scalability of Omni and Omni/ST.

each task size is considerably different. Therefore Omni/ST's merit is conspicuous. Especially Queens show the conspicuous difference, Omni achieves about 25-fold speedup while Omni/ST achieves 46-fold speedup.

Without nested parallelism support of Omni/ST, one might still manually unfold `parallel for` or `parallel sections` to extract more parallelism at outermost level. Such code restructuring is, however, tedious and error prone for the programmer and clearly defeats the benefit of OpenMP.

5   Related Work

5.1   High Performance Fortran

High Performance Fortran (HPF) [7] is the extension of Fortran to extract data parallelism efficiently. HPF targets NUMA architecture multiprocessors, therefore the main concern is which processor data are distributed at. In order to help a compiler to judge the data distribution, programmers insert comment columns following "!HPF$", and instruct the compiler where to distribute the data.

OpenMP targets shared memory multiprocessors, therefore programmers do not have to consider data distribution and it is easier than HPF to make programming.

5.2   Cilk

Cilk [2] is a language for multithreaded parallel programming based on ANSI C. Cilk's scheduler uses the technique of work-stealing based on LTC like Stack-Threads/MP, so it can deal with nested parallelism efficiently.

Cilk's scheduler is closely related with Cilk compiler while StackThreads/MP is provided as a fine-grain thread library. By using StackThreads/MP, we can introduce a mechanism of LTC into existing OpenMP implementation and we can implement nested parallelism easily and efficiently.

5.3   KAI: Workqueuing Model

Shah and others [16] proposed two new pragmas `taskq` and `task` into OpenMP. They are similar to `sections` and `section` in the original OpenMP specification; `taskq` declares a dynamic scope in which new threads are generated and `task`, like `section`, generates an actual thread of control. The main differences are that (1) [16] explicitly states that `taskq` can be nested, and (2) `task` can occur anytime during the execution of a `taskq`, whereas `section` must appear right inside a `sections` clause. Implementation strategy described in the present paper also straightforwardly applies to this model.

As of writing, we do not know the implementation detail of [16]. They only show their result up to four processors, whereas our implementation has shown good scalability up to 60 processors.

5.4   NANOS: NanosCompiler with Nth-Lib

Ayguade and others [1] proposed an extension to OpenMP for nested parallelism. In their proposal, a unit of work in a work-sharing construct (i.e., a chunk of loop iterations or a single `section`) can be explicitly assigned to a group of processors. These processors can execute in parallel another work-sharing construct that appears during the execution of it. This way, the programmer can hierarchically partition processors according to the shape of task graph.

This mechanism is certainly an improvement over a simple load-based inlining described in Section 2, where the programmer has no control over which nested parallel constructs get executed in parallel. The mechanism also enables processor assignments based on the affinity between data and processors. However, it is still unsatisfactory from load balancing point of view. In their execution model, groups of processors are formed in the beginning of a work-sharing construct, and processors assigned to a group cannot migrate to another group later. If distribution of work among groups are not balanced, some groups finish much earlier than others and there are no way to reclaim those processors for other groups. For this mechanism to be effective, therefore, the programmer must assign an appropriate number of processors to each unit of work, which presumes they can approximate the amount of work for each.

Our greedy scheduler needs no annotations from the programmer and the system keeps all the processors busy whenever there are sufficient parallelism.

6   Conclusion and Future Work

This paper discussed the importance of extracting nested parallelism and shows that the implementation of nested parallelism can be both beneficial and simple by using a fine-grain thread library StackThreads/MP. The performance of our implementation is evaluated using several applications with both flat and nested parallelism. The experiments show that our implementation incurs very small overhead for sequential application, does not sacrifice speedup for applications with only flat parallelism, and finally significantly improve scalability of applications with nested parallelism.

Benchmark programs used in this paper are limited to simple application kernels. Our future work includes implementing `taskq` and `task` pragmas, proposing/implementing other dynamic parallelism constructs in general, assessing the importance of these dynamic parallelism managements in real application programs, and comparing various implementation strategies of these constructs.

References

1. Eduard Ayguade, Xavier Martorell, Jesus Labarta, Marc Gonzalez, and Nacho Navarro. Exploiting Multiple Levels of Parallelism in OpenMP: A Case Study. In *the Proceedings of the 1999 International Conference on Parallel Processing*, Aizu (Japan), September 1999.
2. Robert D. Blumofe. *Executing Multithreaded Programs Efficiently*. PhD thesis, Department of Electrical Engineering and Computer Science, Massachusetts Institute of Technology, September 1995.
3. OpenMP Architecture Review Board. A Simple Molecular Dynamics Simulation. `http://www.openmp.org/samples/md.html`.
4. Christian Brunschen and Mats Brorsson. Odinmp/ccp - a portable implementation of openmp for c. In *the Proceedings of First European Workshop on OpenMP EWOMP99*, pages 21–26, Lund, Sweden, September 1999.
5. Andrew. A. Chien, U. S. Reddy, J. Plevyak, and J. Dolby. ICC++ – a C++ Dialect for High Performance Parallel Computing. In *the Proceedings of the Second International Symposium on Object Technologies for Advanced Software*, 1996.
6. Marc Feeley. A Message Passing Implementaion of Lazy Task Creation. In Robert H. Hastead Jr. and Takayasu Ito, editors, *the Proceedings of International*

Workshop on Parallle Symbolic Computing: Languages, Systems, and Applications, number 748 in Lecture Notes in Computer Science, pages 94–107, Springer-Verlag, 1993.

7. High Performance Fortran Forum. High Performance Fortran Language Specification. Technical report, Rice University, 1993. Version 1.0.

8. Seth Copen Goldstein, Klaus Erik Schauser, and David Culler. Lazy Threads: Implementing a Fast Parallel Call. *Journal of Parallel and Distributed Computing*, 37(1):5–20, August 1996.

9. IEEE Standards Department. *POSIX System Application Programming Interface: Threads Extension [C Language]*, posix 1003.4a, draft 8 edition.

10. Eric Mohr, David A. Kranz, and Robert Halstead Jr. Lazy Task Creation: A Technique for Increasing the Granularity of Parallel Programs. *IEEE Transactions on Parallel and Distributed Systems*, 2(3):264–280, July 1991.

11. PGI. PGI workstation. http://www.pgroup.com/.

12. Thuan Q. Pham and Pankaj K. Gargq. *Multithreaded Programming with Win32*. Prentice Hall PTR, November 1998.

13. John Plevyak, Vijay Karamcheti, Xingbin Zhang, and Andrew A. Chien. A hybrid execution model for fine-grained languages on distributed memory multicomputers. In *Supercompuing '95*, 1995.

14. Real World Computing Partnership Omni Compiler Project. Omni OpenMP Compiler. http://pdplab.trc.rwcp.or.jp/pdperf/Omni/.

15. Mitsuhisa Sato, Shigehisa Satoh, Kazuhiro Kusano, and Yoshio Tanaka. Design of OpenMP Compiler for an SMP Cluster. In *the Proceedings of First European Workshop on OpenMP EWOMP99*, pages 32–39, Lund, Sweden, September 1999.

16. Sanjiv Shah, Grant Haab, Paul Petersen, and Joe Throop. Flexible Control Structures for Parallelism in OpenMP. In *the Proceedings of First European Workshop on OpenMP EWOMP99*, pages 60–70, Lund, Sweden, September 1999.

17. Kenjiro Taura. *StackThreads/MP User's Manual*. University of Tokyo, January 1999. http://www.yl.is.s.u-tokyo.ac.jp/sthreads/.

18. Kenjiro Taura, Kunio Tabata, and Akinori Yonezawa. StackThreads/MP: Integrating Futures into Calling Standards. In *the Proceedings of Symposium on Principles and Practice of Parallel Programming*. ACM SIGPLAN, February 1999.

19. Kenjiro Taura and Akinori Yonezawa. SchematicL A Concurrent Object-Oriented Extension to Scheme. In *the Proceedings of Workshop on Object-Based Parallel and Distributed Computation*, number 1107 in Lecture Notes in Computer Science, pages 59–82, Springer-Verlag, 1996.

20. Kenjiro Taura and Akinori Yonezawa. Fine-grain Multithreading with Minimal Compiler Support—A Cost Effective Approach to Implementing Efficient Multithreading Language. In *the Proceedings of Programming Language Design & Implementation*, pages 320–333, Las Vegas, Nevada, June 1997. ACM SIGPLAN.

Adaptive Parallelism
for OpenMP Task Parallel Programs

Alex Scherer[1], Thomas Gross[1,2], and Willy Zwaenepoel[3]

[1] Departement Informatik, ETH Zürich, CH 8092 Zürich
[2] School of Computer Science, Carnegie Mellon University, Pittsburgh, PA 15213
[3] Department of Computer Science, Rice University, Houston, TX 77005

Abstract. We present a system that allows task parallel OpenMP programs to execute on a network of workstations (NOW) with a variable number of nodes. Such adaptivity, generally called *adaptive parallelism*, is important in a multi-user NOW environment, enabling the system to expand the computation onto idle nodes or withdraw from otherwise occupied nodes.

We focus on task parallel applications in this paper, but the system also lets data parallel applications run adaptively.

When an adaptation is requested, we let all processes complete their current tasks, then the system executes an extra OpenMP join-fork sequence not present in the application code. Here, the system can change the number of nodes without involving the application, as processes do not have a compute-relevant private process state.

We show that the costs of adaptations is low, and we explain why the costs are lower for task parallel applications than for data parallel applications.

1 Introduction

We present a system supporting adaptive parallelism for task parallel OpenMP programs running in a multi-user network of workstations environment, permitting the efficient use of a continually changing pool of available machines. As other users start and stop using machines, resources which otherwise would be idle are used productively, while these users retain priority.

Adaptive parallelism also allows for other flexible usage models: A certain percentage of machines may be reserved without having to specify which machines, or a second parallel application may be started without having to abort some on-going long-running program, simply by reducing this application's allocated resources and letting the new application use them.

We have described how we achieve transparent adaptive parallelism for data parallel programs in [15], therefore we focus more on task parallel applications in this paper.

We use the *OpenMP [14]* programming model, an emerging industry standard for shared memory programming. OpenMP frees the programmer from having to deal with lower-level issues such as the number of nodes, the data partitioning or the communication of data between nodes. We recognize that the system can easily adjust the number of compute threads at the boundaries of each OpenMP

S. Dwarkadas (Ed.): LCR 2000, LNCS 1915, pp. 113–127, 2000.

parallel construct *without* having to involve the application. We call such points *adaptation points*.

In task parallel applications, each process solves tasks retrieved from a central task queue, starting with the next assignment whenever one is done. Typically, each process works at its own pace, there is no global barrier-type synchronization, as opposed to data parallel applications. When an adaptation is requested, we let each process complete its current task, then the system creates an adaptation point by executing an *extra* OpenMP join-fork sequence not present in the application code, allowing for a transparent adaptation.

For the application, the only requirement to support adaptivity is for processes to indicate whenever they have completed a task, so the system has the opportunity to transparently insert an adaptation point. For this purpose, one system call is inserted at task boundaries in the application code. This minor code change is done automatically by a preprocessor.

We have tested the system using Quicksort and TSP as example applications running on various NOW environments of PCs with Linux. Even frequent adaptations, such as every 3 seconds, only increase Quicksort's and TSP's runtimes by about 10-20% and 2-5%, respectively.

This paper then presents the following contributions:

1. The design of a transparent adaptive parallel computation system for task parallel applications using an emerging industry-standard programming paradigm (OpenMP). Only one function call is added to the application specifically to obtain adaptivity. This change is done automatically by a preprocessor.
2. Experimental evidence that the system provides good performance on a moderate-sized NOW, even for frequent rates of adaptation.
3. An analysis of the key adaptation cost components, showing why adaptations in task parallel applications are generally cheaper than in data parallel applications.

2   Background

2.1   Related Work

Various approaches have been examined to use idle time on networked nodes for parallel computations.

Much work has been done to support variable resources by using *load balancing*: Systems such as DOME [3], Dataparallel-C [7,13], Charm++ [8,9], and various versions of PVM [10] can adjust the load per node on partially available workstations, but the processor set for the computation is fixed, once started, as opposed to our system.

Cilk-NOW [4] and Piranha [5] support adaptive parallel computation on NOWs in the sense that the pool of processors used can vary during the computation, as in our system. However, the Cilk-NOW system is restricted to *functional* programs, and Piranha requires the adoption of the Linda tuple space as a parallel programming model and special code to achieve adaptivity.

Another class of systems including Adaptive Multiblock PARTI (AMP) [6] and Distributed Resource Management System (DRMS) [12] provide data distribution directives for the reconfiguration of the application to varying numbers of nodes at runtime. Our system distinguishes itself from these approaches by offering fully automatic data management.

All of the above systems require the use of specialized libraries or paradigms, in contrast to our use of an industry-standard programming model.

2.2   OpenMP and Task Parallel Applications

OpenMP uses the fork-join model of parallel execution. In the task queue model, each process [1] executes tasks from a shared queue, repeatedly fetching a new task from the queue until it is empty, no global synchronization between the processes is needed. Therefore, an OpenMP task parallel application typically only has one OpenMP fork at the beginning and one OpenMP join at the end.

2.3   OpenMP on a NOW

We used the TreadMarks DSM system [2] as a base for our implementation. TreadMarks is a user-level software DSM system that runs on commonly available Unix systems and on Windows NT, and it supports an OpenMP fork-join style of parallelism with the Tmk_fork and Tmk_join primitives for the master process, and the Tmk_wait primitive for the slave processes. We use the SUIF compiler toolkit [1] to automatically translate OpenMP programs into TreadMarks code [11]. Each OpenMP parallel construct is replaced by a call to Tmk_fork followed by a call to Tmk_join.

An important advantage of using the shared memory paradigm is the *automatic data distribution*, including the redistribution after an adaptation, relieving the programmer from this task.

2.4   Transparent Support of Adaptivity

In our model, slave processes perform all work either inside tasks or, as in data parallel applications, within other OpenMP parallel sections containing no tasks.

To allow for a transparent adaptation whenever an adapt event occurs while the application is busy with a task queue, we let each process finish its current task, then we let the system execute an *extra OpenMP join-fork sequence*. Having all slave processes' work for the current OpenMP parallel section being contained in the tasks ensures that slave processes do not have any compute-relevant private process state when the adaptation is performed. We introduce a new TreadMarks primitive Tmk_leave which the application calls to indicate completion of a task. This call returns true if a process is to leave, false otherwise. The preprocessor inserts this call at task boundaries. More precisely, the

---

[1]   In our case, "process" and the OpenMP documentation's term "thread" are synonyms. In our implementation of OpenMP, these threads execute as Unix processes on various nodes, where a node is a machine.

Table 1. Loop condition code modifications needed for adaptations. These transformations are done automatically by a preprocessor.

Original code	Automatically modified code
```expr1;``` ```while (expr2) {``` `    statement` `    expr3;` ```}```	```expr1;``` ```while (expr2 && !Tmk_leave()) {``` `    statement` `    expr3;` ```}```
```do {``` `    statement` ```} while(expression);```	```do {``` `    statement` ```} while(expression && !Tmk_leave());```
```for (expr1; expr2; expr3)```	```for (expr1; expr2 && !Tmk_leave(); expr3)```

preprocessor modifies the termination-condition of top-level loops of the functions called by OpenMP forks according to the rules in Table 1. If a forked function does not have any other (compute-relevant) top-level statements besides a loop which retrieves and adds tasks, as in the applications investigated, then the preprocessor can perform the correct code modifications *automatically* (Figure 1).

Adaptations are completely *transparent* to the application, as the only application code modification is the insertion of Tmk_leave. There, leaving processes may terminate while continuing processes experience a slight delay while the system performs the adaptation, and joining processes begin execution of the forked function.

In our current model, task queues are maintained by the application, as the OpenMP standard does not explicitly support task queues. However, KAI have proposed their WorkQueue model [16] as an addition to the OpenMP standard, offering two new pragmas, taskq and task, for task queues and tasks, respectively. Following the acceptance of the proposal, we may modify our system accordingly, *eliminating* the need for the Tmk_leave primitive, as the system will recognize task boundaries through use of the task pragma.

The WorkQueue model allows nested task queues. In our model, we permit adaptations only in top-level task queues, other task queues are completed non-adaptively, avoiding the complexity of dealing with compute-relevant slave process states, such as letting another process complete some half-finished task of a leaving process.

3   Functionality

Processes may be added to or withdrawn from the computation, actions called *join events* and *leave events*, or collectively *adapt events*. The system performs requested adaptations at the next adaptation point. If several processes wish to leave and/or are ready to join when an adaptation point is reached, then these adapt events are all performed simultaneously. Such a scenario is actually much cheaper than performing the events sequentially, as the total cost per adaptation does not vary in proportion to the total number of leaves and/or joins performed

```
Code executed      void _Worker_func(struct Tmk_sched_arg *_my_arguments)
by all threads:    {
                       ...
                       do {
                           if (PopWork(&task) == -1) {
                               break;
                           }
                           QuickSort(task.left, task.right);
                       } while (1);  /* original code */
                       /* modified line below replaces above line */
                       } while (!Tmk_leave());
                   }


Code executed      ...
by master:         Tmk_sched_fork(_Worker_func, &Tmk_arguments);
                   ...
```

Fig. 1. Example structure of a task queue application (Quicksort) showing modification for adaptations according to rules in Table 1.

at once. New processes require about 0.5-1 seconds from the join request until they are ready to join, but during this time all other processes proceed with their computations.

The only limitation in the current implementation is that the master process cannot be terminated.

4   Implementation

We have modified the TreadMarks version 1.1.0 system to support adaptivity. The current version of the system supports adaptive parallelism for both data parallel and task parallel applications, but we focus primarily on task parallel applications in the following description.

Join and leave requests may be sent to the system from any external source via a TCP/IP connection.

4.1   Join Events

For a join event, the master spawns a new process p_{new} on the designated machine and all processes set up network connections to p_{new} while still continuing with their work, i.e. any slow low-level process initializations do not affect the on-going computation. Once p_{new} is ready to begin work, the master starts an *adaptation phase*: It notifies the other processes of the adapt event, whereupon all processes continue until they reach the next *adaptation point*, either Tmk_leave or a regular OpenMP join present in the application code.

Here, all processes perform an OpenMP join and fork, with slaves receiving adaptation information such as new process identifiers. This extra join-fork is initiated by the system and is therefore not in the application source code. Also, the master does not send a pointer with a compute function to the old slaves, only the new process p_{new} receives a pointer to the current compute-function. Now, all old processes perform a garbage collection. This mechanism causes diffs to be fetched and applied, then each node discards internal memory consistency information (such as twins, diffs, write notices, intervals lists [2]). A garbage collection typically costs only a few milliseconds. Thereafter, all shared memory pages are either up-to-date or discarded. In the latter case, an access will cause the page to be fetched from another process with an up-to-date copy.

The system now performs three barrier synchronizations. The first barrier's departure message to the new process includes all non-default page-state information for all pages. This barrier guarantees that garbage collection is completed before page state information is used subsequently.

Next, a second barrier is performed, then all necessary reassignments are performed, including the redistribution of lock managers and lock tokens, and all memory consistency information is cleared. This second barrier ensures that any duplicate departure messages of the first barrier are not sent after some process has already begun with any reassignments.

Thereafter a third barrier is performed, ensuring that no process can proceed with its computation before all processes have performed reassignments and cleared their old consistency information. This barrier concludes the adaptation phase, and processes resume or begin work.

4.2   Leave Events

The handling of leave events is similar to the handling of join events: When a leave request arrives, the master begins the adaptation phase by notifying all processes. Once all processes have reached an adaptation point, an OpenMP join and fork is executed, followed by a garbage collection.

The system then performs three barrier synchronizations as previously, but with some additions: All pages that are exclusively valid on a leaving process must be transfered to a continuing process. For this, all old slaves include page-state information in the arrival-message for the first barrier, then the master allocates an approximately equal number of such pages among the continuing processes and includes this information in the barrier departure messages. This barrier guarantees that garbage collection is completed before page state information is used and before any pages are moved off leaving processes. Processes now in parallel fetch these pages as allocated by the master and assume ownership.

After a second barrier, reassignments are again done and consistency information is cleared. This second barrier ensures that any page transfers off leaving processes are completed, so leaving processes can now terminate, and the third barrier is performed without participation of leaving processes.

4.3   Multiple Adapt Events

Join and leave requests may arrive anytime. Leave requests are always given priority over join requests, as a compute process may need to be cleared off some machine rapidly. Requests are therefore handled according to the policy of including any adapt event that can be included in the current adaptation without

Table 2. Application characteristics and network traffic for 8-thread runs on the non-adaptive or on the adaptive system without any adapt events.

	Size	Network	Shared memory		Avg.	Avg. time (sec.)		Number/amount of transfers			
			# Pages	Page size	# Tasks	Total	Per task	Pages	MB	Messages	Diffs
Traveling	19 cities	100Mbps	108	4k	619	7.63	0.10	7018	28.75	23363	651
Salesman		1Gbps	27	16k	619	5.94	0.08	4320	68.98	15319	654
Quicksort	10'000'000	100Mbps	9798	4k	613	10.86	0.14	31369	124.77	129417	739
	integers	1Gbps	2450	16k	613	6.46	0.08	8882	142.82	40886	1393

delaying any pending leave, other requests are postponed until completion of the adaptation.

The system starts an adaptation phase immediately upon receipt of a leave request, unless the system is already in an adaptation phase or a sequential phase. This policy causes about-to-join processes which, at the adaptation point, are still busy setting up network connections, to be aborted and restarted after the adaptation.

Any deferred or aborted adapt events are performed upon completion of the adaptation phase, with leave requests being handled first.

4.4 Special Cases

Consider the scenario where some processes arrive at an OpenMP join $J1$ belonging to the application while, due to an adapt request, other processes first arrive at the adaptation point and are executing another OpenMP join $J2$ constituting the adaptation point, before having reached $J1$. Space limitation does not permit a detailed discussion here, but the system handles such cases correctly.

Consider further an adaptation request arriving while the system is in a sequential phase, i.e. in-between an OpenMP join and fork. In this case, the adaptation is performed immediately when the sequential phase is over. Any such delay is not so tragic, as a process wishing to withdraw is idle during this phase and is not using compute resources.

5 Overview of Performance

5.1 Experimental Environment

Our testbed consists of 8 400MHz Pentium II machines with 256MB of memory, and we run Linux 2.2.7. For the communication, we use UDP sockets, and the machines are connected via two separate switched, full-duplex Ethernet networks with bandwidths of 100Mbps and 1Gbps, respectively. The 1Gbps network only offers extra bandwidth compared to the 100Mbps network, as the latency is very similar in both networks. We exploit this by increasing the page size from 4K to 16K when using the 1Gbps network.

5.2 Applications

We use the two task queue applications from the standard TreadMarks distribution: Quicksort and TSP (Table 2).

Quicksort sorts an array of integers by adding and retrieving tasks of not-yet-sorted subarrays to and from a central task queue, respectively. Each array is repeatedly split into two subarrays around a selected pivot-value: The shorter one is put on the task queue and the thread recurses on the longer one, until its length falls below a threshold, then it is sorted locally.

TSP uses a branch-and-bound algorithm to solve the traveling salesman problem. Tasks representing partial tours are repeatedly added to and retrieved from a central task queue. Subtours of a given maximum length are solved recursively locally, while longer ones are split into subproblems and added to the task queue.

5.3   No Overhead for Providing Adaptivity

The provision of adaptivity costs virtually nothing compared to the standard non-adaptive TreadMarks system [2] , as no extra messages are sent in the absence of adapt events.

5.4   Measurement Methodologies

For multiple adaptations during the course of execution, we first calculate the average number of processes used during the whole run (e.g. 7.55) by measuring the times in-between each adaptation, then we adjust the runtime to represent a desired average (e.g. 7.5), using a speedup-curve obtained from non-adaptive runs. The adaptation overhead is the difference in runtime compared to a (theoretical) non-adaptive run of the same average, as calculated in the speedup-curve.

To quantify in detail a single adaptation from p to q processes, we collect statistics beginning only at a point immediately preceding the adaptation and compare the results with a non-adaptive run of q processes. We ensure that the number of tasks completed (i.e. the average amount of work done) during statistics measurements is equal in both cases. For the adaptive run, the measured data layout is initially pre-adaptation, but all measured work is done post-adaptation. The difference between the adaptive and non-adaptive run reflects the cost of the adaptation.

Obviously, the two tested applications have a non-deterministic execution, as any task may be executed by any process, and the length and number of individual tasks varies both within one test run and between different test runs, especially for Quicksort, which uses a random input. However, the variations are small enough for our methodologies to show clear trends, especially in combination with the averaging of results obtained from several test runs.

5.5   Cost of Joins and Leaves

To provide an idea of the overhead of adaptations, we periodically caused an adapt event to occur. Figure 2 shows how the total runtime varies as a function of the interval between successive adapt events. Starting with 8 or 4 processes, we let the system alternately perform a leave or a join event at the end of each

---

[2]   Our measurements do not show any difference.

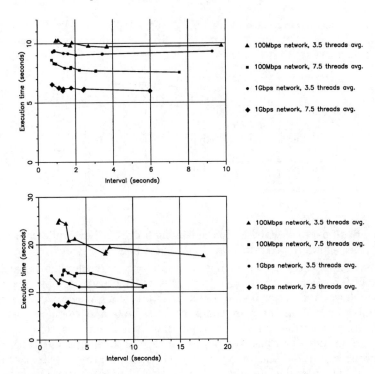

Fig. 2. Execution times for different intervals between adapt events, for TSP (above) and Quicksort (below).

interval, resulting in about 7.5 or 3.5 processes, on average. For the leaves, we let each of the slave processes leave in turn.

Variations in execution time due to the non-deterministic nature of the applications are apparent in Figure 2, as the points in the graphs represent individual test runs. Nevertheless, the trend of an increase in runtime in proportion with an increase in adaptation frequency, as expected, is evident: Every adaptation adds a similar delay to the total runtime.

In TSP, even frequent adaptations of one every second hardly increase the total runtime. In Quicksort, one adaptation every 5 seconds may increase the runtime by perhaps 10%. The graphs also show how adaptations in the 7.5 process runs are cheaper than in the 3.5 process runs, for equal adaptation frequencies, as explained in the next section, and how the faster network offers significantly better performance, both in total runtime and in adaptation costs.

Table 4 provides detailed results for individual adaptations, obtained using the measurement methodology for single adaptations described in the previous section. Table 3 is a summary of Table 4.

We show the number of extra adaptation-induced page fetches occurring during the course of computation after an adaptation (P_{appl} or *Pages Appl.* in the table), as the application experiences extra access misses, and the number of pages explicitly moved off any leaving process by the system (P_{system} or *Pages*

Table 3. Typical average costs (in seconds) per adaptation (For TSP, the exact differences between the various setups are difficult to quantify precisely, as the absolute costs are small in all cases).

	Avg. # procs.	Network	Pre-adapt.-delay cost	Adapt. cost	Total
TSP	3.5 or 7.5	100Mbps or 1Gbps	0.05	0.05	0.1
Quicksort	7.5	100Mbps	0.05	0.5	0.55
	3.5		0.05	1	1.05
Quicksort	7.5	1Gbps	0.05	0.2	0.25
	3.5		0.05	0.4	0.45

System, i.e. all pages of which only the leaving processes have valid copies). The table further shows the cost in seconds for these page transfers [3] .

As both applications execute non-deterministically, such that variations in runtime of 0.5 seconds for identical test runs of Quicksort are not uncommon, we show a lower and upper bound for each adaptation, giving a *range of values*: The numbers were computed by comparing the best- and worst-case adaptive results with the average of the corresponding non-adaptive results. For each adaptation, in different runs, we adapted at several different times during each application's execution, and we repeated each individual test case several times. Negative values show that an adaptation can even lead to less data transfers and an earlier completion of the computation than a comparable non-adaptive run.

The *total cost of an adaptation* is the sum of the cost of the P_{appl} and, if applicable, the P_{system} transfers, plus a *pre-adaptation delay* incurred by waiting at an adaptation point for all processes to arrive. P_{system} page transfers obviously only occur if at least one process is leaving. The pre-adaptation delay is the overall compute time lost before the adaptation begins, i.e. the average of all processes' idle times, occurring after completion of a task, while a process is waiting at the OpenMP join which initiates the adaptation.

The pre-adaptation delay cost obviously varies with the length of the tasks. For the applications tested, it is typically in the range of 0-0.1 seconds, and in a few percent of the cases, it is around 0.2 seconds. Only Quicksort rarely has significantly longer delays: In about 1% of the cases, the cost is on the order of 0.5 seconds.

The results shown in Figure 2, which contain all costs, confirm that the pre-adaptation costs are small: Given the total runtime increase and the frequency of adaptations in the graphs, one can easily estimate an *average cost per adaptation* C_{avg} and verify that these costs are hardly higher than the costs for the P_{appl} plus the P_{system} transfers reported in Table 4. At the same time, these C_{avg} results also validate the measurement methodology for single adaptations used for Table 4.

---

[3] The *Time Pages Appl.* values actually include other adaptation-related costs such as garbage collection and management of data structures. We do not present these separately, as their share of the total costs is minimal, on the order of 1%.

Table 4. Typical costs for various adaptations (excluding pre-adaptation delay) in two test environments, in seconds and number of 4k or 16k pages. For each case, we show the lower and upper bound of values measured in a series of representative tests. We performed one or two leaves from 8 processes (8 → 7, 8 → 6), one or two joins to 8 processes (7 → 8, 6 → 8), one simultaneous leave and join with 8 processes (8 → 8), and one leave from or one join to 4 processes (4 → 3, 3 → 4).

	Traveling Salesman				Quicksort			
	Time Pages Appl.	Pages Appl.	Time Pages System	Pages System	Time Pages Appl.	Pages Appl.	Time Pages System	Pages System
Adaptation								
100Mbps Ethernet environment with page size of 4K								
8 → 8	0.01 0.20	-34 307	0.00 0.00	1 15	0.06 0.19	-264 674	0.30 0.63	874 1781
8 → 7	0.05 0.23	21 367	0.00 0.01	1 28	-0.50 -0.15	-743 586	0.27 0.43	685 1205
8 → 6	0.02 0.05	-35 104	0.00 0.00	1 6	-0.54 -0.26	-1557 -618	0.47 0.83	2168 3676
7 → 8	-0.04 0.05	-61 41	-	-	0.19 0.59	-485 1404	-	-
6 → 8	-0.04 0.05	-41 53	-	-	0.31 0.41	119 1531	-	-
4 → 3	0.03 0.07	15 51	0.00 0.00	0 4	-1.50 0.27	-2204 280	0.36 0.68	1044 1983
3 → 4	-0.01 0.07	4 78	-	-	0.81 2.78	1322 3440	-	-
1Gbps Ethernet environment with page size of 16K								
8 → 8	0.03 0.17	-58 330	0.00 0.00	0 9	-0.08 0.04	-162 91	0.08 0.10	274 354
8 → 7	0.01 0.15	0 309	0.00 0.01	0 18	-0.04 0.04	-137 50	0.07 0.09	252 337
8 → 6	-0.04 0.01	-65 10	0.00 0.00	0 0	-1.30 -0.20	-964 -56	0.07 0.13	394 704
7 → 8	0.02 0.06	10 43	-	-	0.00 0.25	-37 539	-	-
6 → 8	-0.03 0.06	-10 31	-	-	1.17 1.54	710 978	-	-
4 → 3	-0.03 0.02	-42 12	0.00 0.00	0 0	-0.26 0.90	-598 680	0.17 0.21	606 739
3 → 4	-0.01 0.02	-32 10	-	-	-0.64 0.11	-486 365	-	-

We observe that the costs for TSP are very small in all cases, so the absolute values are not very meaningful, especially given the large range of measured values compared to the absolute upper and lower bounds. Table 2 shows that TSP uses little shared memory, causing little data redistribution at an adaptation. The conclusion therefore is that in the absence of large data redistributions, adaptations are very cheap, i.e. there are no significant other costs.

For Quicksort, we observe both positive and negative values. On average, adaptations for this application also cost only a fraction of a second. We analyse the results in more detail in the next section.

Table 4 further shows that the percentage of shared memory pages moved extra due to an adaptation is very small in nearly all cases for Quicksort (a few %), so the absolute costs remain small compared to our previous results of data parallel applications, where redistribution of 30%-60% of all shared memory pages is common [15].

To sum up, Table 4 shows that the costs of an adaptation are typically less than 0.1 seconds for TSP and less than 0.5 seconds for Quicksort even in the slower of the two environments tested, when using around 8 processes.

6   Analysis of Performance

The key cost component of an adaptation is the *additional network traffic* for the data redistribution caused by this event. We therefore analyse the *extra* page transfers attributable to the adaptation, as compared to the non-adaptive case.

Furthermore, we point out the main differences between *independent* and *regular* applications: We call applications where the data layout is independent of process identifiers *independent* applications, as opposed to *regular* applications which have a block or block-cyclic data distribution. In regular applications, a process' data partition is determined by the process identifier and the current number of processes, and the process performs most work using the data in its partition. Adaptations generate a large shift in each process' assigned data partition, and in general all pages that were not in the pre-adaptation data partition have to be fetched extra after the adaptation.

In contrast, in independent applications such as Quicksort and TSP tasks are not bound to processes, any task may be solved by any process, so the probability that a first-time page access of a task is for a locally-valid page depends on issues such as the number of different tasks using the same page and whether pages are mostly read (as in TSP) or also written to (as in Quicksort). As there are no assigned data partitions, an adaptation does not cause data repartitioning.

Adaptations in general are much cheaper when more processes are involved: Not only does a join or a leave of $7 \rightarrow 8$ or $8 \rightarrow 7$ processes cause less data transfer than a join or a leave of $3 \rightarrow 4$ or $4 \rightarrow 3$ processes, but more significantly, with a larger number of processes, the number of page transfers *per process* and equally *per network link* is much lower, so far more page transfers occur in parallel. Table 4 shows that the range of values for P_{appl} transfer costs are higher for less processes involved.

We examine more specific effects of joins and leaves in regular and independent applications in the following two subsections.

6.1   Join Events

Adding new compute processes may cause the following data movements: (1) the faulting-in of pages by the joining processes, as all their pages are invalid initially, and (2) the data redistribution among the "old" processes, when the total number of processes changes, i.e. when the number of joining and leaving processes is not equal.

In regular applications, in most cases all shared memory pages are accessed repeatedly many times. Joining processes therefore generally have to page in the complete partition assigned to them, typically $1/n$ of all pages for n processes, which is more than the number of extra pages fetched by any other process due to the data redistribution. The transfers are less only if not all of the partition's data is accessed anymore during the rest of the computation. As each process typically performs the same amount of work within one OpenMP parallel section, the bottleneck is the process fetching the largest number of pages, i.e. the paging-in of the joining processes' data partitions constitutes the bottleneck.

Independent applications however do not assign data partitions. In TSP, where many tasks reside in the same shared memory page and most accesses are read-only, processes often have a valid copy of most of the pages used overall. Any joining process therefore needs to page-in all these pages extra, so with several processes joining, the total extra data transfer may exceed 100% of the shared memory pages in use. In Quicksort, with many write-accesses to pages, most valid pages are in the exclusive state, only a few in the shared state, and each of n processes typically has about $1/n$ of all used pages valid. As each page is accessed only a few times, as joins occur closer to the end, a new process pages in much less than $1/n$ of all pages in use, as most pages are not needed anymore. Furthermore, due to the absence of data redistribution, independent applications experience less traffic among the "old" processes when adapting, compared to no adaptation: With a join of $m \to n$ processes $(m < n)$, on average more pages are valid per process for m than for n processes. As expected, Table 4 shows that the number of P_{appl} transfers as a percentage of all shared memory pages (cf. Table 2) is much smaller than for regular applications, where percentages of 40-60% are common [15].

Another more significant difference between independent and regular applications is the fact that processes compute tasks at their own pace in independent applications, therefore a larger number of page fetches by one process, such as a join, does not cause all other processes to wait, so only the fetching and the sending process lose compute time, as opposed to regular applications, where all processes lose compute time, waiting at the next OpenMP join.

In conclusion, due to the above reasons join events are significantly cheaper in independent applications than in regular applications.

6.2   Leave Events

A leave of processes may cause the following data movements: (1) All pages P_{system} exclusively valid on the leaving processes are moved to continuing processes, and (2) the data repartitioning among the continuing processes generates page fetches P_{appl}. This may include some of the P_{system} pages, as the system allocates these without knowledge of any data partitioning.

The share of P_{system} transfers is comparable for regular and independent applications: In both cases, in applications with little read-only sharing, given n processes before the adaptation, a leaving process often has about $1/n$ of the pages in use in an exclusively-valid state, so these pages are evenly distributed among the continuing or joining processes. Table 4 shows that the share of P_{system} pages is in the expected percentage range (cf. Table 2), and the numbers for two leaves from $8 \to 6$ processes are about double the numbers for one leave from $8 \to 7$ and $8 \to 8$ processes.

Thereafter, regular applications experience data repartitioning, as in the case of joins. The number of P_{appl} transfers are less than for joins, because generally no process has to page in its complete data partition as a join does, but the data repartitioning still affects around 30-50% of all shared memory pages [15].

In independent applications however, after having received the P_{system} pages, the continuing processes each have about the same share of valid pages as in the corresponding non-adaptive case, where the P_{system} pages are valid on some process already. Therefore, P_{appl} is around zero, as there is also no data repartitioning. Table 4 shows that the P_{appl} values often vary within ranges of both positive and negative values.

When sending P_{system} pages, the system batches several pages into one message, whereas P_{appl} page transfers only contain one page per message. However, all P_{system} pages have to be fetched from the one (or few) leaving process(es), so these transfers occur less in parallel than the P_{appl} transfers. In addition, no process is performing any work while any P_{system} transfers are in progress. In contrast, in independent applications, any P_{appl} transfers occur while other processes continue working (while in regular applications they may be idle).

In conclusion, while the cost of leaves is dominated by the P_{appl} transfer costs in regular applications and this component is around zero for independent applications, while the P_{system} transfer costs are similar in both cases, leave events are generally significantly cheaper in independent applications than in regular applications.

7   Discussion and Conclusions

We have developed a system providing transparent adaptive parallel execution of OpenMP applications on NOWs. Our system combines the convenience of an industry standard programming model, OpenMP, with a flexible and user-friendly usage. Users can easily grant or revoke use of a machine at any time using a graphical user interface, or the system can even be controlled automatically, but we do not analyse user behavior in this paper.

Obviously, the performance of a software DSM system cannot match the performance of a dedicated hardware shared memory system. Rather, our system should be assessed as enabling otherwise idle machines to be used productively - especially for longer-running computations - thanks to the flexibility which adaptivity offers, something previously impossible due to conflicting resource requirements in a multi-user environment. In many cases, our system eliminates the need for a reservation of machines for parallel processing. When using existing NOWs, no hardware costs arise, and running existing OpenMP applications means no software development costs are incurred either.

We have demonstrated that the cost of adaptation is modest and that it is significantly lower for independent applications, where the data distribution is independent of the process identifiers, than for regular applications.

References

1. S. P. Amarasinghe, J. M. Anderson, M. S. Lam, and C. W. Tseng. An overview of the suif compiler for scalable parallel machines. In *Proceedings of the 7th SIAM Conference on Parallel Processing for Scientific Computing*, pages 662–667, San Francisco, February 1995.
2. C. Amza, A.L. Cox, S. Dwarkadas, P. Keleher, H. Lu, R. Rajamony, W. Yu, and W. Zwaenepoel. Treadmarks: Shared memory computing on networks of workstations. *IEEE Computer*, 29(2):18–28, February 1996.
3. J. Arabe, A. Beguelin, B. Lowekamp, E. Seligman, M. Starkey, and P. . Stephan. Dome: Parallel programming in a heterogeneous multi-user environment. Technical Report CMU-CS-95-137, Computer Science Department, Carnegie Mellon University, April 1995.
4. R.D. Blumofe and P.A. Lisiecki. Adaptive and reliable parallel computing on network of workstations. In *Proceedings of the USENIX 1997 Annual Technical Symposium*, pages 133–147, January 1997.
5. N. Carriero, E. Freeman, D. Gelernter, and D. Kaminsky. Adaptive parallelism and piranha. *IEEE Computer*, 28(1):40–49, January 1995.

6. G. Edjlali, G. Agrawal, A. Sussman, J. Humphries, and J. Saltz. Compiler and runtime support for programming in adaptive parallel environments. *Scientific Programming*, 6(2):215–227, January 1997.
7. P. J. Hatcher and M. J. Quinn. *Data-parallel Programming on MIMD Computers*. The MIT Press, Cambridge MA, 1991.
8. L. V. Kalé, B. Ramkumar, A. B. Sinha, and A. Gursoy. The CHARM Parallel Programming Language and System: Part I - Description of Language Features. *IEEE Transactions on Parallel and Distributed Systems*, 1994.
9. L. V. Kalé, B. Ramkumar, A. B. Sinha, and V. A. Saletore. The CHARM Parallel Programming Language and System: Part II - The Runtime System. *IEEE Transactions on Parallel and Distributed Systems*, 1994.
10. R. Konuru, S. Otto, and J. Walpole. A migratable user-level process package for pvm. *Journal of Parallel and Distributed Computing*, 40(1):81–102, Jan 1997.
11. H. Lu, Y. C. Hu, and W. Zwaenepoel. OpenMP on networks of workstations. In *Proc. Supercomputing '98*, Orlando, FL, November 1998. ACM/IEEE.
12. J. E. Moreira, V. K. Naik, and R. B. Konuru. A system for dynamic resource allocation and data distribution. Technical Report RC 20257, IBM Research Division, October 1995.
13. N. Nedeljkovic and M.J. Quinn. Data-parallel programming on a network of heterogeneous workstations. *Concurrency: Practice & Experience*, 5(4):257–268, June 1993.
14. OpenMP Group. http://www.openmp.org, 1997.
15. A. Scherer, H. Lu, T. Gross, and W. Zwaenepoel. Transparent Adaptive Parallelism on NOWs using OpenMP. In *Proceedings of the Seventh ACM SIGPLAN Symposium on Principles and Practice of Parallel Programming (PPOPP)*, Atlanta, May 1999. ACM.
16. S. Shah, G. Haab, P. Petersen, and J. Throop. Flexible Control Structures for Parallelism in OpenMP. In *First European Workshop on OpenMP (EWOMP '99)*, Lund, Sweden, September/October 1999. Kuck & Associates, Incorporated.

Optimizing Mutual Exclusion Synchronization in Explicitly Parallel Programs

Diego Novillo[1], Ronald C. Unrau[1], and Jonathan Schaeffer[2]

[1] Red Hat Canada, Ltd., Toronto, Ontario, Canada
{dnovillo, runrau}@redhat.com
[2] Computing Science Department, University of Alberta, Edmonton, Alberta, Canada T6G 2H1
jonathan@cs.ualberta.ca

Abstract. We present two new compiler optimizations for explicitly parallel programs based on the CSSAME form: Lock-Independent Code Motion (LICM) and Mutex Body Localization (MBL). We have implemented these optimizations on top of the SUIF framework and present performance results for selected SPLASH applications.

1 Introduction

Optimizations for explicitly parallel programs fall into two classes: the adaptation of sequential optimizations to a parallel environment; and the direct optimization of the parallel structure of the program. There have been several recent advances in adapting sequential optimizations such as global constant propagation and dead-code elimination to explicitly parallel programs [6, 10, 13]. There has been less emphasis on optimizing the parallel structure of the program itself.

We build on a concurrent dataflow analysis framework called CSSAME[1][12] to analyze and optimize the synchronization structure of both task and data parallel programs. *Lock-Independent Code Motion* (LICM) is an optimizing transformation that can reduce the size of critical sections in the program. *Mutex Body Localization* (MBL) is a new transformation that converts references to shared memory into references to local memory inside critical sections of the code. We have implemented these algorithms on top of the SUIF framework [5] and apply them to two SPLASH applications [15]: Water and Ocean. We also show that our techniques can be used to automate common optimizations that experienced programmers are currently forced to perform manually.

2 Related Work

Previous work in the area of optimizing explicitly parallel programs has concentrated on the adaptation of sequential optimization techniques to the parallel case. Lee, Midkiff and Padua propose a Concurrent SSA framework (CSSA) for explicitly parallel programs and interleaving memory semantics [9]. They adapt a constant propagation algorithm using the CSSA form. In recent work they have also adapted other SSA-based

---

[1] Concurrent Static Single Assignment with Mutual Exclusion. Pronounced *sesame*.

S. Dwarkadas (Ed.): LCR 2000, LNCS 1915, pp. 128–142, 2000.

techniques including common subexpression elimination and code hoisting [10]. Their work only considers event-based synchronization operations and imposes some restrictions on the input program. Knoop, Steffen and Vollmer developed a bitvector analysis framework for parallel programs with shared memory and interleaving semantics [7]. They use their framework to adapt lazy code motion. However, their framework does not include synchronization operations. This reduces the opportunities for optimization in the general case.

In previous work we have extended the CSSA framework to incorporate mutual exclusion synchronization [13]. Our work extends the analysis techniques proposed by Lee *et al.* and shows the benefit of these extensions in the context of constant propagation for explicitly parallel programs. We also adapt a sequential dead-code removal algorithm that takes advantage of mutual exclusion information and describe an earlier form of the LICM technique that we extend and improve in this paper.

3 The CSSAME Form

The CSSAME form is a refinement of the CSSA framework [9] that incorporates more synchronization analysis to identify memory interleavings that are not possible at runtime due to the synchronization structure of the program. While CSSA only recognizes event synchronization, CSSAME extends it to include mutual exclusion synchronization and barrier synchronization [12]. CSSAME can be applied to both task and data parallel programs.

Like the sequential SSA form, CSSAME has the property that every use of a variable is reached by exactly one definition. When the flow of control causes more than one definition to reach a particular use, merge operators are introduced to resolve the ambiguity. Two merge operators are used in the CSSAME form: ϕ functions and π functions. ϕ functions have the same meaning as in sequential SSA [4]. π functions merge concurrent reaching definitions. Concurrent reaching definitions are those that reach the use of a variable from other threads.

The CSSAME form also examines π functions in critical sections of the code to determine if they can be removed. Since these π functions are in serialized sections of the code, some conflicts inside mutex bodies become superfluous and can be discarded. This pruning process is based on two observations:

1. *consecutive kills*: only definitions that reach the exit points of a critical section can be observed by other threads.
2. *protected uses*: if the use of a variable is protected by a definition local to the critical section, then definitions coming from concurrent critical sections will not be observed in this thread.

These two conditions allow the removal of superfluous conflict edges which in turn may lead to the complete removal of π functions, thus creating more opportunities for optimization [12]. The mutex synchronization analyzer modifies every node in the flowgraph so that they contain a use for each lock variable L (lock and unlock nodes already contain a definition and a use for L). To determine whether or not a flow graph node n is protected by lock L we compute reaching definition information for the use of L at n. If at least one of the reaching definitions comes from an `unlock` node or if there are no reaching definitions, then node n is not protected by lock L [12].

Mutex bodies are defined in terms of lock-protected nodes. In general, a mutex body $B_L(N)$ for lock variable L is a multiple-entry, multiple-exit region of the graph that encompasses all the flowgraph nodes that are protected by a common set of `lock` nodes (N). In contrast, previous work [8, 11] has treated mutex bodies as single-entry, single-exit regions. A mutex structure for a lock variable L is the set of all the mutex bodies for L in the program.

4   Lock-Independent Code Motion

Lock-Independent Code Motion (LICM) is a code motion technique that attempts to minimize the amount of code executed inside a mutex body. This optimization analyzes each mutex body to find code that can be moved outside. If at the end of the transformation a mutex body only contains unlock nodes, then the `lock` and `unlock` instructions are removed.

An expression E inside a mutex body $B_L(N)$ is lock-independent with respect to L if moving E outside $B_L(N)$ does not change the meaning of the program. Similarly, a statement (or group of statements) s is lock independent with respect to L if all the expressions and definitions in s are lock-independent. A flowgraph node n is lock independent if all its statements are lock-independent. The concept of lock-independence is similar to the concept of loop-invariant code for standard loop optimization techniques. Loop invariant computations compute the same result whether they are inside the loop or not. Analogously, lock-independent code computes the same result whether it is inside a mutex body or not. For instance, a statement s that references variables private to the thread will compute the same value whether it is executed inside a mutex body or not. This is also true if s references globally shared variables not modified by any other thread concurrent with s.

Lock-independent code is moved to special nodes called *premutex* and *postmutex* nodes. For every mutex body $B_L(N)$ there is a premutex node, denoted $premutex(n_i)$, for each `lock` node $n_i \in N$. Each premutex node $premutex(n_i)$ immediate dominates its associated `lock` node n_i. Similarly, there is a postmutex node, denoted $postmutex(x_i)$ for every `unlock` node x_i. Postmutex nodes are created as immediate post-dominators of each exit node x_i.

4.1   Moving Statements to Premutex Nodes

Given a lock-independent statement s inside a mutex body $B_L(N)$, LICM will attempt to move s to premutex or postmutex nodes for $B_L(N)$. The selection of `lock` nodes to receive statement s in their premutex node is done satisfying the following conditions (proofs of correctness are available separately [12]):

Protection. Candidate `lock` nodes are initially selected among all the `lock` nodes in N that reach the node containing s (denoted $node(s)$). This condition provides an initial set of candidate `lock` nodes called $protectors(s)$.

Reachability. Since s is reached by all the nodes in $protectors(s)$, there is a control path between each `lock` node in $protectors(s)$ and $node(s)$. Therefore, when statement s is removed from its original location, the statement must be replaced on every path from each `lock` node to $node(s)$. This implies that s may need to be replicated to more than one premutex node.

To determine which `lock` nodes could receive a copy of s we perform reachability analysis among the `lock` nodes reaching s ($protectors(s)$). This analysis computes a partition of $protectors(s)$, called $receivers(s)$, that contains all the `lock` nodes that may receive a copy of statement s. The selection of receiver nodes is done so that (a) there exists a path between s and every `lock` node in $protectors(s)$, and (b) instances of s occur only once along any of these paths (i.e., s is not unnecessarily replicated).

Algorithm 1 computes all the different sets of `lock` nodes that may receive a lock-independent statement s in their premutex nodes. Basically, the algorithm computes reachability sets among the nodes in $protectors(s)$. The set $protectors(s)$ is partitioned into k partitions $P_1, P_2, \ldots P_k$. Nodes in each partition P_j cannot reach each other but put together they reach or are reached by every other node in $protectors(s)$. These partitions are the sets of `lock` nodes that can receive a copy of s in their premutex nodes.

Data Dependencies. When moving a statement s to one of the receiver sets for s, the motion must not alter the original data dependencies for the statement and other statements in the program. If P_j is the selected receiver set for s, two restrictions must be observed:

1. No variable defined by s may be used or defined along any path from $node(s)$ to every node in P_j.
2. No variable used by s may be defined along any path from $node(s)$ to every node in P_j.

These two restrictions are used to prune the set of receiver nodes computed in Algorithm 1. Notice that since the program is in CSSAME form, ϕ functions are also considered definitions and uses for a variable.

When more than one statement is moved to the same premutex node, the original data dependencies among the statements in the same premutex node must also be preserved. This is accomplished by maintaining the original control precedence when moving statements into the premutex node.

It is also possible to move statements forward to postmutex nodes of a mutex body $B_L(N)$. The analysis for postmutex nodes is similar to the previous case. The conditions are essentially the reverse of the conditions required for premutex nodes [12].

The LICMS algorithm scans all the mutex bodies in the program looking for lock-independent statements to move outside the mutex body. Each lock-independent statement s is checked against the conditions described previously. Lines $8-15$ in Algorithm 2 determine the sets of premutex receivers for s. The initial set of candidates computed by Algorithm 1 checks every lock node in a mutex body against each other looking for paths between them.

Notice that it might be possible that a statement can be moved to both the premutex and the postmutex nodes. In that case a cost model should determine which node is more

---

Algorithm 1 Compute candidate premutex nodes (*receivers*).

INPUT: A mutex body $B_L(N)$ and a lock-independent statement s.
OUTPUT: A list of receiver sets. Each receiver set P_i contains `lock` nodes whose premutex nodes may receive s.

1: $protectors(s) \leftarrow$ set of `lock` nodes that reach s.
2: $Q \leftarrow protectors(s)$
3: $k \leftarrow 1$
4: **while** $Q \neq \emptyset$ **do**
5:     $n_i \leftarrow$ first node in Q
6:     $P(k) \leftarrow \{n_i\}$
7:     remove n_i from Q /* Add to $P(k)$ all the nodes that are not *connected* with n_i */
8:     **foreach** node $n_j \in Q$ and $Q \neq \emptyset$ **do**
9:         **if** (there is no path $n_i \rightarrow n_j$) **and** (there is no path $n_j \rightarrow n_i$) **then**
10:             $P(k) \leftarrow P(k) \bigcup \{n_j\}$
11:             remove n_j from Q
12:         **end if**
13:     **end for**
14:     $k \leftarrow k + 1$
15: **end while**
16: **return** $receivers \leftarrow P(1), P(2), \ldots, P(k-1)$

---

convenient. We will base our cost model on the effects of lock contention. Suppose that there is high contention for a particular lock. All the statements moved to premutex nodes will not be affected by it because they execute before acquisition of the lock. However, statements moved to the postmutex node will be delayed if there is contention because they execute after the lock has been released. Therefore, when a statement can be moved to both the premutex and postmutex nodes, the premutex node is selected.

The basic mechanism for moving statements outside mutex bodies can be used to move lock-independent control structures. Control structures are handled by checking and aggregating all the nodes contained in the structure into a single super-node and treating it like a single statement. After this process, Algorithm 2 can be used to hoist the structures outside mutex bodies [12].

4.2   LICM for Expressions

If hoisting statements or control structures outside mutex bodies is not possible, it may still be possible to consider moving lock-independent sub-expressions outside mutex bodies. This strategy is similar to moving statements (Algorithm 2) with the following differences:

1. Sub-expressions do not define variables. They only read variables or program constants.
2. If a sub-expression is moved from its original location, the computation performed by the expression must be stored in a temporary variable created by the compiler. The original expression is then replaced by the temporary variable. This is the same substitution performed by common sub-expression and partial redundancy elimination algorithms [1, 3].
3. Contrary to the case with statements and control structures, expressions can only be moved against the flow of control. The reason is that the value computed by the expression needs to be available at the statement containing the original expression.

Algorithm 2 Lock-Independent Code Motion for Statements (LICMS).

INPUT: A CCFG $G = \langle N, E, Entry_G, Exit_G \rangle$ in CSSAME form with pre and postmutex nodes inserted in every mutex body

OUTPUT: The program with lock-independent statements moved to the corresponding premutex and postmutex nodes

```
 1: foreach lock variable L_i do
 2:    foreach mutex body B_{L_i}(N) ∈ MutexStruct(L_i) do
 3:       n_i ← node(L_i)
 4:       foreach lock-independent statement s reached by n_i do
 5:          D_s ← variables defined by s
 6:          U_s ← variables used by s

 7:          /* Determine which premutex nodes can receive s. */
 8:          P ← receivers of s at premutex nodes (Algorithm 1)
 9:          foreach P_i ∈ P do
10:             foreach node n ∈ P_i do
11:                if (any path between n and node(s) defines or uses a variable in D_s)
                   or (any path between n and node(s) defines a variable in U_s) then
12:                   remove P_i from P
13:                end if
14:             end for
15:          end for

16:          /* Determine which postmutex nodes can receive s. */
17:          X ← receivers of s at postmutex nodes
18:          foreach X_i ∈ X do
19:             foreach node x ∈ X_i do
20:                if (any path between x and node(s) defines or uses a variable in D_s)
                   or (any path between x and node(s) defines a variable in U_s) then
21:                   remove X_i from X
22:                end if
23:             end for
24:          end for

25:          /* Sets P and X contain sets of premutex and postmutex nodes that can receive s. */
26:          if P ≠ ∅ then
27:             select one P_i ∈ P (cost model or random)
28:             remove s from its original location
29:             replicate s to each node n ∈ P_i
30:          else if X ≠ ∅ then
31:             select one X_i ∈ X (cost model or random)
32:             remove s from its original location
33:             replicate s to each node x ∈ X_i
34:          end if
35:       end for

36:       /* Remove the mutex body if it is empty. */
37:       if B_{L_i}(N) = ∅ then
38:          remove all the lock and unlock nodes of B_{L_i}(N)
39:       end if
40:    end for
41: end for
```

Algorithm 3 finds and removes lock-independent expressions from mutex bodies in the program. The process of gathering candidate expressions is similar to that of SSAPRE, an SSA based partial redundancy elimination algorithm [3]. Mutex bodies are scanned for lock-independent first-order expressions, which are expressions that contain only one operator. Higher order expressions are handled by successive iterations of the algorithm.

Once lock-independent expressions are identified, the algorithm looks for suitable premutex or postmutex nodes to receive each expression. We observe that since expressions can only be hoisted up in the graph, it is not necessary to consider postmutex

Algorithm 3 Lock-Independent Code Motion for Expressions (LICME).

INPUT: A CCFG in CSSAME form
OUTPUT: The graph with lock-independent expressions moved to the corresponding premutex nodes

```
 1: repeat
 2:     foreach lock variable Lᵢ do
 3:         foreach mutex body B_{Lᵢ}(N) ∈ M_{Lᵢ} do
 4:             E ← E ⋃ set of lock-independent expressions in B_{Lᵢ}(N).
 5:             if E ≠ ∅ then
 6:                 foreach expression Eⱼ ∈ E do
 7:                     P ← premutex receivers for Eⱼ (Algorithm 1)
 8:                     candidates ← ∅
 9:                     foreach Pᵢ ∈ P do
10:                         if ∀n ∈ Pᵢ : (n DOM node(Eⱼ)) or (node(Eⱼ) PDOM n) then
11:                             candidates ← Pᵢ
12:                             stop looking for candidates
13:                         end if
14:                     end for
15:                     if candidates ≠ ∅ then
16:                         insert the statement tⱼ = Eⱼ in all the premutex nodes for lock nodes in candidates
17:                     end if
18:                 end for
19:             end if
20:         end for
21:     end for
22:     /* Replace hoisted expressions inside each mutex body. */
23:     foreach lock variable Lᵢ do
24:         foreach mutex body B_{Lᵢ}(N) ∈ M_{Lᵢ} do
25:             replace hoisted expressions in B_{Lᵢ}(N) with their corresponding temporaries
26:         end for
27:     end for
28: until no more changes have been made
```

nodes when moving lock-independent expressions. Only lock nodes are considered by the algorithm. Furthermore, the candidate lock must dominate or be post-dominated by the node holding the expression (lines 7 − 13 in Algorithm 3).

The acceptable receiver sets are stored in the set *candidates*. It can be shown that in this case, the algorithm for computing receiver premutex nodes (Algorithm 1) will find none or exactly one set of lock nodes that can receive the expression in their premutex nodes [12].

Figure 1 shows an example program before and after running the LICM algorithm. When LICM is applied to the program in Figure 1(a), the first phase of the algorithm moves the statement at line 6 and the assignment $j = 0$ to the premutex node. The statement at line 10 is sunk to the postmutex node resulting in the equivalent program in Figure 1(b). There is still some lock-independent code in the mutex body, namely the expressions $j < M$ at line 7, the statement j++ at line 7 and the expression $y[j] + sqrt(a) * sqrt(b)$ at line 8. The only hoistable expression is $sqrt(a) * sqrt(b)$ because it is the only expression with all its reaching definitions outside the mutex body (Figure 1(c)). Note that a loop-invariance transformation would have detected this expression and hoisted it out of the loop. LICM goes a step further and hoists the expression outside the mutex body.

The individual LICM algorithms can be combined into a single LICM algorithm. There are four main phases to the algorithm. The first phase looks for mutex bodies

```
 1  double X[]; /* shared */
 2  parloop (i, 0, N) {
 3      double a, b; /* local */
 4      double y[]; /* local */
 5      lock(L);
 6      b = a * sin(a);
 7      for (j = 0; j < M; j++) {
 8          X[j] = y[j] + sqrt(a)
                     * sqrt(b);
 9      }
10      a = y[i];
11      unlock(L);
12  }
```

```
 1  double X[]; /* shared */
 2
 3  parloop (i, 0, N) {
 4      double a, b; /* local */
 5      double y[]; /* local */
 6
 7      ...
 8      b = a * sin(a);
 9      j = 0;
10      lock(L);
11      for (; j < M; j++) {
12          X[j] = y[j] + sqrt(a)
                     * sqrt(b);
13      }
14      unlock(L);
15      a = y[i];
16      ...
17  }
```

```
 1  double X[]; /* shared */
 2  parloop (i, 0, N) {
 3      double a, b; /* local */
 4      double y[]; /* local */
 5      b = a * sin(a);
 6      j = 0;
 7      t_1 = sqrt(a) * sqrt(b);
 8      lock(L);
 9      for (; j < M; j++) {
10          X[j] = y[j] + t_1;
11      }
12      unlock(L);
13      a = y[i];
14  }
```

(a) Program before LICM.   (b) LICM on statements.   (c) LICM on expressions.

Fig. 1. Effects of lock-independent code motion (LICM).

that have nothing but lock-independent nodes. These are the simplest cases. If all the nodes in a mutex body are lock-independent, then the `lock` operations at the lock nodes and the `unlock` operations in the body can be removed. The next three phases move interior lock-independent statements, control structures and expressions outside the mutex bodies in the program.

5   Mutex Body Localization

Consider a mutex body B_L that modifies a shared variable V (Figure 2(a)). With the exception of the definition reaching the unlock node of B_L, all the modifications done to V inside the mutex body can only be observed by the thread. Therefore, it is legal to create a local copy of V and replace all the references to V inside the mutex body to references to the local copy. We call this transformation *mutex body localization* (MBL). While LICM looks for lock-independent code, MBL creates lock-independent code by introducing local copies of a shared variable. The basic transformation is straightforward:

1. At the start of the mutex body a local copy of the shared variable is created if there is at least one use for the variable with reaching definitions outside the mutex body.
2. At the mutex body exits, the shared copy is updated from the local copy of the variable if at least one internal definition of the variable reaches that particular unlock node.
3. All the interior references to the shared variable are modified so that they reference the local copy.

```
double V = 0;          double V = 0;          double V = 0;          double V = 0;
parloop (i, 0, N) {    parloop (i, 0, N) {    parloop (i, 0, N) {    parloop (i, 0, N) {
  double x, y[];          double x, y[], p_V;    double x, y[], p_V;    double x, y[], p_V;
  int i;                 int i;                 int i;                 int i;
                         ...                    ...                    ...
                         lock(L);               lock(L);               p_V = 0;
  lock(L);               p_V = V;               p_V = 0;               i = 0;
  i = 0;                 i = 0;                 i = 0;                 while (p_V <= x) {
  while (V <= x) {       while (p_V <= x) {     while (p_V <= x) {       p_V = p_V + y[i++];
    V = V + y[i++];        p_V = p_V + y[i++];    p_V = p_V + y[i++];   }
  }                      }                      }                      lock(L);
  unlock(L);             V = p_V;               V = V + p_V;           V = V + p_V;
  ...                    unlock(L);             unlock(L);             unlock(L);
}                        ...                    ...                    ...
                         }                      }                      }
```

(a) A mutex body   (b) After localiza-   (c) After reduction   (d) After LICM.
before localiza-   tion.   recognition.
tion.

Fig. 2. Applications of mutex body localization.

Notice that this transformation is legal provided that the affected references are always made inside mutex bodies. Otherwise, the transformation might prevent memory interleavings that were allowed in the original program.

Algorithm 5 makes local copies of a variable a inside a mutex body $B_L(N)$ if the variable can be localized. To determine whether the variable a can be localized it calls Algorithm 4 (a subroutine of Algorithm 5) which returns TRUE if a can be localized inside mutex body $B_L(N)$. The localization algorithm relies on two data structures that can be built during the π rewriting phase of the CSSAME algorithm:

$exposedUses(N)$ is the set of upward-exposed uses from the mutex body $B_L(N)$. This set is associated with the entry nodes in N.

$reachingDefs(X)$ is the set of definitions that can reach the exit nodes X of $B_L(N)$.

Algorithm 5 starts by checking whether the variable can be localized (lines $1 - 4$). It then checks where the local copies are needed. If there are upward-exposed uses of a, a copy is needed at the start of the mutex body (lines $5 - 16$). If there are definitions of a reaching an exit node, the shared copy of a must be updated before exiting the mutex body (lines $17 - 29$). The final phase of the algorithm updates the interior references to a to be references to p_a (lines $30 - 34$). After this phase, the CSSAME form for the program has been altered and it should be updated. The simplest way to do this is to run the CSSAME algorithm again. However, this might be expensive if the localization process is repeated many times.

An alternate solution is to incrementally update the CSSAME form after the variable has been localized. Although this is generally considered a hard problem, the following are some guidelines that should be considered when performing an incremental update of the CSSAME form:

1. If the local copy is created at the start of the mutex body, the statement $p\_a = a$ contains a use of a. This use of a will have the same control reaching definition that the upward-exposed uses of a have. Notice that all the upward-exposed uses of a have the same control reaching definition.

   Since this statement has a conflicting use of a, it requires a π function. The argument list to this π function is the union of all the arguments to all the π functions for a inside the mutex body. Notice that the π functions for a should be for upward-exposed uses of a. This is because the program is in CSSAME form and all conflicting references to a are made inside mutex bodies of the same mutex structure (i.e., a is localizable).

2. All the π functions for a inside the mutex body must disappear because all the interior references to a are replaced by references to p_a.

3. All the interior ϕ functions for a must be converted into ϕ functions for p_a.

4. If the shared copy is updated at the end of the mutex body, the statement $a = p\_a$ contains a use of p_a whose control reaching definition should be the definition of p_a reaching the exit node x.

Algorithm 4 Localization test (*localizable*).

INPUT: A variable a and mutex body $B_L(N)$
OUTPUT: TRUE if a can be localized in $B_L(N)$, FALSE otherwise

```
 1: M_L ← mutex structure containing B_L(N)
 2: /* Check every conflicting reference r to a in the program. All the conflicting */
 3: /* references to a must occur inside mutex bodies of M_L, otherwise a is not localizable. */
 4: foreach conflicting reference r ∈ Refs(a) do
 5:     /* If we cannot find r in any of the mutex bodies of M_L, then a is not localizable. */
 6:     protected ← FALSE
 7:     foreach mutex body B'_L(N') ∈ M_L do
 8:         if node(r) is reached by some lock node in N' then
 9:             protected ← TRUE
10:         end if
11:     end for
12:     if not protected then
13:         return FALSE
14:     end if
15: end for
16: /* All the references to a are protected. Therefore, a is localizable. */
17: return TRUE
```

The MBL transformation by itself does not necessarily improve the performance of a program but it opens up new optimization opportunities. The main benefit of localization is that it might create more lock-independent code. For instance, if a thread contains read-only references to a variable V, localizing V will make those reads into lock-independent operations which in turn might make the whole statement lock-independent. Consider the sample program in Figure 2(a). After localization (Figure 2(b)), most statements inside the mutex body for L are lock-independent. However, none can be moved outside because of the read and write operations to the shared variable V at the fringes of the mutex body. If the compiler incorporates a reduction recognition pass, it is possible to do the reduction locally and only update V at the end (Figure 2(c)). Now all the

---

Algorithm 5 Mutex body localization.

INPUT: (1) An explicitly parallel program P in CSSAME form, (2) A variable a to be localized, (3) A mutex body
$B_L(N)$
OUTPUT: $B_L(N)$ with variable a localized

1: /* Check if a can be localized (Algorithm 4) */
2: **if not** $localizable(a, B_L(N))$ **then**
3:     **return**
4: **end if**
5: /* Check for upward-exposed uses of a. Since the program is in CSSAME form, */
6: /* upward-exposed uses have already been computed. If there are */
7: /* upward-exposed uses of a then we need to make a local copy of a at the start of $B_L(N)$. */
8: $needEntryCopy \leftarrow$ FALSE
9: **foreach** use $u \in exposedUses(N)$ **do**
10:     **if** u is a use of a **then**
11:         $needEntryCopy \leftarrow$ TRUE
12:     **end if**
13: **end for**
14: **if** $needEntryCopy$ **then**
15:     insert the statement $p\_a = a$ at the start of the mutex body
16: **end if**
17: /* Check if any definition of a reaches the exit nodes of $B_L(N)$. */
18: /* Since the program is in CSSAME form, the definitions that reach the exit nodes X */
19: /* have already been computed. If a definition */
20: /* of a reaches x, we need to make a copy of a before leaving the mutex body. */
21: $needExitCopy \leftarrow$ FALSE
22: **foreach** definition $d \in reachingDefs(X)$ **do**
23:     **if** d is a definition of a **then**
24:         $needExitCopy \leftarrow$ TRUE
25:     **end if**
26: **end for**
27: **if** $needExitCopy$ **then**
28:     insert the statement $a = p\_a$ at the exit nodes of the mutex body
29: **end if**
30: /* Update references to a inside the mutex body to reference */
31: /* the local version p_a instead of the shared version a. */
32: **foreach** reference to a inside $B_L(N)$ **do**
33:     replace a with p_a
34: **end for**
35: update CSSAME information for all references to p_a inside $B_L(N)$

---

lock-independent code in the mutex body can be moved to the premutex node resulting in the equivalent program in Figure 2(d).

6   Experimental Results

The algorithms discussed in this paper have been implemented[2] in a prototype compiler for the C language using the SUIF compiler system [5]. Our runtime system leverages on the SUIF runtime system to execute the parallel program.

Once the program has been parsed by the SUIF front-end, the compiler creates the corresponding CCFG and its CSSAME form. We do not transform the input program into SSA form. Instead we use factored use-def chains [17] in the flowgraph and display the source code annotated with the appropriate π and ϕ functions (variables are not renamed but referenced using line number information in the corresponding π or ϕ

---

[2] A preliminary version is available at
http://www.cs.ualberta.ca/~jonathan/CSSAME/

functions). The CCFG can be displayed using a variety of graph visualization systems. The CSSAME form for the program can also be displayed as an option. Finally, the compiler incorporates mutual exclusion validation techniques to warn the user about potential problems with the synchronization structure of the program [14].

Synchronization overhead is sometimes exacerbated by an expensive implementation of `lock` and `unlock` operations. To address this problem, several techniques have been proposed to implement more efficient locking primitives [2, 16]. But there is another source of overhead that even the most efficient implementation cannot alleviate: contention. Lock contention occurs when the demand for a particular lock variable is so high that threads spend a significant amount of time waiting for other threads to release the lock. The techniques for eliminating superfluous synchronization operations developed in this paper can complement the benefits of using an efficient locking mechanism.

6.1 Water

The Water application simulates forces and potentials in a system of liquid water molecules. The simulation is done over a specified number of time-steps until the system reaches equilibrium. Mutual exclusion synchronization is used when computing inter-molecular interactions and for keeping a global sum that is computed every time-step.

To study the effects of LICM in Water, we performed experiments that varied the total number of molecules (N), the number of molecule locks (ML), and, the number of simulation time-steps (TS). Experiments were performed on an SGI PowerChallenge with 8 processors and 384Mb of memory. The implementation uses SGI native threads (`sproc`) and hardware locks (`ulock`). All the experiments were executed on 8 processors with no other system activity.

The first experiment studies the performance effects of LICM as a function of synchronization overhead. As the number of time-steps increases, so does synchronization overhead. Table 1 shows the speedups obtained as a function of the number of time-steps and number of molecules simulated. Notice how the speedups obtained with LICM are lower when a larger number of molecules are simulated. This is caused by the larger computation to synchronization ratio in the larger problem. Also, by restricting the number of molecule locks available we are increasing lock contention. Naturally, as the number of available locks increases, the effects of LICM are diminished.

Table 1. Speedups obtained by LICM on Water as a function of the number of simulation time-steps.

Time steps	64 molecules (10 molecule locks)			216 molecules (10 molecule locks)		
	no LICM time (secs)	with LICM time (secs)	Relative Speedup	no LICM time (secs)	LICM time (secs)	Relative Speedup
70	157	144	1.09	1527	1463	1.04
80	183	171	1.07	1772	1763	1.00
100	235	219	1.07	2344	2285	1.02
120	296	269	1.10	2827	2809	1.00

Since molecule locks are accessed more as the number of time-steps increases, the contention on these locks also increases. To measure lock contention we used the hardware timers provided by the system to measure the average delay of acquiring a lock. We then computed the average delay over the 10 molecule locks. This is shown in Table 2. This table shows how average lock contention on the molecule locks increases as a function of the number of simulation time-steps. Notice that although LICM reduces lock contention significantly, its impact on the runtime of the program may not be too noticeable if the ratio of computation to synchronization is high enough. Again notice how lock contention decreases with the larger problem size. This explains the diminished effects of LICM on large problems.

Table 2. Effects of LICM on lock contention in Water.

	64 molecules			216 molecules		
	no LICM	with LICM		no LICM	with LICM	
Time	avg delay	avg delay	Ratio	avg delay	avg delay	Ratio
steps	(μsecs)	(μsecs)		(μsecs)	(μsecs)	
70	699	72	9.71	561	68	8.25
80	712	73	9.75	575	72	7.99
100	718	71	10.11	557	70	7.96
120	729	85	8.58	564	62	9.10

6.2   Ocean

Ocean studies eddy and boundary currents in large-scale ocean movements. Mutual exclusion is used to update global sums and to access a global convergence flag used in the iterative solver. The update of global sums is done with the same strategy used in Water. A local sum is computed and aggregated to the global sum.

To study the effect of MBL and LICM on this application, we simplified some routines in Ocean to compute global sums directly (the original program computes global sums by aggregating locally computed partial sums). We named this new version Simple Ocean. The intention is to demonstrate how some of the optimizations that are traditionally performed manually by the programmer can be automated using the techniques developed in this paper. Table 3 shows the performance improvements obtained by applying MBL and LICM to Simple Ocean. The program was executed on 8 processors with four different ocean sizes and a time-step of 180 seconds.

The performance improvements obtained on Simple Ocean using MBL and LICM are the same improvements obtained by the manual optimizations done in the original program. The important point of this experiment is to show that using the techniques developed in this paper it is possible to automatically optimize inefficient synchronization patterns. We do not expect experienced programmers to write such inefficient synchronization, but this kind of code could be found in programs written by a less experienced programmer or generated from generic code templates in a programming environment.

Table 3. Effects of MBL and LICM on Simple Ocean.

Ocean size	no MBL+LICM time (sec)	with MBL+LICM time (sec)	Relative Speedup
66×66	21	19	1.11
130×130	69	56	1.23
258×258	258	198	1.30
514×514	865	787	1.10

7   Conclusions and Future Work

We have shown how the CSSAME form allows new optimization opportunities by taking advantage of the semantics imposed by mutual exclusion synchronization. In previous work we have shown how the reduction of memory conflicts across threads can improve the effectiveness of adapted scalar optimization strategies [13]. In this paper, we have introduced two new optimization techniques that are specifically targeted at explicitly parallel programs: *Lock-Independent Code Motion* (LICM) moves code that does not need to be locked outside critical sections and *Mutex Body Localization* (MBL) converts shared memory references into local memory references. We consider these techniques a step towards a unified analysis and optimization framework for explicitly parallel programs. In turn this should facilitate the adoption of high-level systems with language-supported parallelism and synchronization. These systems typically provide powerful abstractions that make parallel programming easier, but those same abstractions often hinder performance. Experienced programmers recognize these limitations and manually circumvent them by removing abstraction layers to speed-up their code. With the techniques developed in this paper, we can transfer the burden of these transformations to the compiler.

References

[1] A. V. Aho, R. Sethi, and J. Ullman. *Compilers: Principles, Techniques, and Tools*. Reading, Mass.: Addison-Wesley, Reading, MA, second edition, 1986.

[2] D. Bacon, R. Konuru, C. Murthy, and M. Serrano. Thin Locks: Featherweight Synchronization for Java. In *ACM SIGPLAN '98 Conference on Programming Language Design and Implementation*, pages 258–268, Montreal, Canada, June 1998.

[3] F. Chow, S. Chan, R. Kennedy, S.-M. Liu, R. Lo, and P. Tu. A new algorithm for partial redundancy elimination based on SSA form. In *ACM SIGPLAN '97 Conference on Programming Language Design and Implementation*, Las Vegas, 1997.

[4] R. Cytron, J. Ferrante, B. Rosen, M. Wegman, and K. Zadeck. Efficiently computing static single assignment form and the control dependence graph. *ACM Transactions on Programming Languages and Systems*, 13(4):451–490, October 1991.

[5] M. Hall, J. Anderson, S. Amarasinghe, B. Murphy, S. Liao, E. Bugnion, and M. Lam. Maximizing Multiprocessor Performance with the SUIF Compiler. *IEEE Computer*, 29(12):84–89, December 1996.

[6] J. Knoop and B. Steffen. Code motion for explicitly parallel programs. In *Proceedings of the Fifth ACM SIGPLAN Symposium on Principles and Practice of Parallel Programming*, Atlanta, GA, May 1999.

[7] J. Knoop, B. Steffen, and J. Vollmer. Parallelism for free: Efficient and optimal bitvector analyses for parallel programs. *ACM Transactions on Programming Languages and Systems*, 18(3):268–299, May 1996.

[8] A. Krishnamurthy and K. Yelick. Analyses and Optimizations for Shared Address Space Programs. *Journal of Parallel and Distributed Computing*, 38:130–144, 1996.

[9] J. Lee, S. Midkiff, and D. A. Padua. Concurrent static single assignment form and constant propagation for explicitly parallel programs. In *Proceedings of the Tenth Workshop on Languages and Compilers for Parallel Computing*, August 1997.

[10] J. Lee, D. A. Padua, and S. Midkiff. Basic compiler algorithms for parallel programs. In *Proceedings of the Fifth ACM SIGPLAN Symposium on Principles and Practice of Parallel Programming*, Atlanta, GA, May 1999.

[11] S. P. Masticola. *Static Detection of Deadlocks in Polynomial Time*. PhD thesis, Department of Computer Science, Rutgers University, 1993.

[12] D. Novillo. *Compiler Analysis and Optimization Techniques for Explicitly Parallel Programs*. PhD thesis, University of Alberta, February 2000.

[13] D. Novillo, R. Unrau, and J. Schaeffer. Concurrent SSA Form in the Presence of Mutual Exclusion. In *1998 International Conference on Parallel Processing*, pages 356–364, Minneapolis, Minnesota, August 1998.

[14] D. Novillo, R. Unrau, and J. Schaeffer. Identifying and Validating Irregular Mutual Exclusion in Concurrent Programs. In *European Conference on Parallel Computing (Euro-Par 2000)*, August 2000.

[15] J. Singh, W. Weber, and A. Gupta. SPLASH: Stanford parallel applications for shared-memory. *Computer Architecture News*, 20(1):5–44, March 1992.

[16] R. Unrau, O. Krieger, B. Gamsa, and M. Stumm. Experiences with Locking in a NUMA Multiprocessor Operating System Kernel. In *Proceedings for the 1st USENIX Symposium on Operating Systems Design and Implementation (OSDI '94)*, pages 139–152, 1994.

[17] M. J. Wolfe. *High Performance Compilers for Parallel Computing*. Reading, Mass.: Addison-Wesley, Redwood City, CA, 1996.

Detecting Read-Only Methods in Java

Jeff Bogda

Department of Computer Science
University of California
Santa Barbara, CA 93106
bogda@cs.ucsb.edu

Abstract. One typically defines a read-only method as a method that does not perform any write operations; however, with respect to a multi-threaded program, we augment this interpretation and let a read-only method be one that does not write to a memory location visible to more than one thread. Such a method can execute concurrently with other read-only methods. With the relaxation of mutual exclusion in mind, we present a read-write analysis that employs the ideas of shape analysis and escape analysis to identify read-only methods in Java. Approximately 31% of the methods in the JDK 1.2 core libraries meets this definition of read-only—nearly 50% more than those that do not perform any write operations.

1   Introduction

Parallel systems of today must be able to execute object-oriented applications efficiently. Programmers write many of these applications in Java [7], a popular object-oriented language that supports multi-threaded behavior at the language level. As a built-in mechanism to protect regions of code from concurrent access, the Java programming language provides the synchronized keyword and associates an implicit lock with each run-time object. When applied to an instance method definition, the synchronized keyword causes two actions to occur. First, upon entering the method, the executing thread acquires the object's lock and flushes its working memory. Second, upon exiting the method, the thread releases the lock and commits its working memory to main memory. Because of this protecting lock, a thread has exclusive access to any synchronized methods invoked on the object.

Depending on the application and the use of a particular run-time object, the above protection may be too strong. It may be meaningful and even beneficial to allow multiple threads to execute some methods concurrently. In particular, code that only reads memory (a reader) can be executed with other code that also only reads memory; however, code that writes to memory (a writer) must have exclusive access to that memory. For example, a multi-threaded program that performs matrix computations can allow threads to read the cells of a shared matrix concurrently.

To implement this multiple-readers/single-writer concept, programmers cannot simply use the implicit locks in Java since they provide a thread exclusive access to an object. Instead, programmers typically resort to run-time libraries that introduce explicit locks in their programs and monitor the invocation of methods. By knowing which methods the run-time system can safely overlap, we can potentially remove this burden from the programmers and still allow the concurrency. For example, at a high level we

S. Dwarkadas (Ed.): LCR 2000, LNCS 1915, pp. 143-154, 2000.

can automatically transform a standard program into one utilizing the multiple-readers/ single-writer protocol. Alternatively, at a low level the run-time system can reduce Java's implicit locks to read-write locks and allow concurrent readers.

We let a read-only method denote a method that the run-time system can execute at the same time as other read-only methods. Traditionally, because of the ease of detection, this has only included methods that do not perform any write operations. We recognize that some writes are still safe, namely writes to memory locations visible only to a single thread. Thus, in this work a read-only method is a method that does not write to static fields or to fields of objects accessible to more than one thread.

We present a whole-program, static analysis (see Section 3) that determines which methods are read-only. Applying this analysis to the example of Section 2 reveals that 31% of the methods are read-only (see Section 4), a significant improvement over an analysis that uses the traditional notion of read-only.

2   Banking Example

Consider the contrived banking program in Figure 1. After spawning twenty threads that repeatedly get the balance of a shared Account object, the main body repeatedly deposits money into the account and prints the account to standard output. It creates an account at line S2 and instantiates the readers at line S3. By invoking the start method of a ReaderThread object, the program causes the run-time system to spawn a thread that executes the object's run method. Thus at run-time the reading of the account may be arbitrarily interspersed with the deposits. The println routine invokes the Account object's toString method, which the compiler most likely translates to

```
String val = String.valueOf( balance );
StringBuffer buf = new StringBuffer( val );
String c = " dollars";
buf.append( c );
return buf.toString();
```

The translated version utilizes a StringBuffer object to synthesize the string.

Since the getBalance, deposit, and toString methods of the Account class are declared synchronized, an Account object is thread-safe. As a result, each thread accesses the account atomically, there is a total ordering to the accesses of the account, and each thread is guaranteed to see the most recent amount in the account. Unfortunately this means that a thread cannot read the account while another thread reads it and that a thread cannot necessarily read the balance currently cached in its working memory. Both actions preserve program semantics. The deposit method is the only method that modifies shared memory—memory accessible to more than one thread—and hence needs exclusive access to that memory. The getBalance and toString methods do not make any changes visible to another thread. We propose an analysis that recognizes getBalance and toString as read-only methods.

3   Read-Write Analysis

The analysis presented here identifies write operations to shared memory and labels methods read-only. It traverses, in reverse topological order, the strongly connected components of the static call graph. Upon analyzing each component, it executes three phases: a shape analysis, a thread-escape analysis, and a read-write analysis. Each underlying analysis iterates over the component until it reaches a fixed point. The shape analysis phase estimates the connectivity of heap objects, the thread-escape analysis

```
public class BankExample {
  private static class Account {
    double balance = 0.0;

    public synchronized double getBalance()
      { return balance; }

    public synchronized void deposit( double amt )
      { balance += amt; }

    public synchronized String toString()      // Compiler rewrites using
      { return balance + " dollars"; }          // a StringBuffer object
  }

  private static class ReaderThread extends Thread {
    Account myCopy;

    public ReaderThread( Account acct )
S1:   { myCopy = acct; }

    public void run() {
      for( int i=0; i<10000; i++ )
        myCopy.getBalance();                    // Perform read
    }
  }

  public static void main( String[] args ) {
S2: Account acct = new Account();

    for( int t=0; t<20; t++ )
S3:   new ReaderThread( acct ).start();         // Spawn reader

    for( int i=0; i<10000; i++ )
      acct.deposit( 50.0 );                     // Perform write

    System.out.println( acct );
  }
}
```

Figure 1. Sample program with a main writer thread and several reader threads.

Table 1. Constraints for the shape analysis phase.

$x = y$ Similarly, $x.f = y$ $y = x.f$	Let the operand $\equiv$ denote the following constraints: $context(x) = context(y)$ $\forall f \in fields(x) \cup fields(y)$ $\quad context(x.f) \equiv context(y.f)$
$foo(a_0,...,a_n)$	$\forall g \in methods\text{-}invoked(foo)$ $\quad \forall i, j, \varphi_i, \varphi_j, \text{ such that } context(p_i.\varphi_i) = context(p_j.\varphi_j)$ $\quad\quad context(a_i.\varphi_i) \equiv context(a_j.\varphi_j)$

phase subsequently determines which objects may be visible outside the currently executing thread, and the read-write analysis phase determines read-only methods. The phases may be carried out at the same time, although for clarity we discuss each phase as being a distinct step in the analysis. Section 3.2 describes an implementation optimization that combines the shape analysis and thread-escape analysis phases.

We make the following assumptions. We treat an array access as a read or write of a single instance field named array, thereby not distinguishing cells of an array. The variables $p_0,...,p_n$ represent a method's formal parameters, while $a_0,...,a_n$ denote the corresponding actual arguments at a given call site. Moreover, a method takes its receiver as its first argument (p_0), the destination variable as its second-to-last argument (p_{n-1}), and the thrown exception as its last argument (p_n).[1] Furthermore, we treat a native method specially. If we know its behavior, we hard-code its results into the analysis; otherwise, we assume the worst results.

3.1 Shape Analysis Phase

A shape analysis [5,6,10,13] statically constructs an approximation of the connectivity of heap objects. We employ it at the method level, and, using the terminology presented in the paper on shape analysis by Wilhelm *et al.* [13], we label each method's resulting snapshot a *shape graph*. A node of a shape graph is an *object context*, which represents one or more objects passing through the method. A directed edge labeled f extends from object context C_i to object context C_j if it is possible that at run-time an object represented by C_j can be accessed through field f of an object represented by C_i.

In presenting the analysis, we follow the format used in [3] and provide a set of constraints (Table 1). Within the constraints, *context*(x.φ) denotes the object context encapsulating any object reachable from the (possibly empty) path φ of field dereferences from the variable x. Also, *field*(x) is the set of fields of x, and *methods-invoked*(foo) is the set of all method implementations named foo that may be reached at a given call site. The analysis assumes incoming objects are not aliased, so each formal parameter initially has its own object context. The callers of the method handle any aliasing.

---

[1] We abuse the semantics of Java here and treat p_{n-1} and p_n as if they were pass-by-reference. This simplifies the presentation and does not adversely affect the analysis.

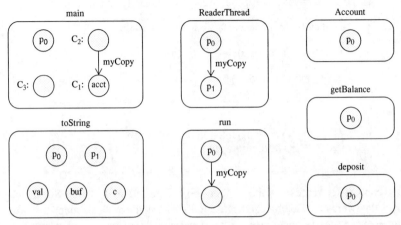

Figure 2. The example's shape graph divided into regions.

The analysis walks the code, manipulating the shape graph as it encounters statements that affect the heap. When it encounters an assignment x = y, where x and y are reference variables, the analysis recursively merges the contexts corresponding to x and to y. Across a method invocation, the analysis maps the structure of a callee's formal parameter contexts to the actual parameter contexts in the caller. If a context does not exist in the caller, one is created. To handle program recursion, if the analysis detects that a context C_i may enter the method being analyzed through parameter a_j, it equates C_i and the context of a_j. Since the number of contexts is finite and the actions only merge nodes of the shape graph, the analysis will reach a fixed point.

After the shape analysis inspects our banking example, the shape graph resembles the diagram in Figure 2.[1] For easy referral, we write the program variable that references an object encapsulated by the context inside the node and an arbitrary label outside. The seven regions of the graph correspond to the seven methods of Figure 1. Since the shape analysis is a backward analysis, each method only knows about objects accessed in the body of the method and objects reachable from formal parameters of called methods.

The final subgraphs corresponding to the Account constructor, getBalance method, and deposit method contain a single context—the context corresponding to the receiver (p_0). The method toString uses objects in addition to the receiver, namely a string to hold the balance (val), a StringBuffer object (buf), a string constant (c), and the returned object (p_1).

Analysis of the ReaderThread constructor reveals that the program stores parameter p_1 into the myCopy field of the receiver at line S1. This relationship indicates that the Account object is accessible through the ReaderThread objects. In run the program merely uses the receiver's myCopy field.

---

[1] For a clearer presentation we ignore exception objects, which do not influence this example, and objects introduced by library classes, which require additional background information.

Table 2. Constraints for the thread-escape analysis phase.

C.f = y (static) y = C.f (static)	Let *markShared* denote the following constraints: shared(context(y)) = T $\forall$ f $\in$ fields(y) markShared(y.f)

foo(a_0,...,a_n)	$\forall$ g $\in$ methods-invoked(foo)
	  $\forall$ i, φ such that shared(context($p_i.\varphi$))
	    markShared($a_i.\varphi$)

In main context C_1 represents the Account object instantiated at line S2, and C_2 encapsulates the twenty thread objects created at S3. The shape analysis maps the structure of the ReaderThread constructor's formal parameters to the actual parameters, causing C_1 to be attached to C_2 via field myCopy. Context C_3 represents the object denoted by System.out.

3.2 Thread-Escape Analysis Phase

The thread-escape analysis [1,2,3,4,12] phase identifies which objects escape a thread, or, in other words, are potentially shared among threads. Immediately after a thread allocates a new object (*i.e.*, invokes the bytecode new), it holds the only reference to the object. Other threads cannot access this object until the creator thread stores the reference in a portion of the heap accessible to other threads. This occurs with a store into a static field or into an instance field of another escaping object.[1] We call such an object *shared* and define the boolean attribute *shared(context(x))* to be true (T) if an object that variable x references may be shared among threads.

The analysis first assumes that no object escapes (*i.e.*, attribute *shared* is false), and then it traverses the code to find places objects may escape. The constraints given in Table 2 guide the analysis. At a static field access, the analysis marks the context representing the data object—as well as all contexts reachable from this context in the shape graph—as being shared. At a method invocation, the contexts of the objects passed into and returned from a callee inherit the *shared* attributes of the corresponding contexts in the callee. Since the attribute *shared* only changes from false to true, the analysis will reach a fixed point.

Because shared objects are essentially global objects, an invaluable optimization is to reuse the contexts of shared objects. Specifically, if a context C_i in a callee has been marked *shared*, the shape analysis can recursively merge the caller's corresponding context with C_i instead of duplicating C_i's structure in the caller. This requires us to combine the shape analysis and thread-escape analysis phases but greatly reduces the space and time usage of the overall analysis.

---

[1] A store into a static field means that multiple threads *can* access the object but does not necessarily imply that multiple threads *will* access the object. A more precise, expensive analysis may be able to ignore the innocuous static field accesses.

Table 3. Constraints for the read-write analysis phase.

x.f = y (instance)	Let *markWrittenTo* denote the following constraints:
	
	if shared(context(x))
	    write(m) = T
	else
	    written-to(context(x)) = T

C.f = y (static)	write(m) = T

foo(a_0,...,a_n)	$\forall$ g $\in$ methods-invoked(foo)
	    if write(g)
	        write(m) = T
	    $\forall$ i, φ such that written-to(context($p_i.\varphi$))
	        markWrittenTo(context($a_i.\varphi$))

Once this phase has reached a fixed point, it has identified those objects, from the perspective of a given method, that may be accessed by more than one thread. When applied to the running example, the analysis deems the contexts labeled C_1, C_2, and C_3 (Figure 2) as shared. C_3 is shared because it encapsulates the object whose reference is stored in the static field System.out. Context C_2 is shared because the program invokes the native method start on it, which we know makes the thread object accessible to multiple threads. Since context C_1 is reachable via field myCopy from context C_2, it also is shared. This signals that the Account object, the ReaderThread objects, and standard output are shared objects and that the memory these objects enclose is global memory. The thread-escape analysis does not mark any other contexts *shared*.

Since the String and StringBuffer objects of the toString method are not shared and not reachable from a formal parameter, they are *thread-local* objects. The memory they enclose are accessible only to the thread executing toString. The read-write analysis phase of the next section allows read-only methods to write into fields of these thread-local objects.

3.3 Read-Write Analysis Phase

The last phase, the read-write analysis phase, determines if a method writes to the heap in such a way that more than one thread can see the effects. We term such a write a *visible write*. Two situations characterize a visible write: a write to a static field and a write to an instance field of a shared object. A method in which no visible write occurs during its execution is a *read-only method*; otherwise, it is a *write method*. This phase initially assumes all methods are read-only and seeks places where visible writes may occur.

The constraints in Table 3 guide the analysis of a method m. We let the boolean attribute *write* be true for m if it or one of its callees writes to a shared object and the boolean attribute *written-to* be true for an object context if the program writes to one of its fields. Initially these attributes are false. When the analysis encounters a write to a static field, it recognizes that the result of the write is visible to other threads and marks m a write method. When the analysis encounters a write to an instance field, it inspects the context representing the base object. If the thread-escape analysis marked its context *shared*, signifying that a portion of the heap is potentially accessible to other threads, m is a write method; otherwise, the analysis sets its context's *written-to* attribute to true. When the analysis discovers a method invocation, it deems m a write method if any callee is a write method; otherwise, it treats the *written-to* contexts in the callee as if the corresponding contexts in m were directly written to. If any of these contexts are marked *shared*, m is a write method. Since the *written-to* and *write* attributes only change from false to true, the analysis reaches a fixed point.

The read-only nature of a method depends on its calling context. A method is always read-only if its *write* attribute is false and if no object context reachable from the contexts of the formal parameters (excluding p_{n-1} and p_n) has its *written-to* attribute set to true. Under no circumstance will such a method perform a visible write. If a method's *write* attribute is false, but it writes to an incoming object, it is read-only if the incoming object is a thread-local object. Therefore, an accurate response to the question "Is this method read-only?" requires us to conservatively assume that all incoming objects are shared.

Consider the results of the read-write analysis on our example. The method getBalance is trivially a read-only method because no writes occur. The method toString only writes to thread-local objects—the String and StringBuffer objects—and hence is also always read-only. On the other hand, method deposit writes to a field of an incoming parameter (the receiver), making it a read-only method only if the receiver is thread-local. Since main invokes deposit on a shared object, the main method is a write method. It would be safe (although less precise) to mistake getBalance and toString as write methods, but it would be incorrect to deem main a read-only method.

4   Evaluation

We ran the analysis on the transitive closure of the banking example using the JDK 1.2.1. Even though these results apply only to this example, we feel they are indicative of results of the core classes pulled in by any multi-threaded application. Table 4 presents the number of read-only methods that the read-write analysis identifies and, for the curious reader, compares these numbers with the number of synchronized methods.

The first column of the table lists the ten classes (with more than ten methods) that have the highest percentage of read-only methods. The second column gives the total number of analyzed non-native methods in the class listed in column one, while column three shows the number of these that are declared synchronized. In the fourth and fifth columns we show the results of an analysis that does not allow a read-only method to perform any writes into the heap. This corresponds to the traditional notion of read-only. The fourth column gives the total number of read-only methods for each class, while the next column shows the number of these read-only methods that are synchronized. The columns entitled "Writes to Local Objects" present the same figures but for the case where read-only methods are allowed to write to thread-local objects. Here all incoming arguments are conservatively assumed to be shared. The final two columns

Table 4. Top JDK library classes, in terms of the percentage of read-only methods.

Class	Meth-ods Anal-yzed	Meth-ods Sync.	Read-Only Methods					
			No Writes		Writes to Local Objects		Writes to Parameters and Local Objects	
			Total	Sync.	Total	Sync.	Total	Sync.
Dec.FormatSymbols	20	0	16	0	17	0	17	0
Character	12	0	10	0	10	0	10	0
GregorianCalendar	30	0	18	0	19	0	23	0
Double	13	0	8	0	8	0	9	0
Signature	12	0	3	0	7	0	10	0
SimpleTimeZone	16	1	6	1	8	1	9	1
BigInteger	25	0	6	0	12	0	22	0
BitArray	15	0	5	0	7	0	10	0
Inflater	13	10	4	4	6	6	7	7
ClassLoader	11	0	3	0	5	0	5	0
Total of all classes	2217	105	481	12	694	18	1024	38
Total without constr. and static initializers	1743	105	442	12	567	18	773	38

show results for the case where all incoming arguments are thread-local objects. The last two rows give the totals for the entire set of 498 classes. The last row ignores constructors and static initializers.

In all, 694, or 31%, of the 2217 methods are always read-only, and 46% are read-only if we know that the objects entering the methods are not shared. In the worst case our analysis recognizes 44% more read-only methods than a traditional analysis, which identifies 481 read-only methods. Constructors, which typically do not require synchronization, account for 17% of the write methods, and static initializers, which are automatically synchronized by the run-time system, account for 6%.

The low percentage of synchronized methods in the core libraries suggests that the classes either entrust mutual exclusion to the programmer or realize mutual exclusion through synchronized blocks. In the latter case, our analysis would greatly profit from the examination of synchronized blocks in addition to synchronized methods. Contrary to this observation, the class java.util.zip.Inflater contains mostly synchronized methods. In fact, all six of the methods deemed read-only are synchronized, suggesting that the locking mechanism is stronger than necessary for these methods.

An optimization can use these results to know when it is safe to overlap execution. Suppose we have a transformation program that automatically replaces Java's synchronization mechanism for the class Account with high-level, reentrant read and write locks that implement the multiple-readers/single-writer paradigm. These locks could be built on top of Java's synchronization primitives to ensure visibility across threads. The read lock would monitor the use of the getBalance and toString methods. For example, the code

```
public double getBalance() {
  readLock.acquire();
  try { return balance; }
  finally { readLock.release(); }
}
```

may reflect an optimized getBalance method. Similarly, the write lock would provide mutual exclusion for the deposit method. For this example, optimizing the Account methods will increase concurrency enough to de-emphasize the overhead of managing high-level locks. In general, however, it is difficult to know which classes will benefit from this optimization.

5   Related Work

As far as we know, our read-write analysis is the first of its kind to be applied to Java. Researchers have thoroughly studied memory access patterns for programs written in C and Fortran, especially in the context of parallelizing compilers. It is our understanding that these studies have focused mostly on inner loops and array accesses of non-object-oriented languages.

Much of the research requires programmers to annotate their code to specify the access patterns of objects. For example, through the keyword const [11], C++ program-mers identify objects that are not written to and member functions that do not modify the state of their receivers. To verify that a program respects its const declarations, the compiler must inspect the writes and invoked methods just as our analysis must.

The work of Yasugi et al. [14], which directly applies to a variant of Java, treats a read-only method as a method that does not write to the instance fields of its receiver. To eliminate the difficulty of aliasing, they rely on the auxiliary keyword internal. Once they determine the status of a method, they decrease the size of critical sections and allow concurrent reading of the receiver's state. Also, they remove mutual exclusion altogether if they conclude a method reads unchangeable fields of the receiver.

With VJava [8], an extension to the Java programming language, the run-time system wishes to allow multiple readers of an object. VJava achieves this by requiring the programmer to specify the view a thread will have of a shared object. The view indi-cates the fields that the thread will read and write. If two views do not write to the same part of an object, the run-time system decides that the threads can access the object concurrently.

An analysis that does not require annotations is the commutativity analysis of Rinard and Diniz [9]. Their analysis groups operations and determines which groups can be ordered arbitrarily. They have applied their analysis to a subset of C++ in order to automatically parallelize code.

6   Conclusions

Parallel systems look to speed up synchronization and to maximize concurrency. Recent Java research has provided static analyses that determine which objects will *not* be shared by multiple threads. With knowledge of such objects, an optimizer may remove lock accesses on these objects. We turn our attention to objects *shared* among threads and strive to speed up multi-threaded programs by allowing threads to execute methods concurrently.

We defined a read-only method to be one in which it and any called methods do not write to a static field or into a shared object. We then described a whole-program static analysis that identifies read-only methods. Results show that approximately 31% of the non-native methods in the JDK 1.2 core libraries meets our definition of read-only. One potential improvement is the ability to analyze synchronized blocks in addition to synchronized methods. As multi-threaded programming in Java gains popularity, more thread-safe libraries will emerge, and the number of synchronized read-only methods will increase.

Identification of read-only methods should give rise to optimizations that allow efficient concurrent access to objects. We know that overlapping the execution of read-only methods can speed up a program, but the question of which methods and which shared objects will benefit most from this optimization still remains.

Acknowledgments

We thank the anonymous reviewers of LCR for their valuable comments on earlier versions of this paper. This work was funded in part by the Stanford/ARPA grant PR-9836 and in part by the NSF grant CCR-9972571.

References

1. Jonathan Aldrich, Craig Chambers, Emin Gun Sirer, and Susan Eggers. Static Analyses for Eliminating Unnecessary Synchronization from Java Programs. In *Proceedings of the Sixth International Static Analysis Symposium (SAS '99)*, Venezia, Italy, September 1999.

2. Bruno Blanchet. Escape Analysis for Object-Oriented Languages. Application to Java. In *Proceedings of Object-Oriented Programming, Systems, Languages, and Applications (OOPSLA '99)*, pages 20-34, Denver, Colorado, 1-5 November 1999.

3. Jeff Bogda and Urs Hölzle. Removing Unnecessary Synchronization in Java. In *Proceedings of Object-Oriented Programming, Systems, Languages, and Applications (OOPSLA '99)*, pages 35-46, Denver, Colorado, 1-5 November 1999.

4. J.-D. Choi, M. Gupta, M. Serrano, V. C. Sreedhar, and S. Midkiff. Escape Analysis for Java. In *Proceedings of Object-Oriented Programming, Systems, Languages, and Applications (OOPSLA '99)*, pages 1-19, Denver, Colorado, 1-5 November 1999.

5. James C. Corbett. *Using Shape Analysis to Reduce Finite-State Models of Concurrent Java Programs*. Technical Report ICS-TR-98-20, Department of Information and Computer Science, University of Hawaii, 14 October 1998.

6. Rakesh Ghiya and Laurie J. Hendren. Is it a Tree, a DAG, or a Cyclic Graph? A Shape Analysis for Heap-Directed Pointers in C. In *Conference Record of the 23rd ACM SIGPLAN-SIGACT Symposium on Principles of Programming Languages (POPL '96)*, pages 1-15, St. Petersburg Beach, Florida, 21-24 January 1996.

7. James Gosling, Bill Joy, and Guy Steele. *The Java Language Specification*. Addison-Wesley: Berkeley, California, 1996.

8. Ilya Lipkind, Igor Pechtchanski, and Vijay Karamcheti. Object Views: Language Support for Intelligent Object Caching in Parallel and Distributed Computations.In *Proceedings of Object-Oriented Programming, Systems, Languages, and Applications (OOPSLA '99)*, pages 447-460, Denver, Colorado, 1-5 November 1999.

9. Martin C. Rinard and Pedro C. Diniz. Commutativity Analysis: A New Analysis Technique for Parallelizing Compilers. *ACM Transactions on Programming Languages and Systems*, pages 942-991, Volume 19, Number 6, November 1997.

10. Mooly Sagiv, Thomas Reps, and Reinhard Wilhelm. Solving Shape-Analysis Problems in Languages with Destructive Updating. In *Conference Record of the 23rd ACM Symposium on Principles of Programming Languages (POPL '96)*, pages 16-31, St. Petersburg Beach, Florida, 21-24 January 1996.

11. Bjarne Stroustrup. *The C++ Programming Language, Third Edition*. Addison-Wesley: Berkeley, California, 1997.

12. John Whaley and Martin Rinard. Compositional Pointer and Escape Analysis for Java Programs. In *Proceedings of Object-Oriented Programming, Systems, Languages, and Applications (OOPSLA '99)*, pages 187-206, Denver, Colorado, 1-5 November 1999.

13. Reinhard Wilhelm, Mooly Sagiv, and Thomas Reps. Shape Analysis. In *Proceedings of the Conference on Compiler Construction*, Berlin, Germany, 27 March - 2 April 2000.

14. Masahiro Yasugi, Shigeyuki Eguchi, and Kazuo Taki. Eliminating Bottlenecks on Parallel Systems using Adaptive Objects. In *Proceedings of the International Conference on Parallel Architectures and Compilation Techniques (PACT '98)*, pages 80-87, Paris, France, 12-18 October 1998.

The Effect of Contention on the Scalability of Page-Based Software Shared Memory Systems

Eyal de Lara[1], Y. Charlie Hu[2], Honghui Lu[1],
Alan L. Cox[2], and Willy Zwaenepoel[2]

[1] Department of Electrical and Computer Engineering
[2] Department of Computer Science
Rice University, Houston TX 77005, USA

Abstract. In this paper, we examine the causes and effects of contention for shared data access in parallel programs running on a software *distributed shared memory* (DSM) system. Specifically, we experiment on two widely-used, page-based protocols, Princeton's home-based lazy release consistency (HLRC) and TreadMarks. For most of our programs, these protocols were equally affected by latency increases caused by contention and achieved similar performance. Where they differ significantly, HLRC's ability to manually eliminate load imbalance was the largest factor accounting for the difference. To quantify the effects of contention we either modified the application to eliminate the cause of the contention or modified the underlying protocol to efficiently handle it. Overall, we find that contention has profound effects on performance: eliminating contention reduced execution time by 64% in the most extreme case, even at the relatively modest scale of 32 nodes that we consider in this paper.

1 Introduction

In this paper, we examine the causes and effects of contention for shared data access in parallel programs running on a software *distributed shared memory* (DSM) system. Specifically, we analyze the execution of a representative set of programs, each exhibiting a particular access pattern that causes contention. In each of these cases, to quantify the effects of contention on performance, we have either modified the application to eliminate the cause of the contention or modified the underlying protocol to efficiently handle that particular access pattern. Overall, we find that contention has profound effects on performance: eliminating contention reduced execution time by 64% in the most extreme case, even at the relatively modest scale of 32 nodes that we consider in this paper.

Our experiments are performed on a network of thirty-two single-processor nodes using both Princeton's home-based (HLRC) protocol [7] [11] and Rice's TreadMarks (Tmk) protocol [6]. Both are widely-used, page-based, multiple-writer protocols implementing Lazy Release Consistency (LRC) [5]. From our experiments, we derive three specific conclusions.

S. Dwarkadas (Ed.): LCR 2000, LNCS 1915, pp. 155–169, 2000.

First, in comparing the results on 8 nodes to 32 nodes, we find that the effects of increasing contention for shared data are evident in the increasing latency to retrieve data. In the worst case, latency increased by 245%.

Second, in one case, the Barnes-Hut program from the SPLASH benchmark suite [9], the HLRC protocol handles contention more effectively than the Tmk protocol. It more evenly distributes the number of messages handled by each node.

Third, the distribution of the number of messages handled by each node is no less important than the total number of messages. For example, in Barnes-Hut, eliminating the message load imbalance under Tmk (through protocol modifications), brought Tmk's performance to the same level as HLRC's, even though Tmk sends 12 times more messages than HLRC.

The rest of this paper is organized as follows. Section 2 provides an overview of TreadMarks and HLRC's multiple-writer protocols. Section 3 discusses the sources of contention in greater detail and defines the notion of protocol load imbalance. Section 4 details the experimental platform that we used and the programs that we ran on it. Section 5 presents the results of our evaluation. Section 6 compares our results to related work in the area. Finally, Section 7 summarizes our conclusions.

2   Background

2.1   Lazy Release Consistency

The TreadMarks (Tmk) protocol [5] and the Princeton home-based (HLRC) protocol [11] are multiple-writer implementations of lazy release consistency (LRC) [5].

Lazy release consistency (LRC) [5] is an algorithm that implements the release consistency (RC) [4] memory model. RC is a relaxed memory model in which ordinary accesses are distinguished from synchronization accesses. There are two types of synchronization access: acquire and release. Roughly speaking, acquire and release accesses are used to implement the corresponding operations on a lock. In general, a synchronization mechanism must perform an acquire access before entering a critical section and a release access before exiting. Essentially, the benefit of RC is that it allows the effects of ordinary memory accesses to be delayed until a subsequent release access by the same processor.

The LRC algorithm [5] further delays the propagation of modifications to a processor until that processor executes an acquire. Specifically, LRC insures that the memory seen by the processor after an acquire is consistent with the happened-before-1 partial order [1], which is the union of the total processor order of the memory accesses on each individual processor and the partial order of release-acquire access pairs.

2.2   TreadMarks and Home-Based LRC

The main difference between Tmk and HLRC is in the location where updates are kept and in the way that a processor validates its copy of a page. In Tmk, processors validate a page by fetching diffs from the last writer or writers to the page. In HLRC, every page is statically assigned a home processor by the programmer. Writers flush their modifications to the home node at release time. To validate a page a processor requests a copy of the entire page from the home. The difference between the protocols is the most evident for falsely shared pages. The home-based protocol uses significantly fewer messages as the number of falsely sharing readers and writers increases. Specifically, for R readers and W writers, the home-based protocol uses at most $2W + 2R$ messages and the Tmk protocol uses at most $2WR$ messages. On the other hand, Tmk's reliance on diffs to validate pages can result in substantial bandwidth savings.

3   Contention and Protocol Load Imbalance

In this section, we introduce the concepts of contention and protocol load imbalance. We give some intuition for the characteristics of Tmk and HLRC that may lead to contention and protocol load imbalance.

3.1   Contention

We define *contention* as simultaneous requests on a node. In our platform, contention can be attributed to limitations in the node or the network. In the former case, the time that the node requires to process a request is longer than it takes for the next request to arrive. In the latter case, the node fails to push out responses fast enough due to bandwidth limitations in the network link. Most systems, under this condition, wait for the interface to free an entry in its output queue. Contention is said to be single-paged, when all requests are for the same page, or multi-paged, when distinct pages are being requested from the same node.

3.2   Protocol Load Imbalance

We refer to the work performed to propagate updates as protocol load (PL). We then define PL imbalance as the difference in PL across the nodes of the system. Under Tmk, PL reflects time spent servicing requests. For HLRC, it also includes time spent pushing modifications to home nodes. As Tmk and HLRC differ in the location where updates are kept, the protocols may have a different effect on the PL balance.

To illustrate the difference, consider a multi-page data structure that has a single writer followed by multiple readers. Both Tmk and HLRC handle each page of the data structure in similar ways. Each reader sends a request message to the processor holding the latest copy of the page. That processor sends back a reply message containing either the changes to the page in Tmk, or a complete copy of the page in HLRC. Where the protocols differ is in the location of the updates. In Tmk, the last writer is the source of the updates, while in HLRC the updates are kept at the home nodes. Hence, Tmk places the load of distributing multiple copies of the entire data structure on the last writer. In contrast, in HLRC, a clever home assignment may result in a more balanced distribution of the load among the nodes.

4   Experimental Environment

4.1   Platform

We perform the evaluation on a switched, full-duplex 100 Mbps Ethernet network of thirty-two 300 MHz Pentium II-based uniprocessors running FreeBSD 2.2.6. On this platform, the round-trip latency for a 1-byte message is 126 microseconds. The time to acquire a lock varies from 178 to 272 microseconds. The time for a 32-processor barrier is 1,333 microseconds. The time to obtain a diff varies from 313 to 1,544 microseconds, depending on the size of the diff. The time to obtain a full page is 1,308 microseconds.

Table 1. Program Characteristics.

Program	Size, Iter.	Seq. Time (sec.)	Home Distr.
SOR	8kx4k, 20	72.23	Block
3D FFT	7x7x7, 10	101.35	Block
Gauss	4096, 1	477.68	Cyclic
Barnes-Hut	65536, 3	125.69	Block

4.2   Programs

We use four programs: Red-Black SOR and Gaussian Elimination are computational kernels that are distributed with TreadMarks; 3D FFT is from the NAS benchmark suite [2]; and Barnes-Hut is from the SPLASH benchmark suite [9].

Table 1 lists for each program the problem size, the sequential execution time, and the (static) assignment strategy of pages to homes for HLRC. These strategies were selected through considerable experimentation and yield the best performance.

Red-Black SOR is a method for solving partial differential equations by iterating over a two-dimensional shared array. Each processor is assigned a band of rows. Communication is limited to the elements in boundary rows.

Gauss implements Gaussian Elimination with partial pivoting on linear equations stored in a two-dimensional shared array. The computation on the rows is distributed across the processors in a round-robin fashion. In addition to the shared array for storing the coefficients of the equations, an index variable storing the pivot row number is also shared.

3D FFT solves a partial differential equation using three-dimensional forward and inverse FFT. The program has two shared data structures, an array of elements and an array of checksums. The computation is decomposed so that every iteration includes local computation and a global transpose.

Barnes-Hut performs an N-body simulation using the hierarchical Barnes-Hut method. There are two shared data structures: a tree used to represent the recursively decomposed subdomains (cells) of the three-dimensional physical domain containing all the particles, and an array of particles corresponding to the leaves of the tree. Every iteration rebuilds the tree on a single node followed by a parallel force evaluation of the particles, during which most of the tree is read by all nodes.

5   Results

In this section, we present the results of running each of the programs on 8 and 32 processors. Figures 1 and 2 present the speedups and a breakdown of the execution time for each of the programs. Table 2 shows the variation in average response time. It also provides the average number of page update requests per node, the total data transferred, and the global message count. Figures 3, 5, 7, 9, and 10 show the response time histograms. Finally, Figures 4,6, 8, 11, and 12 show the protocol load histograms. For brevity, we only provide plots for HLRC when the results differ significantly from Tmk (i.e. Barnes-Hut). For most applications, we only present results for runs on 32 nodes. The response time and protocol load histograms for 8 node runs were all similar to the contention free Red-Black plots (Figures 3 and 4), as in our platform at least, contention effects become significant only at a scale larger than 8 nodes. Some of the above figures and tables also present results for optimized versions of Tmk, which will be discussed in Section 5.2.

The breakdown of the execution time for each program (Figure 2) has three components: `memory` is the time spent waiting to update a page; `synchro` is time waiting for synchronization to complete; and `computation` includes all other time.

The response time histograms plot the time necessary to fulfill every request sent by every node in the system. On the horizontal axis is time in hundreds of microseconds to complete a request. On the vertical axis is the percentage of requests sent by all nodes that required a given amount of time to complete.

The protocol load histograms plot the time spent servicing remote requests by each node. Each bar is composed of three elements: `communication` corresponds to time spent receiving and decoding requests, as well as sending replies; `diff` corresponds to time spent building diffs; and `spin` corresponds to time spent waiting for the network interface to free an entry in its output queue. For Gauss, the protocol load histograms reflect only the time elapsed during the 8th iteration, instead of the entire execution. This finer resolution is necessary to show the imbalance in protocol load that occurs during an iteration.

Red-Black SOR is included as a control program. It is a program that achieves good scalability (with a speedup of 25.7 on 32 processors) and does not suffer from increases in response time, as can be appreciated by the small memory component in Figure 2, as well as by the minor variations in the shape of the response time histograms of Figure 3. Furthermore, it exhibits little contention and has a good balance of protocol load, which is evident in the similar size of the bars of the histogram in Figure 4. For the rest of this section, we will use the Red-Black SOR response time measurements, response time histograms, and the protocol load histograms to illustrate how response time, response time histograms, and protocol load histograms should look in the absence of contention and protocol load imbalances.

We argue that the increase in access miss time experienced by our programs is largely a result of the increase in latency for individual requests due to contention and not solely the result of an increased number of request messages.

This trend is most evident for 3D FFT and Gauss. In 3D FFT, the average number of requests per node drops significantly as the size of the cluster increases. In Gauss, it increases moderately (10.7%). Both programs, however, experience sharp increases in response time. The average request latency increases for 3D FFT and Gauss by 46% and 245%, respectively (see Table 2).

The rest of this section is divided into two parts. First, we talk about the various types of contention exhibited by our programs and how they increase the latency of individual requests. Second, we quantify the effect that contention has on the programs' speedups by eliminating contention manually or automatically.

Table 2. Average response time, average number of pages updated per node, total data transfered and total message count of Tmk, HLRC, and Tmk with optimizations.

Application	Protocol	Avg. resp. time (micro sec.)		Avg. per node updates		Data (MBytes)		Messages (thousands)	
		8	32	8	32	8	32	8	32
SOR	Tmk	1592.33	1668.53	100	125	6	27	2	10
	HLRC	1400.43	1474.77	83	106	7	34	2	10
3DFFT	Tmk	2017.00	2963.19	4041	1125	265	295	66	91
	HLRC	1988.77	2918.72	4041	1125	265	297	65	74
	Opt.	1668.26	1870.31	4041	1125	265	295	66	91
Gauss	Tmk	2595.65	8954.12	8957	9910	357	1581	201	888
	HLRC	2882.89	8640.11	8957	9910	562	2586	201	888
	HLRC	1036.02	1036.02	8957	9910	46	60	73	268
Barnes	Tmk	1630.94	5534.01	2442	2026	130	488	144	1535
	HLRC	1655.81	2033.12	2072	1930	154	529	34	129
	Opt.	1510.39	1734.28	2442	2026	130	448	144	1535

5.1   Types of Contention

3D FFT suffers from multi-page contention. In 3D FFT, processors work on a contiguous band of elements from the shared array. Since HLRC assigns homes

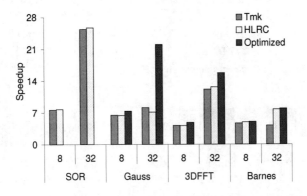

Fig. 1. Speedup of applications for Tmk, HLRC, and Tmk Optimized.

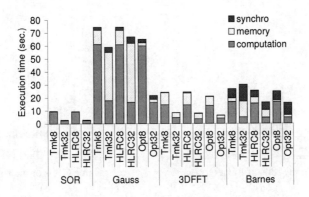

Fig. 2. Execution time breakdown for Tmk, HLRC, and Tmk Optimized.

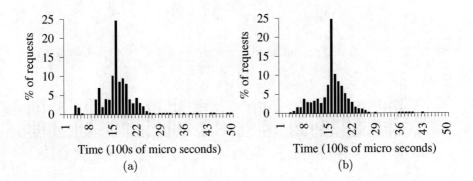

Fig. 3. RB-SOR response time for Tmk with 8 (a) and 32 (b) nodes.

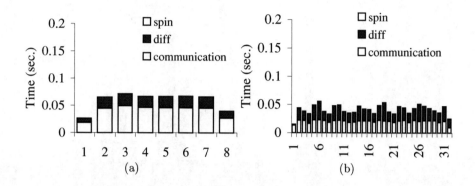

Fig. 4. RB-SOR protocol load for Tmk with 8 (a) and 32 (b) nodes. The plots show the time spent in communication, creating diffs, and waiting for the network interface.

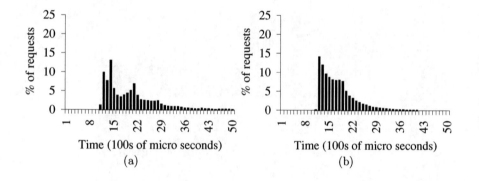

Fig. 5. 3D FFT response time for Tmk (a) and Tmk Optimized (b) on 32 nodes.

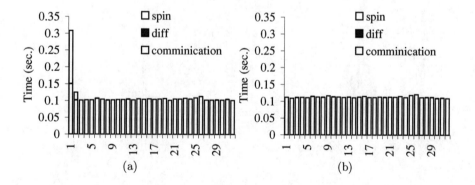

Fig. 6. 3D FFT protocol load for Tmk (a) and Tmk Optimized (b) on 32 nodes.

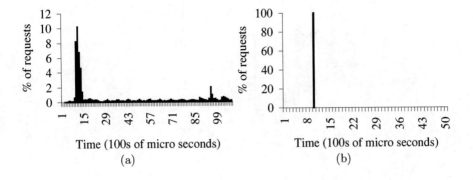

Fig. 7. Gauss response time for Tmk (a) and Tmk Optimized(b) on 32 nodes.

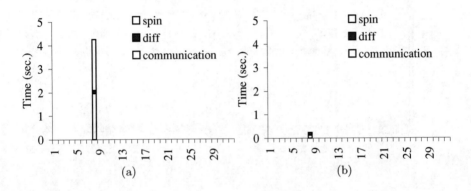

Fig. 8. Gauss protocol load for Tmk (a) and Tmk Optimized (b) on 32 nodes.

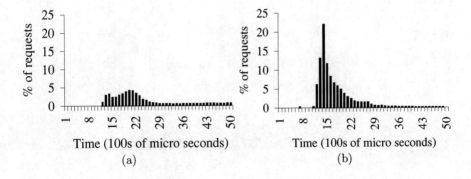

Fig. 9. Barnes-Hut response time for Tmk (a) and Tmk Optimized (b) on 32 nodes.

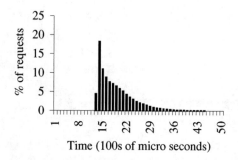

Fig. 10. Barnes-Hut response time for HLRC on 32 nodes.

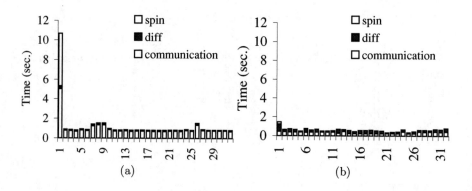

Fig. 11. Barnes-Hut protocol load for Tmk (a) and Tmk Optimized (b) on 32 nodes.

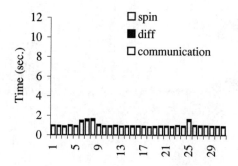

Fig. 12. Barnes-Hut protocol load for HLRC on 32 nodes.

in block fashion, in both protocols the processor modifying the band will be the one hosting the update. The computation on the 3D arrays is partitioned along one axis among the processors. As a result, the global transpose leads to all processors trying to read some pages first from processor 0, then some pages from processor 1, and so on, resulting in a temporal contention at a single processor at a time. The effects of contention are visible in the response time histogram in Figure 5(a). When we compare this plot to the Red-Black SOR response time histogram (Figure 3(b)), we see that it consists of shorter bars that are shifted to the right, which suggest a significant increase in response time.

The effects of contention are also visible in the protocol load histogram (Figure 6(a)), which shows an imbalance in protocol load, with the two left most processors having significant higher loads. This imbalance is somehow surprising, since during an iteration, all nodes service the same number of requests. Closer consideration, however, reveals that, as mentioned above, at the start of an iteration all processors, at once, try to fetch data from processor 0. The simultaneous requests create contention on this processor, as is evidenced by the high spin component in the plot. As processor 0 services these request, however, it staggers the replies, implicitly ordering and distributing them over time. The staggering of replies produces less contention on the next round of communications, as is evidenced by the smaller wait component of the next processor. Processor 1 further accentuates this trend.

Gauss suffers from single-page contention. The access pattern for the pivot row is single-writer/multiple-reader. There are only two such pages for our problem size, but their producer changes on every iteration. The severity of contention in Gauss within each interval is reflected in the large increase in response time shown in Table 2 (almost 245%) and in the response time histogram of Figure 7(a). The large degradation in response is reflected in the shape of this plot, which shows bars that are more spread out, shorter, and shifted to the right, compared to the contention-free Red-Black SOR plot (Figure 3(b)). The increase in response is attributed to the large imbalance in protocol load shown in 8(a), where all the protocol load is concentrated in processor 8, the last writer to the pivot row and pivot index. The large spin component in this Tmk plot results from the backlog of large reply messages containing the pivot row and index in the network interface's output queue.

Barnes-Hut suffers from single-page and multi-page contention. The tree and the array of particles in Barnes-Hut suffer from single-page contention when read in the same order by multiple nodes. Additionally, multi-page contention occurs when updates for multiple parts of the data structures reside at any given node. For Barnes-Hut, there is a significant difference in the rate of latency increase between Tmk and HLRC. While the average response time for HLRC increases slowly, it almost doubles with an increase in the number of nodes for Tmk (see Table 2). This is supported by the rapid dispersion of the bars in the Tmk response time histogram (Figure 9(a)) while the HLRC response time histogram (Figure 10) resembles the contention free Red-Black SOR plot

(Figure 3(b)). We argue in the next section that differences in protocol load balance account for the disparity in response time.

5.2 Quantifying the Effects of Contention

We quantify the effects of contention on our programs by manually tuning the application or the protocol to remove the sources of contention. For each application we describe the contention removal technique we used and discuss the effects on the speedup, load balance and response time. Figures 1 and 2 also include the speedups and breakdown of execution time for the optimized version of Tmk, while Table 2 shows the variations in average response time. Finally, Figures 5(b), 7(b), and 9(b) show the response time histograms, and Figures 6(b), 8(b), and 11(b) show the protocol load histograms.

3D FFT. The contention in 3D FFT can be eliminated by carefully restructuring the transpose loop. By staggering the remote accesses of different consumers such that they access pages on different producers in parallel, the speedup of 3D FFT using Tmk is improved from 12.62 to 15.73 on 32 nodes. The optimization achieves a reduction in response time of 27% (see Table 2), and response time and protocol load histograms that resemble the contention-free case (compare Figures 5(b) and 6(b) to Figures 3(b) and 4(b)).

Gauss. The contention in Gauss can be eliminated by broadcasting the pages containing the pivot row and pivot index. Using a manually inserted broadcast improves Tmk speedup for Gauss from 8.11 to 22.05 on 32 nodes. The optimization achieves a 88% reduction in response time (see Table 2) and 94% in protocol load (compare Figures 8(a) and (b)). Figure 7(b) shows all responses clustered in a single bar at the 1000 microseconds bin. In fact, response times vary within tens of micro seconds, but because of the scaling effects this is not visible. The average response time of 1036 microseconds, which is lower than the contention free time for updating a page, results from the eliminating the request message.

Barnes-Hut. Protocol load imbalance accounts for the difference in speedup (4.18 vs. 7.73) and request latency experienced between Tmk and HLRC for Barnes-Hut.

To prove this claim we added *striping* to the Tmk protocol. Striping reduces contention by automatically eliminating protocol imbalances created by multi-page data structures with a single writer and multiple readers. Striping identifies these data structures and automatically distributes them to other processors (i.e. new homes) at the next global synchronization point. As a result, the writer's effort on behalf of each page that it off-loads is limited to constructing and sending the diff to a single processor. The processor receiving this diff is then responsible for servicing the requests from all of the consumers. Overall, neither the number of messages nor the amount of data transferred is reduced, but the average time that a reader waits for its requested diff drops.

The high load imbalance in Tmk (Figure 11(a)) results from the distribution of the updates for the tree in Barnes-Hut. In Tmk updates are always fetched from the last writer, hence processor 0 has to supply all updates to the tree in Barnes-Hut. As processor 0 gets overwhelmed by requests for updates to the tree, it has to spend an increasing portion of its execution time servicing requests. On the 32 node cluster this time accounts for 35.6% of the total execution time. Of that time, 50.42% is spent blocked waiting for the network interface to clear the output queue.

In contrast (Figure 12), HLRC greatly alleviates the contention for reading the tree by spreading the homes for these data structures across the processors. Specifically, if the tree covers n pages and every processor reads the whole tree, then Tmk requires processor 0 to service $(p-1)*n$ page requests. HLRC instead distributes the tree in $n*(p-1)/p$ messages. After that the load of servicing the tree requests is evenly distributed.

Tmk with striping eliminates protocol load imbalance caused by requests from multiple processors to processor 0 in order to obtain the tree data and achieves response time (Figure 9(b)), protocol load imbalances (Figure 11(b)), and speedups (Figure 1) that are comparable to HLRC.

The results from Tmk with striping demonstrate that (for this application, at least) there is a relationship between protocol balance and response time: as protocol imbalance grows, so does response time. This is an expected result; when the proportion of updates originating from any given node grows, the likelihood of simultaneous requests (i.e., contention) on that node increases. Furthermore, these results show that the distribution of the messages is no less important than the number of messages. For example, Tmk with striping and HLRC transfer roughly equal amounts of data and have identical message distributions. Although Tmk with striping sends 12 times more messages than HLRC, they achieve the same speedup.

Nonetheless, Tmk/stripe and HLRC still suffer from contention, as shown by the difference in average response time when compared to the control (1734.28 for Barnes-Hut vs. 1474.77 for SOR). This contention results from the several nodes transversing the data structures in the same order. As various parts reside in the same node, simultaneous requests for updates may still reach the nodes. That is, the distribution of updates to various processors does not eliminate contention for the data, it only makes it less frequent on a particular node.

6   Related Work

A large number of software shared memory systems have been built. Many of the papers looking at the performance of software DSM on thirty-two or more processors have used SMP-based nodes [7,8,10]. Thus, the actual number of nodes on the network is typically a factor of two to eight less than the number of processors. Because requests for the same page from multiple processors within a node are combined into one, the load on the processor(s) servicing the page may not be as high as when the number of nodes in the network equals the number of processors. These studies have ignored the effects of contention and protocol load imbalance, as these become significant only on a network with a large number of nodes.

Two papers that look at large networks of uniprocessors are Zhou et al. [11] and Bal et al. [3]. Zhou et al. evaluated the home-based lazy release consistency protocol against the basic LRC protocol on an Intel Paragon. The relatively large message latency, page fault, and interrupt times compared with memory and network bandwidth, and the extremely high cost of diff creation on the Paragon architecture are uncommon in modern parallel platforms and favor the HLRC protocol. The high diff cost led the authors to conclude that the performance gap between Tmk and HLRC results from the vast differences in message count. We show that the performance gap results, instead, from the difference in protocol load balance.

Bal et al. evaluated Orca, an object-based distributed shared memory system, on a Myrinet and a Fast Ethernet network of 32 200MHz Pentium Pro computers. The object-based DSM system decreases the number of messages and data resulting from reduced false sharing at the cost of the programmer's extra effort to explicitly associate shared data structures with objects. Objects with low read/write ratio are stored in a single processor, while those with high read/write ratio are replicated on all processors using multicast.

7   Conclusions and Discussion

We show that memory latency increases due to contention and protocol load imbalances are a significant obstacle to the scalability of software DSM systems. For example, in one case, memory latency increased by 245% as the number of nodes increased from 8 to 32. Furthermore, there is relationship between contention and protocol load balance: Higher protocol load imbalance usually results in increased contention. Intuitively, an increase in the proportion of data distributed from a node increases the likelihood of simultaneous requests to that node. Thus, we argue that contention reduction and protocol load balancing should be considered, in addition to message reduction, by designers of scalable DSM systems.

Overall, on our platform, contention has a profound effect on performance even at the modest scale of 32 nodes. In 3D FFT, the contention was caused by multiple processors accessing different single-writer/single-reader pages at the same time. By manually restructuring the transpose loop, we found that the execution time could be reduced by 20% on 32 nodes. In Barnes-Hut, we found that protocol load imbalance caused HLRC to outperform Tmk by 84% on 32 nodes. Eliminating the load imbalance brings the performance of Tmk on par with HLRC. Finally, in Gauss, the contention is due to a single-writer/multiple-reader sharing pattern. In this case, two or three pages are read at a time, and each page is only read once by each processor (other than its producer). Using a manually inserted broadcast, we were able to reduce the execution time on 32 nodes by 64%.

In our future work, we hope to automate the use of broadcast and load balancing to achieve these results transparently.

References

1. S.V. Adve and M.D. Hill. A unified formalization of four shared-memory models. *IEEE Transactions on Parallel and Distributed Systems*, 4(6):613–624, June 1993.
2. D. Bailey, J. Barton, T. Lasinski, and H. Simon. The NAS parallel benchmarks. Technical Report TR RNR-91-002, NASA Ames, August 1991.
3. H.E. Bal, R. Bhoedjang, R. Hofman, C. Jacobs, K. Langendoen, T. Ruhl, and M.F. Kaashoek. Performance evaluation of the Orca shared object system. *ACM Transactions on Computer Systems*, 16(1), February 1998.
4. K. Gharachorloo, D. Lenoski, J. Laudon, P. Gibbons, A. Gupta, and J. Hennessy. Memory consistency and event ordering in scalable shared-memory multiprocessors. In *Proceedings of the 17th Annual International Symposium on Computer Architecture*, pages 15–26, May 1990.
5. P. Keleher, A. L. Cox, and W. Zwaenepoel. Lazy release consistency for software distributed shared memory. In *Proceedings of the 19th Annual International Symposium on Computer Architecture*, pages 13–21, May 1992.
6. P. Keleher, S. Dwarkadas, A. L. Cox, and W. Zwaenepoel. Treadmarks: Distributed shared memory on standard workstations and operating systems. In *Proceedings of the 1994 Winter Usenix Conference*, pages 115–131, January 1994.
7. R. Samanta, A. Bilas, L. Iftode, and J.P. Singh. Home-based SVM protocols for SMP clusters: design and performance. In *Proceedings of the Fourth International Symposium on High-Performance Computer Architecture*, February 1998.
8. D.J. Scales, K. Gharachorloo, and C.A. Thekkath. Shasta: A low overhead software-only approach for supporting fine-grain shared memory. In *Proceedings of the 7th Symposium on Architectural Support for Programming Languages and Operating Systems*, October 1996.
9. J.P. Singh, W.-D. Weber, and A. Gupta. SPLASH: Stanford parallel applications for shared-memory. Technical Report CSL-TR-91-469, Stanford University, April 1991.
10. R. Stets, S. Dwarkadas, N. Hardavellas, G. Hunt, L. Kontothanassis, S. Parthasarathy, and M. Scott. Cashmere-2L: Software coherent shared memory on a clustered remote write network. In *Proceedings of the 16th ACM Symposium on Operating Systems Principles*, October 1997.
11. Y. Zhou, L. Iftode, and K. Li. Performance evaluation of two home-based lazy release consistency protocols for shared virtual memory systems. In *Proceedings of the Second USENIX Symposium on Operating System Design and Implementation*, pages 75–88, nov 1996.

Measuring Consistency Costs for Distributed Shared Data

Christopher Diaz and James Griffioen

Department of Computer Science
University of Kentucky
Lexington, KY 40506 USA
{diaz,griff}@dcs.uky.edu

Abstract. Distributed Shared Memory (DSM) systems typically support one consistency protocol [3,5,6]. However, recent work [1,11,12,14,17] proposes the use of adaptive consistency based on a heuristical analysis of recent access patterns. Although heuristic-based approaches can significantly improve runtime, the access pattern alone does not necessarily define the most appropriate consistency protocol. The size of updates and other factors related to the computing environment, such as heavily loaded links, heavily loaded nodes, bursty traffic patterns, and network latency all affect performance. Multiple access patterns within the application also make it difficult to select the most appropriate consistency protocol. This paper presents a measurement-based approach to the problem of selecting the most appropriate consistency protocol for the current application in the current runtime environment. We show that measurement-based analysis provides an accurate estimate of performance and therefore can be used to select the most appropriate consistency protocol, even in cases where hueristic-based approaches fail to select the appropriate protocol.

1 Introduction

Compute-intensive applications such as hydrodynamics, weather forecasting and genetic analysis play a vital role in scientific communities. These applications often require hours, days, or longer to execute, even on large-scale multicomputers. Performance speedup for these types of applications requires scaling the number of machines. As the number of machines increases, providing consistency among the machines becomes more costly. Consequently, selection of the *most appropriate* consistency protocol becomes very important for large-scale multicomputers.

Past DSM research has resulted in a variety of consistency protocols [5,6,8,13]. However, the most appropriate consistency protocol for a given application is difficult to identify and depends on a wide range of factors. In most systems, the application is stuck with whatever consistency protocol the DSM provides.

Some recent work, however, has explored the concept of adaptive consistency in which the DSM observes the application's access pattern and then selects an appropriate consistency protocol [1,11,12,14,17]. Given an application's recent access pattern, the DSM uses heuristics to map the observed access pattern to

S. Dwarkadas (Ed.): LCR 2000, LNCS 1915, pp. 170–181, 2000.
© Springer-Verlag Berlin Heidelberg 2000

a consistency protocol. For example, if a machine writes to shared data that is subsequently read by N other machines, the DSM may decide to use an update-based approach, such as that used in Eager Release Consistency systems [6,16], where the newly written data is immediately disseminated to the N machines. On the other hand, if a machine writes to shared data that is subsequently read or written by a seemingly random machine, the DSM may take an on-demand approach, like that in Entry Consistency systems [5] or Lazy Release Consistency systems [13] to delay the update until the data is needed.

While heuristic-based approaches can significantly improve performance, they do not always select the best consistency protocol for the application in the current environment. As one example, consider iterative applications that alternate between access patterns, such as the SPLASH2 [20] Water-Nsquared (Water) and NAS [4] Integer Sort (IS) applications. Both applications exhibit an access pattern where shared data is written and then read by a set of machines. Later, both applications exhibit another access pattern where the same set of machines wait, in turn, to write the data. A heuristic-based approach that only analyzes access patterns may choose an update-based protocol because it sees the set requires updates at least some of the time. However, as we show in section 5, the size of updates relative to the network bandwidth or congestion can influence which protocol is most appropriate, and Water exhibits sparse writes compared to IS. Consequently, an update protocol is most appropriate for Water but is often not appropriate for IS.

As a second example, again consider applications with alternating access patterns. A heuristic-based approach may change consistency protocols to react to each change in the access pattern. However, unless the consistency protocol change is made quickly, the access pattern may immediately change again, as in the IS application. Here, such a heuristic-based approach often does not use an appropriate consistency protocol.

As a third example, consider an application where each machine writes to distinct shared data, synchronizes at a barrier, then reads the data written by all other machines. A heuristic-based approach typically selects an update-based protocol for this type of access pattern. However, other factors such as network congestion, caused by the burst of communication activity at the barrier may severely degrade performance to the point where an on-demand consistency protocol would have been better.

This paper presents a new measurement-based adaptive approach to select consistency protocols. The objective is to measure consistency protocol performance to get a clearer picture of an application's performance in the current runtime environment. The DSM estimates application runtime differences between consistency protocols by measuring each protocol's consistency related activity. This approach eliminates the need for an "active user" approach, where the user actively modifies application code, executes the application once with each consistency protocol, notes the runtime for each execution, and finally chooses a protocol. We also note that the appropriate protocol may change over the course of execution because of a remapping of work to machines or a change in the algorithm. In these cases, an active user approach is impractical because the user must detect the change, stop the application, modify application code, then restart or continue the application. To handle these situations, we are currently investigating ways for the DSM to continually reevaluate and rechoose appropriate protocols as necessary.

We present three approaches for measuring consistency overhead. Although these approaches differ in their degree of accuracy, we show that all three approaches can (1) be used to accurately determine the most appropriate consistency protocol for an application in the measured runtime environment, and (2) be used to accurately estimate the expected speedup (or slowdown) of one consistency protocol over another.

The basic mode of operation is quite simple and works as follows. A long running distributed application begins executing. Initially the DSM selects a consistency protocol, say an on-demand one. After some period P, the DSM changes to another consistency protocol. Again, after another period P, the DSM changes to a third consistency protocol. The application is unaware of changes to the consistency protocol. After measuring overhead of each consistency protocol, the DSM computes the expected runtime difference of one protocol over another and selects the protocol with the lowest observed runtime in the current environment.

The paper is organized as follows. Section 2 discusses DSM consistency protocols and other approaches to provide the most appropriate protocol for an application. Section 3 describes our measurement environment and application interface. Section 4 describes the approaches used to measure and estimate consistency costs. Section 5 presents experimental results obtained from a prototype system. Finally, we summarize our work in section 6.

2   Related Work

Traditional DSMs [3,5,6,9,10] each typically provide applications with one consistency protocol. Such systems cannot provide the most appropriate consistency protocol for every application. Systems that provide more than one consistency protocol require the application programmer to specify the desired one, which requires detailed analysis of application or protocol behavior.

Recent works enhance DSM to adaptively choose a consistency protocol for shared data at runtime to provide the most appropriate protocol for runtime speedup. Adaptive consistency may also alleviate the application programmer of burdens such as the need to analyze an application.

Keleher [11,12] modified CVM to provide a heuristic-based invalidate/update hybrid protocol so that after every write to shared data, CVM propagates updates to machines that previously faulted on the data. In situations when a machine does not read every write to shared data, however, the protocol may send unnecessary updates to the machine.

Monnerat and Bianchini presented ADSM [17] to enhance Lazy Release Consistency [13] in TreadMarks [3] with update protocols for lock-protected and barrier-protected data to reduce fault latency. In the case of lock-protected data, when the lock is acquired, ADSM propagates changes made when the lock was previously held. For barrier-protected data, ADSM heuristically analyzes the data's access pattern during the preceding three barriers. If during that period, only one machine modifies the data, ADSM then determines the readers in that same period. After the data is again written, ADSM propagates updates to the readers. If the access pattern changes after only one or two barriers, as in IS, the protocol does not change.

Rice developed ATMK [1,2] to also supplement Lazy Release Consistency in TreadMarks with update protocols for lock-protected and barrier-protected data. ATMK reduces fault latency for lock-protected data with the technique used in ADSM. For barrier-protected data, ATMK heuristically analyzes the data's recent access pattern. At a barrier, ATMK propagates updates for data to machines that previously requested the data. If a machine receives such an update but did not access the previous update, the machine sends a NACK to prevent future propagation. When the access pattern frequently changes, as in IS, ATMK chooses an on-demand protocol when an update-based protocol is appropriate and then chooses an update-based protocol when an on-demand consistency protocol is appropriate.

Tapeworm[14] provides the abstraction of a *tape* for an application to record a series of shared data accesses. When the application later executes the same code, the application "replays" the tape to provide Tapeworm information about forthcoming accesses. The replay suggests which machines may read a write, so when the write reoccurs, Tapeworm sends updates to those machines and reduces fault latency. However, Tapeworm requires additional application code to manipulate tapes.

Lee and Jhon [15] also supplement Lazy Release Consistency with an update protocol. Their work uses application-level annotations of both shared data writes and the machines that read those writes to determine when and where to send updates after a write. To make such annotations, a programmer must understand the access pattern in detail.

These works either use heuristic-based analysis of access patterns to choose a consistency protocol for shared data or require additional application code, the latter which we do not require. While heuristics often choose the most appropriate protocol, they sometimes do not and may cause runtime slowdown. Our system, on the other hand, estimates the runtime differences between consistency protocols to identify which protocol provides the lowest runtime.

3   Measurement Environment and API

Although our measurement-based approach can be applied to the consistency protocols of any system, we will present the methods in the context of the Unify [7] DSM system. Unify provides a segment-based, single global shared address space. Unify provides multiple consistency protocols: an update protocol like that used in Eager Release Consistency systems [6,16], an on-demand protocol like that used in Entry Consistency systems [5], and a protocol that combines both.

To use adaptive consistency protocols, a Unify application must follow semantics similar to Entry Consistency when accessing a shared segment. In short, one or more machines may concurrently read a segment. However, to write a segment a machine must have mutual exclusive access with respect to all other machines that want to read or write the segment. To mark the beginning and end of a shared segment access, a Unify application invokes Read_Begin(seg) and Read_End(seg) to specify the beginning and end, respectively, of a read-only access to a shared segment. Likewise, an application invokes Write_Begin(seg) and Write_End(seg) to specify the beginning and end, respectively, of a read-write access to a shared segment[1]. Access primitives represent points in the application where the DSM may enforce the current consistency protocol. For example, suppose the DSM uses an on-demand protocol. When the application invokes a BEGIN, the DSM retrieves necessary segment updates. Similarly, when the DSM uses an update-based protocol and the application invokes Write_End(seg), the DSM disseminates segment updates to all other machines.

Unify provides a third consistency protocol, called a *Demand-Update Protocol*, that combines on-demand and update-based approaches. When a machine issues a Write_Begin, the DSM provides an on-demand protocol. However, when a machine issues a Read_Begin, the DSM employs an update-based protocol to disseminate updates to machines that previously read the data. The idea behind this dissemination is that if machines concurrently read the data, the first read after a write is a precursor of reads by the other machines. The dissemination then provides consistency more quickly than, say, on-demand approach that updates the machines one at a time. Our measurement system compares all three consistency protocols.

In this paper, we do not elaborate on how the DSM initially selects a consistency protocol. The DSM may select a consistency protocol or decide when to change to another protocol based on heuristical analysis as described in CVM, ADSM or ATMK. Alternatively, the DSM may change protocols after some period P, where P is defined by the system or application as a period of time or other metric. In this study, P is defined by the application as some fixed number of iterations, because behavior in an iteration tends to indicate behavior in successive iterations [18,19]. The goal of this paper is to measure performance of each protocol in the current runtime environment and then recommend the most appropriate protocol for the application in that environment. In this paper, we also assume that the DSM employs exactly one consistency protocol at a time, but we are exploring ways to measure consistency overhead so that each shared segment may be assigned its own appropriate consistency protocol.

4   Measuring Consistency Overhead

This section describes three ways to measure consistency overhead. In the first approach, called *Access Time (AT)*, the DSM measures the wall clock time from a BEGIN to the corresponding END. AT represents a macro analysis, measuring not only consistency costs but all other costs that occur between the BEGIN

---

[1] In the remainder of the paper we will use the term BEGIN to represent either a Read_Begin or Write_Begin and the term END to represent the corresponding Read_End or Write_End.

and END. The motivation of AT is to measure all of the time machine spends accessing shared data. It can be argued this is the "perceived performance" and is what we want to optimize. Unfortunately, it also measures costs not associated with the segment, such as synchronization or changes in machine load. In the case where BEGIN/END pairs are nested, the DSM measures only the outermost BEGIN and END to represent the contributions of all nested accesses to the consistency overhead.

The second approach, *Wait Time (WT)*, measures the wall clock time a machine waits for consistency activity. The idea behind WT is to measure the time a machine is idle due to consistency activity. It can be argued that this is a better measure of consistency cost, but it ignores the consistency protocol's effect on other components of performance, such as prolonged synchronization activity. When an on-demand protocol is used, WT measures the time a machine waits for updates to arrive at the beginning of a shared region access. When using on update-based protocol, WT measures the time a machine waits while the DSM reliably disseminates updates.

The third approach, *Correlated Wait Time (CWT)*, measures the wall clock time of all consistency activity for which a machine *may* block. The idea behind CWT is to not only measure a machine's idle time, but to also measure the time spent propagating updates. Update propagation may slow the sending machine and delay its forward progress. CWT includes WT time but additionally measures the time from the first to last packet a machine receives via an update protocol. When an on-demand protocol is used, CWT measures the time for a machine to send a reply for an update request. Note that a machine may concurrently receive nested updates for two pieces of shared data. CWT measures such nested updates in a manner similar to AT.

5   Analysis of Measurements

We used the SPLASH2 [20] Water-Nsquared (Water), NAS [4] Integer Sort (IS) and Successive-Over Relaxation (SOR, included in the Unify [7] distribution) benchmarks to estimate and compare runtime differences between consistency protocols. Our test environment consisted of twelve 125MHz HyperSparcs, each with 64MB of physical RAM, interconnected by a 100Mb Ethernet. We separately ran each application with an on-demand protocol (OD), an update-based protocol (UB), then a demand-update consistency protocol (DU). During each execution, the DSM measured the consistency overhead for all approaches. We then compared protocols using the actual and estimated runtime differences to see whether our measurements could identify the most appropriate protocol and see how accurately they estimated runtime differences. To obtain "total runtime performance" information, we selected a consistency protocol and ran the application for a period P, defined in this study by the application as some fixed number of iterations. This was done for each application/consistency protocol combination. During each of these runs, we enabled our code to measure AT, WT and CWT consistency costs as well as runtime. Using the AT, WT and CWT measurements, we estimated the relative performance improvement of one consistency protocol over a second protocol by subtracting the measured cost of the first from that of the second. Similarly, actual performance improvement of one protocol over a second protocol is calculated by subtracting the runtime of the first from that of the second. We then compared our estimated improvement against the actual performance improvement.

For each application, we show four graphs. The first graph shows the total runtime of each consistency protocol. The second graph shows the actual improvement UB gives over OD. It also shows the expected improvement predicted by AT, WT and CWT. The third and fourth graphs are similar to the second, but compare UB to DU and DU to OD, respectively.

In the first experiment (figure 1), Water is executed with 2197 molecules for three iterations. Figure 1(a) shows the total runtime for OD, UB and DU as the number of machines scales from two to twelve. As described in section 1, Water contains two distinct access patterns. In the first access pattern, OD suffers because to read, a machine requests updates and waits, possibly for updates to propagate among other machines first. On the other hand, UB and DU disseminate updates to machines that read the molecules, and thereby reduce wait time. In the second access pattern, machines write in turn to molecules. OD or DU appears better, because they send updates to a machine only when needed. However, the writes are sparse, so the size of updates is small. Consequently, UB does not cause excessive overhead because updates may not be overwritten before a machine needs them. As a result, UB scales better than OD, and DU scales similar to UB.

The solid line in figure 1(b) shows the actual runtime performance improvement obtained by using UB rather than OD (taken from figure 1(a)). The remaining lines in figure 1(b) show the improvement predicted by AT, WT and CWT. Note that AT, WT and CWT all predicted that UB is better than OD. Moreover, they accurately predicted how much the improvement would be. In this case, AT and WT are within 20% of the actual difference, and CWT is within about 40%.

Figures 1(c) and 1(d) show similar comparisons for the improvement of UB over DU and DU over OD, respectively. Again, AT, WT and CWT often correctly predict the most appropriate consistency protocol.

IS sorts 2^{24} keys with density 2^{19} 3 times. Figure 2(a) shows the total runtime for OD, UB and DU as the number of machines scales from four to twelve. IS contains access patterns similar to Water, except that writes to shared data overwrite a large portion of the data. As a result, UB does not scale well because the DSM sends large, unnecessary updates to many machines. While OD scales better than UB, OD suffers when each machine reads all shared data and waits for updates to propagate among machines. DU is most appropriate because it employs an on-demand protocol when machines write to shared data in turn and employs an update-based protocol when each machine reads all shared data.

Figure 2(b) shows the improvements obtained by using UB rather than OD. In this case, UB is worse than OD for more than four machines. AT and WT correctly identify OD as the better protocol, usually within 20% of the actual runtime difference. CWT mostly correctly identifies OD as the better protocol

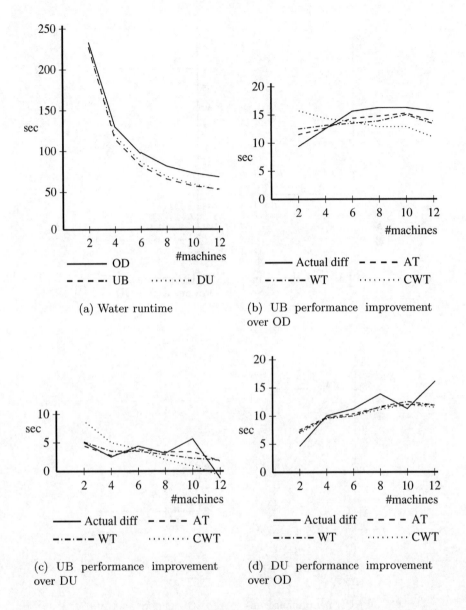

(a) Water runtime

(b) UB performance improvement over OD

(c) UB performance improvement over DU

(d) DU performance improvement over OD

Fig. 1. Measurement analysis of Water: 1(a) runtime in seconds; 1(b) actual and estimated runtime performance of an update-based protocol (UB) over an on-demand protocol (OD); 1(c) actual and estimated performance of UB over a demand-update protocol (DU), and; 1(d) actual and estimated performance of DU over OD.

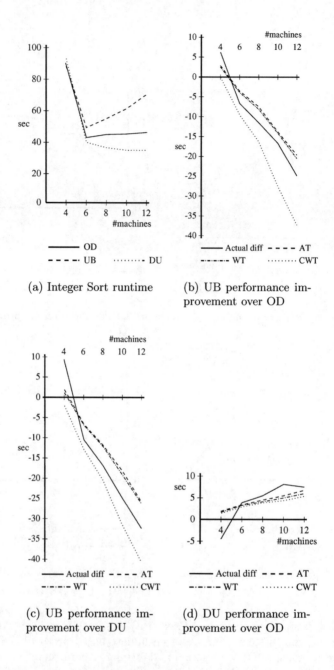

(a) Integer Sort runtime

(b) UB performance improvement over OD

(c) UB performance improvement over DU

(d) DU performance improvement over OD

Fig. 2. Measurement analysis of Integer Sort: 2(a) runtime in seconds; 2(b) actual and estimated runtime performance of an update-based protocol (UB) over an on-demand protocol (OD); 2(c) actual and estimated performance of UB over a demand-update protocol (DU), and; 2(d) actual and estimated performance of DU over OD .

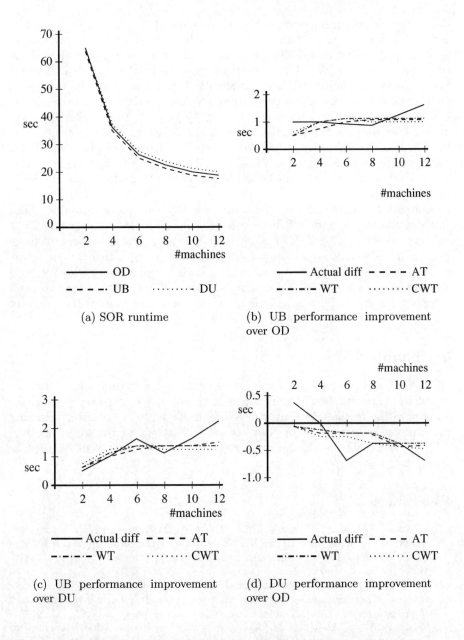

(a) SOR runtime

(b) UB performance improvement over OD

(c) UB performance improvement over DU

(d) DU performance improvement over OD

Fig. 3. Measurement analysis of SOR: 3(a) runtime in seconds; 3(b) actual and estimated runtime performance of an update-based protocol (UB) over an on-demand protocol (OD); 3(c) actual and estimated performance of UB over a demand-update protocol (DU), and; 3(d) actual and estimated performance of DU over OD.

but overestimates the improvement by 50%. Figure 2(c) is similar. In figure 2(d), AT, WT and CWT usually all accurately predict DU as the most appropriate.

SOR is executed on a 1000x1000 grid for 100 iterations. Figure 3(a) shows the total runtime for OD, UB and DU as the number of machines scales from two to twelve. Although UB appears slightly better than OD, the two are so close, it is difficult to accurately predict which one is better. As a result, we see that the improvement predicted in figure 3(b) by AT, WT and CWT dances around 0 seconds. In this case, the system is best off using a *threshold* to say that the predicted improvement is too close to 0 to be accurate. On the other hand, whichever protocol is predicted will not significantly affect performance either way, so either protocol will not be too bad a choice. This situation is similar in figures 3(c) and 3(d).

Out of 51 LAN situations (three each for six Water, five IS and six SOR configurations), AT and WT both correctly identified 48 (94%), while CWT correctly identified 47 (92%). In most cases where a prediction was incorrect, the performance difference was close to zero, and one can argue that the prediction was too close to call. In these cases, an incorrect selection gives roughly the same performance as a correct selection. Furthermore, CWT correctly identifies cases for larger numbers of machines. All approaches estimate runtime improvement usually within 20% to 30% of the actual difference.

6   Summary

We present three approaches for DSM to measure consistency related activity in order to (1) accurately identify the most appropriate consistency protocol for an application in the given runtime environment, and (2) accurately estimate the expected speedup (or slowdown) of one consistency protocol over another. AT, WT and CWT are all good at identifying the most appropriate consistency protocol.

References

1. C. Amza, A. L. Cox, S. Dwarkadas, L.-J. Jin, K. Rajamani, and W. Zwaenepoel. Adaptive protocols for software distributed shared memory. In *Proceedings of IEEE, Special Issue on Distributed Shared Memory*, volume 87, pages 467–475, March 1999.
2. C. Amza, A. L. Cox, S. Dwarkadas, and W. Zwaenepoel. Software DSM protocols that adapt between single writer and multiple writer. In *Proceedings of the Third High Performance Computer Architecture Conference*, pages 261–271, Feb 1997.
3. Cristiana Amza, Alan L. Cox, Sandhya Dwarkadas, Pete Keleher, Honghui Lu, Ramakrishnan Rajamony, Weimin Yu, and Willy Zwaenepoel. Treadmarks: Shared memory computing on networks of workstations. *IEEE Computer*, 29(2):18–28, Feb 1996.
4. D. Bailey, J. Barton, T. Lasinski, and H. Simon. The nas parallel benchmarks. Technical Report TR RNR-91-002, NASA Ames, Aug 1991.
5. Brian N. Bershad, Matthew J. Zekauskas, and Wayne A. Sawdon. The Midway distributed shared memory system. In *Proceedings of the IEEE CompCon Conference*, 1993.

6. John B. Carter, John K. Bennett, and Willy Zwaenepoel. Implementation and performance of Munin. In *Proceedings of 13th ACM symposium on Operating Systems principles*, pages 152–64, Oct 1991.

7. James Griffioen, Rajendra Yavatkar, and Raphael Finkel. Unify: A scalable approach to multicomputer design. *IEEE Computer Society Bulletin of the Technical Committee on Operating Systems and Application Environments*, 7(2), 1995.

8. Liviu Iftode, Jaswinder Pal Singh, and Kai Li. Scope consistency: A bridge between release consistency and entry consistency. In *Proceedings of the Annual ACM Symposium on Parallel Algorithms and Architectures*, Jun 1996.

9. Kirk L. Johnson, M. Frans Kaashoek, and Deborah A. Wallach. CRL: High-performance all-software distributed shared memory. In *Proceedings of the Fifteenth Symposium on Operating Systems Principles*, Dec 1995.

10. P. Keleher. The relative importance of concurrent writers and weak consistency models. In *Proceedings of the International Conference on Distributed Computing Systems*, Dec 1996.

11. Pete Keleher. Update protocols and iterative scientific applications. *The 12th International Parallel Processing Symposium*, March 1998.

12. Pete Keleher. Update protocols and cluster-based shared memory. *Computer Communications*, 22(11):1045–1055, July 1999.

13. Pete Keleher, Alan L. Cox, and Willy Zwaenepoel. Lazy release consistency for software distributed shared memory. In *Proceedings of the International Symposium of Computer Architecture*, pages 13–21, May 1992.

14. Peter J. Keleher. Tapeworm: High-level abstraction of shared accesses. *The 3rd Symposium on Operating System Design and Implementation*, Feb 1999.

15. Jae Bum Lee and Chu Shik Jhon. Reducing coherence overhead of barrier synchronization in software DSMs. *SC98*, Nov 1998.

16. Daniel Lenoski, Kourosh Gharachorloo, James Laudon, Anoop Gupta, John Hennesy, Mark Horowitz, and Monica Lam. The stanford dash multiprocessor. *IEEE Computer*, 25(3):63–79, March 1992.

17. L. R. Monnerat and R. Bianchini. Efficiently adapting to sharing patterns in software DSMs. In *Proceedings of the 4th IEEE International Symposium on High-Performance Computer Architecture*, Feb 1998.

18. Thu D. Nguyen, Raj Vaswani, and John Zahorjan. On scheduling implications of application characteristics. Technical report, University of Washington Department of Computer Science and Engineering.

19. Thu D. Nguyen, Raj Vaswani, and John Zahorjan. Maximizing speedup through self-tuning of processor allocation. In *Proceedings of the International Parallel Processing Symposium*, April 1996.

20. Steven Cameron Woo, Moriyoshi Ohara, Evan Torrie, Jaswinder Pal Singh, and Anoop Gupta. The SPLASH-2 programs: Characterization and methodoligical considerations. In *Proceedings of the 22nd International Synposium on Computer Architecture*, pages 24–36, 1995.

Compilation and Runtime Optimizations for Software Distributed Shared Memory

Kai Zhang, John Mellor-Crummey, and Robert J. Fowler

Department of Computer Science – MS 132
Rice University, 6100 Main, Houston, TX 77005
{kaizhang,johnmc,rjf}@cs.rice.edu

Abstract. We present two novel optimizations for compiling High Performance Fortran (HPF) to page-based software distributed shared memory systems (SDSM). One technique, *compiler-managed restricted consistency*, uses compiler-derived knowledge to delay the application of memory consistency operations to data that is provably not shared in the current synchronization interval, thus reducing false sharing[1]. The other technique, *compiler-managed shared buffers*, when combined with the previous optimization, eliminates fragmentation[2]. Together, the two techniques permit compiler-generated code to efficiently apply multi-dimensional computation partitioning and wavefront parallelism to execute efficiently on SDSM systems.

1 Introduction

SDSM systems implement shared-memory communication abstractions on top of message-passing systems, thus providing a flexible base for developing parallel applications. Shared memory is particularly suited to irregular applications because its dynamic resolution of communication greatly simplifies access to, and management of, irregularly shared data.

Compared with message-passing, however, the range of regular applications that achieve scalability and performance on SDSMs is limited. The regular, data-parallel applications used in the previous studies [20,9,12,7] all had their computations partitioned along the single, slowest varying dimension of the principal array. This is because SDSMs use blocks that are multiples of system page sizes, and partitioning along other dimensions causes a large number of pages to become fragmented with each containing only a few truly shared values along with a large amount falsely shared data. Such fragmentation results in disastrously high communication costs.

In contrast, many applications, such as those common in computational fluid dynamics codes (*e.g.*, [5]), use directional sweeps across several data dimensions.

---

[1] False sharing occurs when two or more processors each accesses mutually disjoint sets of data elements in the same block.

[2] Fragmentation occurs when an entire block of data is communicated to transport only a small fraction its content.

S. Dwarkadas (Ed.): LCR 2000, LNCS 1915, pp. 182–191, 2000.

For these applications, partitioning the data and computation in multiple dimensions reduces serialization.

A multi-dimensional partition is also more scalable than one-dimensional partitioning because it has a smaller communication/computation ratio for large numbers of processors. For these reasons, supporting multi-dimensional partitioning effectively on an SDSM is an important goal.

Furthermore, regular applications in previous studies exhibit loosely synchronous parallelism: specifically, completely parallel loop nests that are separated by synchronization. Noticeably absent are regular applications that require more tightly coupled synchronization such as wavefront parallelizations of applications with loop-carried data dependencies.

In this paper, we describe and evaluate compiler and run-time mechanisms for improving the performance of regular applications on SDSM systems.[3] Our work focuses on reducing the cost of the false sharing and fragmentation that are side effects of multi-dimensional partitioning. We also exploit compiler-derived knowledge of sharing and communication patterns to help choreograph SDSM synchronization and data movement.

In addition, we leverage compiler knowledge of synchronization patterns by extending TreadMarks to support pairwise data-flow synchronization and to support reductions efficiently using an extension of the barrier implementation. Pairwise synchronization usually reduces the number of synchronization messages, but more importantly, it enables us to organize wavefront computation. Collectively, the techniques that we describe here efficiently and effectively support loosely-synchronous parallelism with multi-dimensional computation partitioning and also tightly coupled applications.

The platform for this work comprises the dHPF compiler [3,2,19] and the TreadMarks SDSM system [4], both developed at Rice University.

Previous studies were centered on very small kernel benchmarks or small applications. The study of SDSM performance on large and complicated real applications has been neglected. Our experiments focus on real applications that typify most stencil computations and pipelined computations.

2   Challenges

If SDSM systems are to achieve performance comparable to using direct message passing for a wide variety of regular scientific applications, three major challenges that must be met.

Efficient Synchronization Primitives. In message-passing systems, interprocess synchronization is a side effect of data communication. Synchronization to enforce inter-process data dependencies can be simulated using shared variables and locks; however, these approaches require more than the minimal number of

---

[3] Some of the compiler and run-time mechanisms that we describe have applications to codes with irregular access patterns as well, although irregular applications are outside the scope of this current study.

messages. Direct implementations are required for efficiency. Barriers induce a global order on computations, but they do not map easily onto pipelined computations. Further, using barriers makes it difficult to use wavefront parallelism, in which the shutdown of one pipeline overlaps the startup phase of the next.

Operation Latency. SDSM systems that use invalidation-based memory consistency protocols (*e.g.*, Treadmarks [16]) incur at least one round-trip latency every time a logical block of data is copied between processors. Because data transfers occur on demand, *i.e.*, when a processor faults on a memory location, that round-trip latency cannot be overlapped with computation. For efficiency, round-trip delays should be avoided by replacing them with single messages overlapped with computation, and by aggregating multiple operations into larger ones. Dwarkadas *et al.* [10] have experimented with update protocols as a means of eliminating round trip latencies and overlapping communication with computation. A weakness of this strategy is that, without a precise analysis of sharing behavior, too much data can be sent.

Excess Data Movement. With the exception of a few hardware-dependent systems (*e.g.*, [23]), Shasta [8], and object-based systems [15], most SDSM systems use a software page as the granule of memory consistency. When page-size blocks are larger than the amount of data that actually needs to be communicated, there are two problems: false sharing and fragmentation. Both cause excess communication and consistency operations.

3   Approach

We use an integrated approach involving both compiler and runtime support to address the challenges described in the previous section.

Compiler-Managed Restricted Consistency. Whenever processors synchronize, the multiple-writers protocol used in TreadMarks will re-establish the consistency of all falsely shared pages, even if many of them will continue to be falsely shared. To avoid such unnecessary consistency maintenance, we further the standard lazy release consistency multiple-writer model [4] by augmenting synchronization operations, particularly a `signal` primitive, to create and communicate consistency meta-data *only* for modified pages that *might* be accessed by its synchronization partner(s). In general, the compiler proves that some set of data pages is guaranteed not to be shared between this synchronization operation and the next, and it passes this information to the run-time system, which enforces consistency only for pages outside this set. For regular applications, the dHPF compiler computes precisely the set of pages that must be communicated.

For irregular applications, our analysis is inexact but conservative. Barrier and lock calls are augmented to accept a set of pages that either the compiler or the programmer can prove not to be shared in the coming synchronization interval. The compiler may peel or split a loop when the synchronization intervals in different iterations involve different sets of pages to synchronize. See [24] for details.

Compiler-Managed Shared Buffers. Using multi-dimensional computation partitioning in an SDSM system can cause substantial fragmentation and false sharing. When pages contain only a few shared values, we marshal the actively shared data into separate out-of-band, shared buffers and transform the application to access the data directly out of the shared buffer. The compiler algorithm that detects such data tests whether the array accesses are stride-one in a loop. To minimize false sharing on the buffer, we allocate one new page-aligned buffer per array per destination processor. Moving the actively shared data to a compact set of densely packed pages enables the restricted consistency mechanism to delay or eliminate consistency operations on the fragmented pages. The computational overhead of using compiler-managed shared buffers includes the cost of splitting loops and data copying, which is relatively small.

The shared-buffer strategy also applies to irregular applications. For example, molecular dynamics and fluid dynamics applications often access shared arrays through a level of indirection implemented as an interaction list. For groups of iterations, a processor accesses a fixed set of elements. Excessive false sharing and fragmentation may arise if the indirectly accessed data is scattered throughout the shared arrays. The data of interest to each processor can be relocated to a buffer array accessed only by that processor. Similarly, data that is shared pairwise can be relocated to a page shared only by the two processors involved. This requires that the index sets be pre-computed from the interaction list by a preprocessing loop.

Synchronization Mechanisms. To coordinate the pairwise sharing and enforce data-flow constraints efficiently on the TreadMarks SDSM, we extended the application programming interface with support for point-to-point synchronization primitives `signal` and `wait`. We also extended the barrier mechanism to carry data on the barrier messages. This has many uses, but in our case the motivation was the efficient implementation of *reductions*.

Selective Eager Update. To eliminate round-trip communication for each pairwise-shared page following synchronization operations, we augmented our TreadMarks implementation of point-to-point synchronization to support *selective eager update*. A compiler-specified set of pages is sent to the synchronization partner along with consistency metadata in anticipation of the partner known future requests. The compiler is conservative, such that no data page is pushed that is not accessed after the synchronization. The SDSM runtime decides how many data pages can be pushed without overwhelming the communication subsystem.

4   Experimental Evaluation

To evaluate the effectiveness of our integrated compiler and runtime techniques and to understand the interactions among different optimization techniques, we studied the performance of a set of HPF benchmark codes compiled with our SDSM-version of the dHPF compiler and executed on the enhanced TreadMarks SDSM system. Our experiments were performed on an IBM SP2. The SP2 is a distributed-memory message-passing machine. Our experimental platform was populated with "high" processor nodes, each consisting of 4 PowerPC 604e processors with 1GB of main memory. Nodes are connected by a multi-layer scalable switching fabric. On each multiprocessor high node, we ran only one process to ensure that all messages were transported across the switch and that there was no contention for the network interface. All experiments reported here were performed on 16 high nodes with one process active on each.

In this paper we report only results for BT, an application benchmark from the NAS 2.0 Benchmark suite. We compare the performance of multiple configurations of compiler and runtime optimizations to ascertain the impact of these optimizations both collectively and individually. Additional experiments are described in [24].

NAS-BT is a large, "whole application" benchmark. Our parallel version was constructed by starting with the sequential version of the BT benchmark from the NAS suite [5], adding HPF directives, and interchanging a few loops to adjust the pipeline granularity exploited by dHPF. (These changes are described elsewhere [2].) For those phases in which computation sweeps along a partitioned dimension the compiler can generate pipelined parallelism. By using point-to-point synchronization, this pipelining becomes a wavefront.

In the experiments reported here, we ran the NAS-BT experiments on 16 processors, using the class A problem size and with (*, BLOCK) and (BLOCK, BLOCK) data distributions . The original sequential version runs in 3948 seconds[4]. Table 1 shows the abbreviations used in the subsequent tables presenting performance information.

Table 1. Key for row heading abbreviations in performance tables.

Opts	Meaning
P	point-to-point synchronization
E	eager update
R	restricted consistency
B	compiler-managed shared buffer

Table 2 summarizes the runs with column-wise 1-D partitioning. There is not much false sharing, so the optimizations addressing false sharing give only modest improvements. The message aggregation and latency avoidance of the eager update mechanism do provide significant improvement. The 1-D partitioning leads to longer pipelines (which increase serialization), thus degrading efficiency as more processors are added.

Table 3 summarizes results for (BLOCK,BLOCK) 2D partitioning on 16 processors. False sharing and fragmentation are extensive. Compiler-restricted consis-

---

[4] Because of hardware differences, the results presented here are not directly comparable with the results presented in [2].

Table 2. NAS-BT (16 processes, class A input) with column-wise computation partitioning.

Opts	Time (s)	Msg (K)	Comm (MB)
P	918	6,615	17,063
PE	599	617	17,629
PR	918	6,491	16,932
PRE	591	474	17,687

Table 3. NAS-BT (class A) 4x4 computation partitioning.

Opts	Time (s)	Msg (K)	Comm (MB)
P	926	6,320	14,904
PE	737	3,231	15,052
PR	916	4,674	11,143
PRE	595	754	11,334
PB	1066	6,425	10,689
PEB	852	3,421	10,795
PRB	585	3,252	5,075
PREB	405	247	5,151

tency by itself (PR) hides some of the false sharing, reducing the communication volume by one-third, but it does not address communication latency or fragmentation.

The combination of compiler-managed buffers and compiler-restricted consistency (PRB) works as intended to convert highly fragmented pages into falsely shared ones and then to hide the pages from the consistency mechanism. This eliminates two-thirds of the communication and reduces execution time by over 56%.

Used with any combination of the other mechanisms, eager update decreases communication cost through message aggregation and latency elimination. The best speedup, 10 out of 16, is achieved by applying all of the optimizations (PREB). Once the false sharing and fragmentation problems have been dealt with, the increased parallelism and smaller communication/computation ratio of the 2D partitioning contribute to better overall performance than is achieved using 1D partitioning, as the results in Table 2 show.

5   Related Work

An alternative approach for improving SDSM performance for regular applications is to incorporate message-passing primitives into the SDSM application programming interface [21]. Using this approach, processors cannot write to overlapping sets of data element within a single synchronization interval, since no consistency meta-data is maintained to distinguish the modification order. Since it looks like the processes made independent modifications, the lack of consistency information will cause redundant communication that negates the benefits of message-passing. Unfortunately, the performance evaluation of this approach by Mirchandaney, Hiranandani, and Sethi [21], was incomplete, making it impossible to assess its merits.

In CarlOS [18] the synchronization operations of a lazy release consistent SDSM are built on top of a messages that optionally induce consistency in a shared region of memory. Non-synchronizing messages were used to communicate data in non-shared regions. Using messages to copy data in the shared region, however, would have appeared to the consistency layer to be independent accesses by several processors to the affected data. This would result in redundant consistency operations at the next synchronization point.

Dwarkadas, Cox, and Zwaenepoel [9] proposed a compiler-directed *Fetch_Diffs* operation and a *Push* operation for SDSM. Their Fetch_Diffs primitive has each client request the data it needs at a synchronization point, and bulk transfers move the data. Unlike our eager update protocol, Fetch_Diffs uses round-trip communication to request data and can introduce extra wait time due to blocked signals. The Push operation is also a direct message-passing approach. However, it is based on a global barrier synchronization, and only the synchronous version is supported. In addition, the regular sections used in their work are limited to a contiguous range of memory. Lu *et al.* [20] extended this compiler-directed framework to two irregular applications. As they point out, the disadvantage of their approach is the potential for false sharing overhead when the data set is small or has poor spatial locality. Our techniques can be extended to solve the false sharing problem of irregular codes.

Han and Tseng [11] describe compiler-based techniques for improving performance on software DSM systems. Their techniques focus on reducing synchronization. For a *Jacobi* benchmark, their principal performance improvement comes from eliminating synchronization for anti-dependencies. This technique, however, can only be applied to programs executing on software DSM systems composed of *uniprocessor* nodes. Our synchronization model is more general. It can be used with shared-memory applications running on a cluster of SMP nodes so that processes running within the same SMP node can exploit hardware-based sharing of data in place.

Keleher and Tseng [17] proposed a flush update protocol at barrier synchronization, which is similar to our eager update protocol. Their compiler analysis is not sufficient to prevent unnecessary flush update and their runtime has to maintain a copy set of each page. Like Dwarkadas *et al.* [9], they do not have any support for point-to-point synchronization.

Heinlein *et al.* [14] propose the integration of message passing and cache-coherent shared memory in the Stanford Flash Multiprocessor. In their work, bulk data communication is pipelined to overlap communication with computation. Flash uses a separate hardware controller called MAGIC and data transfer is still a request/reply-based round-trip communication protocol.

The Midway system by Bershad, Zekauskas, and Sawdon [6] supports many different memory consistency models. Their work focused on entry consistency (EC), which enabled programmers to reduce synchronization cost by explicitly associating data with specific synchronization objects. The entry consistency model is similar in some respects to the restricted consistency support that we describe in this work. Exploiting entry consistency in Midway requires additional programming effort. In our work, the compiler determines the association between data and synchronization events, and compiler-restricted consistency is based on lazy release consistency (LRC). Adve, Cox, Dwarkadas, Rajamony, and Zwaenepoel [1] have compared LRC and EC and discovered that neither EC nor LRC consistently outperforms the other. They conclude that EC outperforms LRC if the effect of false sharing within a page dominates. Our work focuses on elimination of false sharing that occurs with page-based distributed memory systems.

Systems that seek to provide fine-grain granularity access control to shared data include Blizzard-E [13], Typhoon-0 [22], and Shasta [8]. Blizzard-E uses ECC bits at the memory level to cause faults on accesses to particular lines Similarly, Typhoon-0 uses hardware at the memory bus to detect an access fault. They all need special hardware support and require precise memory exceptions, which is not supported in many processors (*e.g.*, due to write buffers). Shasta depends on the ATOM toolkit, a facility available only on Alpha platforms, for binary rewriting. Our work continues to use a page-based consistency mechanism that requires only memory management mechanisms that are available on any Unix platform.

6   Conclusions

Our experiments demonstrate that our integrated compiler and runtime augmentations of SDSM can improve the performance of regular applications, including those with loop-carried data dependencies that require tight coupling and pipelined codes to parallelize effectively. The combination of compiler-managed restricted consistency in conjunction with compiler-managed communication buffers is very effective at reducing the amount of false sharing and fragmentation for the applications that we examined. Our optimizations make scalable multi-dimensional computation partitioning feasible on SDSM systems.

Acknowlegements

Alan Cox and Charlie Hu have provided invaluable advice and assistance in the course of this work. The authors are grateful to the people who have contributed to dHPF and TreadMarks.

This research was supported in part by the Texas Advanced Technology Program Grant TATP 003604-017, by DARPA and Rome Laboratory, Air Force

Materiel Command, USAF, under agreement number F30602-96-1-0159, and the Department of Energy's Accelerated Strategic Computing Initiative under research subcontract B347884. The U.S. Government is authorized to reproduce and distribute reprints for Governmental purposes notwithstanding any copyright annotation thereon. The views and conclusions contained herein are those of the authors and should not be interpreted as representing the official policies or endorsements, either expressed or implied, of DARPA and Rome Laboratory or the U.S. Government.

References

1. S. Adve, A. L. Cox, S. Dwarkadas, R. Rajamony, and W. Zwaenepoel. A comparison of entry consistency and lazy release consistency implementations. In *Proceedings of the Second High Performance Computer Architecture Symposium*, pages 26–37, Feb. 1996.
2. V. Adve, G. Jin, J. Mellor-Crummey, and Q. Yi. High Performance Fortran Compilation Techniques for Parallelizing Scientific Codes. In *Proceedings of SC98: High Performance Computing and Networking*, Orlando, FL, Nov 1998.
3. V. Adve and J. Mellor-Crummey. Using Integer Sets for Data-Parallel Program Analysis and Optimization. In *Proceedings of the SIGPLAN '98 Conference on Programming Language Design and Implementation*, Montreal, Canada, June 1998.
4. C. Amza, A. Cox, S. Dwarkadas, P. Keleher, H. Lu, R. Rajamony, W. Yu, and W. Zwaenepoel. TreadMarks: Shared memory computing on networks of workstations. *IEEE Computer*, 29(2):18–28, Feb. 1996.
5. D. Bailey, T. Harris, W. Saphir, R. van der Wijngaart, A. Woo, and M. Yarrow. The NAS parallel benchmarks 2.0. Technical Report NAS-95-020, NASA Ames Research Center, Dec. 1995.
6. B. Bershad, M. Zekauskas, and W. Sawdon. The Midway distributed shared memory system. In *Proceedings of the '93 CompCon Conference*, pages 528–537, Feb. 1993.
7. S. Chandra and J. Larus. Optimizing communication in HPF programs on finegrain distributed shared memory. In *Proceedings of the 6th Symposium on the Principles and Practice of Parallel Programming*, pages 100–111, June 1997.
8. K. G. Daniel J. Scales and C. Thekkath. Shasta: A low overhead, software-only approach for supporting finegrain shared memory. In *Proceedings of the Seventh International Conference on Architectural Support for Programming Languages and Operating Systems*, pages 174–185, Oct. 1996.
9. S. Dwarkadas, A. Cox, and W. Zwaenepoel. An integrated compile-time/run-time software distributed shared memory system. In *Proceedings of the 7th Symposium on Architectural Support for Programming Languages and Operating Systems*, pages 186–197, Oct. 1996.
10. S. Dwarkadas, P. Keleher, A. L. Cox, and W. Zwaenepoel. Evaluation of release consistent software distributed shared memory on emerging network technology. In *Proceedings of the 20th Annual International Symposium on Computer Architecture*, pages 244–255, May 1993.
11. H. Han and C. Tseng. Compile-time synchronization optimizations for software dsms. In *Proceedings of the 12th International Parallel Processing Symposium*, Apr. 1998.

12. H. Han, C.-W. Tseng, and P. Keleher. Eliminating barrier synchronization for compiler-parallelized codes on software DSMs. *International Journal of Parallel Programming*, 26(5):591–612, Oct. 1998. Invited paper from LCPC'97.
13. A. R. L. I. Schoinas, B. Falsafi, S. K. Reinhardt, J. R. Larus, and D. A. Wood. Fine-grain access control for distributed shared memory. In *Proceedings of the Sixth International Conference on Architectural Support for Programming Languages and Operating Systems*, pages 297–306, Oct. 1994.
14. S. D. John Heinlein, Kourosh Gharachorloo and A. Gupta. Integration of message passing and shared memory in the stanford flash multiprocessor. In *Proceedings of the Sixth International Conference on Architectural Support for Programming Languages and Operating Systems*, pages 38–50, Oct. 1994.
15. K. Johnson, M. Kaashoek, and D. Wallach. CRL: High-performance all-software distributed shared memory. In *Proceedings of the 15th ACM Symposium on Operating Systems Principles*, pages 213–228, Dec. 1995.
16. P. Keleher, A. L. Cox, S. Dwarkadas, and W. Zwaenepoel. An evaluation of software-based release consistent protocols. *Journal of Parallel and Distributed Computing*, 29:126–141, October 1995.
17. P. Keleher and C. Tseng. Enhancing software DSM for compiler-parallelized applications. In *Proceedings of the 11th International Parallel Processing Symposium*, Apr. 1997.
18. P. Koch, R. Fowler, and E. Jul. Message-driven relaxed consistency in a software distributed shared memory. In *Proceedings of the First USENIX Symposium on Operating System Design and Implementation*, pages 75–86, Nov. 1994.
19. B. Lu and J. Mellor-Crummey. Compiler optimization of implicit reductions for distributed memory multiprocessors. In *Proceedings of the 12th International Parallel Processing Symposium*, Orlando, FL, Mar. 1998.
20. H. Lu, A. Cox, S. Dwarkadas, R. Rajamony, and W. Zwaenepoel. Software distributed shared memory support for irregular applications. In *Proceedings of the 6th Symposium on the Principles and Practice of Parallel Programming*, pages 48–56, June 1996.
21. R. Mirchandaney, S. Hiranandani, and A. Sethi. Improving the performance of software DSM systems via compiler involvement. In *Proceedings of Supercomputing '94*, 1994.
22. R. W. P. S. K. Reinhardt and D. A. Wood. Decoupled hardware support for distributed shared memory. In *Proceedings of the 23rd Annual International Symposium on Computer Architecture*, pages 34–43, May 1996.
23. I. Schoinas, B. Falsafi, A. R. Lebeck, S. K. Reinhardt, J. R. Larus, and D. A. Wood. Fine-grain access control for distributed shared memory. In *Proceedings of the 6th Symposium on Architectural Support for Programming Languages and Operating Systems*, pages 297–306, Oct. 1994.
24. K. Zhang. Compiling for software distributed-shared memory systems. Master's thesis, Dept. of Computer Science, Rice University, Houston, TX, Apr. 2000.

Run-Time Support for Distributed Sharing in Typed Languages

Y. Charlie Hu, Weimin Yu, Alan L. Cox,
Dan S. Wallach, and Willy Zwaenepoel

Department of Computer Science
Rice University, Houston, Texas 77005
{ychu,weimin,alc,dwallach,willy}@cs.rice.edu

Abstract. We present a new run-time system, DOSA, that efficiently implements a shared object space abstraction underneath a typed programming language. The key insight behind DOSA is that *the ability to unambiguously distinguish pointers from data at run-time enables efficient fine-grained sharing using VM support*. Like earlier systems designed for fine-grained sharing, DOSA improves the performance of fine-grained applications by eliminating false sharing. In contrast to these earlier systems, DOSA's VM-based approach and read aggregation enable it to match a page-based system on coarse-grained applications. Furthermore, its architecture permits optimizations that are not possible in conventional fine-grained or coarse-grained DSM systems.

1   Introduction

This paper addresses run-time support for sharing objects in a typed language between the different computers within a cluster. Typing must be strong enough that it is possible to determine unambiguously whether a memory location contains an object reference or not. Many modern languages fall under this category, including Java and Modula-3. Direct access through a reference to object data is supported, unlike Java/RMI or Orca [2], where remote object access is restricted to method invocation. Furthermore, in languages with suitable multithreading support, such as Java, distributed execution is transparent: no new API is introduced for distributed sharing. This transparency distinguishes this work from many earlier distributed object sharing systems [2,7,14,12].

The key insight in this paper is that *the ability to distinguish pointers from data at run-time enables more efficient fine-grained sharing* than is possible with conventional distributed shared memory (DSM) implementations that do not use type information (e.g., [1,13]). Conventional VM-based DSM systems have only achieved good performance on relatively coarse-grained applications, because of their reliance on VM pages. Although relaxed memory models [9] and multiple-writer protocols [6] reduce the impact of the large page size, fine-grained sharing and false sharing remain problematic [1]. Fine-grained DSM systems have been built using code instrumentation, but they have been limited by the cost of instrumentation and lack of communication aggregation [8]. The system

S. Dwarkadas (Ed.): LCR 2000, LNCS 1915, pp. 192–206, 2000.
© Springer-Verlag Berlin Heidelberg 2000

presented here, DOSA, uses the ability to distinguish pointers from data at run-time to achieve efficient fine-grained sharing *using VM support and without using instrumentation*. It does so by introducing a level of indirection that allows objects to reside at different virtual memory locations with different protection attributes. Compiler optimization reduces the overhead of this level of indirection where necessary.

We have implemented this system, and compared its performance to that of TreadMarks, a state-of-the-art page-based system [1]. We have derived our implementation from the TreadMarks code base, thereby avoiding performance differences due to irrelevant code differences. Our performance evaluation substantiates the following claims:

1. The performance of fine-grained applications is considerably better (up to 98% for Barnes-Hut and 62% for Water-Spatial) than in TreadMarks.
2. The performance of garbage-collected applications is considerably (up to 65%) better than in TreadMarks.
3. The performance of coarse-grained applications is nearly as good as in Tread-Marks (within 6%). Since the performance of such applications is already good in TreadMarks, we consider this an acceptable performance penalty.

No direct comparison with an instrumentation-based DSM system was possible, because no such system is broadly available, but we speculate on the likely outcome of such a comparison in Section 8.

2   Programming Model

No special API is required in languages with suitable typing and multithreading support, such as Java or Modula-3.

The programming model supports a shared space of objects, in which references are distinguishable from data. An object is the unit of sharing. In other words, a single object cannot be written concurrently by different threads, even if those threads modify distinct parts of the object. If two threads write to the same object, they should synchronize between their writes. Arrays are treated as collections of objects, and therefore their elements can be written concurrently. Of course, for correctness, the different processes must write to disjoint elements in the arrays.

The object space is release consistent [9]. In essence, under release consistency, the propagation of updates from one processor to another may be delayed until the processors synchronize. Parallel programs that are properly synchronized (i.e., synchronize between conflicting accesses to shared data) behave as expected on the conventional sequentially consistent shared memory model.

The programmer is responsible for creating and destroying threads of control, and for the necessary synchronization to insure orderly access by these threads to the object space. Various synchronization mechanisms may be used, such as semaphores, locks, barriers, monitors, etc. There is no system-level association between a synchronization variable and a particular object. For instance, a lock may protect a single object, multiple objects, or an array of objects.

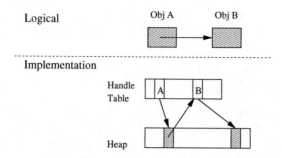

Fig. 1. Objects with handles.

3   Implementation

3.1   Single-Machine Implementation

Consider a single-processor implementation of a typed language using a *handle table*. Each object is identified by an unique object identifier (OID) that is also the index of the object's handle table entry. Thus, all references to the object, in fact, refer to its handle table entry, which in turn points to the actual object (see Figure 1). In such an implementation, relocating objects in memory is easy. It suffices to change its handle table entry. No other changes need to be made, since all references are indirected through the handle table.

3.2   Distributed Implementation

Extending this simple observation allows an efficient distributed implementation of these languages. Specifically (see Figure 2), a handle table representing all shared objects is present on each processor. A globally unique OID identifies each object, and serves as an index into the handle tables. As before, each handle table entry contains a pointer to the memory location where the object resides on that processor. The consistency protocol can then be implemented solely in terms of OIDs, because these are the actual references that appear in any of the objects. Furthermore, the same object may be allocated at different virtual memory addresses on different processors. It suffices for the handle table entry on each processor to point to the proper location. In other words, although the programmer retains the abstraction of a single object space, it is no longer the case that all of memory is virtually shared, and that all objects reside at the same virtual address on all processors, as is the case in a DSM system.

3.3   Fine-Grained VM Access Detection

The ability to locate the same object at different virtual memory addresses on different machines allows us to provide fine-grained access detection using VM techniques as follows. Although only a single physical copy of each object exists

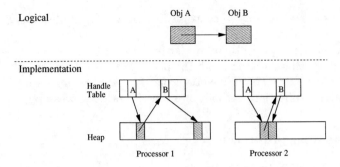

Fig. 2. Shared objects identified by unique OIDs.

on a single processor, each object can be accessed through three VM mappings. All three map to the same physical location in memory, but with three different protection attributes: invalid, read-only, or read-write. A change in access mode is accomplished by switching between the different mappings *for that object only*. The mappings for the other objects in the same page remain unaffected. Consider the example in Figure 3. A page contains four objects, one of which is written on a different processor. This modification is communicated between processors through the consistency protocol, and results in the invalid mapping being set for this object. Access to other objects can continue, unperturbed by this change, thus eliminating false sharing between objects on the same page.

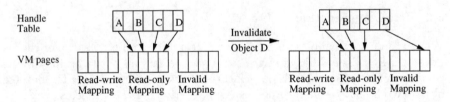

Fig. 3. Access detection using the handle pointers.

3.4 Object Storage Allocation

The ability to allocate objects at different addresses on different processors also suggests that we can delay the storage allocation for an object on a processor until that object is first accessed by that processor. We call this optimization *lazy object storage allocation*. For some programs, it reduces the memory footprint and produces better cache locality. N-body simulations illustrate this benefit. Each processor typically accesses its own bodies, and a small number of nearby bodies on other processors. With global allocation of memory, the remote bodies are scattered in memory, causing lots of misses, messages, and – in the case of

TreadMarks – false sharing. In contrast, in DOSA, only the local bodies and the locally accessed remote bodies are allocated in local memory. As a result of the smaller memory footprint, there are far fewer access misses and messages, and false sharing is eliminated through the per-object mappings. Moreover, objects can be locally re-arranged in memory, for instance to improve cache locality or during garbage collection, without affecting the other processors.

3.5   Consistency Protocol

DOSA, like TreadMarks, uses a lazy invalidate protocol to implement release consistency [1]. Consistency is, however, maintained in terms of objects rather than pages. In other words, consistency messages specify object identifiers instead of page numbers. For individual objects, a single writer protocol is used [11]. For arrays of objects, whether of a scalar type or a reference type, a multiple writer protocol is used [1]. This permits the use of a single OID for the entire array, while still allowing concurrent modifications to distinct objects within the array.

The *lazy* implementation delays the propagation of consistency information until a processor acquires a lock or departs from a barrier. At that time, the last releaser of the lock or the barrier manager processor informs the processor which *objects* have been modified. In particular, invalidations never arrive asynchronously; they only arrive at the time of a synchronization.

An *inverse object table*, implemented as a hash table, is used by the page fault handler to translate a faulting address to an OID.

3.6   Read Aggregation

When a processor faults on a particular object, if the object is smaller than a page, it uses a list of objects in the same page to find all of the invalid objects residing in that page. It sends out concurrent object fetch messages for all these objects to the processors recorded as the last writers of these objects.

By doing so, we aggregate the requests for all invalid objects in the same page. This approach performs better than simply fetching one faulted object at a time. If there is some locality in the objects accessed by a processor, then it is likely that the objects allocated in the same page are going to be accessed closely together in time, in particular given lazy object storage allocation. Some unnecessary objects may be fetched, but the messages to fetch those objects go out in parallel, and therefore their latencies and the latencies of the replies are largely overlapped.

4   Compiler Optimizations

The extra indirection creates a potential problem for applications that access large arrays, because it may cause significant overhead, without any gain from better support for fine-grained sharing. This problem can be addressed using type-based alias analysis and loop invariant analysis to eliminate many repeated indirections.

Consider, a C program with a two-dimensional array of scalars, such as float, that is implemented in the same fashion as a two-dimensional Java array of scalars, i.e., an array of pointers to an array of a scalar type ("scalar_type **a;"). Assume this program performs a regular traversal of the array with a nested for loop.

```
for i
    for j
        ... = a[i][j];
```

In general, a C compiler cannot further optimize this loop nest, because it cannot prove that a and a[i] do not change during the loop execution. a, a[i] and a[i][j] are, however, of different types, and therefore the compiler for a typed language can easily determine that a and a[i] do not change, and transform the loop accordingly to

```
for i
    p = a[i];
    for j
        ... = p[j];
```

resulting in a significant speedup. In the DOSA program the original program takes the form of

```
for i
    for j
        ... = a->handle[i]->handle[j];
```

which, in a typed language can be similarly transformed to

```
for i
    p = a->handle[i];
    for j
        ... = p->handle[j];
```

While offering much improvement, this transformation still leaves the DOSA program at a disadvantage compared to the optimized TreadMarks program, because of the remaining pointer dereferencing in the inner loop. Observe also that the following transformation of the DOSA program is legal but not profitable:

```
for i
    p = a->handle[i]->handle;
    for j
        ... = p[j];
```

The problem with this transformation occurs when a->handle[i]->handle has been invalidated as a result of a previous synchronization. Before the j-loop, p contains an address in the invalid region, which causes a page fault on the first iteration of the j-loop. The DSM runtime changes a->handle[i]->handle to its location in the read-write region, but this change is not reflected in p. As a result, the j-loop page faults on every iteration.

We solve this problem by touching a->handle[i]->handle[0] before assigning it to p. In other words,

```
for i
    touch( a->handle[i]->handle[0] );
    p = a->handle[i]->handle;
    for j
        ... = p[j];
```

Touching a->handle[i]->handle[0] outside the j-loop causes the fault to occur there, and a->handle[i]->handle to be changed to the read-write location. The same optimization can be applied to the outer loop as well.

These optimizations are dependent on the lazy implementation of release consistency. Invalidations can only arrive at synchronization points, never asynchronously, thus the cached references cannot be invalidated in a synchronization-free loop.

5   Evaluation Methodology

A difficulty arises in making the comparison with TreadMarks. Ideally, we would like to make these comparisons by simply taking a number of applications in a typed language, and running them, on one hand, on TreadMarks, simply using shared memory as an untyped region of memory, and, on the other hand, running them on top of DOSA, using a shared object space.

For a variety of reasons, the most appealing programming language for this purpose is Java. Unfortunately, commonly available implementations of Java are interpreted and run on slow Java virtual machines. This would render our experiments largely meaningless, because inefficiencies in the Java implementation would dwarf differences between TreadMarks and DOSA. Perhaps more importantly, we expect efficient compiled versions of Java to become available soon, and we would expect that those be used in preference over the current implementations, quickly obsoleting our results. Finally, the performance of these Java applications would be much inferior to published results for conventional programming languages.

We have therefore chosen to carry out the following experiments. We have taken existing C applications, and re-written them to follow the model of a handle-based implementation. In other words, a handle table is introduced, and all pointers are indirected through the handle table. This approach represents the results that could be achieved by a language or compilation environment that is compatible with our approach for maintaining consistency, but otherwise exhibits no compilation or execution differences with the conventional Tread-Marks execution environment. In other words, these experiments isolate the benefits and the drawbacks of our consistency maintenance methods from other aspects of the compilation and execution process. It also allows us to assess the overhead of the extra indirection on single-processor execution times. The compiler optimizations discussed in Section 4 have been implemented by hand in both the TreadMarks and the DOSA programs.

We have implemented a distributed garbage collector on both TreadMarks and DOSA that is representative of the state-of-the-art. Distributed garbage collectors are naturally divided into two parts: the inter-processor algorithm, which tracks cross-processor references; and the intra-processor algorithm, which performs the traversal on each processor and reclaims the unused memory. Our distributed garbage collector uses a *weighted reference counting* algorithm for the inter-processor part [3,16,17] and a generational, copying algorithm for the intra-processor part. To implement weighted reference counting transparently, we check incoming and outgoing messages for references. These references are recorded in an import table and an export table, respectively.

6   Environment and Applications

Our experimental platform is a switched, full-duplex 100Mbps Ethernet network of thirty-two 300 MHz Pentium II-based computers. Each computer has 256M bytes of memory, and runs FreeBSD 2.2.6.

We demonstrate the performance improvements of DOSA over TreadMarks for fine-grained applications, by using Barnes-Hut and Water-Spatial, both from the SPLASH-2 benchmarks [18]. SOR and Water-Nsquared from the SPLASH benchmarks [15] demonstrate only minimal performance loss for coarse-grained applications.

For each of these applications, Table 1 lists each of the problem sizes and its corresponding sequential execution time. The sequential execution times were obtained by removing all TreadMarks or DOSA calls from the applications. They also include the compile-time optimizations described in Section 4.

Table 1. Applications, problem sizes, and sequential execution time.

Application	Problem Size	Time (sec.) Original	Handle
Small Problem Size			
Red-Black SOR	3070x2047, 20 steps	21.13	21.12
Water-N-Squared	1728 mols, 2 steps	71.59	73.83
Barnes-Hut	32K bodies, 3 steps	58.68	60.84
Water-Spatial	4K mols, 9 steps	89.63	89.80
Large Problem Size			
Red-Black SOR	4094x2047, 20 steps	27.57	28.05
Water-N-Squared	2744 mols, 2 steps	190.63	193.50
Barnes-Hut	131K bodies, 3 steps	270.34	284.43
Water-Spatial	32K mols, 2 steps	158.57	160.39

The sequential timings show that the overhead of the extra level of dereferencing in the handle-based versions of the applications is never more than 5.2% on one processor for any of these four applications. The sequential execution times without handles were used as the basis for computing the speedups reported later in the paper.

To exercise the distributed garbage collector, we use a modified version of the OO7 object-oriented database benchmark [5]. This benchmark is designed to match the characteristics of many CAD/CAM/CASE applications. The OO7 database contains a tree of assembly objects, with leaves pointing to three composite parts chosen randomly from among 500 objects. Each composite part contains a graph of atomic parts linked by connection objects. Each atomic part has 3 outgoing connections.

Ordinarily, OO7 does not release memory. Thus, there would be nothing for a garbage collector to do. Our modified version of OO7 creates garbage by replacing rather updating objects when the database changes. After the new object, containing the updated data, is in place in the database, the old object becomes eligible for collection.

The OO7 benchmark defines several database traversals [5]. For our experiments, we use a mixed sequence of T1, T2a, and T2b traversals. T1 performs a depth-first traversal of the entire composite part graph. T2a and T2b are identical to T1 except that T2a modifies the root atomic part of the graph, while T2b modifies all the atomic parts.

Table 2 lists the sequential execution times for OO7 running with the garbage collector on TreadMarks and DOSA. It also lists the time spent in the memory allocator/garbage collector. DOSA incurs 2% overhead to the copying collector because of extra overhead in handle management; it has to update the handle table entry whenever an object is created, deleted, or moved. Overall, DOSA underperforms TreadMarks by 3% due to handle dereference cost.

Table 2. Statistics for TreadMarks and DOSA on 1 processor for OO7 with garbage collection.

OO7	Tmk	DOSA
Overall time (in sec.)	184.8	190.8
Alloc and GC time (in sec.)	10.86	11.04

7   Results

7.1   Fine-Grained Applications

Figure 4 shows the speedup comparison between TreadMarks and DOSA for Barnes-Hut and Water-Spatial on 16 and 32 processors for small and large problem sizes. Figure 5 shows various statistics from the execution of these applications on 32 processors for both problem sizes.

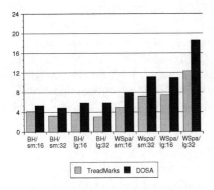

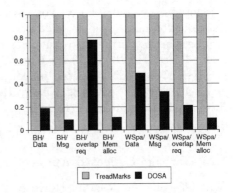

Fig. 4. Speedup comparison between TreadMarks and DOSA for fine-grained applications.

Fig. 5. Statistics for TreadMarks and DOSA on 32 processors for fine-grained applications with large data sizes, normalized to TreadMarks measurements.

We derive the following conclusions from this data. First, from Table 1, the overhead of the extra indirection in the sequential code for these applications is less than 5.2% for Barnes-Hut and 1.1% for Water-Spatial. Second, even for a small number of processors, the benefits of the handle-based implementation are larger than the cost of the extra indirection. For Barnes-Hut with 32K and 128K bodies, DOSA outperforms TreadMarks by 29% and 52%, respectively, on 16 processors. For Water-Spatial with 4K and 32K molecules, DOSA outperforms TreadMarks by 62% and 47%, respectively, on 16 processors. Third, as the number of processors increases, the benefits of the handle-based implementation grow. For Barnes-Hut with 128K bodies, DOSA outperforms TreadMarks by 52% on 16 processors and 98% on 32 processors. For Water-Spatial with 32K molecules, DOSA outperforms TreadMarks by 47% on 16 processors and 51% on 32 processors. Fourth, if the amount of false sharing under TreadMarks decreases as the problem size increases, as in Water-Spatial, then DOSA's advantage over TreadMarks decreases. If, on the other hand, the amount of false sharing under TreadMarks doesn't change, as in Barnes-Hut, then DOSA's advantage over TreadMarks is maintained. In fact, for Barnes-Hut, the advantage grows due to slower growth in the amount of communication by DOSA, resulting from improved locality due to lazy object allocation.

The reasons for DOSA's clear dominance over TreadMarks can be seen in Figure 5. This figure shows the number of messages exchanged, the number of overlapped data requests [1], the amount of data communicated, and the average

---

[1] The concurrent messages for updating a page in TreadMarks or updating all invalid objects in a page in DOSA are counted as one overlapped data request. Since these messages go out and replies come back in parallel, their latencies are largely overlapped.

amount of shared data allocated on each processor. Specifically, we see a substantial reduction in the amount of data sent for DOSA, as a result of the reduction in false sharing. Furthermore, the number of messages is reduced by a factor of 11 for Barnes-Hut/lg and 3 for Water-Spatial/lg. More importantly, the number of overlapped data requests is reduced by a factor of 1.3 for Barnes-Hut/lg and 4.9 for Water-Spatial/lg. Finally, the benefits of lazy object allocation for these applications are quite clear: the memory footprint of DOSA is considerably smaller than that of TreadMarks.

7.2   Garbage Collected Applications

Figure 6 shows the execution statistics on 16 processors for the OO7 benchmark running on TreadMarks and DOSA using the generational, copying collector. We do not present results on 32 processors because the total data size, which increases linearly with the number of processors, is so large that it causes paging on 32 processors.

On 16 processors, OO7 on DOSA outperforms OO7 on TreadMarks by almost 65%. Figure 6 shows that the time spent in the memory management code performing allocation and garbage collection is almost the same for TreadMarks and DOSA. The effects of the interaction between the garbage collector and DOSA or TreadMarks actually appear during the execution of the application code. The main cause for the large performance improvement in DOSA is reduced communication, as shown in Figure 7.

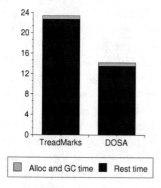
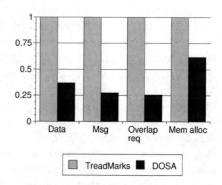

Fig. 6. Time breakdown (in seconds) for the OO7 benchmark on Tread-Marks and DOSA on 16 processors.

Fig. 7. Statistics for OO7 on Tread-Marks and DOSA on 16 processors, normalized to TreadMarks measurements.

The extra communication on TreadMarks is primarily a side-effect of garbage collection. On TreadMarks, when a processor copies an object during garbage collection, this is indistinguishable from ordinary writes. Consequently, when

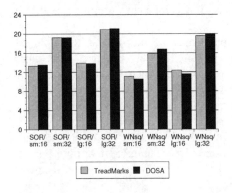

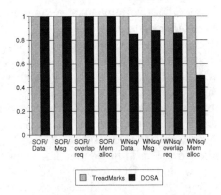

Fig. 8. Speedup comparison between TreadMarks and DOSA for coarse-grained applications.

Fig. 9. Statistics for TreadMarks and DOSA on 32 processors for coarse-grained applications with large data sizes, normalized to TreadMarks measurements.

another processor accesses the object after garbage collection, the object is communicated to it, even though the object's contents have not been changed by the copy. In fact, the processor may have an up-to-date copy of the object in its memory, just at the wrong virtual address. In contrast, on DOSA, when a processor copies an object during garbage collection, it simply updates its handle table entry, which is local information that never propagates to other processors.

The lazy storage allocation in DOSA also contributes to the reduction in communication. In OO7, live objects and garbage may coexist in the same page. In TreadMarks, if a processor requests a page, it may get both live objects and garbage. In DOSA, however, only live objects will be communicated, reducing the amount of data communicated. This also explains why the memory footprint in DOSA is smaller than in TreadMarks.

7.3   Coarse-Grained Applications

Figure 8 shows the speedup comparison between TreadMarks and DOSA for SOR and Water-Nsquared on 16 and 32 processors for small and large problem sizes. Figure 9 shows various statistics from the execution of these applications on 32 processors for both problem sizes.

8   Related Work

Two other systems have used VM mechanisms for fine-grain DSM: Millipede [10] and the Region Trapping Library [4]. The fundamental difference between DOSA and these systems is that *DOSA takes advantage of a typed language to distinguish a pointer from data at run-time and these other systems do not.* This allows DOSA to implement a number of optimizations that are not possible in these other systems.

Specifically, in Millipede a physical page may be mapped at multiple addresses in the virtual address space, as in DOSA, but the similarity ends there. In Millipede, each object resides in its own *vpage*, which is the size of a VM page. Different vpages are mapped to the same physical memory page, but the objects are offset within the vpage such that they do not overlap in the underlying physical page. Different protection attributes may be set on different vpages, thereby achieving the same effect as DOSA, namely per-object access and write detection. The Millipede method requires one virtual memory mapping per object, while the DOSA method requires only three mappings per page, resulting in considerably less address space consumption and pressure on the TLB. Also, DOSA does not require any costly OS system calls (e.g., `mprotect`) to change page protections after initialization, while Millipede does.

The Region Trapping Library is similar to DOSA in that it allocates three different regions of memory with different protection attributes. Unlike DOSA, it doesn't use the regions in way that is transparent to the programmer. Instead, it provides a special API. Furthermore, in the implementation, the read memory region and the read-write memory region are backed by *different* physical memory regions. This decision has the unfortunate side effect of forcing modifications made in the read-write region to be copied to the read region, every time protection changes from read-write to read.

Orca [2], Jade [12], COOL [7], and SAM [14] are parallel or distributed object-oriented languages. All of these systems differ from ours in that they present a new language or API to the programmer to express distributed sharing, while DOSA does not. DOSA aims to provide transparent object sharing for existing typed languages, such as Java. Furthermore, none of Orca, Jade, COOL, or SAM use VM-based mechanisms for object sharing.

Dwarkadas et al. [8] compared Cashmere, a coarse-grained system, somewhat like TreadMarks, and Shasta, an instrumentation-based system, running on an identical platform – a cluster of four 4-way AlphaServers connected by a Memory Channel network. In general, Cashmere outperformed Shasta on coarse-grained applications (e.g., Water-N-Squared), and Shasta outperformed Cashmere on fine-grained applications (e.g., Barnes-Hut). The only surprise was that Shasta equaled Cashmere on the fine-grained application Water-Spatial. They attributed this result to the run-time overhead of the inline access checks in Shasta. In contrast, DOSA outperforms TreadMarks by 62% on the same application. We attribute this to lazy object allocation, which is not possible in Shasta, and read aggregation.

9   Conclusions

In this paper, we have presented a new run-time system, DOSA, that efficiently implements a shared object space abstraction underneath a typed programming language. The key insight behind DOSA is that *the ability to unambiguously distinguish pointers from data at run-time enables efficient fine-grained sharing using VM support.* Like earlier systems designed for fine-grained sharing, DOSA improves the performance of fine-grained applications by eliminating false sharing. In contrast to these earlier systems, DOSA's VM-based approach and read aggregation enable it to match a page-based system on coarse-grained applications. Furthermore, its architecture permits optimizations, such as lazy object allocation, which are not possible in conventional fine-grained or coarse-grained DSM systems. Lazy object allocation transparently improves the locality of reference in many applications, improving their performance.

Our performance evaluation on a cluster of 32 Pentium II processors connected with a 100Mbps Ethernet demonstrates that the new system performs comparably to TreadMarks for coarse-grained applications (SOR and Water-Nsquared), and significantly outperforms TreadMarks for fine-grained applications (up to 98% for Barnes-Hut and 62% for Water-Spatial) and a garbage-collected application (65% for OO7).

References

1. C. Amza, A. Cox, S. Dwarkadas, P. Keleher, H. Lu, R. Rajamony, W. Yu, and W. Zwaenepoel. TreadMarks: Shared memory computing on networks of workstations. *IEEE Computer*, 29(2):18–28, Feb. 1996.
2. H. Bal, R. Bhoedjang, R. Hofman, C. Jacobs, K. Langendoen, T. Ruhl, and M. Kaashoek. Performance evaluation of the Orca shared object system. *ACM Transactions on Computer Systems*, 16(1), Feb. 1998.
3. D. I. Bevan. Distributed garbage collection using reference counting. In *Parallel Arch. and Lang. Europe*, pages 117–187, Eindhoven, The Netherlands, June 1987. Spring-Verlag Lecture Notes in Computer Science 259.
4. T. Brecht and H. Sandhu. The region trap library: Handling traps on application-defined regions of memory. In *Proceedings of the 1999 USENIX Annual Tech. Conf.*, June 1999.
5. M. Carey, D. DeWitt, and J. Naughton. The OO7 benchmark. Technical report, University of Wisconsin-Madison, July 1994.
6. J. Carter, J. Bennett, and W. Zwaenepoel. Techniques for reducing consistency-related information in distributed shared memory systems. *ACM Transactions on Computer Systems*, 13(3):205–243, Aug. 1995.
7. R. Chandra, A. Gupta, and J. Hennessy. Cool: An object-based language for parallel programming. *IEEE Computer*, 27(8):14–26, Aug. 1994.
8. S. Dwarkadas, K. Gharachorloo, L. Kontothanassis, D. J. Scales, M. L. Scott, and R. Stets. Comparative evaluation of fine- and coarse-grain approaches for software distributed shared memory. In *Proceedings of the Fifth International Symposium on High-Performance Computer Architecture*, pages 260–269, Jan. 1999.
9. K. Gharachorloo, D. Lenoski, J. Laudon, P. Gibbons, A. Gupta, and J. Hennessy. Memory consistency and event ordering in scalable shared-memory multiprocessors. In *Proceedings of the 17th Annual International Symposium on Computer Architecture*, pages 15–26, May 1990.
10. A. Itzkovitz and A. Schuster. Multiview and millipage – fine-grain sharing in page-based DSMs. In *Proceedings of the Third USENIX Symposium on Operating System Design and Implementation*, Feb. 1999.

11. P. Keleher. The relative importance of concurrent writers and weak consistency models. In *Proceedings of the 16th International Conference on Distributed Computing Systems*, pages 91–98, May 1996.

12. M. C. Rinard and M. S. Lam. The design, implementation, and evaluation of Jade. *ACM Transactions on Programming Languages and Systems*, 20(3):483–545, May 1998.

13. D. Scales, K. Gharachorloo, and C. Thekkath. Shasta: A low overhead software-only approach for supporting fine-grain shared memory. In *Proceedings of the 7th Symposium on Architectural Support for Programming Languages and Operating Systems*, Oct. 1996.

14. D. J. Scales and M. S. Lam. The design and evaluation of a shared object system for distributed memory machines. In *Proceedings of the First USENIX Symposium on Operating System Design and Implementation*, pages 101–114, Nov. 1994.

15. J. Singh, W.-D. Weber, and A. Gupta. SPLASH: Stanford parallel applications for shared-memory. *Computer Architecture News*, 20(1):2–12, Mar. 1992.

16. R. Thomas. A dataflow computer with improved asymptotic performance. Technical Report TR-265, MIT Laboratory for Computer Science, 1981.

17. P. Watson and I. Watson. An efficient garbage collection scheme for parallel computer architectures. In *PARLE'87—Parallel Architectures and Languages Europe*, number 259 in Lecture Notes in Computer Science, Eindhoven (the Netherlands), June 1987. Springer-Verlag.

18. S. C. Woo, M. Ohara, E. Torrie, J. P. Singh, and A. Gupta. The SPLASH-2 programs: characterization and methodological considerations. In *Proceedings of the 22nd Annual International Symposium on Computer Architecture*, pages 24–36, June 1995.

InterWeave: A Middleware System for Distributed Shared State[*]

DeQing Chen, Sandhya Dwarkadas, Srinivasan Parthasarathy,
Eduardo Pinheiro, and Michael L. Scott

Computer Science Department, University of Rochester
{lukechen,sandhya,srini,edpin,scott}@cs.rochester.edu

Abstract. As an alternative to message passing, Rochester's InterWeave system allows the programmer to map shared segments into programs spread across heterogeneous, distributed machines. InterWeave represents a merger and extension of our previous Cashmere and InterAct projects, combining hardware coherence within small multiprocessors, Cashmere-style lazy release consistency within tightly coupled clusters, and InterAct-style version-based consistency for distributed shared segments.

In InterWeave, each shared segment evolves through a series of consistent versions. When beginning a read-only critical section on a given segment, Inter-Weave uses a programmer-specified predicate to determine whether the currently cached version, if any, is "recent enough" to use. Inter-segment consistency is maintained by means of hashed vector timestamps. Automatic data conversions allow each program to employ its own natural data format, byte order, and alignment, with full support for intra- and inter-segment pointers. Timestamping is used to determine and communicate only those pieces of a segment that are different from the cached copy.

A preliminary implementation of InterWeave is currently running on our AlphaServer cluster. Driving applications include data mining, intelligent distributed environments, and scientific visualization.

1 Introduction

Advances in processing speed and network bandwidth are creating new interest in such ambitious distributed applications as interactive data mining, remote scientific visualization, computer-supported collaborative work, and intelligent environments. Most of these applications rely, at least in the abstract, on some notion of distributed shared state. When one of their processes must access data that are currently located elsewhere, one has the option of moving the process to the data or moving the data to the process. Either option may make sense from a performance point of view, depending on the amounts of data and computation involved, the feasibility of migration, and the frequency of data updates.

The first option—move the process to the data—corresponds to remote procedure call or remote method invocation, and is supported by widely available production-quality systems. The second option—move the data to the process—is not so well

---

[*] This work is supported in part by NSF grants EIA–9972881, CCR–9702466, CCR–9705594, and CCR-9988361; and an external research grant from Compaq.

S. Dwarkadas (Ed.): LCR 2000, LNCS 1915, pp. 207–220, 2000.

understood. It still tends to be achieved through special-purpose, application-specific message-passing protocols. The creation of these protocols is a time-consuming, tedious, and error-prone activity. It is complicated by the need, for performance reasons, to cache copies of data at multiple locations, and to keep those copies consistent in the face of distributed updates.

At Rochester we have been discussing these issues with colleagues in data mining, scientific visualization, and distributed intelligent environments, all of whom have very large distributed data sets. To support their applications, we are developing a system, known as InterWeave, that allows the programmer to map shared segments into program components regardless of location or machine type. InterWeave represents a merger and extension of our previous Cashmere [39] and InterAct [30] projects. Once shared segments have been mapped, InterWeave can support hardware coherence and consistency within multiprocessors (*level-1* sharing), Cashmere-style software distributed shared memory within tightly coupled clusters (*level-2* sharing), and InterAct-style version-based consistency across the Internet (*level-3* sharing) for these segments (see Figure 1).

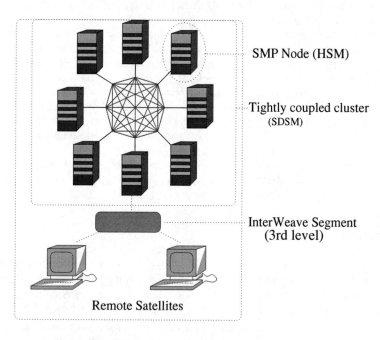

Fig. 1. InterWeave's target environment.

At the third level, each segment in InterWeave evolves through a series of consistent versions. When beginning a read-only critical section on a given segment, InterWeave uses a programmer-specified predicate to determine whether the currently cached version, if any, is "recent enough" to use. Several coherence models (notions of "recent enough") are built into the InterWeave system; others can be defined by application programmers. When the application desires causality among segments, to avoid causality loops, we invalidate mutually-inconsistent versions of other segments, using a novel hashing mechanism that captures the history of each segment in a bounded amount of space.

Like CORBA [29] and many older RPC systems, InterWeave employs a type system based on a machine- and language-independent interface description language, in our case Sun XDR [40]. We do not require that programmers adhere to an object-oriented programming style. We simply ensure that the version of a segment cached by a given program component is appropriate to the component's language and machine architecture. When transmitting data between machines, we convert to and from a standard wire format. We also swizzle pointers [45], so that references to data currently cached on the local machine are represented as machine addresses. We even allow programs to organize dynamically-allocated data within a segment in different ways on different machines, for the sake of spatial locality.

We describe the design of InterWeave in more detail in Section 2, covering synchronization, coherence, consistency, heterogeneity, and integration with existing shared memory. Our initial implementation and preliminary performance results are described in Section 3. We compare our design to related work in Section 4 and conclude with a discussion of status and plans in Section 5.

2   InterWeave Design

The unit of sharing in InterWeave is a self-descriptive data segment within which programs allocate strongly typed blocks of memory. Every segment has an Internet URL. The blocks within a segment are numbered and optionally named. By concatenating the segment URL with a block number/name and offset (delimited by pound signs), we obtain a machine-independent pointer: "http://foo.org/path#block#offset". To accommodate heterogeneous data formats, offsets are measured in primitive data units—characters, integers, floats, etc.—rather than in bytes. To create and initialize a segment in C, we execute the following calls:

```
IW_handle_t h = IW_create_segment (url);
IW_wl_acquire (h);
my_type* p = (my_type *) IW_malloc (h, my_type_desc);
*p = ...
IW_wl_release (h);
```

Every segment is managed by an InterWeave server at the IP address indicated in the segment's URL. Assuming appropriate access rights, the IW_create_segment call communicates with the server to create an uninitialized segment, and allocates space to hold (the initial portion of) a local cached copy of that segment in the caller's address space. The handle returned by IW_create_segment is an opaque, machine-dependent type that may be passed to IW_malloc, along with a type descriptor generated by our XDR compiler. Copies of a segment cached by a given process need not necessarily be contiguous in the application's virtual address space, so long as individually malloced blocks are contiguous; the InterWeave library can expand a segment as needed using unrelated address ranges.

Once a segment has been initialized, a process can create a machine-independent pointer to an arbitrary location within one of its allocated blocks:

```
IW_mip_t m = IW_ptr_to_mip (p);
```

This machine-independent pointer can then be passed to another process through a message, a file, or even console I/O. Given appropriate access rights, the other process can convert back to a machine-specific pointer:

```
my_type *p = (my_type *) IW_mip_to_ptr (m);
```

The IW_mip_to_ptr call reserves space for the specified segment if it is not already locally cached (communicating with the server if necessary to obtain layout information for the specified block), and returns a local machine address. Actual data for the segment will not be copied into the local machine until the segment is locked. The mechanism used to specify and verify access rights is still under development.

Any given segment A may contain pointers to data in some other segment B. The pointer-swizzling and data-conversion mechanisms described in Section 2.3 below ensure that such pointers will be valid local machine addresses, and may freely be dereferenced. It remains the programmer's responsibility, however, to ensure that segments are accessed only under the protection of reader-writer locks. To assist in this task, InterWeave allows the programmer to identify the segment in which the datum referenced by a pointer resides:

```
IW_handle_t h = IW_get_handle (p);
```

2.1 Coherence

Given the comparatively high and variable latencies of local-area networks, traditional hardware-inspired consistency models are unlikely to admit good performance in a distributed environment. Even the most relaxed of these models, release consistency [16], guarantees a coherent view of *all* shared data among *all* processes at synchronization points, resulting in significant amounts of communication.

Fortunately, processes in distributed applications can often accept a significantly more relaxed—and hence less costly—notion of consistency. Depending on the application, it may suffice to update a cached copy of a segment at regular (temporal) intervals, or whenever the contents have changed "enough to make a difference", rather than after every change.

The server for a given segment in InterWeave is responsible for the segment's coherence. This coherence is based on the notion that segments move over time through a series of internally consistent states, under the protection of reader-writer locks.

When writing a segment, a process must have exclusive access to the most recent version (we do not support branching histories). When reading a segment, however, the most recent version may not be required. InterWeave inherits five different definitions of "recent enough" from its predecessor system, InterAct. It is also designed in such a way that additional definitions (coherence models) can be added easily. Among the current models, *Full coherence* always obtains the most recent version of the segment; *Null coherence* always accepts the currently cached version, if any (the process must employ additional, explicit library calls to obtain an update); *Delta coherence* [38] guarantees that the segment is no more than x versions out-of-date; *Temporal coherence* guarantees that it is no more than x time units out of date; and *Diff-based coherence* guarantees that no more than $x\%$ of the segment is out of date. In all cases, x can be specified by the process.

When a process first locks a shared segment, the InterWeave library obtains a copy from the segment's server. At each subsequent read-lock acquisition, the InterWeave library checks to see whether the local copy of the segment is "recent enough". If not, it obtains a version update from the server. Twin and diff operations [8], extended to accommodate heterogeneous data formats (Section 2.3), allow InterWeave to perform an update in time proportional to the fraction of the data that has changed.

The relaxed semantics of read locks imply that a process may hold a write lock (with exclusive access to the current version of the segment) even when other processes are reading older versions. To support concurrent access by readers that need to exclude any writer, InterWeave also supports a strict read lock.

Unless otherwise specified, newly-created segments employ Full coherence. The creator of a segment can specify an alternative default if desired. An individual process may then override this default for its own lock operations. Different processes may therefore use different coherence models for the same segment. These are entirely compatible: the server for a segment always has the most recent version; the model used by a given process simply determines when it decides whether its own cached copy is recent enough.

The server for a segment need only maintain a copy of the segment's most recent version. Older versions are not required, because the API specifies that the current version of a segment is always acceptable, and since processes cache whole segments, they never need an "extra piece" of an old version. To minimize the cost of segment updates, the server maintains a timestamp on each block of each segment, so that it can avoid transmitting copies of blocks that haven't changed.

As noted in Section 1, a Cashmere-style "level-2" sharing system plays the role of a single node at level 3. A process in a level-2 system that obtains a level-3 lock does so on behalf of its entire level-2 system, and may share access to the segment with its level-2 peers. The runtime system guarantees that updates are propagated consistently, and that protocol overhead required to maintain coherence is not replicated at levels 2 and 3. Further details appear in Section 3.

2.2 Consistency

While InterWeave's predecessor, InterAct, has proven useful for many applications (in particular, we have used it successfully for interactive datamining [30]), it does not respect causality: in the face of multi-version relaxed consistency, the versions of segments currently visible to a process may not be consistent with what Lamport called the "happens-before" relationship [26]. Specifically, let A_i refer to version i of segment A. If B_j was created using information found in A_i, then previous versions of A are causally incompatible with B_j; a process that wants to use B_j (and that wants to respect causality) should invalidate any cached segment versions that predate the versions on which B_j depends.

To support this invalidation process, we would ideally like to tag each segment version with the names of all segment versions on which it depends. Then any process that acquired a lock on a segment would check to see whether it depends on newer versions of any segments currently locally cached. If so, the process would invalidate those segments.

The problem with this scheme is that the number of segments in the system—and hence the size of tags—is unbounded. One simple solution is to hash the information. We let every segment version S_i carry an n-slot vector timestamp, and choose a global hash function h that maps segment identifiers into the range $[0..n-1]$. Slot j in the vector indicates the maximum, over all segments P whose identifiers hash to j, of the most recent version of P on which S_i depends. When acquiring a lock on S_i, a process checks each of its cached segment versions Q_k to see whether k is less than the value in slot $h(Q)$ of S_i's vector timestamp. If so, the process invalidates Q_k.

To support the creation of segment timestamps, each process maintains a local timestamp that indicates (in hashed form) the most recent segment versions it has read. When releasing a write lock (thereby creating a new segment version), the process increments the version number of the segment itself, updates its local timestamp to reflect that number, and attaches this new timestamp to the newly-created segment version. We have developed refinements to this scheme to accommodate roll-over of the values within timestamps, and to reduce the chance that hash collisions will cause repeated extraneous invalidations of a segment that seldom changes.

To support operations on groups of segments, we allow their locks to be acquired and released together. Write locks released together make each new segment version appear to be in the logical past of the other, ensuring that a process that acquires the locks together will never obtain the new version of one without the other. To enhance the performance of the most relaxed applications, we allow an individual process to "opt out" of causality on a segment-by-segment basis. For sharing levels 1 and 2, consistency is guaranteed for data-race-free [1] programs.

2.3   Heterogeneity

The Internet is highly heterogeneous. Even our local-area network includes Suns, Linux and Windows 2000 PCs, SGI machines, Macintoshes, Alphas, and a variety of special-purpose peripherals. To accommodate such a variety of architectures, remote procedure call systems usually incorporate a language- and machine-independent notation to describe the types of parameters, together with a stub compiler that automatically translates to and from a universal "wire format". Any system for distributed shared state must provide a similar level of support for heterogeneity.

Segments in InterWeave are currently similar to those in InterAct, and are derived from a C++ base class with special constructor, destructor, and synchronization methods. InterWeave uses the C++ reflection mechanism to obtain type information and to identify intra- and inter-segment pointers, so that data can be translated appropriately when sent from one machine to another. Other systems such as Orca [4] provide similar representations for address-independent segments.

We are in the process of eliminating our dependence on C++ by using Sun's XDR language to define the types of data within segments. Pointer swizzling [45] will be used to accommodate reference types. Briefly, swizzling uses type information to find all (machine-independent) pointers within a newly-acquired segment, and converts them to pointers that work on the local machine. Pointers to segments that are not (yet) locally cached point into reserved but unmapped pages where data will lie once properly locked. The set of segments currently cached on a given machine thus displays an "expanding frontier" reminiscent of lazy dynamic linking. As noted at the beginning of this section, each segment is structured as a heap in which blocks may be allocated dynamically. Further detail can be found in our paper at WSDSM 2000 [33]. In keeping with our work on InterAct, we will allow compilers and smart applications to control the relative placement of blocks within the heap, to maximize cache performance under different traversal orders. The code that transfers segments from one machine to another will automatically re-order items in the heap according to local preference, as part of the swizzling process.

3   Implementation and Performance

In this section, we describe the current version of our implementation prototype, and present preliminary performance data for remote visualization of an N-body simulation.

3.1   Implementation

Our current implementation (see Figure 2) employs a server process for each segment. The server keeps metadata for each active client of the segment, as well as a master copy of the segment's data. Communication with each client is managed by a separate thread.

Each segment client can be either a single process or a tightly coupled cluster. When a client obtains a write lock, it uses virtual memory mechanisms to identify pages of the segment's local copy that are about to be modified. For each such page it creates a pristine copy (called a *twin*) before allowing modification. At the time of the write lock release, the runtime library uses the twins and other local meta-data (specifically, type descriptors) to construct a *machine-independent diff* that describes changes in terms of field offsets within blocks. Blocks above a certain minimum size are logically subdivided into "chunks" so that a small change to a very large block need not create a large diff. The machine-independent diff is sent back to the segment server to update its master copy.

When a tightly coupled cluster, such as a Cashmere-2L system, uses an InterWeave segment, the cluster appears as a single client to the segment server. The InterWeave system uses cluster-wide shared memory for the segment local copy. Our goal is to minimize any additional overhead due to incorporating the third level into the system. In the current implementation, we designate a node inside the cluster as the cluster's manager node. All of the third level interactions with the segment server go through the manager node. During the period between a write lock acquire and release, the same twins are used by both the second and third level systems (see [39] for details on the

Segment Data:

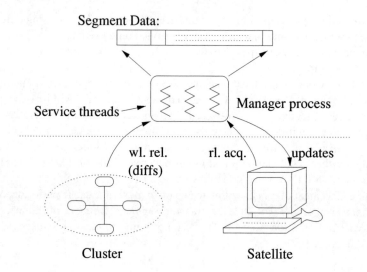

Fig. 2. Current InterWeave implementation.

Cashmere-2L implementation). At a second level release, in addition to sending diffs to the second level home node, the runtime system sends a third level diff to the manager node. The manager node merges all of these diffs and sends them to the segment server at the time of the third level write-lock release. One optimization would be to have the second level home nodes maintain the cumulative third level diffs. This would eliminate communication with a possibly separate manager node entirely. We are currently incorporating this optimization into our system.

3.2 Experiments

To evaluate our prototype implementation of InterWeave, we have collected performance measurements on a remote visualization of the Splash-2 [46] Barnes-Hut simulation. The simulation runs on a 4-node, 16-processor Cashmere system. Each node is an AlphaServer 4100 5/600, with four 600 MHz 21164A processors, an 8 MB direct-mapped board-level cache with a 64-byte line size, and 2 GBytes of memory. The nodes are connected by a Memory Channel 2 [13] system area network. The simulation repeatedly computes new positions for 16,000 bodies. These positions may be shared with a remote visualization satellite via an InterWeave segment. The simulator uses a write lock to update the shared segment, while the satellite uses a relaxed read lock with temporal coherence to obtain an effective frame rate of 15 frames per second. Under human direction, the visualization satellite can also steer the application by acquiring a write lock and changing a body's data.

When we combine the high performance second level shared memory (Cashmere) with the third level shared memory (InterWeave), it would be ideal if there were no degradation in the performance of the second level system. To see how closely we approach this ideal, we linked the application with the InterWeave library, but ran it without connecting to a visualization satellite. Communication with the server running on another Alpha node was via TCP/IP over Fast Ethernet. Relatively little communication occurs in the absence of a satellite, due to a *sole-sharer* optimization that avoids the transmission of diffs when there is only a single known copy of the data.

Execution times for the no-satellite experiment appear in Figure 3. Each bar gives aggregate wall-clock time for ten iteration steps. In each pair of bars, the one on the right is for the standard Cashmere system; the one on the left is for Cashmere linked with the InterWeave library and communicating with a server. The left-hand bars are subdivided to identify the overhead due to running the third-level protocol code. This overhead is negligible for small configurations, but increases to about 11% for 16 processors on 4 nodes. This non-scalability can be explained by our use of a single manager node within the Cashmere cluster. As the number of processes increases, the manager has to spend more time collecting diffs, which makes the system unbalanced. As described in Section 3.1, we are working to eliminate this bottleneck.

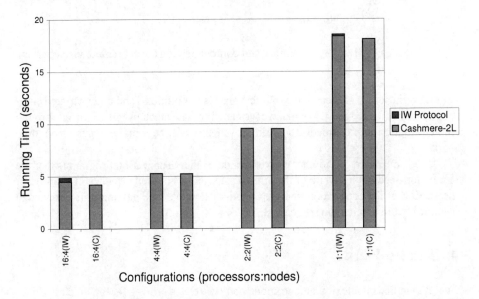

Fig. 3. Overhead of InterWeave library without a satellite.

We also measured the simulator's performance when communicating with a single satellite. Specifically, we compared execution times using InterWeave to those obtained by augmenting user-level code with explicit TCP/IP messages to communicate with the satellite (directly, without a server), and then running the result on the standard Cashmere system. Preliminary results appear in Figure 4. In all cases the satellite was running on another Alpha node, communicating with the cluster and server, if any, via TCP/IP over Fast Ethernet. We have again subdivided execution time, this time to separate out both communication and (for the left-hand bars) InterWeave protocol overhead. The overhead of the InterWeave protocol itself remains relatively small, but communi-

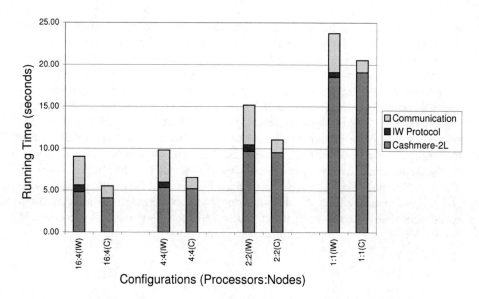

Fig. 4. Overhead of InterWeave library and communication during remote visualization.

cation overhead is significant, due to InterWeave's unoptimized and unaggregated communication with the server. We believe we can eliminate much of this overhead through implementation improvements; such improvements will be a major focus of ongoing work.

A key advantage of the InterWeave version of the visualization program is that the simulation need not be aware of the number of satellites or the frequency of sharing. In the version of the application that uses hand-written message passing, this knowledge is embedded in application source code.

4   Related Work

InterWeave finds context in an enormous body of related work—far too much to document thoroughly here.

Most systems for distributed shared state enforce a strongly object-oriented programming model. Some, such as Emerald [23], Argus [27], Ada [22], and ORCA [42], take the form of an explicitly distributed programming language. Some, notably Amber [10] and its successor, VDOM [11], are C++-specific. Many in recent years have been built on top of Java; examples include Aleph [20], Charlotte [5], Java/DSM [48], Javelin [7], JavaParty [31], JavaSpaces [41], and ShareHolder [18].

Language-independent distributed object systems include PerDiS [12], Legion [17], Globe [44], DCOM [35], and various CORBA-compliant systems [29]. Globe replicates objects for availability and fault tolerance. PerDiS and a few CORBA systems (e.g., Fresco [25]) cache objects for locality of reference. Thor [28] enforces type-safe object-oriented access to records in a heterogeneous distributed database.

At least two early software distributed shared memory (S-DSM) systems provided support for heterogeneous machine types. Toronto's Mermaid system [49] allowed data to be shared across more than one type of machine, but only among processes created as part of a single run-to-completion parallel program. All data in the same VM page was required to have the same type, and only one memory model—sequential consistency—was supported. CMU's Agora system [6] supported sharing among more loosely-coupled processes, but in a significantly more restricted fashion than in InterWeave. Pointers and recursive types were not supported, all shared data had to be accessed indirectly through a local mapping table, and only a single memory model (similar to processor consistency) was supported.

Perhaps the two projects most closely related to InterWeave are Khazana [9] and Active Harmony [21]. Both are outgrowths of previous work in software distributed shared memory. Both support distributed sharing without enforcing an object-oriented programming style. Khazana proposes a global, 128-bit address space for all the world's shared data. It does not impose any structure on that data, or attempt to translate it into locally-appropriate form. Active Harmony is more explicitly oriented toward high-performance parallel execution. Early work appears to have focussed primarily on load balancing and process management. Various Linda systems [32,37] also provide a non-object-oriented distributed shared store.

Interface description languages date from Xerox Courier [47] and related systems of the early 1980s. Precedents for the automatic management of pointers include Herlihy's thesis work [19], LOOM [24], and the more recent "pickling" (serialization) of Java [34]. Friedman [15] and Agrawal et al. [2] have shown how to combine certain pairs of consistency models in a non-version-based system. Alonso et al. [3] present a general system for relaxed, user-controlled coherency. We explore a real implementation of a dynamically adjustable coherence mechanism in an environment that allows tightly-coupled sharing in addition to the relaxed coherence in a more distributed environment. Several projects, including ShareHolder, Globus [14], and WebOS [43], use URL-like names for distributed objects or files. Khazana proposes the use of multiple consistency models.

5   Status and Plans

A preliminary version of InterWeave is up and running on Rochester's AlphaServer cluster. It provides full support for user-specified coherence predicates, but does not yet implement inter-segment coherence. The type system is currently based on C++, rather than XDR, and though we support user-specified data layouts (rearrangement of blocks in the heap), we have not yet implemented data conversions for heterogeneous machine architectures. The current system supports working demonstrations of remote interactive parallel association mining and visualization of a parallel N-body simulation, demonstrating the utility of the system in combining distributed sharing with tightly-coupled coherence.

Once the basic features of InterWeave are in place, we expect to turn to several additional issues, including security, fault tolerance, and transactions. We hope to leverage the protection and security work of others, most likely using a group-based system reminiscent of AFS [36]. Toleration of client failures is simplified by the version-based programming model: a segment simply reverts to its previous version if a client dies in the middle of an update. Server faults might be tolerated by pushing new versions through to stable storage. Ultimately, a true transactional programming model (as opposed to simple reader-writer locks) would allow us to recover from failed operations that update multiple segments, and to implement two-phase locking to recover from deadlock or causality violations when using nested locks.

References

1. S. V. Adve and M. D. Hill. A Unified Formulation of Four Shared-Memory Models. *IEEE Trans. on Parallel and Distributed Systems*, 4(6):613–624, June 1993.
2. D. Agrawal, M. Choy, H. V. Leong, and A. K. Singh. Mixed Consistency: A Model for Parallel Programming. In *Proc. of the 13th ACM Symp. on Principles of Distributed Computing*, Los Angeles, CA, Aug. 1994.
3. R. Alonso, D. Barbara, and H. Garcia-Molina. Data Caching Issues in an Information Retrieval System. *ACM Trans. on Database Systems*, 15(3):359–384, Sept. 1990.
4. H. E. Bal, M. F. Kaashoek, and A. S. Tanenbaum. Orca: A Language for Parallel Programming of Distributed Systems. In *IEEE Trans. on Software Engineering*, pages 190–205, June 1992.
5. A. Baratloo, M. Karaul, V. Keden, and P. Wyckoff. Charlotte: Metacomputing on the Web. *Intl. Journal on Future Generation Computer Systems*, 15(5-6):559–570, 1999.
6. R. Bisiani and A. Forin. Multilanguage Parallel Programming of Heterogeneous Machines. *IEEE Trans. on Computers*, 37(8):930–945, Aug. 1988.
7. P. Cappello, B. O. Christiansen, M. F. Ionescu, M. O. Neary, K. E. Schauser, and D. Wu. Javelin: Internet-Based Parallel Computing Using Java. In *1997 ACM Workshop on Java for Science and Engineering Computation*, Las Vegas, NV, June 1997.
8. J. B. Carter, J. K. Bennett, and W. Zwaenepoel. Implementation and Performance of Munin. In *Proc. of the 13th ACM Symp. on Operating Systems Principles*, pages 152–164, Pacific Grove, CA, Oct. 1991.
9. J. Carter, A. Ranganathan, and S. Susarla. Khazana: An Infrastructure for Building Distributed Services. In *Intl. Conf. on Distributed Computing Systems*, pages 562–571, May 1998.
10. J. S. Chase, F. G. Amador, E. D. Lazowska, H. M. Levy, and R. J. Littlefield. The Amber System: Parallel Programming on a Network of Multiprocessors. In *Proc. of the 12th ACM Symp. on Operating Systems Principles*, pages 147–158, Litchfield Park, AZ, Dec. 1989.
11. M. J. Feeley and H. M. Levy. Distributed Shared Memory with Versioned Objects. In *OOPSLA '92 Conf. Proc.*, pages 247–262, Vancouver, BC, Canada, Oct. 1992.
12. P. Ferreira, M. Shapiro, X. Blondel, O. Fambon, J. Garcia, S. Kloosterman, N. Richer, M. Roberts, F. Sandakly, G. Coulouris, J. Dollimore, P. Guedes, D. Hagimont, and S. Krakowiak. PerDiS: Design, Implementaiton, and Use of a PERsistent DIstributed Store. Research Report 3525, INRIA, Rocquencourt, France, Oct. 1998.
13. M. Fillo and R. B. Gillett. Architecture and Implementation of Memory Channel 2. *Digital Technical Journal*, 9(1):27–41, 1997.
14. I. Foster and C. Kesselman. Globus: A Metacomputing Infrastructure Toolkit. *Intl. Journal of Supercomputer Applications*, 11(2):115–128, 1997.
15. R. Friedman. Implementing Hybrid Consistency with High-Level Synchronization Operations. In *Proc. of the 12th ACM Symp. on Principles of Distributed Computing*, Ithaca, NY, Aug. 1993.

16. K. Gharachorloo, D. Lenoski, J. Laudon, P. Gibbons, A. Gupta, and J. L. Hennessy. Memory Consistency and Event Ordering in Scalable Shared-Memory Multiprocessors. In *Proc. of the 17th Intl. Symp. on Computer Architecture*, pages 15–26, Seattle, WA, May 1990.

17. A. S. Grimshaw and W. A. Wulf. Legion — A View from 50,000 Feet. In *Proc. of the 5th Intl. Symp. on High Performance Distributed Computing*, Aug. 1996.

18. J. Harris and V. Sarkar. Lightweight Object-Oriented Shared Variables for Distributed Applications on the Internet. In *OOPSLA '98 Conf. Proc.*, pages 296–309, Vancouver, Canada, Oct. 1998.

19. M. Herlihy and B. Liskov. A Value Transmission Method for Abstract Data Types. *ACM Trans. on Programming Languages and Systems*, 4(4):527–551, Oct. 1982.

20. M. Herlihy. The Aleph Toolkit: Support for Scalable Distributed Shared Objects. In *Workshop on Communication, Architecture, and Applications for*, Orlando, FL, Jan. 1999.

21. J. K. Hollingsworth and P. J. Keleher. Prediction and Adaptation in Active Harmony. In *Proc. of the 7th Intl. Symp. on High Performance Distributed Computing*, Chicago, IL, Apr. 1998.

22. International Organization for Standardization. Information Technology — Programming Languages — Ada. Geneva, Switzerland, 1995. ISO/IEC 8652:1995 (E). Available in hypertext at http://www.adahome.com/rm95/.

23. E. Jul, H. Levy, N. Hutchinson, and A. Black. Fine-Grained Mobility in the Emerald System. *ACM Trans. on Computer Systems*, 6(1):109–133, Feb. 1988. Originally presented at the *11th ACM Symp. on Operating Systems Principles*, Nov. 1987.

24. T. Kaehler. Virtual Memory on a Narrow Machine for an Object-Oriented Language. In *OOPSLA '86 Conf. Proc.*, pages 87–106, Portland, OR, Sept. – Oct. 1986.

25. R. Kordale, M. Ahamad, and M. Devarakonda. Object Caching in a CORBA Compliant System. *Computing Systems*, 9(4):377–404, Fall 1996.

26. L. Lamport. Time, Clocks, and the Ordering of Events in a Distributed System. *Comm. of the ACM*, 21(7):558–565, July 1978.

27. B. Liskov. Distributed Programming in Argus. *Comm. of the ACM*, 31(3):300–312, Mar. 1988.

28. B. Liskov, A. Adya, M. Castro, M. Day, S. Ghemawat, R. Gruber, U. Maheshwari, A. C. Myers, and L. Shrira. Safe and Efficient Sharing of Persistent Objects in Thor. In *Proc. of the 1996 ACM SIGMOD Intl. Conf. on Management of Data*, Montreal, Canada, June 1996.

29. Object Management Group, Inc. The Common Object Request Broker: Architecture and Specification, Revision 2.0. Framingham, MA, July 1996.

30. S. Parthasarathy and S. Dwarkadas. InterAct: Virtual Sharing for Interactive Client-Server Applications. In *4th Workshop on Languages, Compilers, and Run-time Systems for Scalable Computers*, May 1998.

31. M. Philippsen and M. Zenger. JavaParty — Transparent Remote Objects in Java. *Concurrency — Practice and Experience*, 9(11):1125–1242, Nov. 1997.

32. G. P. Picco, A. L. Murphy, and G. Roman. Lime: Linda meets mobility. In *Proc. of the 21st Intl. Conf. on Software Engineering*, pages 368–377, Los Angeles, CA, May 1999.

33. E. Pinheiro, D. Chen, S. Dwarkadas, S. Parthasarathy, and M. L. Scott. S-DSM for Heterogeneous Machine Architectures. In *Proc. of the 2nd Workshop on Software Distributed Shared Memory*, Santa Fe, NM, May 2000. In conjunction with the *14th Intl. Conf. on Supercomputing*.

34. R. Riggs, J. Waldo, A. Wollrath, and K. Bharat. Pickling State in the Java System. *Computing Systems*, 9(4):291–312, Fall 1996.

35. D. Rogerson. *Inside COM*. Microsoft Press, Redmond, Washington, Jan. 1997.

36. M. Satyanarayanan. Integrating Security in a Large Distributed System. *ACM Trans. on Computer Systems*, 7(3):247–280, Aug. 1989.

37. Scientific Computing Associates Inc. Virtual Shared Memory and the Paradise System for Distributed Computing. Technical Report, New Haven, CT, April 1999.

38. A. Singla, U. Ramachandran, and J. Hodgins. Temporal Notions of Synchronization and Consistency in Beehive. In *Proc. of the 9th Annual ACM Symp. on Parallel Algorithms and Architectures*, Newport, RI, June 1997.

39. R. Stets, S. Dwarkadas, N. Hardavellas, G. Hunt, L. Kontothanassis, S. Parthasarathy, and M. Scott. Cashmere-2L: Software Coherent Shared Memory on a Clustered Remote-Write Network. In *Proc. of the 16th ACM Symp. on Operating Systems Principles*, St. Malo, France, Oct. 1997.

40. *Network Programming Guide—External Data Representation Standard: Protocol Specification*. Sun Microsystems, Inc., 1990.

41. Sun Microsystems. JavaSpaces Specification. Palo Alto, CA, Jan. 1999.

42. A. S. Tanenbaum, M. F. Kaashoek, and H. E. Bal. Parallel Programming Using Shared Objects and Broadcasting. *Computer*, 25(8):10–19, Aug. 1992.

43. A. Vahdat, T. Anderson, M. Dahlin, D. Culler, E. Belani, P. Eastham, and C. Yoshikawa. WebOS: Operating System Services for Wide Area Applications. In *Proc. of the 7th Intl. Symp. on High Performance Distributed Computing*, Chicago, IL, July 1998.

44. M. van Steen, P. Homburg, and A. S. Tanenbaum. Globe: A Wide-Area Distributed System. In *IEEE Concurrency*, pages 70–78, Jan.-Mar. 1999.

45. P. R. Wilson. Pointer Swizzling at Page Fault Time: Efficiently and Compatibly Supporting Huge Address Spaces on Standard Hardware. In *International Workshop on Object Orientation in Operating Systems*, page 244ff, Paris, France, Sept. 1992.

46. S. C. Woo, M. Ohara, E. Torrie, J. P. Singh, and A. Gupta. Methodological Considerations and Characterization of the SPLASH-2 Parallel Application Suite. In *Proc. of the 22nd Intl. Symp. on Computer Architecture*, Santa Margherita Ligure, Italy, June 1995.

47. Xerox Corporation. Courier: The Remote Procedure Call Protocol. Technical Report XSIS 038112, Dec. 1981.

48. W. Yu and A. Cox. Java/DSM: A Platform for Heterogeneous Computing. *Concurrency—Practice and Experience*, 9(11), Nov. 1997.

49. S. Zhou, M. Stumm, K. Li, and D. Wortman. Heterogeneous Distributed Shared Memory. In *IEEE Trans. on Parallel and Distributed Systems*, pages 540–554, 1992.

Run-Time Support for Adaptive Heavyweight Services

Julio C. Lopez and David R. O'Hallaron

Carnegie Mellon University, Pittsburgh PA 15213, USA
{jclopez,droh}@cs.cmu.edu

Abstract. By definition, a heavyweight network service requires a significant amount of computation to complete its task. Providing a heavyweight service is challenging for a number of reasons. First, since the service can typically not be provided in a timely fashion using a single server at the remote site, multiple hosts at both the server and client sites must be employed. Second, the available compute and network resources change with respect to time. Thus, an effective service must be adaptive in the sense that it is able to transparently aggregate the available resources and react to the changing availability of these resources. In this paper we present a framework that allows us to build these kinds of adaptive heavyweight services. Experimental results with a distributed visualization service suggest that the cost imposed by the new capability is reasonable

1 Introduction

Existing Web-based network services are typically *lightweight* in the sense that servers do a relatively small amount of work in order to satisfy each request. This is primarily due to concerns about minimizing response latency for clients and not overloading the compute resources of high-volume servers. If these concerns were addressed, service providers could also offer *heavyweight* services that require significant amounts of computation per request. Examples include search engines with advanced IR algorithms, data mining, and remote visualization of large datasets.

Providing heavyweight services is challenging for a number of reasons: (1) Service providers can only contribute so many compute resources, and often these resources will be insufficient; (2) For a given service, the available compute and network resources are often quite different, and can also change over time. For example, different clients will have different rendering and compute power and available memory and disk storage; paths to different clients will have different bandwidth and latency; server loads and hence the number of available server cycles will vary.

There a number of implications: (1) Clients must contribute significant compute resources; (2) Services must be able to aggregate the compute resources made available by the individual clients; (3) Services must be able to adapt to different resources. The bottom line is that no single server design is appropriate for all conditions. Heavyweight services must be *performance-portable*, adapting automatically to different levels of available resources.

In this paper we describe a run-time system and its API for building heavyweight network services. The system is based on the notion of *active frames*, which are mobile

S. Dwarkadas (Ed.): LCR 2000, LNCS 1915, pp. 221–234, 2002.

code and data objects that hop from host to host in a computational grid [4] (Section 2). Adaptivity is achieved by allowing application-level scheduling [3] of the work performed at each hop and the location of the next hop (Section 3). The active frame system is the basis for a remote visualization application (Section 4). In section 5 we evaluate the active frame system as a mechanism to aggregate resources in two different setups.

2   Active Frames

An *active frame* is an application-level transfer unit that contains program and associated application data. Frames are processed by compute servers called *frame servers*. The frames are transfered among servers using TCP/IP over a best-effort internet. The program and data contained in the frame are read by servers, which interpret and execute the program (See figure: 1). The active frame interface declares a single `execute` method, which is used as the entry point for the frame execution.

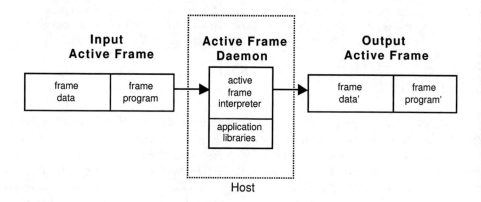

Fig. 1. Active frame and server

```
interface ActiveFrame {
  HostAddress execute(ServerState state);
}
```

The `execute` method operates on the input data and produces output data. The frame has access to the state of the server where it is executing through the `state` parameter passed to the execute method. After the frame execution the server sends the frame to the address returned by the `execute` method.

2.1   Frame Server API

The frame server defines a small set of primitives shown in Table 1. The application running on a host can either start a new server on its local host or access an already running server on the same machine. The application then creates a frame and uses the send primitive to initiate the frame's processing. The send primitive on the server calls the frame's execute method and sends the frame to the returned address if it is not null. Here is how an application might create and start a frame server:

Table 1. Frame server API

Method	Description
void send(ActiveFrame frame)	Execute and send an active frame to the server returned by its execute method.
Object get(String id)	Retrieve an object from the server soft storage
void put(String id)	Add an object to the server soft storage

```
1:FrameServer server=new FrameServer(3000);
2:ActiveFrame frame =new SampleFrame();
3:server.send(frame);
```

The application starts a server on the local host using port 3000 (line 1), and then creates and sends a new active frame (lines 2,3). An active frame executing at a server calls these primitives through the reference to the server's state passed to the execute method. Here is a sample frame that uses soft storage to keep state between execution of frames:

```
1:class SampleFrame
2:   implements ActiveFrame {
3:   HostAddress execute(ServerState state) {
4:   Integer estimate    = (Integer)state.get(ESTIMATE_ID);
    ... // set app parameters
5:   Integer execTime    = compute();
6:   Integer newEstimate\\
                  = computeEstimate(estimate, execTime);
7:   state.put(ESTIMATE_ID, newEstimate)
    ...
   }
 }
```

The frame uses the get method (line 4) to obtain a previously stored estimate of the time it will take to complete a computation. After the frame finishes the computation (line 5) it updates and stores the estimate in the server's soft storage using the put method (lines 6-7).

With this simple mechanism the application can exploit the compute resources of the frame servers by shipping part of the computation along with the data to the servers. In order to provide more sophisticated services to the application, the servers can be extended with application specific libraries. This is a crucial feature because it allows the use of existing packages and integration with other systems. For example a visualization program can use packages like vtk [7] or openDX [1]. In our current implementation the servers load these libraries at startup time and active frames can access the libraries throughout their execution.

3   Scheduling with Active Frames

The scheduler interface defines a single method:

```
interface Scheduler {
    HostAddress getHost(int hopCount);
}
```

The getHost method returns the address of the next host the frame should be sent to. It takes a single integer argument that specifies the number of servers the frame has visited. A zero argument indicates that the frame is at the *source server*.

The scheduler is transmitted along with the frame program. The getHost method is called by every server the frame visits. This mechanism permits the implementation of various scheduling policies, allowing the application to make decisions at different points during its execution. Here are some examples.

Static scheduling: In this scenario the application uses the same host assignment for all frames of the same type. Each frame visits the same set of servers and executes the same set of calculations. The application can exploit information about its own resource demands to create the schedule. However it cannot adapt to dynamic resource availability. The following example shows the implementation of a static scheduler:

```
1:class StaticScheduler
2:     implements Scheduler {
3: StaticScheduler(HostAddress[] list) {
4:   this.hosts = list;
     }
5: HostAddress getHost(int hopCount) {
6:   if(hopCount<numberOfHosts) {
7:     return this.hosts[hopCount];
     }
8:   return null;
     }
   }
...
9: HostAddress[] list  = getHostList();
10:Scheduler sched     = new StaticScheduler(list);
11:ActiveFrame frame   = new SampleFrame(sched);
12:server.send(frame);
```

---

[1] http://www.research.ibm.com/dx

The application computes the list of hosts to execute once and then uses that set of hosts for all frames. The scheduler carries the list of host addresses and returns the appropriate address from that list.

Scheduling at frame creation time: In this scenario, the frames are scheduled at the source server. The scheduler can combine application-specific information with data from a resource monitoring system such as Remos [5] or NWS [8] to make scheduling decisions. This scheme adds some degree of adaptivity to the application, because different frames may follow different paths and use different compute resources. However, since the schedule for any individual frame is static, this adaptation only occurs at the source. In the following example the scheduler generates the path of compute hosts at the source (hopCount==0) and uses that path for the frame transmission.

```
1:class AtCreationTimeScheduler
2:    implements Scheduler {
   ...
3: HostAddress getHost(int hopCount) {
4:  if(hopCount==0) {
5:    this.hosts = computePath();
   }
6:  if(hopCount<numberOfHosts) {
7:    return this.hosts[hopCount];
   }
8:  return null;
  }
 }
```

Scheduling at frame delivery time: In this scenario, the application can make scheduling decisions just before the active frame is delivered to the next server. The application can react to changing resource conditions even if the frame is in flight. This offers the highest degree of adaptivity, but might introduce significant overhead depending on the complexity of the decision making procedure.

```
1:class AtDeliveryTimeScheduler
2:    implements Scheduler {
3: HostAddress getHost(int hopCount) {
4:    if(hopCount<numberOfHosts) {
5:      return getHostNow();
   }
6:    return null;
  }
 }
```

4 Motivating Remote Viz Service

We have the active frame system to implement a general remote visualization service called Dv [1]. The specific viz application (Quakeviz) produces an animation of the ground motion during the 1994 Northridge earthquake [2].

Each Quakeviz input dataset consists of a 3D tetrahedral mesh and a sequence of frames, where each frame describes the magnitude of the earth's displacement at each node in the mesh at a particular point in time. Ranging in size from hundreds of GB to TBs, the datasets are generally too massive to copy from the remote supercomputer site where they are computed to our local site. We must manipulate them remotely, and thus the need for a remote viz service.

The Quakeviz input datasets for the examples in this paper were produced by our 183.equake benchmark program in the SPEC CPU2000 benchmark suite [6]. The visualization of the 183.equake dataset produces a 3D animation of the wave propagation during the first 40 seconds of a quake.

Figure 2 shows the transformations that are applied to each frame in the dataset to produce a frame in the animation. The first step selects a region of interest both in time and space from the dataset after it is loaded from a file. The next step finds regions in the dataset with similar features to generate isosurfaces. The final tasks apply a color map to the values in the dataset, synthesize a scene, and then render the final image.

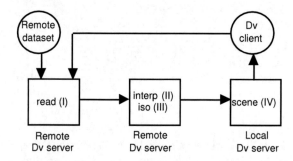

Fig. 2. A QuakeViz application implemented with Dv

4.1   Dv

Dv is a toolkit built on top of the active frame system that enables a user to visualize and interact with datasets stored at remote sites [1]. Figure 2 shows an example Quakeviz application implemented with Dv. This particular instance of the visualization runs on three hosts: (1) a *source host* that reads the dataset; (2) a *compute host* where the isosurface extraction is performed and a client host that that performs isosurface extraction; and (3) a *client host* that performs the scene synthesis and rendering. Each Dv server is a frame server that is extended with existing visualization libraries. The Dv client sends a special type of active frame, called a *request frame*, to the source host. The request server reads the dataset and generates a series of *response frames* that are sent back to the client. Examples of these frames are shown below.

```
1:class RequestFrame
2:   implements ActiveFrame {
```

```
3: HostAddress execute(ServerState state) {
4:   Source source = new QvDataSource();
     ...
5:   while (moreFrames()) {
6:    Dataset data
7:       = source.getFrame(roi_parameters);
8:    ResponseFrame fr=new ResponseFrame();
9:     fr.setData(data);
10:   Scheduler sched = createScheduler();
11:    fr.setScheduler(sched);
12:    state.getServer().send(fr);
     }
     ...
13:  return null;
     }
   }
```

The request frame creates a source object (lines 4–7), which is defined in the visualization library, to access the dataset. Then it creates a response frame (line 8) and a scheduler (line 10). The request frame sends the response with its scheduler (lines 11-12) using the frame server API. The request frame returns null (line 13) after it has sent the response frames back to the client.

```
1:class ResponseFrame
2:      implements ActiveFrame {
     ...
3:   HostAddress execute(ServerState state) {
     ...
4:     Filter filter = new Filter();
5:     filter.setInput(this.data);
6:     filter.compute();
7:     this.data = filter.getOutput();
     ...
8:     return scheduler.getHost(hopCount);
     }
   }
```

The response frame uses a filter from the visualization library to process the dataset (lines 4-6), and then it updates the frame data with filter output (line 7). Finally the response frame calls the scheduler to obtain the address of the next host and returns it.

5   Evaluation

It is clear that the active frame system provides a flexible mechanism for application-level scheduling. In this section we begin to evaluate the costs and benefits of this flexibility.

5.1   Single-Host Setup

This section characterizes the execution time on a single host of the visualization described in Section 4, using a relatively small dataset as input. The input dataset contains `183.equake` ground motion data with 30K unstructured mesh node and 151K tetrahedral elements. The size of each frame data is 120 KB. The dataset contains 165 frames, each containing a scalar value for the horizontal displacement of each node in the mesh. The region of interest specified for the animation includes the complete volume of the basin and all the frames in the dataset. The measurements shown below were taken on a Pentium-III/450MHz host with 512 MB of memory running NT 4.0 with a Real3D Starfighter AGP/8MB video accelerator.

Table 2. Mean execution time (local)

Isosurfaces Operation	10 time (ms)	20 time (ms)	50 time (ms)
Read frame data	584.35	582.65	586.13
Isosurface extraction	1044.37	1669.73	3562.36
Rendering	55.72	63.73	125.77
Total	1684.44	2316.11	4274.26
Frames per second	0.59	0.43	0.23

Table 2 summarizes the cost of running a purely sequential C++ version of the visualization on a single host. The application pays an average one-time cost of 5.389 seconds to load the mesh topology (not shown in table). The application caches the mesh information since it is the same for all frames. To process a frame, the application spends an average of 583.78 ms loading the data for each frame.

Figures 3 and 4 show the execution time of isosurface extraction and rendering. Execution time for each tasks depends on the *number-of-isosurfaces* parameter (See table 2). The isosurface extraction task produces a more complex output dataset with finer granularity and a greater number of polygons as the number-of-isosurfaces parameter increases, which in turn slows down the rendering task. Figure 4 shows that the execution time of the rendering task is affected by the content of the dataset. During the initial time steps only the ground close to the epicenter is moving. As time passes the wave propagates to the surface, which affects a larger region of the dataset. Toward the end, the effect of the wave is dampened and only the ground near the surface is still shaking.

These results suggest that (1) additional resources are needed; and (2) expected execution time of a task can be controlled by varying application parameters. In order to achieve interactivity, the application must be responsive to the user's input. The total time required to process a single frame (See Table 2) is too large for interaction. By varying application parameters such as number-of-isosurfaces, the application can either produce a higher quality version of the visualization when enough resources are available, or it can reduce the frame's processing time to meet the frame's deadline.

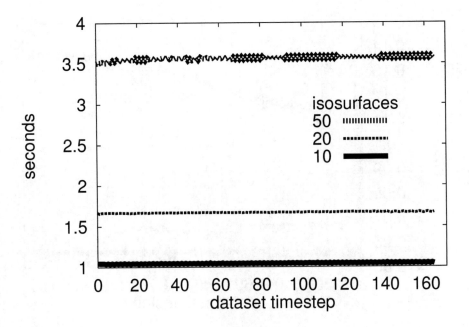

Fig. 3. Isosurface extraction (local).

5.2 Pipeline Setup

To try to make the animation more responsive, we can switch (*without changing the application source code*) from the single-host setup to a three-host setup. Two of these hosts are used as compute servers and the other as a display client. The client host is the same as in Section 5.1. The two additional compute servers are 550 MHz Pentium III processor machines with Ultra SCSI hard disks running version 2.0.36 of the Linux kernel. The server hosts are connected using a 100 Mbit switched Ethernet. The client communicates with the servers through a 10Mbit Ethernet.

The scheduler used in this configuration assigns the tasks to the three hosts as follows (See figure 5): One of the hosts contains the dataset to visualize. The other compute host performs the isosurface extraction. The client host performs the remaining tasks, including scene generation and rendering to the screen.

Table 3 shows the time required to complete each of the operations, including the additional transfer of the data and program from the source to the compute server (marked as s-s) and from the server to the client (s-c). Note that the transfer of the program is significantly slower from the source to the compute server than from the compute server to the client. The compute server becomes the bottleneck of the execution (See table 4) and the task receiving the frame must compete for compute resources to demarshall the frame program and data. The time to transfer the data from the compute server to the client is significantly higher for the extraction of 50 isosurfaces because the polygonal structure is much more detailed and complex in this case, requiring more bandwidth.

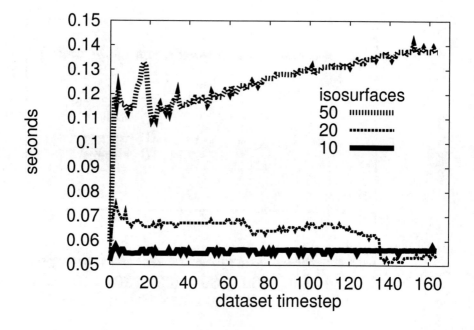

Fig. 4. Rendering (local).

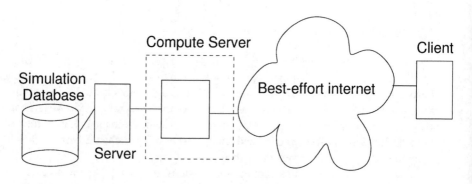

Fig. 5. Pipeline setup

Despite the additional cost of transferring the data and the program, it is possible to obtain the benefits of resource aggregation. Table 4 shows the time each host spends processing a single frame and the respective frame rate each host can produce. For all cases, the compute server has the slowest frame rate, which determines the overall frame rate of the pipeline. Another significant advantage over the local setup is that the client now has plenty of spare cycles for interaction with the user (i.e., Rotate, zoom-in).

Figure 6 shows time to the render a frame at the client throughout the animation. The rendering of a frame is slower and more variable in this setup than in the single-

Table 3. Mean elapsed time (pipeline)

# Isosurfaces Operation	10 time (ms)	20 time (ms)	50 time (ms)
Read frame data	286.21	285.98	287.11
program transfer(s-s)	110.14	94.47	86.51
Data transfer(s-s)	118.88	116.92	119.52
Isosurface extraction	696.43	1152.03	2561.41
Program transfer(s-c)	39.54	44.13	46.40
Polys transfer	175.10	435.66	1700.59
Render	64.99	162.32	340.40
Total	1491.29	2291.51	5141.95

Table 4. Mean frame rate (pipeline)

	Processing time (ms)			Frames per second		
# isos	10	20	50	10	20	50
Source	515.23	497.37	493.15	1.94	2.01	2.03
Server	1140.09	1843.21	4514.44	0.88	0.54	0.22
Client	279.63	642.11	2087.40	3.58	1.56	0.48
Max frame rate				0.88	0.54	0.22

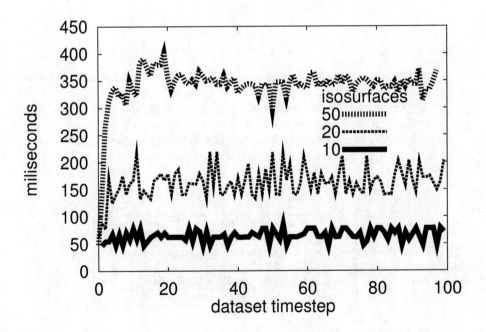

Fig. 6. Render (pipeline).

host setup because the rendering task shares compute resources with the frame transfer task.

5.3   Fan Setup

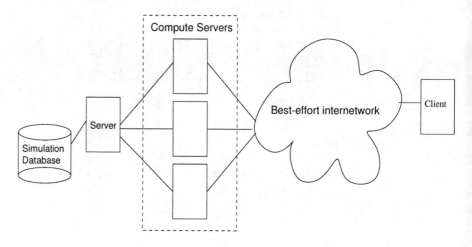

Fig. 7. Fan setup

In this setup, two additional compute servers, with the same specifications as described in the previous section, are used to execute the application. For each frame, the source server reads the dataset and the client generates and renders the scene. The scheduler uses the remaining servers to execute the isosurface extraction by sending each server a different frame in a round-robin fashion (See figure 7). The frames are collected, reordered if necessary, and rendered by the client.

Table 5. Mean frame rate (fan)

# isos	Processing time (ms)			Frames per second		
	10	20	50	10	20	50
Source	413.43	414.85	418.24	2.42	2.41	2.39
Server x 3	1209.77	1746.87	4590.96	2.48	1.72	0.65
Client	525.96	701.03	2345.04	1.90	1.43	0.43
		Max frame rate		1.90	1.43	0.43

Table 5 shows that the client host is saturated, which causes the whole system to slow down. In this case both the program and data transfer operations are slowed down at the client (See Table 6). However, by using application-specific information in the scheduler, the total frame rate is increased by a factor of 3 in two out of the three cases and double in the other case, compared to the single-host setup.

Table 6. Mean execution time (fan)

Isosurfaces Operation	10 time (ms)	20 time (ms)	50 time (ms)
Read data	283.46	283.58	284.52
Program transfer(s-s)	13.61	15.09	17.73
point data transfer	116.36	116.18	115.99
Isosurface	677.09	1098.01	2384.19
program transfer(s-c)	65.26	83.47	173.76
polys transfer	337.45	434.13	1899.29
Render	123.24	183.44	271.99
Total	1616.47	2213.88	5147.48

The rendering time is increased even further (See Table 6) and exhibits higher variability (See Figure 8), because the client host is under high load, which causes the rendering task to be preempted more often.

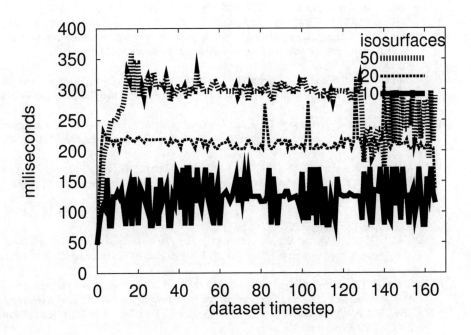

Fig. 8. Render (fan).

6 Conclusions

In order to provide heavyweight services in the future, we must build them so that they are performance-portable, in the sense that they can adapt to heterogeneous and dynamically changing resources. The approach we described here, based on the active frame mechanism, supports various levels of adaptivity, including completely static scheduling, scheduling at request time, and scheduling at frame delivery time.

Our evaluation suggests that remote viz is an example of a heavyweight service that benefits from this adaptivity. We evaluated the remote viz service under two different resource configurations. Although the flexibility of the mechanism introduces non-negligible overhead, in all cases the service obtains the benefits of resource aggregation.

References

1. AESCHLIMANN, M., DINDA, P., KALLIVOKAS, L., LOPEZ, J., LOWEKAMP, B., AND O'HALLARON, D. Preliminary report on the design of a framework for distributed visualization. In *Proceedings of the International Conference on Parallel and Distributed Processing Techniques and Applications (PDPTA'99)* (Las Vegas, NV, June 1999), pp. 1833–1839.
2. BAO, H., BIELAK, J., GHATTAS, O., KALLIVOKAS, L., O'HALLARON, D., SHEWCHUK, J., AND XU, J. Large-scale simulation of elastic wave propagation in heterogeneous media on parallel computers. *Computer Methods in Applied Mechanics and Engineering 152* (Jan. 1998), 85–102.
3. BERMAN, F., AND WOLSKI, R. Scheduling from the perspective of the application. In *Proceedings of the Fifth IEEE Symposium on High Performance Distributed Computing HPDC96* (August 1996), pp. 100–111.
4. FOSTER, I., AND KESSELMAN, C., Eds. *The Grid: Blueprint for a New Computating Infrastructure*. Morgan Kaufman, 340 Pine Street, Sixth floor, San Francisco, CA 94104-3205, 1999.
5. LOWEKAMP, B., MILLER, N., SUTHERLAND, D., GROSS, T., STEENKISTE, P., AND SUBHLOK, J. A resource query interface for network-aware applications. In *Proc. 7th IEEE Symp. High-Performance Distr. Comp.* (jul 1998).
6. O'HALLARON, D. R., AND KALLIVOKAS, L. F. The SPEC CPU2000 183.equake benchmark. http://www.spec.org/osg/cpu2000/CFP2000/, 2000.
7. SCHROEDER, W., MARTIN, K., AND LORENSEN, B. *The Visualization Toolkit: An Object-Oriented Approach to 3D Graphics*, second ed. Prentice Hall PTR, Upper Saddle River, NJ, 1998.
8. WOLSKI, R. Forecasting network performance to support dynamic scheduling using the network weather service. In *Proceedings of the 6th High-Performance Distributed Computing Conference (HPDC97)* (Aug. 1997), pp. 316–325. extended version available as UCSD Technical Report TR-CS96-494.

An Infrastructure for Monitoring and Management in Computational Grids

Abdul Waheed[1], Warren Smith[2], Jude George[3], and Jerry Yan[4]

[1] MRJ Technology Solutions, NASA Ames Research Center, Moffett Field, CA 94035-1000
waheed@nas.nasa.gov

[2] Computer Sciences Corp., NASA Ames Research Center, Moffett Field, CA 94035-1000
wwsmith@nas.nasa.gov

[3] FSC End2End, Inc., NASA Ames Research Center, Moffett Field, CA 94035-1000
jude@nas.nasa.gov

[4] NASA Ames Research Center, Moffett Field, CA 94035-1000
yan@nas.nasa.gov

Abstract. We present the design and implementation of an infrastructure that enables monitoring of resources, services, and applications in a computational grid and provides a toolkit to help manage these entities when faults occur. This infrastructure builds on three basic monitoring components: sensors to perform measurements, actuators to perform actions, and an event service to communicate events between remote processes. We describe how we apply our infrastructure to support a grid service and an application: (1) the Globus Metacomputing Directory Service; and (2) a long-running and coarse-grained parameter study application. We use these application to show that our monitoring infrastructure is highly modular, conveniently retargettable, and extensible.

1   Introduction

A typical computational grid is characterized by distributed *resources*, *services*, and *applications*. Computational grids consist of large sets of diverse, geographically distributed resources that are grouped into virtual computers for executing specific applications. The diversity of these resource and their large number of users render them vulnerable to faults and excessive loads. Suitable mechanisms are needed to monitor resource usage for detecting conditions that may lead to failures. Grid resources are typically controlled by multiple, physically separated entities that constitute value-added services. Grid services are often expected to meet some minimum levels of quality of service (QoS) for desirable operation. Appropriate mechanisms are needed for monitoring and regulating system resource usage to meet QoS requirements. The complexity of grid applications, which are built on distributed resources and services, stems from their typically large size and inherently distributed structure. This complexity contributes to a possibility of encountering failures. Therefore, grid applications also require mechanisms to detect and recover from failures.

The National Aeronautics and Space Administration (NASA) is building a computational grid, called the Information Power Grid (IPG). Currently, the IPG consists of resources at NASA's Ames, Glenn, and Langley research centers and will grow to contain resources from many NASA centers. As part of this effort, we are developing an infrastructure to monitor resources, services, and applications that make up the IPG and to detect excessive resource usage patterns, faults, or deviations from required QoS levels. This grid monitoring infrastructure is also capable of invoking recovery mechanisms for possible fault management or QoS regulation. In this paper, we present the design of this infrastructure and describe its implementation for fault detection and management of a grid service and an IPG application.

We require a framework for monitoring and fault management that is scalable, extensible, modular, secure, and easy to use. Our infrastructure must scale to the large number of entities to be monitored and managed in the IPG. Our framework must also be extensible because entities to be monitored, failure modes, and methods for fault recovery or QoS regulation are likely to change over time. As a means to several ends, we require that our grid monitoring infrastructure is modular to allow new components to be added and existing components to be modified without changing the rest of the code. Modularity helps lower the software complexity by allowing a user to include only those components that they wish to use. We also require support for several levels of security built atop the basic IPG security infrastructure: none, authentication and authorization, and finally authentication, authorization, and encrypted communication.

We examined a number of existing monitoring systems and found that they did not fulfill the above requirements. A majority of existing monitoring systems, such as NetLogger [15], Paradyn [12], AIMS [17], Gloperf [10], and SPI [1] can collect data from distributed systems for analyzing them through their specific tools. However, these monitoring systems cannot serve as data collection components for other tools and applications that may wish to use this information. Some of the existing monitoring systems do support external tools or applications for fault detection, resource scheduling, and QoS management. The Heart Beat Monitor (HBM) is an extension of Globus that periodically sends "heartbeats" to a centralized collector and provides a fault detection service in a distributed system [14]. While heartbeats are often used for periodically determining the status of a remote node, relying only on one type of "sensor" (i.e., heartbeats generated by local monitors) contributes to inaccuracies in fault detection. The Network Weather Service (NWS) measures available network bandwidth and system load to predict their future states. Future state predictions can be used by a scheduler to reserve and allocate these resources in an efficient manner [16]. If we consider a state estimator as a special type of sensor, we could use its future state predictions for the benefit of several real-time applications that often rely on dynamic scheduling of resources. Dinda et al. compare and evaluate several time-series modeling techniques to predict future system loads, which can be applied to dynamic resource management [5]. The Dynamic Soft Real-Time (DSRT) scheduling tool relies on a customized CPU monitor to implement various specific scheduling policies of this tool [4]. JEWEL/DIRECT is an example where a monitoring system can be used as a part of a feedback loop in control systems [7,9]. However, the complexity of this monitoring system makes it a challenge to use. RMON monitors the resource usage for distributed multimedia systems running RT-Mach [11]. Information collected by the monitoring system is specifically used for adaptively managing the system resources through real-time features of the operating system. Autopilot integrates dynamic performance instrumentation and on-the-fly performance data reduction with configurable resource management and adaptive control algorithms [13]. However, in this case data collection is specifically geared toward providing adaptive control and it is not obvious if underlying data gathering services can be used for other applications. Java Agents for Monitoring and Management (JAMM [3]) is another effort in the same direction, which addresses the needs of only Java based applications. SNMP based tools are widely used for network monitoring and management. Similarly, monitoring, fault notification, and web-based system and network administration tools, such as Big Brother [2] are also useful for distributed systems. However, these tools cannot provide application-specific event notification, which is supported in our monitoring and management infrastructure.

Our infrastructure is built on three basic modules: *sensors*, *actuators*, and a *grid event service*. Sensors are used to measure properties from a local system. Since there are many properties that could be measured, our monitoring infrastructure defines a common application programming interface (API) for sensors. In this way, we can implement some set of sensors for measuring basic properties and other users can add sensors for other properties that they wish to monitor. Actuators perform actions from a local system. Similar to sensors, there are many different actuators that all share a common API. The grid event service provides communication of monitoring and fault management events from producers to consumers. Atop these basic modules, higher-level modules can be constructed. For example, we describe a *sensor manager* component that facilitates the building of customized monitoring systems. Our monitoring infrastructure is described in Section 2. Section 3 describes a service and an application that we are supporting with our infrastructure. We conclude with a discussion of future directions of this effort in Section 4.

2   Monitoring Infrastructure

Our grid monitoring infrastructure includes three basic components: sensors, actuators, and an event service. Figure 1 depicts a typical monitoring scenario built on these basic components. These components are typically located on multiple hosts that interact with one another through the event service as shown in the figure. Further description of three basic components follows.

Sensors: A sensor can measure the characteristics of a target system resource. A sensor typically executes one of Unix utilities, such as *df*, *ps*, *ping*, *vmstat*, or *netstat*, and extracts sensor-specific measurements. These measurements are represented as values of sensor-specific attributes. In addition to these *external sensors*, we also provide *internal sensors* that can collect resource usage information from within the calling process.

Actuators: An actuator is invoked in a similar fashion to a sensor except that it uses the shell to perform specific configuration, process control, or other user-defined tasks. Some of the actuators that we are implementing include: kill process, send mail, execute a shell command, *lightweight directory access protocol* (LDAP) server queries, and some Globus commands.

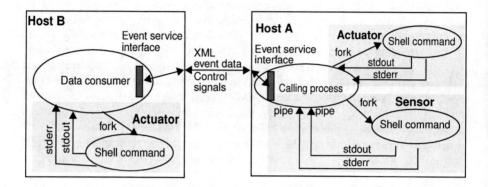

Fig. 1. A prototype implementation of a monitoring system using three basic components of grid monitoring infrastructure: sensors, actuators, and grid event service.

Event Service: This facility provides a mechanism for forwarding sensor-collected information to other processes that are interested in that information. Event service supports a publisher-subscriber paradigm for a client to request specific information and a server to forward that information. Event service also facilitates forwarding of application-specific event data from a user process to a consumer process.

These basic monitoring services can be invoked through APIs. Common APIs to sensors and actuators allow us to implement new sensors or actuators without changing the code that uses them. We also implement the APIs as stand-alone utilities so that they can be invoked on the command-line. We have implemented these components on three platforms: Irix, Solaris, and Linux. We represent the monitored data using eXtensible Markup Language (XML).

A number of higher level components can be built using the basic monitoring components. We have implemented a local *sensor manager* that can execute user-specified sensors and forward event data. We have also developed a generic *data collector* component for gathering the information forwarded by local monitoring servers. We are in the process of developing *data archives* and *query servers* to extend monitoring and management infrastructure to support tools and applications that do not use publisher-subscriber paradigm. Figure 2 presents an overview of the software architecture of monitoring and fault management infrastructure. Prototypes for the three basic components are built on Globus middleware services for communication and security. Higher level components are based on the three basic components. Distributed applications, management tools, and monitoring tools can either use high level components or directly access basic components for a greater degree of customizability.

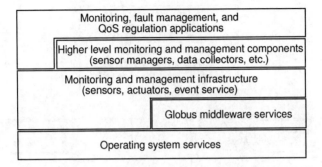

Fig. 2. Software architecture of monitoring and management infrastructure for computational grids.

3   Applications of the Infrastructure

We are currently applying our infrastructure to one grid service and one grid application to provide fault handling and application status tracking. The following subsections present an overview of these uses of our infrastructure.

3.1   Fault Management for Metacomputing Directory Service

The *metacomputing directory service* (MDS) is the LDAP-based grid information service of the Globus toolkit [6]. In a Globus based computational grid, the MDS maintains dynamic information about resources, services, and applications. Many services and applications utilize this information and it is thus critical that this information be available. An MDS server may become inaccessible for queries due to several reasons including: (1) large log files resulting in high disk usage and I/O failures; (2) excessive CPU load; (3) excessive number of clients trying to query MDS; (4) network failures; and (4) LDAP server failures. In order to provide a reliable directory service in a production grid environment, we need to detect, report, and manage these MDS faults.

Figure 3 describes the architecture of an MDS fault manager based on our grid monitoring and management components. Each host running a LDAP server for the MDS contains a monitor and a fault manager. The monitor periodically invokes sensors to collect information on disk usage, CPU usage, number of active TCP connections to the MDS host, and the status of the LDAP server process. This information is received by the local fault manager which checks this information against predefined fault conditions. If a fault condition occurs, the fault manager uses actuators to take the specified actions. For example, if the LDAP log files exceed their allocated disk space, older log files are moved to tape or if the LDAP server process disappears, the LDAP server is restarted. The fault manager is a separate process from the monitor for security reasons: the fault manager requires root privileges to start the LDAP server and therefore the fault manager should be as simple as possible for verification.

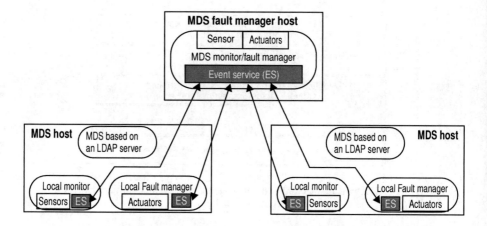

Fig. 3. Architecture of an MDS fault manager using grid monitoring infrastructure.

Much of the monitoring and fault management in this example takes place on the local machine, but a remote monitor and fault manager is used to monitor the hosts that are running the LDAP servers. The local monitor on the LDAP server host is sending periodic heartbeat messages to the MDS fault manager on a remote host. If the MDS fault manager stops receiving heartbeats from a local monitor, it will see if the host running the local monitor can be contacted. If the host is not accessible and does not become accessible within a specified period, an email is sent to the MDS administrators so that they can correct this problem.

Figure 4 depicts the temporal analysis of trace data obtained from a four day long test of MDS fault manager. Clearly, the inter-arrival times of a majority of heartbeat sensor messages at the MDS fault manager are close to their actual sampling period of 10 sec with only a few exceptions that exceed timeout value of 12 sec. Using this consistency in inter-arrival times, some of the existing fault management facilities rely on periodic heartbeats and use "unusual" delay in the arrival of these messages to establish fault occurrence [14]. For this test, using a heartbeat based approach alone would have erroneously detected this late arrival as a failure. The MDS fault manager uses a *ping* sensor to confirm if the MDS host is actually unreachable and distinguish a failure from late-arriving heartbeat. In the case shown in Figure 4(a), it was simply a late-arriving heartbeat. Figure 4(b) shows that the available disk space remained below the minimum value of 100 MBytes during this experiment; so no faults occurred. Figure 4(c) shows that most of the time, the number of TCP connections remained below an arbitrarily selected limit of 40.

Fig. 4. Temporal analysis of three types of sensor messages sent to the central MDS fault manager during a four day long test. A sensor time period of 10 sec is used. (a) A majority of the heartbeat messages are received by the fault manager within a 12 sec allowable inter-arrival time. (b) Free disk space remains above the 100 MB limit. (c) Number of TCP connections exceeded the limit for a small interval of time.

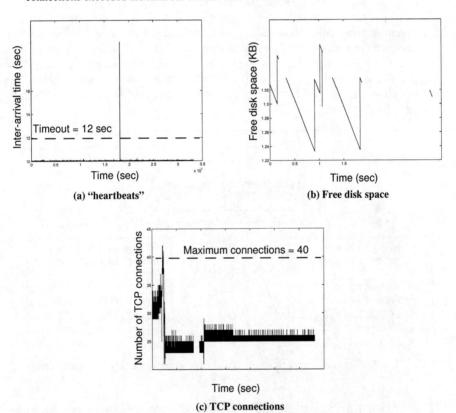

(a) "heartbeats"

(b) Free disk space

(c) TCP connections

3.2   Monitoring and Fault Management of a Parameter Study Application

Parameter studies are often considered suitable applications for distributed computing platforms due to their coarse-grain parallelism. For this parameter study application, sensors monitor processes state, free disk space, file staging, host status, and application execution progress. Monitoring is needed to detect faults related to host accessibility, disk space availability, and application process status during an execution. In this subsection, we describe how to use our infrastructure to perform monitoring and fault management for a parameter study application.

Figure 5 depicts the architecture of a monitoring and fault notification system for a parameter study application. The front end of the parameter study application, called *ILab*, distributes the individual processes on multiple parallel systems in a computational grid. A shell script on the front-end host of each parallel system determines the process IDs for relevant processes and uses a command-line implementation of *process status* sensor, which periodically sends the process state information from front-end host to the *ILab* host. A *disk space* sensor is also invoked to monitor the disk usage. This process and disk usage information is used by the *ILab* front-end to determine if a process has terminated or excessive disk space has been used. In case of process termination, *ILab* uses a separate script to examine the process output file to determine if it was terminated normally or abnormally. In case of an abnormal termination, *ILab* can try to further analyze the cause of this condition and may alter the future course of job submissions. Similarly, if the disk usage on a particular file system exceeds a specified value, subsequently launched processes are configured to write their output to a different file system. Thus using monitoring and fault detection through grid monitoring components, selected fault conditions can be automatically managed.

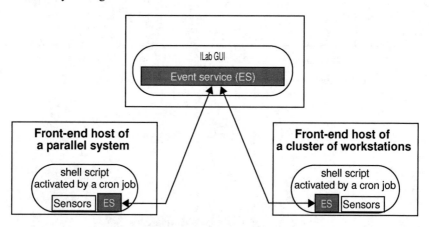

Fig. 5. Architecture of a monitoring and fault reporting facility for a parameter study application.

We tracked the disk space usage and status of a particular application process during one experiment with the parameter study application. Figure 6 presents plots of this information over the application execution time. Using this information, the *ILab* front-end detects the condition when a particular process terminates and it can proceed with its test to decided whether or not it terminated normally.

In addition to monitoring system level resource usage, our monitoring and fault management infrastructure can dynamically monitor application-specific events occurring in distributed processes. This is accomplished through internal sensors and the event service API. Distributed application processes are instrumented by embedding internal sensors in the code to publish desired information, which is collected by a client. Client process subscribes to the publisher to asynchronously receive the desired event data. This is essentially a traditional application monitoring scenario, which is implemented using a publisher-subscriber paradigm. This type of information can be used for performance monitoring or to allow client to steer the application.

Fig. 6. Disk usage and process status information collected during the execution of a parameter study application. (a) Inter-arrival times of heartbeat messages. (b) Free disk space. (c) Status of one of the application processes. A value of 1 indicates that the process is running and 0 indicates that it has terminated.

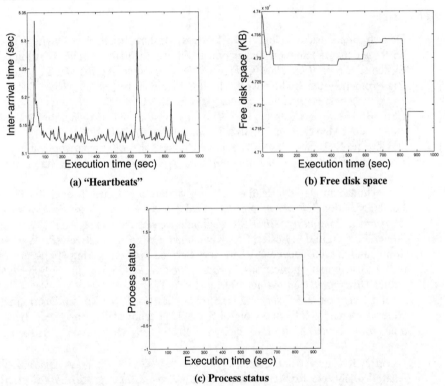

(a) "Heartbeats"   (b) Free disk space

(c) Process status

4   Discussion

In this extended abstract, we outlined a grid monitoring and fault management infrastructure to provide modular, retargettable, and extensible data collection components to enable higher level fault handling and management services in a computational grid. In addition to performing the traditional task of a monitoring system to gather system- and application-specific information, this infrastructure can be employed in high level data consumers that use monitored information for accomplishing fault management, decision making, or application steering tasks. We presented two applications of this monitoring infrastructure to provide such services for specific distributed applications.

Currently, our infrastructure uses a publisher-subscriber paradigm for event notification. We plan to enhance it to other data forwarding models, such as querying archives of monitored information. We will also use rule-based fault detection mechanisms that are based on prediction of future system states through appropriate time-series models. Fault detection and management mechanisms are based on characterization and understanding of conditions that lead to failures. We are using application and system level monitoring to characterize fault occurrences and to glean better understanding of conditions that lead to faults.

References

[1]   Devesh Bhatt, Rakesh Jha, Todd Steeves, Rashmi Bhatt, and David Wills, "SPI: An Instrumentation Development Environment for Parallel/Distributed Systems," *Proc. of Int. Parallel Processing Symposium*, April 1995.

[2]   Big Brother System and Network Monitor, available from http://maclawran.ca/ bb-dnld/bb-dnld.html.

[3]   Chris Brooks, Brian Tierney, and William Johnston, "Java Agents for Distributed System Management," LBNL Technical Report, Dec. 1997.

[4]   H. Chu and K. Nahrstedt, "CPU Service Classes for Multimedia Applications," *Proc. of IEEE Multimedia Computing and Applications*, Florence, Italy, June 1999.

[5]   Peter Dinda and David O'Hallaron, "An Evaluation of Linear Models for Host Load Prediction," *Proc. of the 8th IEEE Symposium on High-Performance Distributed Computing (HPDC-8)*, Redondo Beach, California, Aug. 1999.

[6]   Steven Fitzgerald, Ian Foster, Carl Kesselman, Gregor von Laszewski, Warren Smith, and Steven Tuecke, "A Directory Service for Configuring High-Performance Distributed Applications," *Proc. of the 6th IEEE Symp. on High-Performance Distributed Computing*, 1997, pp. 365–375.

[7]   Martin Gergeleit, J. Kaiser, and H. Streich, "DIRECT: Towards a Distributed Object-Oriented Real-Time Control System," Technical Report, 1996. *Available from* http://borneo.gmd.de:80/RS/Papers/direct/direct. html.

[8]   David J. Korsmeyer and Joan D. Walton, "DARWIN V2 — A Distributed Analytical System for Aeronautical Tests," *Proc. of the 20th AIAA Advanced Measurement and Ground Testing Tech. Conf.*, June 1998.

[9]   F. Lange, Reinhold Kroger, and Martin Gergeleit, "JEWEL: Design and Implementation of a Distributed Measurement System,". *IEEE Transactions on Parallel and Distributed Systems*, 3(6), November 1992, pp. 657-671. *Also available on-line* from http://borneo.gmd.de:80/RS/Papers/JEWEL/ JEWEL.html.

[10]   Craig A. Lee, Rich Wolski, Ian Foster, Carl Kesselman, and James Stepanek, "A Network Performance Tool for Grid Environments," Proc. of SC'99, Portlan, Oregon, Nov. 13–19, 1999.

[11]   Clifford W. Mercer and Ragunathan Rajkumar, "Interactive Interface and RT-Mach Support for Monitoring and Controlling Resource Management," *Proceedings of Real-Time Technology and Applications Symposium*, Chicago, Illinois, May 15-17, 1995, pp. 134–139.

[12]   Barton P. Miller, Jonathan M. Cargille, R. Bruce Irvin, Krishna Kunchithapadam, Mark D. Callaghan, Jeffrey K. Hollingsworth, Karen L. Karavanic, and Tia Newhall, "The Paradyn Parallel Performance Measurement Tool," *IEEE Computer*, 28(11), November 1995, pp. 37–46.

[13] Huseyin Simitci, Daniel A. Reed, Ryan Fox, Mario Medina, James Oly, Nancy Tran, and Guoyi Wang, "A Framework for Adaptive Storage Input/Output on Computational Grids," *Proc. of the 3rd Workshop on Runtime Systems for Parallel Programming (RTSPP)*, April 1999.

[14] Paul Stelling, Ian Foster, Carl Kesselman, Craig Lee, and Gregorvon Laszewski, "A Fault Detection Service for Wide Area Distributed Computations," *Proc. of the 7th IEEE Symp. on High Performance Distributed Computing*, 1998, pp. 268-278.

[15] Brian Tierney, William Jonston, Brian Crowley, Gary Hoo, Chris Brooks, and Dan Gunter, "The NetLogger Methodology for High Performance Distributed Systems Performance Analysis," *Proc. of IEEE High Performance Distributed Computing Conference (HPDC-7)*, July 1998.

[16] Rich Wolski, Neil T. Spring, and Jim Hayes, "The Network Weather Service: A Distributed Resource Performance, Forcasting Service for Metacomputing," *Journal of Future Generation Computing Systems*, 1999.

[17] Jerry C. Yan, "Performance Tuning with AIMS—An Automated Instrumentation and Monitoring System for Multicomputers," *Proc. of the Twenty-Seventh Hawaii Int. Conf. on System Sciences*, Hawaii, January 1994.

Realistic CPU Workloads
through Host Load Trace Playback*

Peter A. Dinda[1] and David R. O'Hallaron[2]

[1] School of Computer Science, Carnegie Mellon University
amd Department of Computer Science, Northwestern University
pdinda@cs.nwu.edu
[2] School of Computer Science and Department of Electrical
and Computer Engineering, Carnegie Mellon University
droh@cs.cmu.edu

Abstract. This paper introduces *host load trace playback*, a new technique for generating a background workload from a trace of the Unix load average that results in realistic and repeatable CPU contention behavior. Such workloads are invaluable for evaluating various forms of distributed middleware, including resource prediction systems and application-level schedulers. We describe the technique and then evaluate a tool, *playload*, that implements it. *Playload* faithfully reproduces workloads from traces on the four platforms on which we have evaluated it. Both *playload* and a large set of host load traces are publicly available from the web at the following URL: http://www.cs.cmu.edu/~pdinda/LoadTraces

1 Introduction

Being able to generate a realistic and repeatable background CPU workload is a necessary prerequisite to evaluating systems such as application-level schedulers [3], dynamic load balancers [1,12], distributed soft real-time systems [4], and resource prediction systems [7,14]. Systems such as these react to the CPU contention produced by other running programs in an effort to improve the performance of the applications they serve. To evaluate them, a mechanism to produce realistic and repeatable CPU contention is necessary.

This paper introduces *host load trace playback*, a new technique for generating a background workload that results in realistic and repeatable contention for the CPU. The workload is generated according to a trace of the Unix load average, which measures the time-varying CPU contention that was caused by a real workload running on a real machine. The objective of the playback process is to reproduce this contention as accurately as possible given the playback host and the machine on which the trace was recorded. The playback process can be configured to operate in a time-based manner, where the contention only

---

* This research was sponsored by the Defense Advanced Research Projects Agency (DARPA) and the Air Force Research Laboratory (AFRL), the Office of Naval Research (ONR) and the Space and Naval Warfare Systems Center (SPAWARSYSCEN), the Air Force Materiel Command (AFMC), the National Science Foundation, and through an Intel Corporation Fellowship.

S. Dwarkadas (Ed.): LCR 2000, LNCS 1915, pp. 246–259, 2000.

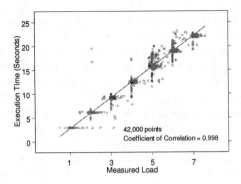

Fig. 1. Relationship between load and running time.

persists for the period of time reflected in the trace, or in a work-based manner, where any additional contention due to the foreground workload elongates the contention period of the trace.

We have developed a tool, *playload*, that implements our technique and collected a large and interesting family of traces with which to drive it. Both are publicly available on the web at http://www.cs.cmu.edu/~pdinda/LoadTraces/. In this paper, we describe the technique, and demonstrate how the tool performs on four different operating systems.

2   Why Host Load Trace Playback?

Consider the problem of predicting the running time of a compute-bound real-time task on each host in a shared, unreserved distributed computing environment. The goal is to schedule the task on the host where it is most likely to meet its deadline [4,6]. The running time on a particular host is almost entirely determined by the CPU contention the task will encounter, which is well measured by host load, the Unix load average. Specifically, we focus on the Digital Unix five second load average, sampled at 1 Hz. This resource signal [6] is interesting because the running time of a compute-bound task is directly related to the average load that it encounters during execution. For example, Figure 1 plots the running time and average load encountered by 42,000 randomized tasks on a Digital Unix machine. The coefficient of correlation between these quantities is nearly 1.0.

An example of a trace of host load can be seen in Figure 6(a). We have developed a system that predicts the future behavior of this resource signal and then transforms the prediction into a running time estimate [7,6]. To evaluate our system, we must be able to produce realistic contention behavior on a host. The unique requirements of workload generation to evaluate workload prediction systems motivated the technique and software described in this paper.

A common approach to generating workloads is to create a statistical model based on the measurement of real systems. If the resulting model captures the relevant statistical properties of the workload, then it can be used to generate

new workloads that also exhibit these properties. The problem lies in determining
which properties are relevant and whether all of the possibly relevant properties have been discovered. Both the networking and load balancing communities
have histories of choosing the wrong properties, resulting in unfortunate system
designs that have only recently been corrected [13,8].

When we studied the statistical properties of host load signals, we found
complex properties such as a strong autocorrelation structure, self-similarity and
epochal behavior [5]. Predictive models use these properties to create forecasts,
and thus it is vital to get them right in the model that the workload generator
uses. However, fixing the model in this way effectively pre-ordains the performance of different predictors on the generated workload. Furthermore, there may
be other, undiscovered properties that are relevant to prediction.

To avoid this conundrum, we decided to directly use traces of the host load
signal to create workloads. The traces undeniably show real contention on real
machines. Using the technique described in this paper, we can reconstruct this
contention by using a family of processes with carefully modulated busy loops.
The resulting host load can be measured and compared with the original load
trace to see how accurate the playback process is.

It is important to point out that this process has limits. Only CPU contention
is reproduced. The busy loops obviously do not reproduce any contention for
the memory system, disk, or the network that may have existed during the
time the trace was recorded. Furthermore, we assume that all the processes that
significantly contributed to the contention recorded in the trace ran at the same
priority level. Low priority processes increase the load average out of proportion
to their actual contention effects on higher priority processes.

Trace-based workload generation is not a new idea, but this is the first work of
which we are aware that uses the Unix load average, a measure of contention, to
recreate CPU contention through purely application-level means. Previous work,
such as DWC [9] and that of Kyung and Hollingsworth [11], creates contention
based on utilization measures. DWC uses in-kernel mechanisms to replay extremely fine grain traces of CPU utilization. The target utilizations in the traces
are "doctored" using process counts in order to model how this workload would
contend with additional processes. Kyung and Hollingsworth's application-level
workload generator uses course grain traces of CPU utilization to parameterize
a stochastic model that decides the length of fine grain CPU bursts. No provision appears to be made to adjust the target utilization to reflect the actual
contention that new processes would see. Our work is also in the spirit of trace
modulation, which is used to create realistic traffic in mobile networks [10].

3   Load Trace Playback

To describe host load trace playback, we shall focus on a periodically sampled
trace, $\langle z_i' \rangle$, captured with a period of $\Delta/2$ seconds. The technique and our implementation can also operate with non-periodically sampled traces.

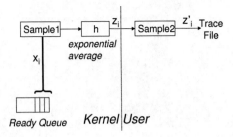

Fig. 2. Sampling process.

3.1   The Playback Algorithm

The Unix load average is an exponential average of the number of processes in the operating system's ready-to-run queue. Conceptually, the length of the ready queue is periodically sampled, and these samples, $\langle x_i \rangle$, flow through an exponential filter

$$z_i = (e^{-\Delta/\tau_{record}})z_{i-1} + (1 - e^{-\Delta/\tau_{record}})x_i \tag{1}$$

where Δ is the sampling interval and the application-visible load average is the $\langle z_i \rangle$ series. A load trace, $\langle z_i' \rangle$, is gathered at the application level by periodically sampling the the load average that the kernel makes available and recording the time-stamped samples to a file. The sample rate should be at least twice as high as the sample rate of the in-kernel process, so we rewrite the above equation as

$$z_i' = (e^{-\Delta/2\tau_{record}})z_{i-1}' + (1 - e^{-\Delta/2\tau_{record}})x_i'. \tag{2}$$

For the Digital Unix traces we use in this paper, $\Delta/2 = 1$ Hz. The sampling process used to generate a load trace is illustrated in Figure 2.

The goal of host load trace playback is to force the measured load average to track the load average samples in the trace file. To do this, we treat the x_i' in the above equation is the *expected* run-queue length during the last $\Delta/2$ seconds. To determine the x_i', we can simply rewrite Equation 2 as

$$x_i' = \frac{z_i' - (e^{-\Delta/2\tau_{record}})z_{i-1}'}{1 - e^{-\Delta/2\tau_{record}}}. \tag{3}$$

This operation was first described by Arndt, et al [2] as a way of achieving a more dynamic load signal ($\langle x_i' \rangle$) on typical Unix systems. All that is necessary to perform this step is knowledge of the smoothing constant, τ_{record}, for the machine on which the trace was taken. For Digital Unix, τ_{record} is 5 seconds. On most other Unix systems, τ_{record} is 60 seconds. A larger τ_{record} value indicates that the load average will behave more smoothly.

We treat the value x_i' as the expected amount of contention the CPU saw for the the time interval—the expected run queue length during the interval. To reproduce this contention, we split the interval into smaller subintervals, each of which is larger than the scheduler quantum, and then stochastically

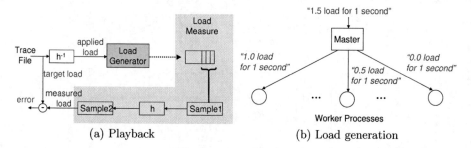

(a) Playback   (b) Load generation

Fig. 3. Playback process.

assign subprocesses to either work or sleep during the subintervals. For example, suppose $x'_i = 1.5$. We would assign subprocess 0 to work during a subinterval with probability 1, and subprocess 1 to work during a subinterval with probability 0.5.

After each individual x'_i value has been played, the load average on the system is measured. This measurement, m_i, can then be compared with the target z'_i value from the load trace if the smoothing constant of the playback machine, $\tau_{playback}$, is the same as that of the trace machine. If $\tau_{playback} \neq \tau_{record}$ then it is necessary to compute an appropriate z'_i from x'_i using Equation 2 and $\tau_{playback}$. The resulting $\langle z'_i \rangle$ is the trace that would have resulted given the smoothing of the playback machine. Figure 3 illustrates the playback process we have just described for a machine where $\tau_{playback} = \tau_{record}$.

3.2   Work-Based versus Time-Based Playback

Most likely, there will be other processes on the system—the tasks we will run during the evaluation, for example—and so it is important to understand how the contention that the load playback tool generates reacts to the contention produced by these processes. Two modes of operation are possible, time-based and work-based.

In the time-based mode of operation, the contention probabilities implied by the x'_i value last only until the end of x''_i's interval in real time. Essentially, this means that the other load on the machine can only amplitude modulate the played back load. For example, suppose there is a uniform 1.0 load on the machine and the load trace dictates a 1.0 load from 0 to 1 second and zero elsewhere. Then, the measured load will (ideally) be 2.0 from 0 to 1 second and 1.0 elsewhere. Figure 4(a) shows an example where a real load trace (target load) is being played back using the time-based mode in competition with an external continuous 1.0 load, resulting in an amplitude modulated measured load.

In the work-based mode of operation, the load is interpreted as work that must always be done, but which may be slowed down by other load. This means that the other load on the system can also frequency modulate the played load. Using the same example as the previous paragraph, the measured load would be 2.0 from 0 to 2 seconds and 1.0 elsewhere. Figure 4(b) shows an example where a real load trace (target load) is being played back using the work-based mode

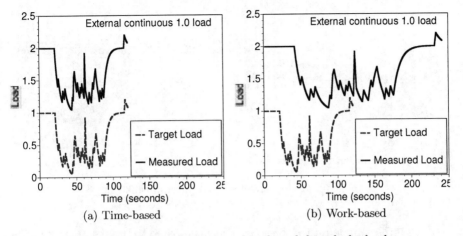

Fig. 4. Example of time-based and work-based playback.

in competition with an external continuous 1.0 load, resulting in an amplitude and frequency modulated measured load.

3.3 Sources of Playback Error

The measured load during playback tracks the desired load only approximately in some cases. The most obvious reason is that there are other processes on the playback machine. The additional contention they introduce can drastically affect the measured load. However, even on a reasonably idle machine, errors do occur. This is mainly because the OS's scheduler is functioning both as a sampling processes and as part of the sampled process.

The sampling process that produces the x_is in Equation 1 is the OS's scheduler, which sees only integer numbers of processes on the ready queue. We treat our sample of x_i, x_i', as the expected value of x_i, $E\{x_i\}$. In playing back x_i' we contrive to make the value that the scheduler samples this expected value. However, the second moment, $E\{x_i^2\}$, is nonzero, so the actual value that is sampled may be different even if the playback applies the correct work at the correct times.

Consider the following contrived example. Suppose $x_i' = 0.5$, we have a sub-process spend 50% of its time sleeping and 50% working, and we alternate randomly between these extremes. The expected run queue length the scheduler would see is then $E\{x_i\} = (0.5)(1) + (0.5)(0) = 0.5$. However, the scheduler will really sample either 1 or 0. The effect on the load average in either case will be drastically different than the expected value, resulting in error. Furthermore, because the load is an exponential average, that error will persist over some amount of time (it will decline to 33% after $\tau_{playback}$ seconds). Another way of thinking about this is to consider the second moment, $E\{x_i^2\}$. For this example, $E\{x_i^2\} = (0.5)(1)^2 + (0.5)(0)^2 = 0.5$, so the standard deviation of the distribution of $E\{x_i\}$ is $\sqrt{E\{x_i^2\} - E\{x_i\}^2)} = \sqrt{0.5 - 0.25} = 0.5$ which explains the variability in what the scheduler will actually sample.

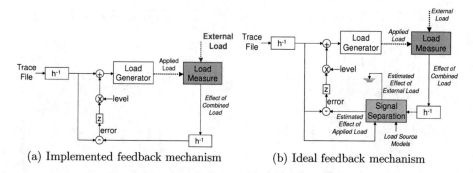

(a) Implemented feedback mechanism   (b) Ideal feedback mechanism

Fig. 5. Negative feedback mechanisms

Even if the sample rate of the trace is low compared to the sample rate of the scheduler, resulting in the x_i''s corresponding measurement being the aggregate of several observations by the scheduler, any extant error is still propagated by the exponential filter.

Another source of error is that an actual process on the ready queue may not consume its full quantum.

3.4 Negative Feedback

It is reasonable to view host load playback as a control system in which the goal is to force the output host load measurements to accurately track the input measurements in the load trace. It is natural to consider using negative feedback to achieve more accurate operation. Our implementation of host load playback, which will be described shortly, supports a negative feedback mechanism. Using this mechanism, it can sometimes more accurately track the load average in a trace.

There are, however, two problems with relying on this mechanism. First, the frequency of the control loop is the measurement frequency, which is considerably lower than the frequency at which work is applied. This makes feedback unstable. It would appear to be possible to up-sample the trace and implement measurement at a finer granularity to avoid this problem. However, the second problem with feedback is somewhat more daunting. The measurements are of the *total* load on the system, but the goal of feedback is to control merely the load being applied by the playback tool, not the external load produced by foreground processes. To determine the real playback errors, it would be necessary to separate the measured load into the contributions of the host load playback tool and of other processes running on the host. In general, this is difficult because so much information has been lost by the time measurements are taken.

Figure 5 shows both our implemented feedback mechanism (a) and what an ideal feedback mechanism would look like (b). Implementing the box denoted "Signal Separation" in Figure 5(b) is necessary both for making feedback useful when there is external load and for accurately determining the effect of the predicted load on a new process when the host is heavily utilized. Because of its broad utility, we are currently exploring ways to achieve this functionality.

Because of these difficulties, we do not use negative feedback in the evaluation that follows.

3.5   Real Traces versus Synthetic Traces

In almost all cases, when a real load trace that has been sampled at a sufficiently high rate is played, the x_i's are close to integers. Intuitively, this makes sense—the scheduler can only observe integral numbers of processes on the ready queue, and if our estimates of its observations (the x_i's) are accurate, they should also mostly be integers.

It's easy to construct synthetic traces that are actually not sensible in terms of short term behavior. One such trace is the continuous 0.5 example discussed in the previous section. Deconvolving that trace produces x_i's slightly above 0.5. Load playback reasonably produces a situation where the expected ready queue length is 0.5 by having a process spend half of its time working and half sleeping. However, the observations the kernel (the x_is) will make will be either 0 or 1. Thus the measured load trace will vary widely. The average load average will match to the 0.5 we desire, but the short term behavior will not. It's important to note that the load playback tool is doing what the user probably wants (keeping the CPU 50% busy, which can be verified with vmstat.) It is simply the case that the load average fails to be a good measure for how well the generated load conforms.

Another way a synthetic trace can fail is to have very abrupt changes. For example, a square wave will be reproduced with lots of overshoot and error. In order for the abrupt swings of a square wave to have been the output of the exponential smoothing, the input x_i must have been much more abrupt, and the estimate x_i' will also be quite large. This means load playback has to have many processes try to contend for the CPU at once, which raises the variability considerably.

The best way to produce synthetic traces is to create a string of integer-valued x_is and smooth them with the appropriate τ_{record}. Another possibility is to present these x_is directly to load playback with a very small τ_{record} trace value.

3.6   Implementation

We implemented the host load trace playback technique in a tool called *playload*. *Playload* consists of approximately 2600 lines of ANSI C and uses only standard Unix calls. We have successfully ported it to a number of platforms, including Digital Unix, Solaris, FreeBSD, and Linux.

Because it is vital that τ_{record} be known, we provide a tool which estimates this value using the decay time after a CPU burst on the otherwise unloaded machine. Another implementation issue is how many subintervals should be generated for each sample in the load trace. More subintervals tend to smooth out kernel sampling fluctuations, but, on the other hand, fewer subintervals reduce the overhead of the system. We have resolved this tension experimentally, finding approximately 120 subintervals per second to be appropriate for Digital Unix, and about 30 subintervals per second to be appropriate for the other platforms.

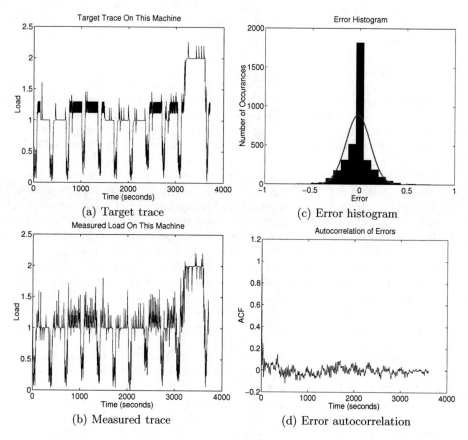

Fig. 6. Trace playback on a Digital Unix Machine.

4   Evaluation

In this section, we evaluate the performance of *playload* on Digital Unix, Solaris, FreeBSD, and Linux. The evaluation is based on a playing back a one hour trace (3600 samples) recorded on a Digital Unix workstation in the Pittsburgh Computing Center's Alpha cluster on August 23, 1997. In each case, the playback is work-based, no feedback is used, and the machine is otherwise quiescent.

Figure 6 illustrates the performance of *playload* in playing back the trace on another Digital Unix machine. The format of the figures for the other machines will be the same. Figure 6(a) shows the target signal on the machine, $\langle z_i' \rangle$. It is identical to the signal recorded in the load trace because this machine has a smoothing constant that is identical to that of the trace machine. Figure 6(b) shows the measured result, $\langle m_i \rangle$. As we can see, the measured signal closely tracks the target signal, with the exception of occasional outliers. Most of these are associated with target loads that are non-integral, resulting in the kind of sampling errors described above. Figure 6(c) shows the distribution of all of the playback errors, $\langle m_i - z_i' \rangle$. The distribution is approximately normal. As we can

Environment	Target		Measured		Error	
	Mean	StdDev	Mean	StdDev	Mean	StdDev
Alpha/DUX 4.0	1.065	0.465	1.047	0.442	-0.018	0.127
Sparc/Solaris 2.5	1.047	0.376	1.122	0.356	0.076	0.061
PII/FreeBSD 2.2	1.047	0.376	1.123	0.361	0.076	0.124
PII/Linux 5.2	1.047	0.376	1.131	0.360	0.084	0.164

Fig. 7. Cumulative errors (3600 samples).

see, most errors are actually quite small. Furthermore, the errors are essentially uncorrelated over time, as can be seen by their autocorrelation function, plotted in Figure 6(d).

Figure 7 presents summary statistics for the target, measured, and error signals on all the machines we tested. For playback under Digital Unix, note that the mean and standard deviation of the target and measured signals are nearly identical, which shows that *playload* is reconstructing all of the trace's work and dynamics. The mean error is slightly less than zero, which indicates that either *playload* is overall producing slightly less work than needed. The error's high standard deviation reflects the outliers.

Using the same format as before, Figure 8 shows how *playload* performs on a Solaris machine. The target signal for Solaris is considerably smoother than that for Digital Unix because Solaris uses a 60 second smoothing constant, as do the remainder of the machines in this evaluation. We can see that playback works beautifully on this machine, producing a nearly normal distribution of errors with few outliers. The errors are slightly more correlated over time than on Digital Unix, however. Also, as we can see from Figure 7, slightly more work than desired is being generated.

Figure 9 shows playback on a FreeBSD machine. This machine exhibits considerably more error than the Solaris machine. However, the error distribution is nearly normal and a bit less correlated over time. In terms of the cumulative error, we can see from Figure 7 that playback produces slightly more work than desired. The error is biased slightly positive, showing that, overall, about 7–8% more contention is being observed than desired. This is similar to the Solaris and Linux machines. The Solaris machine shows the lowest variability in error, while the FreeBSD machine has about the same error variability as the Digital Unix machine.

Figure 10 shows how *playload* performs on a Linux machine. *Playload* performs more poorly on Linux than on any of the other machines we have tested. However, the measured load signal does track the general outline of the target load signal. The error distribution is not even approximately normal, and is obviously biased toward positive errors. This leads to the cumulative error being about 8% higher than desired, and to a much greater variability in that error, as can be seen in Figure 7. However, it is important to point out that, as with all the other machines, *playload* on Linux produces a measured load signal which exhibits the desired variability. At this point, we do not understand exactly why *playload* behaves so differently on Linux.

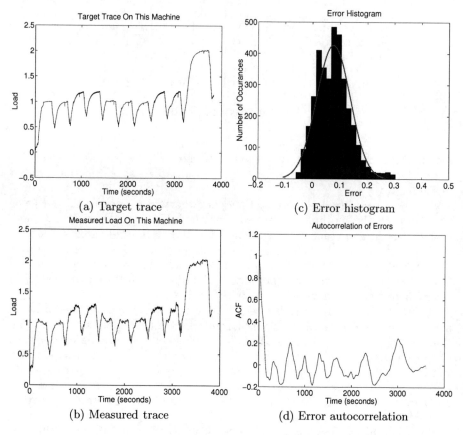

Fig. 8. Trace playback on a Solaris Machine.

5   Conclusions and Future Work

We have introduced *host load trace playback*, a new technique for generating a background workload from a trace of the Unix load average that results in realistic and repeatable contention for the CPU. We described the technique and then evaluated the performance of an implementation on several different platforms. The implementation, *playload*, works quite well in reproducing the overall behavior of the trace in terms of low, roughly normally distributed error that has little correlation over time. *Playload* works better on Digital Unix, Solaris, and FreeBSD machines than on Linux machines, but at this point we don't know why. We have used *playload* extensively in our evaluation of a real-time scheduling advisor based on the on-line prediction of task running time [6].

There are several ways in which we are planning to extend the work described in this paper. First, we hope to understand and improve the inferior performance we see on Linux. Second, we are exploring how to separate out the effects of load applied by *playload* and external load applied by other programs. If this can be done, it would let us use negative feedback to make playback even more

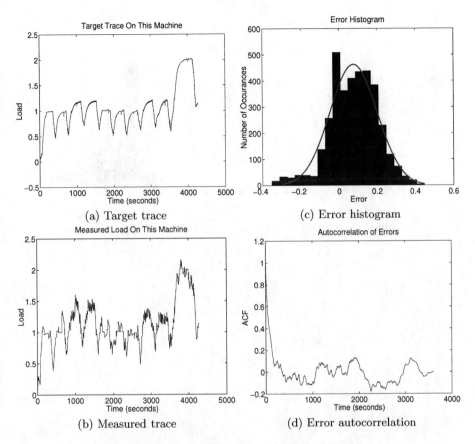

Fig. 9. Trace playback on a FreeBSD Machine.

accurate. Furthermore, this signal separation step would be extremely helpful in the context of prediction-based systems, where it is often necessary to decompose predictions into contributions by individual applications. The third way in which we intend to build on this work is to explore the finer grain measurement facilities that are available on some operating systems, perhaps developing some such facilities ourselves. Using these mechanisms would allow us to provide workloads that are more appropriate for evaluating systems that use very short-lived tasks. Finally, we plan to look at developing and integrating trace playback tools for disk, memory, network, and other workloads.

Playload and a large collection of host load traces that we described in an earlier paper [5] are available from the web at the following URL:
http://www.cs.cmu.edu/~pdinda/LoadTraces
We hope that the combination of *playload* and these traces can serve as the basis for standardized benchmarks to evaluate the tools of the distributed computing community.

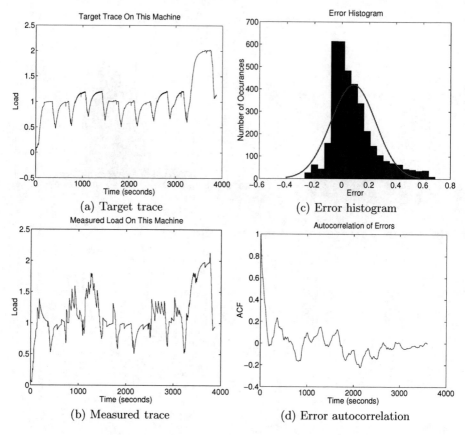

Fig. 10. Trace playback on a Linux Machine.

References

1. ARABE, J., BEGUELIN, A., LOWEKAMP, B., E. SELIGMAN, M. S., AND STEPHAN, P. Dome: Parallel programming in a heterogeneous multi-user environment. Tech. Rep. CMU-CS-95-137, Carnegie Mellon University, School of Computer Science, April 1995.
2. ARNDT, O., FREISLEBEN, B., KIELMANN, T., AND THILO, F. Dynamic load distribution with the winner system. In *Proceedings of Workshop Anwendungsbezogene Lastverteilung (ALV'98)* (March 1998), pp. 77–88. Also available as Technische Universitt Mnchen Technical Report TUM-I9806.
3. BERMAN, F., AND WOLSKI, R. Scheduling from the perspective of the application. In *Proceedings of the Fifth IEEE Symposium on High Performance Distributed Computing HPDC96* (August 1996), pp. 100–111.
4. DINDA, P., LOWEKAMP, B., KALLIVOKAS, L., AND O'HALLARON, D. The case for prediction-based best-effort real-time systems. In *Proc. of the 7th International Workshop on Parallel and Distributed Real-Time Systems (WPDRTS 1999)*, vol. 1586 of *Lecture Notes in Computer Science*. Springer-Verlag, San Juan, PR, 1999, pp. 309–318. Extended version as CMU Technical Report CMU-CS-TR-98-174.

5. DINDA, P. A. The statistical properties of host load. *Scientific Programming 7*, 3,4 (1999). A version of this paper is also available as CMU Technical Report CMU-CS-TR-98-175. A much earlier version appears in LCR '98 and as CMU-CS-TR-98-143.

6. DINDA, P. A. *Resource Signal Prediction and Its Application to Real-time Scheduling Advisors*. PhD thesis, School of Computer Science, Carnegie Mellon University, May 2000. Available as Carnegie Mellon University Computer Science Department Technical Report CMU-CS-00-131.

7. DINDA, P. A., AND O'HALLARON, D. R. An evaluation of linear models for host load prediction. In *Proceedings of the 8th IEEE International Symposium on High Performance Distributed Computing (HPDC '99)* (August 1999), pp. 87–96. Extended version available as CMU Technical Report CMU-CS-TR-98-148.

8. HARCHOL-BALTER, M., AND DOWNEY, A. B. Exploiting process lifetime distributions for dynamic load balancing. In *Proceedings of ACM SIGMETRICS '96* (May 1996), pp. 13–24.

9. MEHRA, P., AND WAH, B. Synthetic workload generation for load-balancing experiments. *IEEE Parallel and Distributed Technology 3*, 2 (Summer 1995), 4–19.

10. NOBLE, B. D., SATYANARAYANAN, M., NGUYEN, G. T., AND KATZ, R. H. Trace-based mobile network emulation. In *Proceedings of the ACM SIGCOMM Conference* (Cannes, France, September 1997).

11. RYU, K. D., AND HOLLINGSWORTH, J. K. Fine-grain cycle stealing for networks of workstations. In *Proceedings of ACM/IEEE SC98 (Supercomputing '98)* (November 1998), pp. 801–821.

12. SIEGELL, B., AND STEENKISTE, P. Automatic generation of parallel programs with dynamic load balancing. In *Proceedings of the Third International Symposium on High-Performance Distributed Computing* (August 1994), pp. 166–175.

13. WILLINGER, W., TAQQU, M. S., LELAND, W. E., AND WILSON, D. V. Self-similarity in high-speed packet traffic: Analysis and modeling of ethernet traffic measurements. *Statistical Science 10*, 1 (January 1995), 67–85.

14. WOLSKI, R., SPRING, N., AND HAYES, J. Predicting the CPU availability of time-shared unix systems. In *Proceedings of the Eighth IEEE Symposium on High Performance Distributed Computing HPDC99* (August 1999), IEEE, pp. 105–112. Earlier version available as UCSD Technical Report Number CS98-602.

Thread Migration and Load Balancing in Heterogeneous Environments

Kritchalach Thitikamol and Peter J. Keleher

University of Maryland
Department of Computer Science, University of Maryland
College Park, MD 20742
{kritchal,keleher}@cs.umd.edu

Abstract. Networks of workstations are fast becoming the standard environment for parallel applications. However, the use of "found" resources as a platform for tightly-coupled runtime environments has at least three obstacles: contention for resources, differing processor speeds, and processor heterogeneity. All three obstacles result in load imbalance, leading to poor performance for scientific applications. This paper describes the use of thread migration in transparently addressing this load imbalance in the context of the CVM software distributed shared memory system. We describe the implementation and performance of mechanisms and policies that accommodate both resource contention, and heterogeneity in clock speed and processor type. Our results show that these cycles can indeed be effectively exploited, and that the runtime cost of processor heterogeneity can be quite manageable. Along the way, however, we identify a number of problems that need to be addressed before such systems can enjoy widespread use.

1 Introduction

The realities of fast and cheap communication networks, combined with the emergence of the Internet as a commodity workspace, have led to a new emphasis on parallel and distributed applications and systems. Dedicated, homogenous parallel systems will always be an option, but the sheer number of cycles available in non-dedicated environments dwarfs those available in dedicated environments. The advent of fast commodity networks has made these cycles available.

The drawback is that these environments are usually heterogeneous in both resource capacities, such as otherwise-identical systems with differing clock speeds, and in terms of resource types, such as between Pentiums and Alphas. Moreover, such applications usually need to co-exist with other applications running on the same systems. This is especially troublesome for tightly-coupled applications, i.e. those that communicate with fine granularity.

This paper presents a case study in the utility of such environments for running parallel programming systems normally associated with more tightly-coupled environments, such as SP-2's or clusters of workstations on the same high-speed LAN.

S. Dwarkadas (Ed.): LCR 2000, LNCS 1915, pp. 260-271, 2000.

We are specifically interested in the extent to which we need special operating system and programming model support. We evaluate mechanisms and policies that support automatic reconfiguration of software distributed shared memory (SDSM) applications in such heterogeneous environments.

We focus on SDSM applications in order to have a demanding application base. While some would argue that SDSM systems have little utility even in dedicated, homogenous environments, much less the heterogeneous environments that are investigating, we believe that long-term trends point the other direction. These trends are (i) the increasing ubiquity of small-scale shared-memory multiprocessors, (ii) the convergence between hardware and software implementations of DSM, and (iii) the similarity in application-restructuring principals needed for large-scale hardware DSM and small-scale software DSM.

First, dual and quad-processor shared memory machines are now appearing on desktops. As parallel, multi-threaded applications become the norm rather than the exception, the ability to extend the same (or a similar) programming paradigm across network boundaries becomes more important. Second, the boundaries between hardware and software DSM are becoming more blurred. The FLASH [1] multiprocessor uses a protocol processor that looks and acts suspiciously like the user-programmable Lanai communications coprocessor used in Myrinet networks [2]. Finally, applications often need to be restructured in order to perform well on SDSM systems. However, the immediate goal of the restructuring is to improve data locality, precisely the same restructuring that needs to be done in order to get good performance on large-scale hardware DSMs [3], such as a 128-node SGI Origin.

There are two concerns when trying to exploit this type of environment. First, the parallel jobs may have to compete with other jobs for resources. Handling this type of contention is more complicated than merely scaling down the expected performance by the percentage of CPU cycles that the parallel job's process can be expected to get. Fine-grained parallel applications usually need each constituent process to be responsive, i.e. to handle incoming requests promptly. Such responsiveness is compromised if the parallel process is not scheduled when requests arrive.

Second, heterogeneity poses a whole slew of problems. We distinguish between systems with *heterogeneous capacities*, and those with *heterogeneous processor types*. Systems with heterogeneous capacities are binary-compatible machines with potentially differing clock rates, network interfaces, and disks. This creates load-balancing problems for parallel applications that statically distribute work.

Systems with heterogeneous processor types can have the former's differences, but may also include mutually incompatible processor types, such as Pentiums, Power2's, Alphas, and SPARC's. Machines frequently differ in such basic matters as byte ordering, floating point formats, and even data type size.

Matters are further complicated by the general lack of high-speed connections between different types of machines. Many locations use high-speed networks within clusters, which are usually homogeneous, but not between clusters.

Despite these obstacles, there are reasons to be hopeful. We are attempting to exploit "found" resources. While high efficiency is desirable, any advantage that we obtain is worthwhile because the resources are otherwise idle.

Section 2 characterizes the applications, the environments, and the SDSM system that we will use. Section 3 discusses mechanisms and policies useful in implementing load-balancing through thread migration. Section 4 shows preliminary performance on heterogeneous machines. Section 5 discusses related work and Section 6 concludes.

2 Applications, System, and Environments

Our platform is the CVM software distributed shared memory system [4], modified to work in our target environment. The modified version of CVM supports multiple threads per node, thread migration, and heterogeneous sets of machines.

2.1 System Characterization

Most of our performance results are based on 100Mbit Fast Ethernet, although the heterogeneous configuration uses only 10 Mbit links. Finding an acceptable network configuration was a non-trivial exercise. Although we have a number of high-performance networks in our department, all connect homogeneous sets of machines. Our solution was to use Fast Ethernet with small numbers (4) of processors. Using fewer machines prevents network contention and allows us to put together configurations with equal numbers of each type of machine. Our homogenous configuration, *conf-hom*, consists of our 266 MHz Pentium II machines. Configuration *conf-het* consists of one UltraSPARC 270 MHz, one 275 MHz Alpha, one 66 MHz Power2, and one 133 MHz Pentium.

Fig. 1 shows relative processor capacities on our suite of applications (discussed below). The bars represent average speedup, and minimum and maximum speedups are shown in the error bars. For example, the PentiumII ranges from almost five times faster than the Pentium to only 50% faster. The inescapable conclusion of this data is that load-balancing in heterogeneous environments must be driven by dynamic infor-

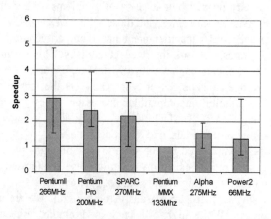

Fig. 1: Average speedup (min,max in error bars)

Sources	msg type	Destinations (µsec)					
		SPARC	Power2	Alpha	Pentium	Pentium Pro	Pentium II
SPARC	page	33	9657	9195	3196	Performance of bcopy() and htonl() conversions of 8192 bytes showed on the diagonal.	
	diff	200	3376	3200	2125		
	lock		1808	1630	986		
Power2	page	9474	37	10254	9563		
	diff	3283	680	3743	3423		
	lock	1674		1740	1628		
Alpha	page	9707	10915	112	9425		
	diff	3296	3859	488	3252		
	lock	1720	1945		1622		
Pentium	page	3572	10489	9157	104	8107	2031
	diff	2042	3416	3153	547	1873	981
	lock	1117	1804	1587		1287	356
Pentium Pro	page	PentiumII bcopy() and htonl() times are 15 and 245 usecs, respectively.			7793	45	7654
	diff				1987	330	1721
	lock				620		507
Pentium II	page				1650	7702	1357
	diff				1055	1652	647
	lock				372	506	227

Table 1: Micro-benchmarks: remote request latency

mation. Static estimates of relative capacity reflect only average performance, and hence might be highly inaccurate for a given application.

Table 1 shows the result of several benchmark tests. The boxes on the diagonal give costs of performing a bcopy() and htonl() (Section 4) on 8192-byte pages. Numbers off the diagonal show average round-trip latency seen by the requester for remote page, *diff*, and lock requests. A diff is a summary of the modified bytes on a single page. Lock requests are "1-hop", meaning that they are immediately satisfied by the destination rather than being forwarded. Note that links to and from the Alpha and Power2 machines are 10 Mbit/sec.

2.2 Application Characterization

Our application suite consists of applications from a number of places. water, spatial, barnes, and fft are ubiquitous applications from the Splash-2 suite [5]. tsp, an implementation of the travelling salesman problem, and Gauss, which performs Guassian elimination with partial pivoting, are both from Rice. expl and adi are dense stencil kernels typical of iterative PDE solvers, parallelized by the SUIF [6] compiler. swm contains a mixture of stencils and reductions, and is from the SPEC benchmark suite. Table 2 summarizes input sets and shared segments sizes.

Apps	Description	Problem Sizes	Shared Pages
Adi	ADI integration kernel	64K	2321
expl	Explicit hydrodynamics	512×512	2509
fft	3-D fast Fourier transform	64×64×128	3587
gauss	Gaussian elimination	2048x2048	2050
sor	Successive Over-Relaxtion	2048x2048	4097
tsp	Traveling salesman problem	19 cities	99
spatial	Spatial Water molecular dynamic	4096 mols	339
swm	Shallow-water model	512	2006
water	molecular dynamic simulation	512 mols	43

Table 2: Application characteristics

Fig. 2 shows four-processor speedup of the applications on `conf-hom`, connected by FastEthernet and UDP/IP over FastEthernet. The speedup of each is broken down into categories with size proportional to their contribution to execution time. The components are `comp`, the time spent running application code, `segv`, the time spent incurring and servicing segv signals (page faults), `sigio`, the time spent servicing remote requests, `barrier`, the average time spent waiting at barriers due to load imbalance, and `lock`, the time spent waiting for remote lock requests to succeed. The same categories will be used throughout this paper. Six of the eight applications get speedups of at least 3.0 on the four processors. The exceptions are `fft` and `swm`, which share large amounts of data and consequently have large `segv` times. The largest overhead category for most of the applications is `barrier`, which implies load imbalance. Note that this balance is not necessarily due to imbalance in the work assigned to nodes. Instead, imbalance is often created by unequal distributions of consistency actions, page faults either incurred or serviced. The largest overhead in `fft` and `swm` is caused is `segv`, corresponding to page faults. These applications share far more data than any of the others, and hence incur many more page faults.

We also ran the applications on UDP/IP over Myrinet [7]. This configuration made

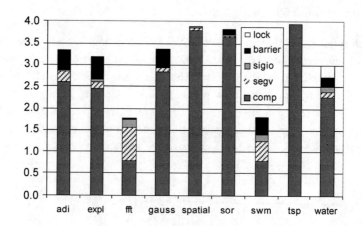

Fig. 2: 4-Processor application speedup

little difference, as the Myrinet IP stack is slower than FastEthernet for small messages. Note that `tsp` is included primarily as an example of an application that balances load implicitly, and therefore does not need system-level load-balancing support.

3   Multi-threading and Thread Migration

Load balancing of iterative scientific codes is generally not necessary on dedicated, homogenous clusters. Scientific codes are usually balanced already, and dedicated clusters do not add any sources of imbalance.

However, all three environmental challenges considered in this paper, resource contention and heterogeneity of both capacity and processor type, result in differing execution rates across nodes. Since the majority of our applications use barrier synchronization in order to avoid data races, either the application or the system must balance load in order to use resources efficiently.

Reconfiguration of running applications is usually accomplished inside the program. For example, the `tsp` application discussed in this paper uses a centralized task queue that balances load implicitly. However, most scientific codes use a more static computation model.

We perform online reconfiguration transparently to the application via thread migration. Thread migration is the obvious choice because threads are visible to the system, and generally each has work statically assigned to it. Moving a thread, therefore, also moves the work. All of our applications can already be parameterized to run on different numbers of processors. Since sharing between threads is through a shared segment that is visible on all nodes, running with 8 threads on each of four processors can be made indistinguishable (except for performance) from having 1 thread on each of 32 processors.

To summarize, our runtime strategy is to: i) derive relative processor capacities through online measurement, ii) derive mappings of individual threads to nodes by using online data-sharing information, and iii) perform a single migration phase where threads are reshuffled. We discussed the information derivation phase in [8].

4   Heterogeneous Processors

While the potential advantages of exploiting heterogeneous environments are clear, conventional wisdom holds that they are outweighed by the disadvantages. Approaches to handling heterogeneity in distributed systems range from prohibition (the majority), to implementation in a type-safe language (such as Java, Modula-3, or Emerald [9]), to language-independent approaches that require the user to explicitly identify all types as part of communication operations (MPI and PVM).

We summarize the problems in Table 3. The first three problems relate to differences in data representation on distinct machines. A data type might differ in size, precision, and byte ordering. Differences might exist not only between machines, but

Problem	Solution
differing data formats	Each page and diff translated as it is transmitted.
differing data precision	Notify user.
differing data sizes	Padded allocation and prohibiting certain types of constructs, such as pointers into arrays of such types.
identifying heap data	Extra parameters to dynamically allocated shared data, segregating shared variables into typed regions.
identifying stack data	Migrating threads only at well-known places, explicit identification of stack data.
differing page sizes	Using the maximum page size of all systems.
differing shared addresses	Either prohibiting pointers or requiring all systems to use a well-known address.

Table 3: Summary of problems and approaches relating to processor heterogeneity

also between compilers on the same machine and operation system. Results in this paper assume gcc on all platforms.

Table 4 shows a hex dump of several differently-typed scalars on all four platforms. Note that the float and double values are implemented with the same precision on all platforms, differing only in byte order. The value represented on each system is the same except for the pointer variable, which points to the short variable. All types are the same size across systems except for the long and char * types, which are eight bytes on the Alpha.

Translating from one representation to another requires not only swapping bytes, but adjusting data type sizes and pointer values. Byte swapping is simple and efficient, but adjusting address spaces to accommodate variables whose sizes are location-dependent is not generally possible with untyped languages like C and C++. The Tui system [10] performs elaborate compiler analysis in order to restrict off-the-shelf programs as little as possible, but must still impose a number of restrictions.

Rather than require compiler analysis (and hence restrict the system's usefulness), we set out to find a fairly minimal set of programmer restrictions that would allow a useful system to be built. Inspection of our application code revealed a number of useful properties.

First, our programs use only int, float, double and char *, types. Int and float variables have the same size on all platforms, and can both be translated

Data Type	Pentium II	SPARC	Alpha	Power-2
short	0x2211	0x1122	0x2211	0x1122
int	0x44332211	0x11223344	0x44332211	0x11223344
long	0x44332211	0x11223344	0x4433221100000000	0x11223344
float	0x0050c347	0x47c35000	0x0050c347	0x47c35000
double	0x00000000d012634	0x416312d0000000	0x00000000d012634	0x416312d000000000
char *	0x5c960408	0x00020ac4	0x2000004001000000	0x20000640

Table 4: Differences in data formats

between different machine representations by reversing the byte ordering of each four-byte quantity. Double variables can be handled similarly, except that the two words need to be swapped after the byte reordering is accomplished.

Pointer values additionally need to be adjusted to reflect changes in the base address of variables. Note that a strategy of allocating the largest possible size for each data type will not work. An array of pointers, for example, must have four bytes per element added when moving from an Intel platform to an Alpha platform, or compiler-generated code will be incorrect. However, inspection of our code reveals that pointer values are stored in shared memory for some systems, but are static after initialization in all but one case. We therefore disallow long's and pointer values in shared memory, resulting in all shared data being of type int, float, or double. Restructuring our code in order to meet this restriction was trivial in all cases.

This restriction allows us to translate all data with the following two-step process. First, all data transmitted to and received from the network has each four-word quantity translated to or from network byte-ordering format, if the system is in heterogeneous mode (automatically detected at startup). Second, the two halves of each double value are swapped, if necessary, when the data is copied.

Double values must be identified in order to be swapped. Our system provides an interface that allows type information to be passed to the system on a word-by-word basis. For reasons of efficiency, however, our altered applications segregate all double values from ints and floats by allocating them in a separate segment via calls to cvm_alloc_double(). Incoming pages containing double values with an ordering different from the local ordering are swapped in place.

One last concern with double is that it changes the granularity with which the system allows false sharing. We altered the diff creation routine to add modified data to diffs eight bytes at a time, instead of the four assumed for the rest of the shared segment.

4.1 Heterogeneous Thread Migration

CVM's heterogeneous thread migration mechanism is identical to the homogeneous mechanism except in handling the stack. In addition to being copied between machines, the stack must be translated to accommodate differing data types and sizes. Additionally, stacks commonly hold other data, such as temporary compiler data and prologue data used by the system to initialize state.

Taking these problems in order, the translation process is similar to that discussed above for shared data. The main difference is that stacks often contain pointer values that point to the stack itself (self-referential stack pointers). Re-structuring code to eliminate all these uses would be non-trivial. Furthermore, data of all types can occur consecutively in a stack, unlike in the shared segment.

We accommodate pointers in this environment by restricting migration to occur only at a single point in each application, usually the beginning or end of a scientific application's main iteration loop. We require all stack data (local variables, parameters) to be explicitly identified to the system at startup. Each function that might have

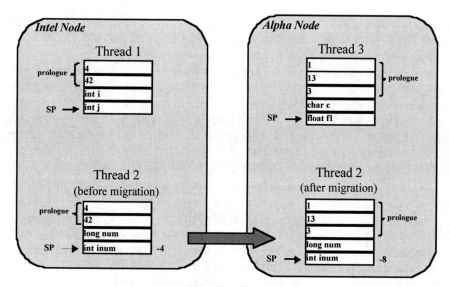

Fig. 3: Heterogeneous thread migration

a frame on the stack when the migration occurs must have pre-identified its variable's offsets through calls to `cvm_stack_vars()`. There are never more than two such functions in any of our applications.

Above this data, the stack consists of operating system-specific data common to all stacks on a single machine. On each machine, CVM records a snapshot of this prologue code the first time any local thread reaches the migration point. Note that the single snapshot is per architecture, not per thread. When a thread migrates to a node from another architecture, a stack is created by combining the prologue from the snapshot with the typed data from the incoming thread that was described by the `cvm_stack_vars()` calls. This technique not only reduces complexity, but it also significantly reduces the number of bytes that need to be copied.

The example in Fig. 3 shows migration of Thread 2 from an Intel node to an Alpha node. The variables `num`, and `inum` are described to the system by `cvm_stack_vars()` calls. The initial snapshot on the Alpha captured the prologue code, containing words '1', '13', and '3' in this case. This prologue is combined with translated versions of the stack variables to form the new stack on the Alpha machine. The offset of `inum` is modified on the Alpha to account for the differently sized `inum` variable. The prologue from the Intel node is discarded.

Fig. 4 shows speedup of `conf-hetero` relative to the speed of the SPARC for the auto and "best" thread distribution. When averaging across all applications, sequential execution times imply that the theoretical capacity of the four machines is 2.96 times greater than the SPARC's alone. Five of the eight applications speed up by at least a factor of two, with `expl` speeding up almost 3.5 times. Note that 2.96 is an *average*; the theoretical speedup is higher for some applications.

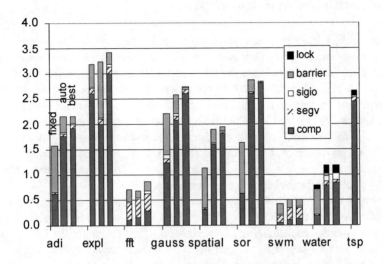

Fig. 4: Heterogeneous speedup (relative to fastest node)

The runtime impact of heterogeneity consists of changes to three modules: translation to and from network order on all message sends and receives, word-swapping on page-faults for pages containing `double`'s, and slightly different diff creation and application code. The latter difference is negligible. As full-page faults occur only the first time a page is accessed by a processor, this overhead is also negligible. The remaining cost is for translation to and from network order. This cost is only incurred on the Alpha and Pentium-based machines, and peaks at 6.6% for `adi`. The cost was never more than 2.5% for the others, and the average cost was 2.1%.

5   Related Work

Heterogeneous SDSM has been studied before. Mermaid [11] is an early system that ran on two distinct architectures. Although Mermaid could migrate threads before they started, running threads could not be moved. Stardust [12] uses a simple language to describe shared data types. A *heterogeneous page* is used to ensure that a given page contains the same number of elements on all architectures, despite differences in the size of primitive data types. However, this paper gave no performance results for heterogeneous applications. Arachne [13] is a package that allows threads to migrate across heterogeneous machine boundaries. Correctness is maintained by aggressively instrumenting all code.

6   Implications and Conclusions

Many researchers have proposed ways to exploit otherwise-idle resources in non-dedicated environments [14]. However, most investigated sequential or coarse-grained distributed applications because of the inherent overheads in such environments.

Conventional wisdom holds that tightly coupled applications can only be profitably parallelized on sets of roughly comparable machines that are connected by fast networks. However, in one case we were able to obtain performance improvement even from a machine five times slower than the fastest in the configuration. The key to evaluating performance in this environment, however, is in remembering that these resources *are* otherwise idle. Any use of found resources that improves execution time is well spent; linear parallel speedup is not necessary.

This paper has described the performance of nine demanding applications running on top of a modified version of the CVM SDSM in such environments. We separate the key performance challenges into three categories: contention for the CPU resource, heterogeneous processor capacity, and heterogeneous processor types. Most of the applications achieved good speedup relative to the fastest constituent node, despite the tight coupling of processes and fine-grained communication required by the SDSM system.

CVM performs well by balancing load through thread migration. The automatic thread distribution mechanism performed well for all but a few of the applications running in non-dedicated environments. Our future work will include investigation into the use of multiple rounds of reconfiguration as a means of narrowing the gap even further.

A second major issue addressed in this work is the use of SDSM systems in heterogeneous environments. Though this issue has been addressed before, none performed as extensive of a study. We added several restrictions to the programming model and showed that the direct costs of heterogeneity can be thereby minimized. It remains to be seen whether these restrictions can be eased without hurting performance, but the current programming model required very few changes to our suite of nine applications.

References

1. Kuskin, J. and D.O.e. al. The Stanford FLASH Multiprocessor. in *Proceedings of the 21st Annual International Symposium on Computer Architecture*. April 1994.
2. Boden, N.J., et al., Myrinet: A Gigabit-per-second Local Area Network. *IEEE Micro*, 1995. **15**(1): p. 29-36.
3. Jiang, D. and J.P. Singh. Scaling Application Performance on a Cache-coherent Multiprocessors. in *Proceedings of the 26th Annual International Symposium on Computer Architecture*. May 1999.
4. Keleher, P. The Relative Importance of Concurrent Writers and Weak Consistency Models. in *Proceedings of the 16th International Conference on Distributed Computing Systems*. 1996.

5. Woo, S.C., et al. The SPLASH-2 Programs: Characterization and Methodological Considerations. in *Proceedings of the 22nd Annual International Symposium on Computer Architecture*. June 1995.
6. Wilson, R.P., et al., SUIF: An Infrastructure for research on parallelizing and optimizing compilers. *ACM SIGPLAN Notices*, December 1994. **29**(12): p. 31-37.
7. Boden, N.J., et al., MYRINET: A Gigabit Per Second Local Area Network. *IEEE-Micro*, 1995. **15**(1): p. 29-36.
8. Thitikamol, K. and P.J. Keleher. Active Correlation Tracking. in *The 19th International Conference on Distributed Computing Systems*. June 1999.
9. Steensgaard, B. and E. Jul. Object and Native Code Thread Mobility Among Heterogeneous Computers. in *Proceedings of the 15th ACM Symposium on Operating Systems Principles*. 1995.
10. Smith, P. and N.C. Hutchinson, Heterogeneous Process Migration: The Tui System, February 1996, Department of Computer Science, University of British Columbia.
11. Zhou, S., et al., Heterogeneous distributed shared memory. *IEEE Trans. on Parallel and Distributed Systems*, May 1991. **3**(5): p. 540-554.
12. Cabillic, G. and I. Puaut, Stardust: An Environment for Parallel Programming on Networks of Heterogeneous Workstations. *Journal of Parallel and Distributed Computing*, 1997. **40**(1): p. 65-80.
13. Dimitrov, B. and V. Rego, Arachne: A Portable Threads System Supporting Migrant Threads on Heterogeneous Network Farms. *IEEE Transactions on Parallel and Distributed Systems*, May, 1998. **9**(5): p. 459-469.
14. Litzkow, M., M. Livny, and M. Mutka. Condor - A Hunter of Idle Workstations. in *International Conference on Distributed Computing Systems*. 1988.

Toward Compiler Support for Scalable Parallelism Using Multipartitioning*

Daniel Chavarría-Miranda and John Mellor-Crummey

Department of Computer Science, Rice University
{danich,johnmc}@cs.rice.edu

Abstract. Strategies for partitioning an application's data play a fundamental role in determining the range of possible parallelizations that can be performed and ultimately their potential efficiency. This paper describes extensions to the Rice dHPF compiler for High Performance Fortran which enable it to support data distributions based on multipartitioning. Using these distributions can help close the substantial gap between the efficiency and scalability of compiler-parallelized codes for multi-directional line sweep computations and their hand-coded counterparts. We describe our the design and implementation of compiler support for multipartitioning and show preliminary results for a benchmark compiled using these techniques.

1 Introduction

Strategies for partitioning an application's data and computation play a fundamental role in determining the application's possible parallelizations and ultimately its parallel efficiency. High Performance Fortran (HPF) and OpenMP, two standard high-level models for parallel programming, provide a narrow set of choices for data partitioning and computation partitioning, respectively. While these partitionings can lead to good performance for loosely synchronous computations, they are problematic for more tightly-coupled codes.

One important class of tightly-coupled computations not well supported by the HPF and OpenMP partitioning models are those that use line sweeps to solve one-dimensional recurrences along each dimension of a multi-dimensional discretized physical domain. Alternating Direction Implicit (ADI) integration

---

* This work has been supported by NASA Grant NAG 2-1181, sponsored by DARPA and Rome Laboratory, Air Force Materiel Command, USAF, under agreement number F30602-96-1-0159, and supported in part by the Los Alamos National Laboratory Computer Science Institute (LACSI) through LANL contract number 03891-99-23, as part of the prime contract (W-7405-ENG-36) between the Department of Energy and the Regents of the University of California. The U.S. Government is authorized to reproduce and distribute reprints for Governmental purposes notwithstanding any copyright annotation thereon. The views and conclusions contained herein are those of the authors and should not be interpreted as representing the official policies or endorsements, either expressed or implied, of DARPA and Rome Laboratory or the U.S. Government.

S. Dwarkadas (Ed.): LCR 2000, LNCS 1915, pp. 272–284, 2000.
© Springer-Verlag Berlin Heidelberg 2000

is a common technique for solving partial differential equations that uses this solution style [14]. Two of the NAS parallel benchmarks [5], SP and BT, use ADI integration to solve the Navier-Stokes equation in three dimensions. Fractional step methods and other solution techniques that use line sweeps are described by Naik et al. [14]. For this class of computations, applying a standard block partitioning to any of the spatial dimensions is problematic—recurrences along the partitioned dimension partially serialize execution.

Prior to the new work described in this paper, the Rice dHPF compiler used a coarse-grain pipelining strategy for parallelizing line sweep computations [1]. Figure 1 shows a 16-processor execution trace for NAS SP using this approach.[1] Block partitionings introduce serialization that coarse-grain pipelining can only partially overcome. Commercial HPF compilers such as PGI's pghpf [7] lack support for coarse-grain pipelining. To support the NAS benchmarks, PGI reworked variants of these codes to use full transposes between directional sweeps. Neither coarse-grain pipelining, nor transpose provides ideal scalability.

Hand-coded message-passing versions of the NAS SP and BT benchmarks (version NPB2.3b2) use a sophisticated data distribution known as "multipartitioning" that involves a skewed-cyclic distribution of data blocks [17]. (Multipartitioning is described in more detail in Section 2.) Multipartitioning offers two key advantages for parallelizing line sweep computations. First, a multipartitioned distribution of k-dimensional data arrays ensures that for each partitioned dimension, each processor owns a data block in each of the $k-1$ dimensional slabs defined by the partitioning. Computation within a slab is fully parallel, so line sweep computations can be parallelized effectively using this partitioning. Figure 2 shows a 16-processor execution trace that shows the balanced parallelism achieved using multipartitioning for NAS SP. Second, this parallelization only requires coarse-grain communication, unlike pipelining. For these reasons, multipartitioning can provide better scalability and speedup on large systems [19].

More generally, many data and computation partitioning problems partitioning a domain into blocks with one or more blocks per processor. We refer to such techniques collectively as *overpartitioning*. Examples in the literature include virtual processor approaches for cyclic and block-cyclic distributions [3,12], support for dynamic and non-uniform computation partitioning of data-parallel programs on heterogeneous systems [18], and support for managing computation on out-of-core arrays [6].

This paper describes our design and implementation of multipartitioning in the Rice dHPF compiler. (A description of the principal analyses and optimizations supported in the dHPF compiler can be found elsewhere [1,2] We view this as a first step towards supporting a general overpartitioning framework. We describe several compiler and runtime techniques necessary to generate code

---

[1] We show execution behavior using space-time diagrams visualized using the AIMS toolkit [20]. Each horizontal line in the diagram represents a time line showing the activity of a processor. Time increases to the right. Along a processor's time line, solid bars represent computation, and blank spaces represent idle time. Edges between process time lines represent messages between processors.

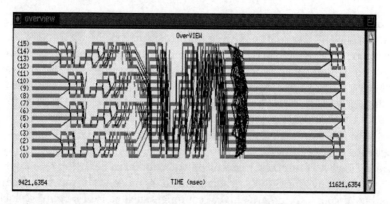

Fig. 1. dHPF-generated NAS SP using block partitioning and coarse-grained pipelined communication.

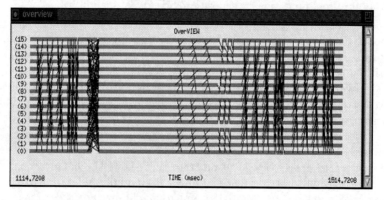

Fig. 2. Hand-coded NAS SP using 3D multipartitioning.

for this class of distributions. Our implementation performs the analysis and code generation necessary to realize multipartitioning computation partitionings; however, as described in Section 5, further communication optimization will be necessary to achieve the scalability of hand-coded implementations.

Section 2 provides an overview of multipartitioning. Section 3 describes our implementation of multipartitioning in dHPF. Section 4 describes key implementation issues that arose in this work. Section 5 describes our preliminary experimental results. Section 6 provides a capsule summary of related work. We conclude with a description of the remaining challenges and our ongoing work.

2   Multipartitioning Overview

Multipartitioning [16,14] is a strategy for partitioning multidimensional arrays. Its main property is that for any directional sweep across the array, all processors are active in each step of the computation, there is perfect load-balance, and only coarse-grain communication is needed.

Multipartitioning achieves this balance by partitioning data into $p^{\frac{d}{d-1}}$ tiles, where p is the number of processors and d is the number of partitioned array dimensions. Each processor is assigned $p^{\frac{1}{d-1}}$ tiles along diagonals through each of the partitioned dimensions. Figure 3 shows a 3D multipartitioning distribution for 16 processors; the number in each tile represents the processor that owns the block.

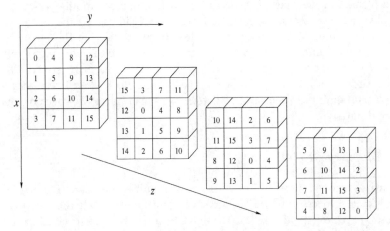

Fig. 3. 3D Multipartitioning on 16 processors.

For an n-dimensional multipartitioning on p processors, the expression $p^{\frac{1}{n-1}}$ must be an integer. Thus, a 3D multipartitioning requires the number of processors to be a perfect square. However, multipartitioning can be applied to any two dimensions of an n-dimensional array allowing use of an arbitrary number of processors.

3   Multipartitioning in dHPF

To specify that multipartitioning should be used to distribute a multidimensional array, we extended the dHPF compiler to accept the *MULTI* keyword as a distribution specifier.

Because multipartitioning involves distributing each partitioned array dimension across all of the processors, our implementation enforces several restrictions. First, an HPF processor array onto which a multipartitioned distribution is mapped must be a one-dimensional array containing all the processors. Second, if the *MULTI* distribution specifier is used for an array or template, neither *BLOCK* nor *CYCLIC* can be used in the same distribution. Finally, the *MULTI* keyword must be used in at least two dimensions of a distribution.

3.1   Virtual Processors

The integer set analysis framework used by dHPF [2] supports *BLOCK* partitionings of arbitrary size onto a symbolic number of processors. To support multipartitioning we extended this model to treat each tile in a multipartitioned array as a block in a *BLOCK* partitioned array, mapped to an array of $p^{\frac{d}{d-1}}$ virtual processors.

Implementing this virtual processor model, requires mapping between virtual and physical processors. Each virtual processor is identified by its *tile position indices*, a d-dimensional tuple representing its coordinates in the virtual processor array (in column-major order). We use these indices to index into a *virtual to physical processor mapping*. When a tile needs data from another tile, the other tile's coordinates are computed from the data indices, the virtual to physical processor mapping is then used to determine which physical processor owns the required data.

3.2   Memory Model

A multipartitioned distribution of an array, requires the allocation of $p^{\frac{1}{d-1}}$ tiles per physical processor. Each tile's data is contiguous. Each tile is extended as necessary with overlap areas [11] to facilitate access to data received from neighboring tiles. On each processor, all local tiles for a multipartitioned array are dynamically allocated as contiguous data. Storage is indexed in column-major order, where the leftmost dimensions are the original array dimensions and a new rightmost dimension corresponds to the *local tile index*.

3.3   Code Generation

Code generation for multipartitioning is a generalization of code generation for *BLOCK* partitioning. Within dHPF the integer set framework is used to generate code for blocks of arbitrary but uniform size at arbitrary positions. We use the generated computational and communications code for such a block, as the kernel code for each tile of the multipartitioned distribution.

All communication and computation performed for a tile is defined in terms of the data mapped to that tile. Since more than one virtual processor is assigned to each physical processor, the tile position indices have to be adjusted on each physical processor as it cycles through its tiles. Computation for a loop nest occurs by having each processor perform the computations for each of its owned tiles.

To generate code that handles multiple tiles per processor, we wrap a tiling loop that iterates over all the tiles assigned to a physical processor around the kernel code for a tile. The order in which a physical processor must iterate over its tiles, is determined by the data dependences present in the loop nest. Since multipartitioning is a multidimensional distribution, the data dimension in which the outermost dependence is carried is the one that determines the iteration sequence. The order in which each processor iterates over its tiles corresponds to the loop direction and must satisfy the loop-carried dependences present in the loop body. (If there are no loop-carried dependences then the iteration sequence follows the outermost loop index that indexes a multipartitioned dimension within the array.) As shown in Figure 3, the tiles for a processor fall along a diagonal which spans the d dimensions of the array. We use modular arithmetic (modulo number of tiles) to compute the following tile indices from the values of the current ones. The value of the dependence-carrying loop index is what is used to index into the tile dimension of the array. The iteration must begin with the first tile at the appropriate end of the selected dimension.

3.4   Communication Model

Communication generation for multipartitioned distributions, is a direct extension of the model used to generate communication events for $BLOCK$ distributions. For communication loop nests, we applied the same strategy we used for computational loop nests: we extend the basic single tile instance communications loop kernel to support multiple tiles.

For communication that is vectorized outside of all computational loops over data dimensions, we generate a simple tile loop around the communications kernel, applying the same sort of adjustments described for computational loops.

For communication pinned inside a loop by a data dependence, it would be incorrect to wrap the communication event in a tiling loop because dependences would not be satisfied. Code generation for computational loops will have wrapped a tile loop outside the dependence-carrying loop. Thus, no additional tile loop is required for the inner communications kernel code.

In general, a single communication event for a tile may require interaction with multiple communication partners. To manage these interactions, multipartitioning requires a flexible buffering scheme, that supports dynamic allocation of multiple buffers per communication event, for each tile.

Since each physical processor performs communication on behalf of each of its tiles, care must be taken to ensure that messages received are delivered to the appropriate tile. To avoid mixing up messages, we use a message tagging scheme, which uniquely identifies the originating tile and communication event. Each message is labeled with a unique tag consisting of an integer identifying the communication event plus another integer that identifies the originating tile in terms of a unique global number computed from its tile position indices.

3.5   Runtime Support

Our main runtime components required to support the multipartitioned code generated from the dHPF compiler are a function to compute virtual-to-physical processor mappings and support for managing multiple dynamic buffers. Each multipartitioned template distribution requires a different virtual-to-physical processor map. We associate maps with their corresponding template runtime descriptor. These maps are computed once, at the start of program execution, with very little overhead, since their sizes depend on the number of tiles.

4   Key Implementation Issues and Insights

Scheduling Tiles. With multipartitioning, managing each tile as a virtual processor that performs its own computation and communication introduces a scheduling problem that is not present with simple block distributions. In a loop nest with carried dependences, such as each of the loop nests in NAS SP that perform a line sweep, communication operations must occur inside the loop nest. With multipartitioning, a tile iteration loop is wrapped around the computational loop nest. During a sweep, each physical processor will perform computation for multiple tiles. If unbuffered communication is used, any simple sequential ordering of the tiles will result in deadlock.

Consider a 2D multipartitioning involving the x and y dimensions of a 3D array. In the first time step of a sweep along the x direction, each processor will perform the computation on its leftmost tile. The boundary values for each of these tiles are needed for the computation on the next column of tiles along the x direction. Thus, the tile computation must send its boundary values to the processor that will compute the neighboring tile. If it uses unbuffered communication to send these values, a tile's communication will block until the matching receive is posted for the neighboring tile. However, if each processor performs an unbuffered blocking send on behalf of its first tile, deadlock will occur since the matching receive not be posted until each processor begins its second tile.

This problem can be solved by using a multithreaded model, that assigns a separate thread to execute each tile. This threads should execute using run-until-block semantics with respect to the communication library involved. This implies that the underlying communication library has to be thread aware to some degree.

As an alternative to implementing a threaded execution model for our experiments, we used buffered communication. This introduces some overhead in the communication, but relieves the compiler from dealing with the problem in its more general complexity.

Set Constraints. Since we are compiling for a symbolic number of processors, the information available inside our integer set analysis framework is weaker than when the number of processors is known. This has implications in terms of the complexity of the underlying iteration and communication sets, particularly with regard to determining sizes and ranges of the data blocks.

Imprecision in the communication sets makes them more general than necessary and can lead to overly complex code. In particular, this imprecision can make it difficult to determine that a communication event involves only a single communication partner. The imprecision can be reduced when we can determine that the communication is flowing only along one of the virtual processor dimensions. This implies that the virtual processor indices for the other dimensions are the *same* as for the current processor, thus avoiding enumeration loops for those dimensions.

We can also avoid processor enumeration loops for the dimension in which communication is flowing, if the subscript value of the reference for that dimension is invariant with respect to the loop index at that level. If this is the case then we can compute the processor index for this dimension precisely, without needing to create an enumeration loop.

Availability Analysis. Set imprecision for symbolic numbers of processors also creates a problem for availability analysis. This analysis determines when non-local data is available locally because it has been computed previously as a result of non-owner-computes computation partitionings. Availability analysis inspects each read reference and compares its communication set with the data computed by the non-owner-computes partitioning. If the needed data is a subset of the non-owner-computes generated data, then communication is *NOT* needed for this reference and the compiler can avoid generating communication statements for it. Without availability analysis, the NAS SP application benchmark would require bidirectional communication at tile boundaries during its sweep computations, which would result in deadlock without a threaded execution model as described in the tile scheduling section above.

5   Experimental Results

We have implemented prototype support for multipartitioning within the Rice dHPF compiler. We present experimental results for the NAS SP application benchmark. In order to evaluate the benefits of the compiler support, we compare our compiler-generated multipartitioning with its hand-coded counterpart.

Our scalability experiments were performed on an SGI Origin 2000 node of ASCI Blue Mountain (128 250MHz R10000, 32KB (I)/32KB (D) L1, 4MB L2 (unified)) using 1, 4, 9, 16 and 25 processors for each execution instance.

5.1   NAS SP Class 'A'

The NAS SP application benchmark [4] is a realistic code for computing numerical solutions to differential equations. The SP code solves a scalar pentadiagonal system in 3D. This code employs multiple forward and backward sweeps over the arrays along each of the spatial directions. The hand-coded MPI version of this benchmark uses a 3D multipartitioning distribution to achieve very high performance and scalability.

From a compiler's point of view, the NAS SP benchmark presents a significant challenge for achieving high performance. To generate efficient parallel code from a lightly modified serial version of this benchmark with the BLOCK distribution, requires the use of several advanced compilation strategies [1] including non-owner-computes computation partitionings, complex patterns of computation replication to reduce communication for privatizable arrays and other

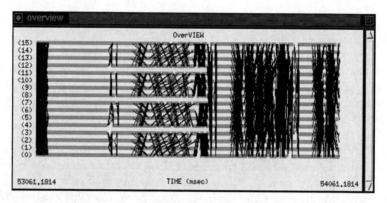

Fig. 4. dHPF-generated NAS SP using 3D multipartitioning.

loop independent data reuse, aggressive communication coalescing, coarse grain pipelining, and interprocedural computation partitioning. These optimizations together yield reasonably good performance even with BLOCK partitioning, within about 20% of the handcoded message-passing version on 32 processors, where the number of processors is a known compile-time constant. The scalability of the code, however, falls substantially short of the handcoded version because of inherent serialization induced by the *BLOCK* partitioning.

Figure 4 shows a 16-processor parallel execution trace for two iterations in the steady-state section of the NAS SP class 'A' execution, for the compiler-generated multipartitioned code. By comparing this execution trace with that of the hand-coded MPI version shown in Figure 2, one can see that dHPF-generated code achieves the same qualitative parallelization. Comparing this multipartitioned version with the coarse-grain pipelining code for a BLOCK distribution shown in Figure 1, it is clear that the new compiler-generated multipartitioning code has less serialization.

Despite the fact that the dynamic communication patterns of our compiler-generated parallelization using multipartitioning resemble those of the hand-coded parallelization, there is still an important performance gap between our dHPF-generated code and the hand-coded MPI. Figure 5 shows speedup measurements taken in June 2000 on an SGI Origin 2000 system equipped with MIPS R10000 processors. All speedups shown in the figure are relative to the performance of the sequential code for SP from the NAS 2.3-serial distribution.

The most significant difference between the performance of the codes is that the dHPF-generated code does not yet have the same scalability as the hand-generated code. The performance gap is primarily due to insufficient aggregation of communication. First, in the dHPF-generated code, communication that has been fully vectorized outside all loops over spatial dimensions is performed by each processor one tile at a time rather than once for all tiles. For 3D multipartitioning, when shifting array values along a spatial dimension this effect causes $O(p^{\frac{1}{2}})$ messages instead of the $O(1)$ messages in the hand-coded multi-

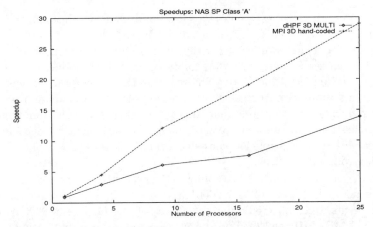

Fig. 5. Speedups for MPI hand-coded multipartitioning and dHPF-generated multipartitioning versions of NAS SP benchmark (class A).

Metric	Hand-MPI	dHPF-MPI
cycles	.94	1.22
grad. instr.	.94	1.07
grad. loads.	.92	.96
L1 misses	.95	.98
L2 misses	.94	1.04
prefetches	1.02	.08

Table 1. Ratio of performance metrics for single-processor executions of parallelized versions of the NAS SP benchmark relative to those for the original sequential code.

partitioning. Enhancements to dHPF's communication generation and run-time libraries are underway to enable messages to be sent on a per-processor rather than a per-tile basis. Second, in the dHPF-generated code, separate messages are used to move data for each array that must be communicated. Such messages should be coalesced. Finally, communication for references involved in carried data dependences along a partitioned dimension may not be fully fused when the references require communication in different sets of iterations.

In January 2000, first detailed measurements of the scalar performance of the dHPF-generated code for multipartitionings showed that its scalar performance was a factor of 2.5 slower than the original sequential code. Careful analysis of overhead in the generated code showed that the main contributing factors were high primary data cache miss rates, excessive instruction counts due to complex addressing using linearized subscripts and overly complicated communication code, and excessive code replication.

To address these issues, we developed a number of compiler refinements including communication hoisting (which makes it possible to nest loops according to their natural memory order rather than constraining communication-carrying loops to be outermost), array padding for dynamic arrays to reduce cache conflict misses, data indexing using Cray pointers rather than linearized storage to help the back-end compiler optimize array subscript calculations, communication set splitting to avoid complex code that comes from having a single communication event orchestrate data movement across multiple partitioned dimensions, and code generation for multiple loop nests at a time to reduce code replication that can arise from guard lifting.

Table 1 uses several metrics to compare the performance of hand-coded MPI, dHPF-generated MPI (as of May 2000), and the original sequential code. These measurements were collected on a single node of an SGI Origin 2000 equipped with a 300 MHz MIPS R12000 processor. All code was compiled using the SGI Fortran 77 compiler version 7.3.1.1.[2]

The overall scalar performance of the dHPF-generated code is competitive with both the hand-coded MPI and the original sequential code. The number of graduated instructions, graduated loads, and cache misses measured for the dHPF-generated code are within 4–7% of the values measured for the sequential code. However, the overall performance of the dHPF-generated code was 22% slower than the sequential code. The primary contributing factor was that the SGI compiler failed to generate data prefetches for the dynamic arrays in the dHPF-generated code.

6   Related Work

Multipartitioning, described by Naik [16,14], is a generalization of a 3D partitioning first used by Bruno and Capello [8]. Naik studied the performance and scalability characteristics of multipartitioning for a general class of computational fluid dynamics (CFD) applications and compared it to alternative "unipartitioning" (*i.e.*, *BLOCK* partitioning) strategies. He presents a detailed analysis of load balancing for five static partitioning schemes for parallel CFD applications [15]. His findings show that 3D multipartitioning and 3D unipartitioning are the most tolerant to load imbalance. Another study by Van der Wijngaart [19] of implementation strategies for Alternating Direction Implicit Integration (ADI) found that 3D multipartitioning was superior to both static block partitionings using a wavefront parallization strategy, as well as a dynamic block partitioning strategy where repartitioning was performed by transposing between phases of the computation. Our work on multipartitioning in the dHPF compiler was inspired by this record of success using hand-coded multipartitioning for line-sweep algorithms.

---

[2] The compiler flags used were `-64 -r12000 -OPT:Olimit=0 -NC200 -OPT:alias=cray_pointer -LNO:prefetch=2 -O3` in order to attain high performance

The closest similar distributions supported by parallelizing compilers in the literature are the generalized block distribution and variants thereof, including a general BLOCK distribution specified as an approved extension in the HPF2 standard [9,13,10]. These distributions divide an array into rectangular blocks of potentially unequal size, and assign a single block per processor. In contrast, multipartitioning assigns multiple blocks of identical size to each processor.

7   Conclusions

We have succeeded in providing the compiler support for automatically exploiting multipartitioned data distributions. While end-to-end performance and scalability are not yet satisfactory, we believe that the better parallelism, load balance and coarse-grain communication afforded by multipartitioning will yield superior compiler-generated code after refining our code generation strategy to address performance concerns.

The support we have implemented for multipartitioning in the Rice dHPF compiler was devised to serve as the basis for a general framework to support overpartitioning. Overpartitioning, has a range of additional applications. An application of overpartitioning that we intend to explore in the future is using it as the basis for generating multi-threaded, latency-tolerant programs suitable for computing on wide-area computational grids.

Support for overpartitioning has been added to the dHPF compiler in such a way that it is largely orthogonal to sophisticated analysis and code generation techniques already in place. The abstract analysis and code generation framework based on manipulation of sets of integer tuples [2] made this possible. Even with multipartitioning, the dHPF compiler is able to exploit sophisticated parallelization strategies including use of non-owner computes computation partitionings and partial replication of computation to reduce communication.

Acknowledgments

We thank Vikram Adve for his involvement in the early design and implementation discussions of this work.

References

1. V. Adve, G. Jin, J. Mellor-Crummey, and Q. Yi. High Performance Fortran Compilation Techniques for Parallelizing Scientific Codes. In *Proceedings of SC98: High Performance Computing and Networking*, Orlando, FL, Nov 1998.
2. V. Adve and J. Mellor-Crummey. Using Integer Sets for Data-Parallel Program Analysis and Optimization. In *Proceedings of the SIGPLAN '98 Conference on Programming Language Design and Implementation*, Montreal, Canada, June 1998.
3. S. Amarasinghe and M. Lam. Communication optimization and code generation for distributed memory machines. In *Proceedings of the SIGPLAN '93 Conference on Programming Language Design and Implementation*, Albuquerque, NM, June 1993.

4. D. Bailey, J. Barton, T. Lasinski, and H. Simon. The NAS parallel benchmarks. *International Journal of Supercomputing Applications*, 5(3):63–73, Fall 1991.
5. D. Bailey, T. Harris, W. Saphir, R. van der Wijngaart, A. Woo, and M. Yarrow. The NAS parallel benchmarks 2.0. Technical Report NAS-95-020, NASA Ames Research Center, Dec. 1995.
6. R. Bordawekar, A. Choudhary, K. Kennedy, C. Koelbel, and M. Paleczny. A model and compilation strategy for out-of-core data parallel programs. In *Proceedings of the Fifth ACM SIGPLAN Symposium on Principles and Practice of Parallel Programming*, pages 1–10, Santa Barbara, CA, July 1995.
7. Z. Bozkus, L. Meadows, S. Nakamoto, V. Schuster, and M. Young. Compiling High Performance Fortran. In *Proceedings of the Seventh SIAM Conference on Parallel Processing for Scientific Computing*, pages 704–709, San Francisco, CA, Feb. 1995.
8. J. Bruno and P. Cappello. Implementing the beam and warming method on the hypercube. In *Proceedings of 3rd Conference on Hypercube Concurrent Computers and Applications*, pages 1073–1087, Pasadena, CA, Jan. 1988.
9. B. Chapman, P. Mehrotra, and H. Zima. Extending hpf for advanced data parallel applications. Technical Report TR 94-7, Institute for Software Technology and Parallel Systems, U niversity of Vienna, Austria, 1994.
10. N. Chrisochoides, I. Kodukula, and K. Pingali. Compiler and runtime support for irregular and adaptive applica tions. In *Proceedings of the 1997 ACM International Conference on Supercomputing*, pages 317–324, Vienna, Austria, July 1997.
11. M. Gerndt. Updating distributed variables in local computations. *Concurrency: Practice and Experience*, 2(3):171–193, Sept. 1990.
12. S. K. S. Gupta, S. D. Kaushik, C. Huang, and P. Sadayappan. Compiling array expressions for efficient execution on distributed-memory machines. *Journal of Parallel and Distributed Computing*, 32(2):155–172, Feb. 1996.
13. A. Müller and R. Rühl. Extending high performance fortran for the support of un-structu re computations. Technical Report TR-94-08, Ecole Polytechnique Fedérale de Zurich, November 1994.
14. N. Naik, V. Naik, and M. Nicoules. Parallelization of a class of implicit finite-difference schemes in computational fluid dynamics. *International Journal of High Speed Computing*, 5(1):1–50, 1993.
15. V. Naik. Performance effects of load imbalance in parallel CFD applications. In *Proceedings of the Fifth SIAM Conference on Parallel Processing for Scientific Computing*, 1992.
16. V. Naik. Scalability issues for a class of CFD applications. In *Proceedings of the 1992 Scalable High Performance Computing Conference*, Williamsburg, VA, Apr. 1992.
17. V. Naik. A scalable implementation of the NAS parallel benchmark BT on distributed memory systems. *IBM Systems Journal*, 34(2), 1995.
18. N. Nedeljkovic and M. J. Quinn. Data-parallel programming on a network of heterogeneous workstations. *Concurrency: Practice and Experience*, 5(4):257–268, June 1993.
19. R. F. Van der Wijngaart. Efficient implementation of a 3-dimensional ADI method on the iPSC/860. In *Proceedings of Supercomputing 1993*, pages 102–111. IEEE Computer Society Press, 1993.
20. J. C. Yan, S. R. Sarukkai, and P. Mehra. Performance measurement, visualization and modeling of parallel and distributed programs using the aims toolkit. *Software—Practice and Experience*, 25(4):429–461, Apr. 1995.

Speculative Parallelization of Partially Parallel Loops

Francis H. Dang and Lawrence Rauchwerger *

Dept. of Computer Science
Texas A&M University
College Station, TX 77843-3112
{fhd4244,rwerger}@cs.tamu.edu

Abstract. Current parallelizing compilers cannot identify a significant fraction of parallelizable loops because they have complex or statically insufficiently defined access patterns. We have previously proposed a framework for their identification. We speculatively executed a loop as a doall, and applied a fully parallel data dependence test to determine if it had any cross–processor dependences; if the test failed, then the loop was re–executed serially. While this method exploits doall parallelism well, it can cause slowdowns for loops with even one cross-processor flow dependence because we have to re-execute sequentially. Moreover, the existing, partial parallelism of loops is not exploited. In this paper we propose a generalization of our speculative doall parallelization technique, named Recursive LRPD test, that can extract and exploit the maximum available parallelism of *any* loop and that limits potential slowdowns to the overhead of the run-time dependence test itself, i.e., removes the time lost due to incorrect parallel execution. The asymptotic time-complexity is, for fully serial loops, equal to the sequential execution time. We present the base algorithm and an analysis of the different heuristics for its practical application. Some preliminary experimental results on loops from Track will show the performance of this new technique.

1 Efficient Run-Time Parallelization Needed for All Loops

To achieve a high level of performance for a particular program on today's supercomputers, software developers are often forced to tediously hand–code optimizations tailored to a specific machine. Such hand–coding is difficult, increases the possibility of error over sequential programming, and the resulting code may not be portable to other machines. Restructuring, or parallelizing, compilers address this problem by detecting and exploiting parallelism in sequential programs written in conventional languages as well as parallel languages (e.g., HPF). Although compiler techniques for the automatic detection of parallelism have been studied extensively over the last two decades (see, e.g., [7,12]), current parallelizing compilers cannot extract a significant fraction of the available parallelism in a loop if it has a complex and/or statically insufficiently defined access pattern. Typical examples are complex simulations such as SPICE [6], DYNA–3D [11], GAUSSIAN [4], and CHARMM [1]. Run–time techniques can succeed where static compilation fails because they have access to the input data. For example, input dependent or dynamic data distribution, memory accesses guarded by run–time

* Research supported in part by NSF CAREER Award CCR-9734471, NSF Grant ACI-9872126, NSF Grant EIA-9975018, DOE ASCI ASAP Level 2 Grant B347886 and a Hewlett-Packard Equipment Grant

S. Dwarkadas (Ed.): LCR 2000, LNCS 1915, pp. 285–299, 2000.

dependent conditions, and subscript expressions can all be analyzed unambiguously at run–time. In contrast, at compile–time the access pattern of some programs cannot be determined, sometimes due to limitations in the current analysis algorithms but most often because the necessary information is just not available, i.e., the access pattern is a function of the input data.

In previous work we have taken two different approaches to run time parallelization. First, we have employed the LRPD test [9], to speculatively execute a loop as a doall and subsequently test whether the execution was correct. If not, the loop was re-executed sequentially. While for fully parallel loops the method performs very well, partially parallel loops will experience a slow-down equal to the speculative parallel execution time (the loop has to be re-executed sequentially). Second, for loops which were presumed to be partially parallel we have developed an inspector/executor technique [8] in which we record the relevant memory references and then employ a sorting based technique to construct the iteration dependence graph of the loop. Then the iterations are scheduled in topological order. The major limitation of this method is its assumption that a proper inspector loop exists. If there is a dependence cycle between data and address computation of the shared arrays then a proper, side-effect free inspector of the traversed address space cannot be obtained. (It would be most of the analyzed loop itself.) Furthermore, the technique requires large additional data structures (proportional to the reference trace).

In this paper we will present a new technique to extract the maximum available parallelism from a partially parallel loop that removes the limitations of our previous techniques, i.e., it can be applied to any loop and requires less memory overhead. We propose to transform a partially parallel loop into a sequence of fully parallel loops. At each stage, we speculatively execute all remaining iterations in parallel and the LRPD test is applied to detect the potential dependences. All correctly executed iterations (those before the first detected dependence) are committed, and the process recurses on the remaining iterations. The only limitation is that the loop has to be statically block scheduled in increasing order of iteration. The negative impact of this limitation can be reduced through dynamic feedback guided scheduling, a dynamic load balancing technique described in Section 4.1.

An additional benefit of this technique is the overall reduction in potential slow-downs that simple doall speculation can incur when the compiler and/or user guesses wrong. In effect, by applying this new method exclusively we can remove the uncertainty or unpredictability of execution time – we can guarantee that a speculatively parallelized program will run at least as fast as its sequential version and with some additional testing overhead.

The remainder of this paper will first present the technique as an extension of the LRPD test and several implementation issues. We will introduce a performance model that guides our strategy for applying the various flavors of the technique. Finally we will validate the model and present some experimental results on a real code.

2   The Recursive LRPD Test (R-LRPD)

In our previous work [9] we have described the LRPD test as a technique for detecting doall loops. When the compiler cannot perform classical data dependence analysis it can speculatively transform a loop for parallel execution. At run-time, it executes a loop in parallel and tests subsequently if any data dependences could have occurred. If the test fails, the loop is re–executed sequentially. To qualify more parallel loops, *array privatization* and *reduction parallelization* can be speculatively applied and their validity tested after loop termination.[1] For simplicity, we will not present reduction parallelization in the following discussion; it is tested in a similar manner as independence and privatization. We have also previously shown that by using a *processor-wise* test we can reduce the overhead of the test as well as qualify more loops as parallel by checking only for cross-processor dependences rather than loop carried dependences (as classical data dependence does). We have further shown that we can increase the number of loops found parallel by testing the *the copy-in* condition in combination with privatization. Privatization testing will detect if a read memory location is referenced by *(Write—Read)* sequence in every iteration (and therefore remove this type of dependence by allocating private storage on each processor). However, if a memory location is first read (any number of times in any number of iterations) before it becomes privatizable, i.e., it has a reference pattern of the form $(Read^*|(Write|Read)^*)$, then the memory location can be transformed for safe parallel execution by privatizing it and initializing it with the original shared data previous to the start of the loop. More formally, in addition to the privatization condition, we need to test at run-time if the highest consecutive read iteration (maximum read) is lower than the earliest (minimum) writing iteration - for all references of the loop. In a processor-wise test (always preferable) we have to schedule the loop statically (blocked). While this is a limitation it also simplifies the tested conditions: Highest reading processor $\leq$ lowest writing processor. The initialization of the private arrays can be done either before the start of the speculative loop or, preferably, as an 'on-demand copy-in' (read-in if the memory element has not been written before). It follows that the only reference pattern that can still invalidate a speculative parallelization is a flow dependence between processors (a write on a lower processor matched by a read from a higher processor) – all other dependences have been removed through privatization and copy-in.

We now make the crucial remark that in any block-scheduled loop executed under the processor-wise LRPD test, the chunks of iterations that are less than or equal to the source of the first detected dependence arc are always executed correctly. Only the processors executing iterations larger or equal to the earliest sink of any dependence arc need to re-execute their portion of work. This leads to the conclusion that only the remainder of the work (of the loop) needs to be re-executed, which can represent a significant saving over the previously presented LRPD test method (which would re-execute the whole loop sequentially). To re-execute the fraction of the iterations assigned to the processors that may have worked off erroneous data we need to repair the unsatisfied dependences. This can be accomplished by initializing their privatized memory with the data produced by the lower ranked processors. Alternatively, we can commit (i.e., copy-out) the correctly computed data from private to shared storage and use on-demand copy-in during re-execution. Furthermore, we do not need to re-execute the remainder of the loop serially. If we re-apply the LRPD test on the remaining pro-

---

[1] *Privatization* creates, for each processor cooperating on the execution of the loop, private copies of the program variables. A shared variable is privatizable if it is always written in an iteration before it is read, e.g., many temporary variables. A *reduction variable* is a variable used in one operation of the form $x = x \otimes exp$, where $\otimes$ is an associative and commutative operator and x does not occur in exp or anywhere else in the loop. There are known transformations for implementing reductions in parallel [10,5,3].

cessors we can in fact speculatively re-execute in parallel. This procedure is applied recursively until all processors have finished correctly their work. For loops with cross-processor dependences we can expect to finish in only a few parallel steps.

To better understand the technique let us consider a do loop for which the compiler cannot statically determine the access pattern of a shared array A (Fig. 1(a)). We allocate the shadow arrays for marking the write accesses, A_w, and the read accesses, A_r. The loop is augmented with marking code (Fig. 1(b)) and enclosed in a while loop that repeats the speculative parallelization until the loop completes successfully. We use two bits for Read and Write: If on a processor the Read occurs before the Write then both bits will remain set – which means the reference is not privatizable. If the Write occurs first, then any subsequent Read will not set the read bit. Repeated references of the same type to an element on a processor will not cause a change in the shadow arrays. The array A is first privatized. Read-first references will copy-in on-demand the content of the shared array A. Array B, which is not tested (it is statically analyzable), is checkpointed. The result of the marking after the first speculative doall can be seen in Fig. 1(c). After the analysis phase we copy (commit) the elements of A that have been computed on processors 1 and 2 to their shared counterpart (by taking their last written value). This step also insures that flow-dependences will be satisfied during the next stage of parallel execution (we will read-in data produced in the previous stage). We further need to restore the section of array B that is modified/used in processors 3 and 4 so that a correct state is established for all arrays. (In our simple example this is not really necessary because we would overwrite B). Finally, after re-initializing the shadow arrays on processors 3 and 4 a new parallel loop is started on the last two processors for the remainder of the iterations (5-8). The final state is shown in Fig. 1(d). At this point all data can be committed and the loop finishes in a total of two steps of two iterations each.

In Fig. 1(e) we adopt a different strategy (RD): Instead of re-executing only on the processors that have incorrect data and leaving the rest of them idle (NRD), we redistribute at every stage the remainder of the work across all processors (while keeping the rest of the procedure the same). There are pros and cons for this approach. Through redistribution of the work we employ all processors all the time and thus the execution time of every stage decreases (instead of staying constant, as in the NRD case). The disadvantage is that we may uncover new dependences across processors which were satisfied before by executing on the same processor. Moreover, there is a 'hidden' but potentially large cost associated with work redistribution: more remote misses during loop execution due to data redistribution between the stages of the test. In the next section we will model these two strategies and devise a method to decide between them.

3   The Model

We have previously shown [9] that if the LRPD test passes, i.e., the loop is in fact fully parallel, then the speedups obtained range from nearly 100% of the ideal in the best case, to *at least* 25% of the ideal in the worst case. The overhead spent performing the single stage (original) LRPD test scales well with the number of processors and data set set size of the parallelized loop. We can break down the time spent testing and running a loop with the LRPD (single stage) test in the following *fully parallel* phases:

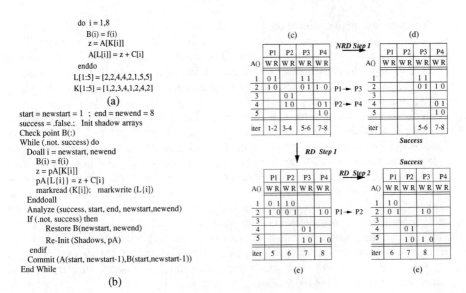

```
do i = 1,8
    B(i) = f(i)
    z = A[K[i]]
    A[L[i]] = z + C[i]
enddo
L[1:5] = [2,2,4,4,2,1,5,5]
K[1:5] = [1,2,3,4,1,2,4,2]
            (a)
```

```
start = newstart = 1  ;  end = newend = 8
success = .false.;   Init shadow arrays
Check point B(:)
While (.not. success) do
    Doall i = newstart, newend
        B(i) = f(i)
        z = pA[K[i]]
        pA{L{i}} = z + C[i]
        markread (K[i]);   markwrite (L{i})
    Enddoall
    Analyze (success, start, end, newstart,newend)
    If (.not. success) then
        Restore B(newstart, newend)
        Re-Init (Shadows, pA)
    endif
    Commit (A(start, newstart-1),B(start,newstart-1))
End While
            (b)
```

Fig. 1. Do loop (a) transformed for recursive speculative execution, (b) the `markwrite` and `markread` operations update the appropriate shadow arrays. The test is repeated until *success* becomes true. B is an independent array that is checkpointed and partially restored at every stage. pA is the privatized array A that is initialized to A and partially committed at every stage. (c) State of shadow arrays after first LRPD test. Note the cross-processor dependences. (d) State of shadow arrays after second (and successful) LRPD test on processors 3 and 4 only (NRD). (e) State of shadow arrays after second LRPD test when remainder of work is redistributed (RD) on all processors. Note the newly uncovered dependences. (f) Final state of shadow arrays after the second (and successful) LRPD test with work redistribution (RD).

The *initialization of shadow structures* is proportional to the dimension of the shadow structures. For dense access patterns we initialize shadow arrays dimensioned to conform to the tested arrays.

The work associated with *checkpointing* the state of the program before entering speculation is proportional to the number of distinct shared data structures that may be modified by the loop. For dense access patterns it is proportional to the dimension of all shared arrays that may be modified during loop execution. The actual time spent saving the state of the loop at every stage will depend on how the checkpointing is implemented as a separate step before loop execution or 'on-the-fly', during loop execution, before modifying a shared variable.

The overhead associated with the execution of the *speculative loop* is equal to the time spent marking (recording) relevant data references. It is proportional to the dynamic count of these memory references. For dense access patterns it can be approximated by the number of references to the tested arrays.

The final *analysis of the marked shadow structures* will be, in the worst case, proportional to the number of distinct memory references marked in each processor and to the (logarithm of the) number of processors that have participated in the speculative parallel execution. For dense access patterns this phase may involve the merge operation of p (number of processors) shadow arrays.

The recursive application of the LRPD test adds some additional components which must be accounted for in the performance analysis. The following breakdown will always depend on the fraction of the successfully completed work which in turn depends on the data dependence structure of the loop. It is important to note that in dynamic programs the data dependence structure of a loop is extremely input dependent and varies during program execution.

If cross-processor dependences are detected then a *Data Restoration* phase will restore the state of the shared arrays that were modified by the processors whose work cannot be committed. It is time proportional to the number of elements of the shared arrays that need to be copied from their checkpointed values. If dependences are detected and re-execution is needed, then the shadow arrays will be *re-initialized*. The *Commit* phase transfers the last data computed (last value) by the earlier processors from private to shared memory. Its cost is proportional to the number of written array elements. Each of these steps is *fully parallel* and scales with the number of processors and data size. Furthermore, the commit, re-initialization of shadow arrays and restoration of modified arrays can be done concurrently as two tasks on the two disjoint groups of processors, i.e., those that performed a successful computation and those that have to restart. These issues will be explained in more detail in Section 4.

The number of times re-execution is performed, as well as the work performed during each of them, depends on the strategy adopted: with or without work redistribution. As mentioned earlier, when we do not redistribute work (NRD), the time complexity of the technique is the cost of a sequential execution in the worst case. We will have at most p steps performing n/p work, where p is the number of processors and n is the number of iterations. In the RD (with redistribution) case we will take progressively less time because we execute in p processors decreasing amount of work. We are always guaranteed to finish in a finite number of steps because we are guaranteed that the first processor is always executing correctly. Let us now model more carefully the tradeoff between these two strategies.

Initially, there are n iterations which are equally distributed among the processors. The computation time for each iteration is ω, yielding a total amount of (useful) work in the loop as ωn. In the following discussion we assume that we know ω, the cost of useful computation in an iteration, ℓ, the cost of redistributing the data for one iteration to another processor, and s, the cost of a barrier synchronization.

For the purpose of an efficient speculative parallelization we classify loop types based on their dependence distribution in the following two classes: (a) **geometric** (α) loops where a constant fraction $(1 - \alpha)$ of the current *remaining* iterations are completed during each speculative parallelization (step), and (b) **Linear** (β) loops where a constant fraction $(1 - \beta)$ of the *original* iterations are completed during each speculative parallelization (step).

No Redistribution of Data Between Speculative Parallelizations (NRD). If $\omega \leq \ell + s$, then it does not pay to redistribute the remaining iterations among the p processors after a dependence is detected during a speculative parallelization attempt. That is, the overhead of the redistribution (per iteration) is larger than work of the iteration. In this case, the total time required by the parallel execution is simply

$$T_{\text{static}}(n) = \sum_{i=0}^{k_s} \left(\frac{n\omega}{p} + s \right) = \frac{n\omega k_s}{p} + k_s s \qquad (1)$$

where $k_s \leq p$ is the number of steps required to complete the speculative parallelization. Thus, to determine the time $T_{\text{static}}(n)$ we need to compute the number of steps k_s (the number of speculative parallelization attempts needed to execute the loop). We consider two cases (the α and β loops) and determine the value of k_s for each.

For the α loops, we assume a constant fraction $(1 - \alpha)$ of the *remaining work* is completed during each speculative parallelization step. In this case, $n\omega\alpha^i$ work remains to be completed after i steps. Thus, the final (k_s-th) step will occur when $n\omega\alpha^{k_s} = \frac{n\omega}{p}$ (since then all remaining iterations reside on one processor because we do not re-distribute). So, solving for k_s, we get $k_s = \log_{\frac{1}{\alpha}} p$. For example, if $\alpha = \frac{1}{c}$, then $k_s = \log_c p$, for constant c.

For the β loops, we assume a constant fraction $(1 - \beta)$ of the *original work* is completed successfully in each speculative parallelization step (i.e., a constant number of processors successfully complete their assigned iterations). In this case, $n\omega(1 - \beta)i$ work is completed after i steps. Thus, all the work will be completed when $n\omega(1 - \beta k_s) = n\omega$, or when $k_s = \frac{1}{(1-\beta)}$. For example, for a fully parallel loop, $\beta = 0$ and so $k_s = 1$ and $T_{\text{static}}(n) = \frac{n\omega}{p} + s$, and for a sequential loop, $\beta = \frac{p-1}{p}$ and so $k_s = p$ and $T_{\text{static}}(n) = n\omega + ps$.

Redistribution of Data Between Speculative Parallelizations (RD). If $\omega > \ell + s$, then it may pay to redistribute the remaining iterations among the p processors after a dependence is detected during a speculative parallelization attempt. The difference here as opposed to the no redistribution case is that in each subsequent step the processors will have a smaller number of iterations assigned to them. In this case, the total time required by the parallel execution is

$$T_{\text{dyn}}(n) = \sum_{i=0}^{k_d} \left(\frac{n_i\omega}{p} + \frac{n_i\ell}{p} + s \right) = \frac{(\omega + \ell)}{p} \left(\sum_{i=0}^{k_d} n_i \right) + k_d s \qquad (2)$$

where n_i is the number of iterations remaining to be completed at the start of the i-th speculative parallelization step, and k_d is the number of speculative parallelization steps completed to this point using redistribution.

Even if redistribution is initially useful, there comes a point when it should be discontinued. In particular, it should occur only as long as the time spent (per processor) on useful computation is larger than the overhead of redistribution and synchronization. That is, redistribution should occur as long as the first term in the first sum in Eq. 2 is larger than the sum of the last two terms, or equivalently, as long as

$$n_{k_d} \geq \frac{ps}{\omega - \ell}. \qquad (3)$$

Note that this condition can be tested at run-time since it only involves the number of uncompleted iterations which is known at run-time and p, s, ω, and ℓ, which we assume are known *a priori*, and can be estimated through both static analysis and experimental measurements.

Thus, in summary, for the first k_d steps, the remaining iterations should be redistributed among the processors. After that, no redistribution should occur. From this point on, we are in the case described as T_{static} above, but starting from $n' = n_{k_d}$ instead of n. Thus, the total time required will be

$$T(n) = T_{\text{dyn}}(n) + T_{\text{static}}(n_{k_d}) = \frac{(\omega + \ell)}{p} \left(\sum_{i=0}^{k_d} n_i \right) + \frac{n_{k_d} \omega k_s}{p} + (k_d + k_s)s \quad (4)$$

where n_i, k_d and k_s are as defined above.

To compute an actual value for $T(n)$, we need to determine n_i, k_d, and k_s, and substitute them in Eq. 4. For example, consider the geometric loops in which a constant fraction $(1 - \alpha)$ of the current work is completed during each speculative parallelization attempt.[2] In this case, $n_i = n\alpha^i$, and $\sum_{i=0}^{k_d} n_i = \sum_{i=0}^{k_d} n\alpha^i = n \left(\frac{\alpha^{k_d+1} - 1}{1 - \alpha} \right)$. Using $n_{k_d} = n\alpha^{k_d}$ in Eq. 3, and solving for k_d we obtain $k_d = \log_\alpha \left[\left(\frac{s}{\omega - \ell} \right) \frac{p}{n} \right]$. Finally, $k_s = \log_{\frac{1}{\alpha}} p$ as described above.
Thus, the total time required will be

$$T(n) = \frac{n}{p}(\omega + \ell) \left(\frac{\alpha^{k_d+1} - 1}{1 - \alpha} \right) + \frac{n\alpha^{k_d} \omega k_s}{p} + (k_d + k_s)s$$

where k_d and k_s are computed as defined above based on the known values of n, ω, ℓ, s, and α. In general, one may not know α exactly, however, in many cases reasonable estimates can be made in advance, and recomputed during execution (e.g., as an average of the α values observed so far).

Experimental Model Validation. The graph in Fig. 2 illustrates the loop, testing overhead, and redistribution overhead time (mostly due to remote cache misses) for each restart of Recursive LRPD test of a synthetic loop executed on 8 processors of HP-V2200 system. We assume that the fraction of remaining iterations is 1/2. The initial speculative run is assumed not to incur a redistribution overhead. We have performed three experiments to illustrate the performance of the following three strategies: The *never* case means that we use the NRD strategy, i.e., we never redistribute the remaining work. *Adaptive* redistribution means that redistribution is done as long as the previous speculative loop time is greater than the sum of the overhead and incurred delay times of the previous run. *Always* redistribution means 'always' redistribute. Fig. 2(a) shows the execution time breakdown of our experiment. At each stage of the R-LRPD test we measure the time spent in the actual loop and the synchronization and redistribution overhead. In Fig. 2(b) we show the cumulative times spent by the test during its four stages. The "adaptive" redistribution method begins to have shorter overall execution times compared to the "always" redistribution method after the failure on processor 8. The NRD method (never redistribute) performs the worst, by a wide margin. It should be noted however that our synthetic loop assumes, for simplicity, that α and β are constant. In practice we would have to adjust the model parameters at every stage of the R-LRPD test.

---

[2] The case in which a constant fraction of the original work is completed during each speculative parallelization is not realistic here since the number of iterations each processor is assigned varies from one speculative parallelization to another.

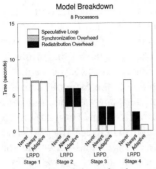
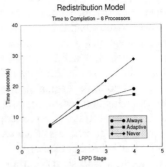

(a) Execution time breakdown for three strategies   (b) Time to completion for three strategies

Fig. 2. Selection strategy between RD and NRD re-execution technique.

4 Implementation and Optimizations

We have implemented the Recursive LRPD test in both RD and NRD flavors and applied several optimization techniques to reduce the run-time overhead of checkpointing and reduce the load imbalance caused by the block scheduling of the parallelized irregular loops. As previously mentioned block scheduling is a requirement of the R-LRPD test and thus load balancing is an important issue. The implementation (code transformations) is mostly done by our run-time pass in Polaris (it can automatically apply the simple LRPD test) and additional manually inserted code for the commit phase and execution of the `while` loop shown in Fig. 1(b). We have then applied our technique to the most important loops in TRACK, a Perfect code. In the remainder of this section we will present two optimizations which we have found to be the most effective in reducing the run-time overhead of our technique.

On-Demand Checkpointing and Commit. In Section 3 we have already mentioned the need to optimize checkpointing because its work is approximatively proportional to the working set of the loop. At every stage of the test we find a contiguous number of processors (processors executing a contiguous block of iterations) that have executed without uncovering any dependences between them and a remainder block of processors which have to re-execute their work. Thus we need to save the data residing in the shared arrays before it is modified by the speculative execution. There are two types of shared variables: Variables that are under test because the compiler cannot analyze them and variables proven by the compiler to be either independent (accessed in only one iteration (processor) or read-only) or privatizable. Saving state or preserving a safe state can be done in two ways: (a) We can write into un-committed private storage which we later either commit by copying it out to the shared area or delete. (b) We can copy the data that *may* be modified by the speculative loop to another, safe, memory storage and then either delete it (if we commit the results of the speculation) or copy back from the original variables (in case we have to restore state).

Both the copy-in/copy-out mechanism and the copying to a safe area can be done in two ways: (i) Before the speculative loop the *entire* working set of the loop is saved or copied-in or (ii) *On-demand*, during loop execution. Performing this activity before the loop always adds to the critical path-length of the program and, in the case of sparse reference patterns, generate more work and consume more memory than necessary. It is however fully parallel and the per operation cost is small (block copy). The on-demand strategy has many advantages: It performs the copy operations only when and if they are needed, which in case of sparse codes, can be orders of magnitude less than a 'wholesale' approach. Moreover, because it is done during loop execution, it may not actually add to the critical path of the program due to the exploitation of low level parallelism. However, each operation has to be initiated separately and may have to be guarded. We need to save data (or copy-in) only at the first write (or read) reference. To accomplish this 'first access' filter we have to distinguish between *variables under test*, i.e., those variables that cannot be analyzed by the compiler and which are shadowed during execution and shared variables that have been analyzed statically. From these variables only the independent ones need attention (read-only and privatized variables don't modify state and don't need to be restored). An independent variable references its location in only one iteration (or processor) and its location can be extracted by the compiler. The 'referenced first' filter can be generated also by the compiler either through peeling it off (in case of nested loops) or using a guard and a very simple shadow (or tag). If the code is such that there is only statement per distinct reference in an iteration then the filter becomes trivial.

The commit and restoration phase needed after the analysis region of each stage of the R-LRPD test depends on the strategy used for checkpointing. For Committing data we need to copy out the last value written (in the sequential semantics). For independent arrays (not under test) this either accomplished by a compiler generated loop (in case we used copy-in) or by simply deleting the corresponding saved data (if the wholesale copy before the loop strategy is used).

In the experiments shown in Section 4.1 we have implemented on demand copy-in, last-value-out for the arrays under test and on-demand checkpointing with release of back-up storage at commit phase because it proved to be the most cost-effective for the application studied.

Feedback-Guided Load Balancing. One of the drawbacks of the R-LRPD test is the requirement that the speculative loop needs to be statically block scheduled in order to commit partial work. Due to the fact that the target of our techniques are irregular codes load balancing does indeed pose some performance problems. We have independently developed and implemented a new technique similar to [2] that adapts the size of the blocks of iterations assigned to a processor such that load balancing is achieved at every stage of the R-LRPD test. Briefly this how are technique works:

At every instantiation of the loop we measure the execution time of each iteration. After the loop finishes we compute the prefix sums of the total execution time of the loop as well as the 'ideal', perfect balance, execution time per processor, i.e., the average execution time per processor ($\frac{total\_time}{number\_of\_processors}$). Using the prefix sums we can then compute a block distribution of iterations that would have achieved perfect load balance. We then save this result and use it as a first order predictor for the next instantiation of the loop. When the iteration space changes from one instantiation to another we scale the block distribution accordingly. The implementation is rather simple: We instrument the loop with low overhead timers and then use a parallel prefix routine to compute the iteration assignments to the processors. In the near future we will improve this technique by using higher order derivatives to better predict trends in the distribution of the execution time of the iterations. The overhead of the technique is relatively small and can be further decreased. Another advantage of the method is its tendency to preserve locality.

4.1 Experimental Results

Our experimental test-bed is a 16 processor ccUMA HP-V2200 system running HPUX11. It has 4Gb of main memory and 4Mb single level caches. We have applied our techniques to the most important loops in TRACK, a Perfect code. Track is a missile tracking code that simulates the capability of tracking many boosters from several sites simultaneously. The main loops in this program are DO 400 in subroutine EXTEND and DO 300 in NLFILT and DO 300 in FPTRAK. They account for $\approx 95\%$ of sequential execution time We have modified the original inputs which were too small for any meaningful measurement. We have also created several input files to vary the degree of parallelism of some of its loops. The loops under study are instantiated ≈ 56 times. To better gauge the obtained speedups we define a measure of the parallelism available in a loop over the life of the program as the *parallelism ratio*

$$PR = \frac{total\ number\ of\ instantiations}{total\ number\ of\ restarts + total\ number\ of\ instantiations}$$

For example, a fully parallel loop has a $PR = 1$ and a partially parallel loop has a $PR > 1$. In the case of the NRD strategy, a fully sequential loop has a $PR = 1/p$, while the RD case it can be much lower.

We will now briefly analyze the loop from subroutine NLFILT and show the effect of the various optimizations we have applied.

NLFILT DO 300. The compiler un-analyzable array that can cause dependences is NUSED. Its write reference is guarded by a loop variant condition. We have shadowed and marked NUSED according to the rules previously explained. The dependences are mostly of short distance. Fig. 3(a) presents the effect of the input sets on the the resulting execution ratio (PR) when the number of processors is varied. It is important to remark that the PR is dependent on the number of processors because only interprocessor dependences affect the number of restarts (stages) of the R-LRPD test. Furthermore, when feedback guided scheduling is performed the length of iterations blocks assigned to processors is variable which can lead to a variable PR. Fig. 3(b) shows the best obtained speedups (all optimizations turned on) for the tested input sets. The speedup numbers include all associated overhead.

The next figures, present the importance of our optimizations to the quality of our parallelization. Fig.s 4 compare the execution time breakdown of our method when the checkpointing is done (a) before the speculative loop and (b) on-demand, i.e., during the speculative loop. It is quite obvious that the on-demand strategy generates much less overhead and drastically reduces the overall execution time. Fig. 5(a) compares the execution time per processor when the iteration space is equally distributed to the processors with the time per processor when feedback guided scheduling is employed. We can clearly see that our loop balancing technique 'flattens' the execution profile and thus balances the irregular loop. Fig. 5(b) compares the effectiveness of the various optimizations techniques. The input set is 16-400, i.e., a moderate number of dependences are uncovered almost independent of the of processors used in the experiment. Clearly, due to the large state of the loop and its conditional modification the on-demand-checkpointing is the most important optimization. The load balancing technique is very important when redistribution (RD) is used. RD vs. NRD strategy has here a lesser impact because we use only 16 processors.

EXTEND DO 400. This loop has mostly independent array references. It reads data from a read-only part of an array and always writes at the end of the same arrays that are being extended at every iteration. It first extends them in a temporary manner by one slot. If some loop variant condition does not materialize then the newly created slot (track) is re-used (overwritten) in the next iteration. This implies that at most one element of the track arrays needs to be privatized. These arrays are indexed by a counter (LSTTRK) that is incremented conditionally. It is in fact a conditionally incremented induction variable and thus does not have a closed form. Because it is used as an index into the arrays, data dependence analysis is difficult. It cannot be pre-computed through loop distribution because its guarding condition is loop variant. Our solution was to speculatively let all processors compute it from a zero offset. At the same time we privatize and shadow the arrays in question and collect their reference ranges [13]. After the first parallel execution we obtain the per processor offsets of the induction variable (the prefix sums of LSTTRK) and show that all read references to the array do not intersect with any of the writes, i.e., maximum read index < minimum write (which occurs in the first iteration). All other write references are indexed higher by LSTTRK because it is a (not strictly) monotonic induction variable. Finally, in the second `doall` we repeat the execution using the correct offsets for LSTTRK. Last value assignment commits the arrays to their shared storage. In a future implementation we will process the loop only once - only the last value needs to be committed after computing the actual values of the induction variables. In Figuress 6(a) and (b) we show the PR and the best obtained speedup for these inputs. We obtain about 60% of the speedup obtainable through hand-parallelization because our compiler cannot yet recognize and deal with conditional induction variable.

FPTRAK DO 300. This loop is very similar to yet simpler than EXTEND DO 400 The array under test has a read-only front section which is conditionally extended by appending a new element. The array under test is privatized with the copy-in/last-value out method and shadowed. The same two stage approach as in EXTEND is employed here. Figures 7(a) and (b) show the PR and the best obtained speedup for these inputs.

PROGRAM TRACK. The execution profile of the **entire TRACK code** for different input sets given in Fig. 8(b) shows how input sensitive this program is. However, regardless of input, almost all the execution time is spent in the previously discussed loops. The overall speedup for input 16-400 and shown in Fig. 8(a) is scalable and is quite impressive, especially given the fact that these are only preliminary results with minimal compiler support.

5   Conclusion

In this paper we have shown how to exploit parallelism in loops that are less than fully parallel and thus cannot be parallelized with either compile time analysis nor with the original LRPD test. We have also shown how to overcome some of the overheads associated with this method. Moreover, some of these optimizations have general applicability, e.g., load balancing of irregular applications and checkpointing for various applications.

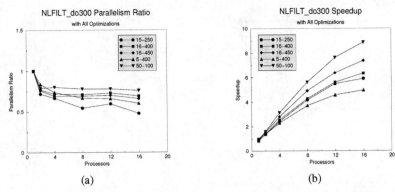

Fig. 3. . NLFILT DO 300: (a) Execution ratio for different inputs. (b) Obtained speedups.

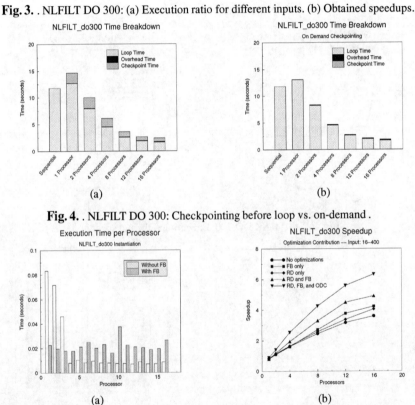

Fig. 4. . NLFILT DO 300: Checkpointing before loop vs. on-demand .

Fig. 5. . NLFILT DO 300: (a) Feedback guided load balancing, (b) Optimization contribution .

References

1. Charmm: A program for macromolecular energy, minimization, and dynamics calculations. *J. of Computational Chemistry*, 4(6), 1983.
2. J. Mark Bull. Feedback guided dynamic loop scheduling: Algorithms and experiments. In *EUROPAR98*, Sept., 1998.

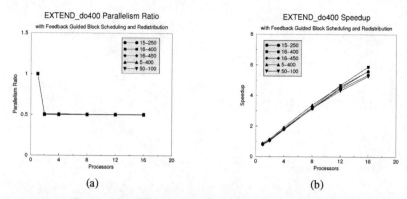

Fig. 6. . EXTEND DO 400: Execution ratio and speedup.

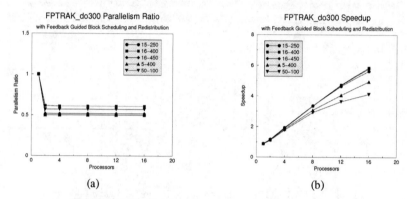

Fig. 7. . FPTRAK DO 300: Execution ratio and speedup.

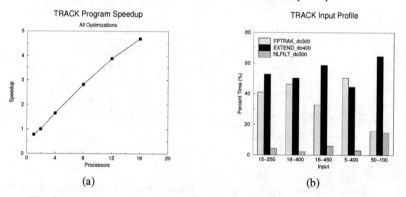

Fig. 8. . TRACK (a)Speedup and (b) Execution Profile for entire program

3. Zhiyuan Li. Array privatization for parallel execution of loops. In *Proc. of the 19th Int. Symp. on Computer Architecture*, pp. 313–322, 1992.
4. M. J. Frisch et. al. *Gaussian 94, Revision B.1*. Gaussian, Inc., Pittsburgh PA, 1995.
5. D. Maydan, S. Amarasinghe, and M. Lam. Data dependence and data-flow analysis of arrays. In *Proc. 5th Workshop on Languages and Compilers for Parallel Computing*, Aug. 1992.

6. L. Nagel. *SPICE2: A Computer Program to Simulate Semiconductor Circuits*. PhD thesis, University of California, May 1975.
7. D. A. Padua and M. J. Wolfe. Advanced compiler optimizations for supercomputers. *Communications of the ACM*, 29:1184–1201, Dec. 1986.
8. L. Rauchwerger, N. Amato, and D. Padua. A scalable method for run-time loop parallelization. *Int. J. Parallel Programming*, 26(6):537–576, July 1995.
9. L. Rauchwerger and D. Padua. The LRPD Test: Speculative Run-Time Parallelization of Loops with Privatization and Reduction Parallelization. *IEEE Trans. on Parallel and Distributed Systems*, 10(2), 1999.
10. P. Tu and D. Padua. Automatic array privatization. In *Proc. 6th Workshop on Languages and Compilers for Parallel Computing*, Portland, OR, Aug. 1993.
11. R. Whirley and B. Engelmann. *DYNA3D: A Nonlinear, Explicit, Three-Dimensional Finite Element Code For Solid and Structural Mechanics*. L. Livermore National Lab., Nov., 1993.
12. M. Wolfe. *Optimizing Compilers for Supercomputers*. The MIT Press, Boston, MA, 1989.
13. Hao Yu and L. Rauchwerger. Run-time parallelization overhead reduction techniques. In *Proc. of the 9th Int. Conf. on Compiler Construction (CC2000), Berlin, Germany*. Lecture Notes in Computer Science, Springer-Verlag, March 2000.

Author Index